The High Performance Organization

Creating dynamic stability and sustainable success

Linda Holbeche

ELSEVIER

BUTTERWORTH
HEINEMANN

AMSTERDAM BOSTON HEIDELBERG LONDON NEW YORK OXFORD
PARIS SAN DIEGO SAN FRANCISCO SINGAPORE SYDNEY TOKYO

Elsevier Butterworth-Heinemann
Linacre House, Jordan Hill, Oxford OX2 8DP
30 Corporate Drive, Burlington, MA 01803

First published 2005

Permissions may be sought directly from Elsevier's Science and Technology Rights
Department in Oxford, UK: phone: (+44) (0) 1865 843830; fax: (+44) (0) 1865
853333; e-mail: permissions@elsevier.co.uk. You may also complete your request
on-line via the Elsevier homepage (www.elsevier.com), by selecting 'Customer
Support' and then 'Obtaining Permissions'

British Library Cataloguing in Publication Data
A catalogue record for this book is available from the British Library

Library of Congress Cataloguing in Publication Data
A catalogue record for this book is available from the Library of Congress

ISBN 0 7506 5620 4

For information on all Elsevier Butterworth-Heinemann
publications visit our website at www.elsevier.com

Typeset by Charon Tec Pvt. Ltd, Chennai, India
www.charontec.com
Printed and bound in Great Britain

Contents

Acknowledgements

I should like to thank a number of people for their support during the writing of this book. Maggie Smith and Ailsa Marks of Butterworth-Heinemann, together with Francesca Ford and Claire Hutchins, have shown generosity and forbearance in waiting for this text. My colleagues at Roffey Park have been an endless source of ideas and practical support. Val Hammond and her successor as Chief Executive of Roffey Park, John Gilkes, have encouraged the project.

I should also like to thank all those people who have participated in the Roffey Park research projects over the years whose findings I refer to in this book. I am very grateful to all the writers who have kindly allowed me to draw on their ideas. In particular, I would like to thank Professor W. Warner Burke for permitting me to include the Burke–Litwin Organizational Performance Model. Thanks are also due to Dr Meredith Belbin for his valuable comments on the text.

Above all, I would like to thank my husband Barney and my mother Elsie for their unfailing support and encouragement during the writing of this book.

Linda Holbeche

Part One: Building Dynamic Stability

Section 1: The High Performance Organization

1

Introduction: towards the high performance organization

Investors will reward a successful downsizing program, but they place a much higher value on companies that improve their bottom line by increasing revenues.

Pathways to Growth, Mercer Management
Journal, *3, 9 (1994)*

In a fast-moving economic climate, organizations in every sector are having to change just to stand still. Against the backdrop of an increasingly volatile global economy, the focus of many business leaders and investors in recent years has become ever more short term. Increased global competition and the effect of customer choice are driving organizations to reinvent themselves and compete on the basis of speed, cost, quality, innovation, flexibility and customer responsiveness. Technology is leading to shorter cycle times, and new working patterns (such as sun-time working and teleworking) have been introduced in response to increasing consumer demands for cheaper, better, faster and round-the-clock availability of quality products and services. In this context, change-as-an-event is being replaced by change-as-the-norm.

The ability to manage continuous change has become the lifeblood of business success. However, it has also become the Achilles Heel for organizations unable to change fast and effectively. Unless an organization can flex in line with the changing needs of its customers and the driving forces in the environment, it soon finds itself out-of-step and forced to implement major 'transformational' change.

The challenge of managing change

Given the drivers for business flexibility, organizations need to change in order to remain successful. Change is not something to be managed just when there is a major crisis or when a new chief executive arrives and embarks on an ambitious change initiative, hoping to make his or her mark. Change management is an ongoing challenge and a prerequisite for organizational survival. What makes this a tough challenge is that, despite the sheer volume of change activity undertaken in recent years, the sad fact of the matter is that most organizational change efforts fail. Various reports suggest that 75 per cent of all transformation efforts fail, as do 50–75 per cent of all-re-engineering efforts. In mergers in particular, even those companies that manage to achieve short-term benefits from the integration usually fail to realize the longer-term value potential of the deal. Why should this be so, especially as it might be presumed that business leaders reach their positions on the basis of strong business judgement?

Several factors are known to contribute to failure, including inappropriate business strategies. Decisions can be made too late, based on faulty information, driven by egos or fad, or may simply be the wrong course of action for that time. What is becoming self-evident is that in a fast-moving economic climate, great business strategies alone are no guarantee of long-term success. The strategic planning timeframe has become very short term, with the challenge being less about choosing a strategic direction and more about implementing the latest chosen strategy.

However, most theorists now recognize that the main causes of failure are in the human domain. Change is a profoundly human process, requiring people to change their behaviours if the change effort is to be successful. The most effective change occurs when employees commit to the change effort. Resistance to change is common despite (or perhaps because of) people's familiarity with change. In today's workplace, people are expected to absorb large amounts of change without difficulty. Given the sheer volume of change activity, employees may experience multiple challenges – the need to master new skills, forge new relationships, even develop a new workplace identity. Essentially, managing change is about managing people through change.

In order for successful change to occur, employees need to be willing and able to adapt their behaviours and skills to respond to changing business needs. Organizations need to be 'dynamically stable' (Abrahamson, 2000). Ironically, the very process of changing can also destabilize the foundations of future success by destroying the currency on which employee motivation is based – trust. Successive waves of change – restructurings, redundancies, delayerings – have swept through organizations in recent years, leading to a severe erosion of the 'psychological contract' – the set of unwritten mutual expectations between employers and their employees. This represents a real threat and risk factor for continued business success since at the heart of the psychological contract is *trust*, which change research suggests can be a major enabler of change while, conversely, a low trust level is one of the greatest barriers to change.

The old relational contracts of the past, where employees expected continuity of employment and the possibility of promotion in return for unstinting loyalty and hard work, have largely been swept away. Notions of job security and conventional career growth have been replaced by messages about 'employability' at a time when many people have experienced increased workloads, uncertainty about pensions and a sense that their employer considers them to be an expendable 'resource' rather than a valued contributor.

Consequently, the psychological contract has become more transactional than in the past. Employees are more obviously taking responsibility for managing their own interests, including their career. Employees who believe themselves to be employable elsewhere do not place commitment to any one employer high on the agenda unless that employer offers something the employee values.

Ironically, in the emerging knowledge economy, where skill gaps exist and key employees with marketable skills are hard to find, the power balance is tipping in favour of employees, forcing employers to put the needs of employees higher up their agendas. Recruitment and retention (increasingly referred to as 'talent management') are becoming major challenges, and organizations are being driven to develop new and more meaningful relationships with such employees in order to recruit, retain and reap the benefit of the best available talent. I shall argue that it is in an organization's best interests to focus on building a partnership with employees on issues such as careers and work–life balance if the organizations themselves are to survive and thrive in future.

This highlights the paradoxical nature of change: without change an organization is likely to stagnate, yet the way the change process itself is handled can fundamentally undermine the basis of future high performance by damaging or destroying the employment relationship between employers and employees. Another paradox is inherent in the way most organizations function: managers aim to maintain and stabilize operations, rather than change them. For managers at all levels, managing change in ways that retain employee commitment, keep 'business as usual' going, yet produce new, value-added ways of operating, is a key challenge.

Attention is therefore shifting instead to building a more sustainable approach to change, based on organizational culture and reflected in management and employee behaviour and practice.

Types of change

Change is not uniform – there are many types of change producing different effects on businesses and their employees. For example, many employees will have experienced incremental change efforts aimed at improving current operations. The use of technology in particular has brought with it the demand for new skills, methods and working hours. Typical changes of this sort are the introduction of new IT systems, outsourcing, the increasing use of contractors, call centres, the introduction of flexible working, and virtual teams. Such changes require people to develop flexible mindsets and the willingness to learn and be able to work effectively in new working patterns and across organizational cultures.

Rather than leading to increased leisure hours, as was predicted decades ago, technology has added to workloads by enabling new working arrangements, the non-stop flow of e-mail traffic, and the removal of barriers of time and place. Work can be, and is often expected to be, carried out anytime, anywhere.

At one level people seem to adapt relatively effortlessly to such changes. The sight of business travellers using mobile phones and laptops as they travel, downloading e-mails at every conceivable opportunity, is now commonplace. So too is the endless pressure to perform and, with it, the danger that life can become dangerously skewed towards continuous working patterns.

Many employees will also be familiar with the sorts of transformational changes needed when an organization falls out of step with its environment and needs to regain strategic alignment (sometimes requiring a new business model). Transformational change often tends to be driven by necessity rather than preference. It usually has an air of urgency about it, and can involve major restructuring, replacement of personnel, the selling off of some parts of the business or some other major strategic shift. For employees, such changes can present the challenge of coping with possible trauma during downsizings and readjustments to new working practices and jobs. They can also provide positive boosts to morale if transformation leads to new growth, energy and renewal for the organization and for individuals.

In addition, many employees will have experienced more radical forms of change, such as a merger or acquisition. Such changes force people out of comfort zones. Even employees from the acquiring company may find that the old pecking order is disturbed and that they have to start again to build relationships and re-establish themselves in the new scenario. In the public sector the need for 'joined up' delivery is bringing about many types of cross-organizational partnering, rather than full mergers. For some employees, working in strategic alliances, partnerships and joint ventures with other organizations offers unparalleled opportunities for personal development, as well as the challenges of working with ambiguity and retaining good 'home' connections while forging new relationships and directions.

What is clear is that change is not neutral in its effects on people. It tends to have an unpredictable impact that is both substantive and emotional. Managing change effectively requires more than an intellectual understanding of the processes involved. It requires, in the jargon of the day, real emotional, political and, some would argue, spiritual intelligence on the part of those leading change.

Change, productivity and performance

Despite the volume of change and the valiant attempts to reorganize to meet marketplace demands in recent years, many organizations find that sustainable business success remains as elusive as ever. In trying to understand why this should be so, we shall explore the link between change, organizational performance and business success. It is possible that, by 'unblocking' some of the perceived barriers to high performance, positive change will flow more freely, providing a better platform for business success.

For example, whatever the strategic drivers for change, if we look at the wave upon wave of initiatives of recent years, we are likely to find that change tends to be aimed at achieving immediate synergies and business improvements. Ironically, implementing change for short-term gain has proved the undoing of many a good company. This is largely because a short-term perspective on change tends to result from knee-jerk reactions to business pressures, or to the latest business fad. Constant and multiple change initiatives appear to take their toll on employees and the organizations that employ them. No sooner has one change initiative begun than another one gets under way. There is often little real communication about why change is taking place, and after a while no-one seems to bother to find out if the change is working. In consequence, change-weary employees lose sight of the goal, customer service standards suffer and disgruntled customers go elsewhere.

A law of diminishing returns

Looked at from an employee perspective, there can often appear to be little coherence between change projects or progress being made as a result of change. Instead, change seems to result in greater pressure on individuals as their workloads increase and targets become ever more stretching. Against a backdrop of uncertainty, company politics become an additional source of pressure as individuals strive to protect their own position. 'Blame culture' and scapegoating tend to lead to risk aversion. In such a context, it is hardly surprising that people dislike the increased levels of accountability and seek to pass the buck. Innovation, which requires a degree of risk-taking, seems unlikely in such circumstances.

In turn, managers, frustrated as employees' lack of accountability, become less likely to delegate. Quite the contrary; they start to take back jobs, interfere and 'micro-manage'. Rather than increasing productivity, this can actually contribute to productivity losses as work becomes centred on managers. At some

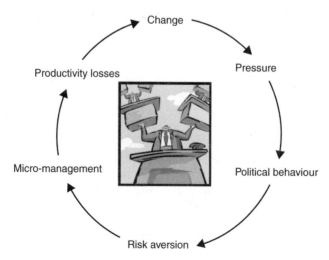

Figure 1.1 A law of diminishing returns.

point the system gives way and another change initiative begins in order to try and address the problems, so the vicious cycle begins over again. It is perhaps little wonder that so much change effort appears to achieve so little.

Even Michael Hammer (2001), one of the co-authors of *Reengineering the Corporation* (Hammer and Champy, 1993), suggested that business process re-engineering during the 1990s went too far, in some cases cutting into not just the 'fat' of the organization but also its bones and sinews. Corporate 'anorexia' and 'amnesia' became symptoms of organizations that were becoming too lean to be able to respond flexibly and innovatively in an increasingly competitive global marketplace. With many key employees amongst those who left, organizations had to reinvent wheels, at some expense, since corporate knowledge went with these individuals.

Therefore, if change is to result in an organization strengthening its position over time, it will need to be managed with an eye to the future; from the perspective of an investor more than that of an asset-stripper.

Is the new trend towards high performance organizations just another management fad? My hunch is that, while some guru-led management fashions may have come and gone over the last 20 years or so, the aspiration towards sustainable high performance is a more enduring theme, underpinning much of what has gone before, and one that needs redefinition in today's volatile economic context.

In the UK, the search for sustainable high performance has been given particular focus by the much reported productivity gap between the UK and other European economies. While economists may argue about how productivity should be measured and the extent of the gap, the fact that one exists is undeniable and is causing concern amongst ministers and officials alike. A host of research projects has spun off this concern, investigating why, if UK workers are reported to work far longer hours than their European counterparts, UK productivity still lags behind.

A degree of consensus seems to be emerging, both about the reasons for the reported shortfall and about what needs to be done to narrow the productivity gap. One element is the skills gap, with one in three of the UK's top board directors saying that skills shortages are the most important problem facing their company. One in five UK adults are reported to lack the literacy or numeracy of secondary-school starters; French and German workers are better educated; and government estimates suggest that, by 2010, 70 per cent of new jobs in the UK will need degree-level skills. At the same time, sickness absence levels in the UK have grown exponentially in the early years of the millennium, especially among younger workers, mirroring the largest increases in staff dissatisfaction levels regarding workload and working hours in Europe. Attempts are being made to plug the skills gap directly by opening up the UK labour market to workers from new entrant countries to the European Union.

Another key factor is lack of investment in the future, through research and development. This is another reflection of the short-termist approaches of many companies, whose directors are often rewarded according to their companies' performance in share price terms. To some extent it follows that the actions that boost share price, such as stringent cost savings and radical overhauls of business direction, will be the ones that drive management actions but may do damage to the longer-term revenue-generating potential of the company.

There is now greater awareness in the management community that great outputs in terms of business results need great 'inputs'.

In today's so-called 'knowledge economy', the key production factor is people, and this is one factor that does not lend itself to being traded like a commodity. The source of improved productivity lies in raising the performance of the workforce. The link between good people management practice and organizational success is now widely recognized in UK government and management circles. There has been a long tradition of measuring company performance primarily in financial terms. There is a growing appreciation that such measures do not reflect a company's true competitiveness and provide little real guide to future performance. The 'Accounting for People' Taskforce, led by Denise Kingsmill, explored how companies should go about measuring their human capital and communicating the value of their people in their annual report and accounts, and so raise the status of people assets in the investment community.

For Kingsmill, 'Human Capital Management', or 'the way organizations manage, recruit, retain, train and develop employees ... is about looking at people as a valuable business asset, not just a cost. It is about making sure that you have people with the right skills and experience to deliver your business strategy, both today and in the future' (Kingsmill, 2003). This is because it is now recognized that intellectual capital and the potential for innovation are key to the long-term health of a business, and that people – or 'human capital' – are the source of both assets.

The Balanced Business Scorecard, EFQM and other measurement frameworks have successfully reinforced the importance of managing the internal supply chain well (i.e. providing employees with the skills and leadership they require in order to provide great customer performance and achieve great business results). The input side of the equation appears to centre on the 'deal' for employees in terms of the nature of the organizational context and climate in which work will take place, and the elements needed for high performance work practices to occur. It also appears to concentrate on whether employees feel they are consulted or even involved in decision-making, and whether employees feel that their organization is a 'great place to work'.

Yet typical management practice remains different from what these models suggest. Particularly when times are hard, people are almost always treated as a cost and as expendable. If change results in a poorer deal for employees, little wonder if they feel less committed to their organization.

In another initiative that recognized the vital link between employees, organizational factors and productivity, the UK government invited the US guru of competitive advantage, Michael Porter, to advise on the quality of leadership required to make UK plc successful. Leadership has been the focus of several major studies in the UK in recent times (including those conducted by the Council for Excellence in Management and Leadership and also by the Chartered Management Institute). The assumption is that better leadership will help to close the UK's productivity gap with other developed countries.

Perhaps some of the clearest evidence of a causal link between people and performance is evident in the 2003 UK list 'The 50 Best Companies to Work For'. This list builds on the experience of the list 'The 100 Best Companies to Work For' in the United States, published through *Fortune* magazine. The share performance of the 'best companies to work for' in the US has consistently outperformed the S&P 500 to a significant degree. This same phenomenon is also strongly reflected in the first UK list (Crouch, 2003).

This is where a more holistic view is needed in terms of management theory and practice, placing business strategy considerations alongside the key organizational 'input' elements that appear to lead to great and sustainable business results. This is why Roffey Park's model of the elements of sustainable high performance more obviously puts employee needs and expectations alongside organizational needs and business challenges. Roffey Park's own research programme, notably our annual *Management Agenda* survey, which explores employee perceptions of the changing workplace, points to a range of factors that may make a positive difference to productivity and aid organizations in their aspirations towards sustainable high performance. These factors form the basis of the high performance organization model explored throughout this book.

Towards the high performance organization

While there may be no single magic formula for maintaining margins and competitive edge in such a turbulent context, there has been no shortage of ideas on the subject. Over the last three decades, executives have looked to a variety of management theories in the desperate search for the blueprint for sustainable business success. Thus, theories and management tools of the 1970s (such as strategic planning, value chain, matrix management and participative management) were succeeded by the excellence and entrepreneurship theories, and the focus on leadership and customer service of the 1980s. These in turn were superseded by the learning organization, re-engineering, core competency, systems thinking, agile company and empowerment theories of the 1990s.

In the current era, complexity brings a new perspective to many of the preceding theories. In a context that is fast-moving, complicated and unpredictable, the notion of organizations as living, complex, adaptive systems seems particularly apt. Rather than continuing to reproduce and rely on success patterns from the past, organizations, like organisms, need to embark on a path of self-renewal. Rather than setting course for the future through sticking rigidly to a fixed strategic plan, organizations need also to adapt to their changing environment by scanning and planning continuously, rather than simply on a once-a-year basis. Rather than focusing only on improving the *status quo*, for example in terms of operational efficiency, organizations need also to work in ways that are 'sustainable' or, like living organisms, they will die if they fail to find new sources of sustenance for the future. Rather than caring only about the needs of external stakeholders, organizations need also to recognize the symbiotic relationship between the ability to survive and thrive (achieve business success), the health of the organism itself (culture), and the way in which the constituent parts (employees) are nourished and nurtured.

This is where emerging notions of a high performance organization may complement some of the elements of earlier approaches while putting a greater emphasis on the question of sustainability. In high performance organizations the focus is on reconciling seemingly incompatible needs – to be both short and long term; both fixed and continuously changing; both externally and internally facing; both directed to the needs of the organization as a whole and to the needs of individuals; and intent on both harvesting the fruits of yesterday's labours and planting for tomorrow.

Defining the high performance organization

So what is a high performance organization? This book combines elements of high performance organization theory with a look at how the theory can work in practice. It draws on a variety of key sources, including a wide range of research initiatives on productivity and leadership, amongst other themes, some of which are indicated in this chapter. In particular I have drawn from Roffey Park's own research programme, notably the annual *Management Agenda* survey, which looks at the cross-sectoral experience of people working in over 700 organizations. I have attempted to extract from these various sources some of the factors that appear to make a positive difference to productivity and, from an employee standpoint, contribute to business success and sustainability. In developing the high performance organization input model, some of the literary sources that have helped shape my thinking include the following:

- Pettigrew and Whipp (1991), who have argued that competitive performance is linked to a firm's ability to adapt to major changes in the environment and thus, by implication, to its level of learning. Rowden (2001) argues that in unpredictable and highly turbulent business conditions, an organization's capacity to learn as it goes may be the only true source of competitive advantage. Schein (1993) suggests that, in order to survive and thrive in an ever-changing world, organizations have to adapt faster than the pace of change or else they will go under in the economic evolutionary process. Learning is therefore not only a source of competitive advantage but also an absolute necessity for survival. Senge (1990) believes that in the future there will be only two types of company: failures, which die slowly or suddenly, and learning organizations, which have the ability to learn and react more quickly to a fluid market than their competitors.
- Ashkenas *et al.* (1998). Sustainable success in the medium to longer term comes from an organization's ability to leverage its resources in a changing economic context. In *The Boundaryless Organization* (Ashkenas *et al.*, 1998), the authors suggest that the reason many organizations fail to move short-term cost management to longer-term sustainability through resource

leverage is that the form of management required for the latter is very different from what most people have experienced to date. They argue that the basis of leverage is having the capability to learn, share and deploy knowledge in ways that transcend current administrative boundaries.

- Vecchio and Appelbaum (1995), who believe that high performing organizations focus on implementing solutions to problems – management has a deliberate bias towards action that ensures goal attainment. Such firms manage performance in supportive and stimulating ways that enable empowerment and accountability at the right levels. They also suggest that the most sustainably successful organizations improve performance by achieving agreement or consensus of employees – where managers and employees work together to achieve mutually agreed performance goals. Good information flow is a prerequisite, employee suggestions are actively sought, and a positive work group-spirit is encouraged.
- The Gallup Survey on Trust (2002). Increasingly, surveys suggest that trust is perhaps the key component of a high performing organization. If colleagues trust one another and management, they are more willing to share information, develop team projects and 'go the extra mile' without fear that their goodwill and achievements will be exploited by others. In general, levels of trust seem to be in decline. A Gallup survey (2002) suggests that trust in many key institutions, large national organizations and capitalism has fallen to critical proportions, with citizens having as much trust in the media as they do in their national governments. The way change is handled does much to destroy trust.
- Dunphy et al. (2003). Leaders in particular have a key role to play in rebuilding organizational communities in which people are right to trust one another. They need to engage people to do willingly and well what needs to be done. This requires a determined effort because 'trust does not grow automatically; in organisational life, it is built consciously, purposefully over time by those who care' (Dunphy et al., 2003). The authors also argue that corporate sustainability is intimately linked to global issues of ecological sustainability, human resource management, corporate citizenship and community renewal.

High performance organizations recognize the need to move swiftly into new modes of operating more appropriate to the world we trade in today. If organizations wish to be able to compete successfully in the global marketplace, they need to develop innovative products and services quickly and cost-effectively. They need to be able to operate beyond their own boundaries and maximize potential synergies.

High performance organizations are able to transform their structures and working practices. In Jim Collins' (2001) study of 'great' companies (the 11 out of 1435 that achieved breakthrough performance that continued to exceed industry standards), 'relentless commitment' to excellence, rather than a grand strategic programme, was part of their secret of success. Rather than focusing exclusively on short-term success, high performance organizations operate on a 'both/and' basis – building the foundations for longer-term viability while delivering success in the here and now.

High performance organizations have employees who are willing to be flexible and able to deploy their talents to the organization's advantage. Employees are customer-focused, aware of the need to respond proactively in a changing marketplace and able to act responsibly and be accountable for their actions. Their organization's culture and management practices support and value these behaviours.

Finding the keys to sustainable success becomes even more critical in turbulent times, as is evident in the urgency behind various UK government initiatives. At the basis of these initiatives is an assumption that sustainable high performance is linked to the way people are managed, developed and led. Other government-backed initiatives aim to upgrade the quality of leadership in all sectors, especially amongst small and medium-sized enterprises. Similarly, initiatives are underway on employee consultation and work–life balance to address some of the organizational climate issues which are the legacy of an extended period of industrial transformation.

Attention is therefore shifting instead away from 'slash and burn' approaches to change towards a more sustainable approach, based on organizational culture and reflected in management and employee behaviour and practice. Attention is also shifting to a more inclusive approach to leading and managing business, taking into account a wider group of stakeholders and an organization's responsibilities to its broader community and environment.

What do high performance organizations do?

In their seminal study of so-called 'excellent' companies in the early 1980s, Peters and Waterman (1982) identified the role of culture as the key variable in achieving high performance. They recognized that consistently successful companies in the *Fortune* Top 500 had strong alignment between their business strategy, and internal elements such as their systems, structure, leadership style, and the skills and style of staff. Most of these successful companies were characterized by a strongly shared mindset and culture.

1. High performance organizations focus on the 'right things'

High performance organizations develop strong cultures and practices, which attract good people to work for them and thus make them successful in their markets. Collins and Porras (1994) studied 18 exceptional companies (which they called 'visionary'), with an average age of nearly 100 years, and compared their performance to that of 18 similar or good competitors. They found that it was these organizations' cultures that distinguished the best from the rest. In companies such as IBM, Merck, and Johnson and Johnson, the belief in company values is described as almost 'cult-like'. Cultural attitudes and practices make these companies good at managing for change. They are financially conservative. Rather than focusing purely on the bottom line, which is evident in other organizations in attitudes such as recruitment treated as gap filling and 'we're too busy to train', the visionary companies tend not to focus on profit for its own sake. Indeed, such companies recognize their responsibilities as corporate citizens, developing and implementing live policies on diversity, corporate social responsibility and other ethical considerations.

Collins and Porras explain the lasting success of the 'visionary' companies by their strong and relatively non-changing core purpose. 'Visionary' companies change their strategies and, in some cases, their values, but they stick firmly to their core purpose. They are able to distinguish between 'core' and 'non-core', between what should never change and what should be open to change. The authors illustrate this as follows:

> *Johnson and Johnson used the concept to challenge its entire organization structure and revamp its processes while preserving the core ideals embodied in the Credo. 3M sold off entire chunks of its company that offered little opportunity for innovation – a dramatic move that surprised the business press – in order to refocus on its enduring purpose of solving problems innovatively.*

Visionary companies are careful to select people who can work successfully within such environments. Similarly, Jim Collins' study of 'great' companies (2001) explains the importance of starting with the 'who' – 'getting the right people on the bus' – and determining your strategy thereafter. Such companies have strong leadership, good products, successful market insights and high levels of profits. These profits are the results of such cultures, rather than the driving force behind them.

In another study, the research firm ISR (Maitland, 2002) identified a number of factors that differentiate high performance organizations from others. These all demonstrate:

- An obsession with quality. High performance companies obsess over the quality of what they do. Employees are much more likely to feel that achieving high quality is a priority in their day-to-day work, and that their company's products and services have a good reputation. They do not feel under pressure to sacrifice quality in order to save costs.
- Innovation. The best companies innovate and then they innovate again. Employees believe that their company outperforms its competitors in the rapid development of new products and services, in responding quickly to market changes and in technological innovation.

In a US study, Mark Huselid (1995) explored the impact of high commitment work practices using measures of financial performance. He produced a sophisticated index, which showed that a one standard deviation increase of high commitment work resulted in an annual increase in sales of over \$27 000 per employee. What was interesting about this study was that it was found that the effectiveness of these work practices was not contingent on a firm's strategy, but consistently led to performance improvements.

2. High performance organizations reconcile different, potentially conflicting stakeholder needs

Competitive pressures are driving even well established industries such as oil and pharmaceuticals, with their relatively longer-term business cycles, to cut down lead times and get products to market fast. These market demands mean that the emphasis on the short term is driven even deeper into the business psyche. In today's global marketplaces, businesses are usually only as good as their last results and investment analysts rarely look beyond current and short-term financial projections to make their assessment of a company's worth.

The search for shareholder value underpins much cost-cutting and the more radical re-engineering exercises of the 1990s. From a shareholder's or financial analyst's perspective the loss of jobs in order to improve the book value of a company makes sense, whereas to affected employees and the local community such decisions can seem disastrous. While longer-term sustainability of the enterprise may be important to employees, management and the community, it may be far less important to investors, who may view a company as no more than a bunch of assets to be realized.

Senior managers are usually caught between the need to please shareholders by driving costs down and increasing profitability, and the needs of the organization and its employees. Whilst shareholder value has been the Holy Grail for companies in recent decades, the view that this should take precedence over other interests is starting to be challenged. Ongoing business success requires organizations to be closely connected with the changing environment and to change strategy if required. If change is driven solely from a shareholder perspective it is more likely to provoke employee resistance and thus slow down the organization's ability to change rapidly.

High performance organizations have customer-focused purpose

Successful organizations focus intensely on customers and their needs. They invest in ways to improve products and provide superior customer service. They do not forget that clients and their needs underpin their organization's existence. They focus on retaining customer loyalty as much as on attracting new customers. For example, the fortunes of Marks & Spencer started to revive when a radical strategic overhaul placed the tastes and preferences of the customer at the centre of investment decisions.

In the ISR research, high performance companies exist in order to serve their customers, not their shareholders. In Roffey Park research (2004) too, high performance is strongly correlated to customer-focused purpose. Significantly greater numbers of employees think that their organization is customer-oriented, that it provides better customer service than its competitors, and that its customers hold it in high regard.

Ignoring customer needs is not an option. In some ways these are remarkably consistent: customers always want the highest-quality goods, when they want them, at a price they can afford.

However, focusing on customers' needs and preferences can be frustrating and costly, especially as these change over time and can seem fickle and fashion-led. Responding to tough competition from all corners means that company margins get squeezed and the race is on to be the first in the marketplace with new goods that will attract customers. Witness the battle between BA and Virgin Atlantic in the race to attract the lucrative market in business class travellers. Prior to the partial collapse of transatlantic travel following the events of 11 September 2001, the two airlines were competing neck and neck to provide fully reclinable seats and other expensive benefits to the traveller. Now that confidence in long-haul air travel appears to have returned the race is on yet again, even if both companies have seen their profits drop dramatically with the fall-off in transatlantic trade.

The ideas of Michael Hammer, the 'father' of re-engineering, have come in for much criticism. Hammer himself accepts that the concept of radical re-engineering started to turn sour by the late 1990s. In his 2001 book *The Agenda: What every business must do to dominate the decade*, Michael Hammer focuses on how the world's major organizations build a business strategy. He has identified nine steps, of which the major point is that in order to activate the 'customer is king' principle, fundamental change is required both within and between organizations. He outlines a vision for a business landscape defined by collaboration. He urges companies to build collaborative relationships with their partners and re-design inter-enterprise processes to cut down duplication. This would require data to be shared openly and work to be relocated to whoever can carry it out best.

Whilst many of the theorists of high performance argue in favour of balancing different stakeholder needs, Richard Ellsworth in *Leading with Purpose* (2002), a study of 20 major organizations that have stood the test of time, suggests that having clarity of purpose is essential to business success. For Ellsworth, the most effective vision for change is customer focused. Ellsworth suggests that companies with a customer-focused purpose:

- Found change easier to manage
- Had employees who experienced work as more meaningful
- Achieved higher shareholder returns over the long term
- Had stronger cultures
- Had more internal alignment.

It is important to understand the customer's world, including the customer's end-user. Building a customer-focused vision invariably means that one change will lead to another as customers' needs change.

High performance organizations value employees

Harvard Business School Professors John Kotter and James Heskett found a correlation in 1992 between companies who valued employees, and business success. The authors asked industry analysts a series of questions about the culture of 22 companies, which the interviewees had to rate from 1 (definitely not) to 7 (absolutely, yes). Regarding the question 'How highly does (a specified organization) value its employees?', the 12 better-performing firms averaged a score of 5.8 while the lower 10 scored an average of 4.1.

In the ISR research, high performance companies know that their employees are their most important asset and invest in employees. They don't only say this, they mean it – and they invest accordingly. Employees are much more likely to feel that their contribution is recognized, that they have good opportunities for promotion and that they are able to develop and grow in their work. Employees who feel this way are far more likely to rally round in bad times and to stick around in good times – two of the reasons why employers that invest in their people are more successful than those that hire and fire at will.

Jim Collins, in *Good to Great* (2001), suggests that truly 'great' companies tend to surpass merely 'good' companies in terms of hard business outcomes, such as cumulative stock returns relative to the market. For Collins, greatness is not a function of circumstance but a conscious choice, even though luck is still a variable. For him, great companies practise timeless principles of good people management. Greatness is a cumulative process, which requires pushing consistently in an intelligent direction, with disciplined people, thought and action. Leaders therefore become rigorous rather than ruthless, aiming to keep the right people 'on the bus', in the 'right seats' for a long time. Only when you have the right people on board is it time to focus on the strategy.

3. High performance organizations aim for sustainable success over the long-term

Arie de Geus (1997), formerly coordinator in charge of corporate planning for Royal Dutch/Shell, has written in his book *The Living Company* about the research commissioned by Shell to identify what differentiated large companies that had survived for 100 years or longer with their identities intact from those that had disappeared. The study discovered 40 such organizations, including Rolls Royce, Du Pont and Sumito. In contrast, the lifespan of other large organizations averaged a mere 40 years. While longevity alone is not necessarily a recommendation, these companies have also managed to ride the economic uncertainties of different eras and remain successful.

De Geus found that all the 'living' companies had certain characteristics:

- They were conservative in financing. Having money 'in the pocket' gave these organizations control of their timing.
- They were sensitive to the world around them. Their top leaders were part of the wider world and aware of the changing environment.
- They had a sense of cohesion and corporate identity. Both employees and leaders had a good understanding of what the company stands for. Leaders and employees were happy to act consistently with these values.
- They had a management style that was tolerant of experimentation and eccentricity 'at the margin'. They had decentralized structures and delegated authorities. They left space in the organization, and controlled the context rather than the contents.

These qualities form the basis of developing the organization's capacity for reshaping itself. De Geus has developed the premise that if companies are to survive they need to give up a purely economic model of corporate success and should cultivate the characteristics of a living being.

In the ISR research, high performance companies have a healthy culture and are fulfilling places to work. Employees are not asked to sacrifice or compromise their personal standards and values in order to achieve organizational objectives. On the contrary, the best companies set an example for employees to aspire to. Employees are much more likely to believe their organization operates with integrity, both internally and externally.

Similarly, research carried out by Collins and Porras (*Built to Last*, 1994) suggests that success for commercial companies in the past, whether measured in terms of longevity, profitability or both, was linked to their ability to establish themselves as a human community of successive generations of people. In the 19 'visionary' companies studied, success was not dependent on putting the maximization of profits/shareholder value as the top managerial priority. Human sustainability involved developing the social capital of employees.

These studies suggest that bigger commercial wins are more likely to be achieved when employees feel committed to their organization, are well led, and have the skills and flexibility needed to build competitive advantage for the future. High performance organizations focus on building their people asset for today and tomorrow. This calls for a truly strategic perspective on investment decisions relating to the recruitment, development and retention of skilled employees.

High performance organizations grow leadership

Similarly, it is not leadership in itself that matters, but rather the inner ambition that counts. Collins suggests that what he calls 'Level 4' leadership (charismatic) can become a liability for organizations, making the system dependent on the leader as a catalytic force. Collins notes that in great companies it is 'Level 5' leadership, rather than Level 4, that is in evidence. This is when a leader demonstrates a paradoxical combination of general personal humility, being ambitious for the cause rather than self, together with a strong will to make good on the cause. Such leaders give credit elsewhere and will take the blame if things go wrong, whereas in Collins' comparison companies the reverse was more common. In the great companies most of the CEOs were grown from within the organization, with a few exceptions such as Lou Gerstner of American Express and IBM.

The high performance organization input model

Roffey Park's high performance organization model, more obviously than many previous management theories, places employee needs and expectations in the balance, alongside organizational needs. Based on Roffey Park research into the changing workplace, since 1996, the model focuses on issues that affect employees' attitudes and behaviours, their willingness to commit and give of their best. It also focuses on how organizations and their employees will increasingly need to operate, in order to be successful in today's changing context.

The elements of this model are cultural 'inputs' which I believe underpin sustainable business results over the long term. For example, if people are the source of intellectual capital and innovation, then an organization which becomes a great place to work will attract and retain the right employees, will have the right organizational context and climate for work to take place, and will be likely to find that employees are willing to commit to the organization and provide the high performance required of them. However, the model's elements can also be outputs, since becoming known as a great place to work is likely to enhance an organization's brand value. All the elements combined should enable an organization to adapt and change effectively while maintaining high performance, thus providing the change-able organization with sustainable competitive advantage.

Creating sustainable high performance is fundamentally about culture-building. In practice, this involves shaping artefacts of culture to be coherent and consistent with the desired endgame. To borrow from McKinsey's 7S model, it involves having a customer-focused *strategy* that is in tune with the changing economic environment. It requires aligning and integrating *structures, systems* and *processes* that have clarity and flexibility built in. In particular it requires excellent communication processes. *Staff* (including managers) need the *skills* and *styles* of operating conducive to high performance. Above all, they need genuinely *shared values* which form the basis of conduct and represent the best of the brand – to customers, employees and other stakeholders.

The key elements of the model are as follows:

- Developing organizational change-ability (or how to develop flexibility, speed and learning)
- Creating a knowledge-rich context for innovation (or how to stimulate business breakthroughs and continuous improvement)
- Creating a boundaryless organization (or how to maximize potential synergies)
- Stimulating people to sustainable levels of high performance (or how to enable people willingly to release 'discretionary effort')
- Becoming a great place to work (or how to provide the right employee value proposition or 'deal')
- Becoming a values-based organization (or how to connect with employees and other stakeholders at a deeper level of meaning).

The underpinning features of our model are:

- Appropriate management and leadership
- Built-in flexibility
- A fair employee 'deal'
- Empowerment and accountability.

We shall be exploring the different elements of this model in detail throughout the book, examining how each can be brought to life in practical terms. I will draw on a variety of Roffey Park research projects, in particular the *Management Agenda* survey from the period 2000–2004, unless otherwise stated. I shall be using examples from organizations and individuals who have contributed to research on high performance by way of illustration.

A brief synopsis of each of the elements follows.

Developing organizational change-ability

In Roffey Park's model of high performance organization, we have integrated what employees tell us about how change can be effectively handled with what they consider helps them to give of their best. With so much change driven top-down, people often find themselves unable to influence their own destinies. When people feel disempowered, it is hardly surprising that they become resistant to change. Developing change-ability is about creating a context where change is no longer seen as simply a source of added pressure, but as a source of ongoing renewal – as much for individuals as for the organization.

Two key elements of organizational change-ability that we will explore in this book are:

1. How to handle change in a way that engenders employee ownership and commitment while achieving improved results
2. How to build flexibility into planning, systems, processes, structures and mindsets.

Creating a knowledge-rich context for innovation

This is about developing working practices and management approaches that are conducive to breakthrough ideas, as well as continuous improvement. It is in the nature of innovation that there is a high degree of failure, risk, uncertainty and complexity. Developing new behaviour patterns among those involved can take time. Weak strategic oversight, organizational politics, blame culture and risk-averse senior managers are only some of the blockers of innovation and learning. Leaders in particular have a key role to play in leading rather than supervising, providing clarity of direction and parameters within which experimentation is encouraged. Key areas we shall explore are:

1. How to develop working practices and management approaches that are conducive to breakthrough ideas, as well as continuous improvement
2. How to maximize the potential value of shared knowledge
3. How to manage for diversity.

Creating a boundaryless organization

This is about reaping the benefits of diversity in a context where organizations and employees are increasingly required to operate effectively across mindset, functional, corporate and geographic boundaries. It is about using technology and teamworking to provide greater 'reach' and flexibility for employees and the organization, while maximizing potential synergies. In practice, many organizations struggle to maximize the potential of cross-boundary working, whether the context is merger integration, joint ventures, teleworking, international teamworking or implementing diversity policies. Often employees find working in ambiguous or remote relationships difficult, and managers too are frequently challenged by managing 'new' forms of teams, made up of contractors and people working remotely or on various forms of flexible work patterns alongside full-time employees. Therefore, we will be exploring:

1. How to operate effectively across mindset, functional, corporate and geographic boundaries
2. How to use technology and teamworking to provide greater 'reach' and flexibility for employees and the organization, while maximizing potential synergies.

Stimulating people to sustainable levels of high performance

This is about designing organizational structures and job roles that support high performance, but most of all it is about building an organizational climate conducive to high performance. It is about making the most of employee talents and accountabilities, and managing performance in ways that unleash, rather than constrain, employee potential. Various research projects suggest that in many organizations the workplace climate actually works against employees being willing to release so-called 'discretionary effort'. In Roffey Park's *Management Agenda* survey, for instance, people report that they are not empowered to do their jobs. The main barriers to empowerment include heavy workloads, organizational politics, risk-averse senior management, interference by managers, and blame cultures. Key factors we shall examine include:

1. How to build roles that make the most of employee talents and accountabilities
2. How to manage performance in ways that unleash, rather than constrain, employee potential
3. How to build empowerment and accountability.

Becoming a great place to work

When the psychological contract is weak, the cost to the organization is felt when it becomes difficult to recruit and retain key people. This is forcing organizations to develop new and more meaningful relationships with such employees if they are to recruit, retain and reap the benefit of their talent. Becoming a great place to work is about developing a new 'employee deal' which responds to employee needs for work–life balance, development and career growth. In conjunction with a good workplace climate, this deal is likely to go some way towards repairing damaged trust and forming the basis of employee commitment and retention. We shall explore:

1. How to develop a 'new deal' that responds to employee needs for work–life balance, development and career growth
2. What organizations can do to operate as 'partners' to employees on the 'new deal'.

Becoming a values-based organization

This is about building an organization to which key employees want to belong. For managers and leaders this means going beyond the rhetoric of values statements and corporate social responsibility policies; it is about how to 'walk the talk'; how to build a new basis for trust.

Roffey Park surveys suggest that many employees want to see a more open, democratic and ethical style of leadership, which treats employees as adults. Under such leadership employees develop a strong, shared sense of purpose to which they can readily subscribe. In such contexts, employees are more likely to commit to the organization and want to give of their best. Conversely, when values are merely paid lip service and a leadership vacuum exists, employee cynicism is more likely to rise and commitment to the organization to fall. While organizations in every sector have explicit sets of values, some are more vigorous than others in ensuring that these are practised. Safeway, the supermarket chain, prior to its acquisition by Morrisons, for instance, held a 'meeting for everyone' every two weeks to demonstrate the company values, rather than merely discussing them. We will look at:

1. How to become an organization to which key employees want to commit
2. What this means in practical terms for management and leadership
3. How to go beyond the rhetoric of values statements and corporate social responsibility policies; how to 'walk the talk' and build a new basis for trust.

While many *Management Agenda* respondents tell us that, in practice, their daily experience of the workplace is very far from the ideal described above, all is not lost. This book is designed to point to some of the practical actions that can help executives, managers, HR professionals and employees as a whole to break away from the law of diminishing returns described earlier and produce a more virtuous cycle instead.

Overview of this book

This book is designed to complement a related book, *Understanding change: theory, implementation and success* (Holbeche, 2005), which looks as the theory behind change and high performance cultures and at some of the different ways in which change can be managed so as to lay the foundations for high performance. In contrast, this book is designed to address some of the practical process considerations related to building a high performance culture. Using data amassed from research, literature and consultancy practice, I will highlight some of the key issues that appear to undermine high performance. At the same time, I will suggest ways in which the gap can be bridged between the intention to achieve sustainable high performance, and implementation.

Building a high performance culture takes time, and is likely to involve changes – planned and intended, accidental and emergent – in the way organizations operate. Of course, all stakeholders in any organization are actively engaged in building and perpetuating culture through their day-to-day activities. However, leaders and other change agents, whether line managers, HR professionals or others, have special roles to play in designing and enabling high performance practices. Most management attention is generally given to the grander aspects of strategy and change, yet it is my contention that small-scale but significant day-to-day actions and effective policies can more substantially contribute to building a change-friendly culture in which people are willing and able to give of their best.

Some of the action areas I will suggest are intended for executives, while others are more likely to be the responsibility of HR or line managers. Finally, some of the actions proposed are relevant to individuals who wish to operate from a high performance model.

Part One of this book is about building organizational adaptability. In the first section, *The High Performance Organization*, we will explore issues relating to culture-building. We shall look at how organizational cultures can be understood, how they evolve, and if, and how, they can be shaped or changed. We shall look at some of the approaches used to analyse culture in order to gain an understanding of which aspects of culture can be strengthened to support high performance. Then we shall look at a planned approach to changing culture through organization design.

In the next section, *Creating Dynamic Stability*, we shall look at how to create organizational change-ability through building flexibility into organizational processes and creating a shared sense of ownership of change through employee involvement. Then we shall examine some of the ways in which innovation and effective knowledge management can be supported.

In the third section, *The Boundaryless Organization*, we shall look at how organizations can develop effective cross-boundary working. We shall explore the nature of working in partnering arrangements, looking in particular at strategic alliances, and then at how technology is dissolving boundaries of time and space, considering how organizations can transform themselves in the context of e-business and international working.

In the *High Performance Management Practices* section we shall look at how employees can be stimulated to achieve high performance by appropriate management practices and an appropriate work climate. We shall also look at performance management and ways in which measures can be used strategically, rather than defensively. We shall examine the role of Human Resources professionals in building systems, policies and practices supportive of high performance working.

Part Two concentrates on building positive psychological contacts. We shall start by looking at issues relating to employer brand, or how organizations can recruit and retain the talent they need. We then look at the key psychological contract issues of work–life balance and careers. The focus is both on what employees say they need, and what organizations can do to act in partnership with employees on these matters. We shall look at what employees can do for themselves with regard to developing the key skills required to be successful in changing organizations.

Next, we shall consider how positive psychological contracts need to be built on the basis of trust and mutual respect. We will look at how the rhetoric of organizational values can be converted into practice and how work can become more meaningful. Finally, we shall explore the essential role and nature of leadership required for building sustainable high performance. In particular, we shall consider how meaning lies at the heart of the positive psychological contract, creating the basis of employee commitment and engagement.

2

Building culture

Introduction

What makes seemingly similar firms in similar markets with similar products and brands nevertheless different? What is going to make them stand out? What makes sophisticated, high performing companies, trusted and invested in by the market, suddenly lose the market's confidence? What makes the difference is the way those organizations operate – what is valued, encouraged or tolerated. In other words, 'culture' counts. Interest in the role played by organizational culture in business success has been growing since the 1980s. In this chapter we shall explore what theorists commonly define as organizational culture and look at how cultures form. We shall then examine the debate around whether cultures can be deliberately changed, and look at the roles of various change agents/culture builders, especially leaders, HR professionals and line managers.

Culture as competitive advantage

The concept of culture being the great variable in what makes one company succeed while another fails is the rationale for focusing on building a performance culture. As Johan Nel, global HR Director of brewer SABMiller suggests (Nel, 2003):

It is easy to replicate a brewery or any kind of manufacturing infrastructure. What is not so easily copied, is how well those assets are managed, and how effectively that organization engages in innovative numerator activities. That comes from people's creativity and motivation.

An assumption behind the high performance organization input model is that if you get some of the organizational elements right, sustainable business success will follow – in particular, if you create a culture conducive to high performance, employees will 'naturally' want to give of their best and be enriched by the performance process.

Defining organizational culture

Organizational cultures, often described as 'the way we do things around here', are multifaceted and notoriously difficult to grasp. Culture provides a sense of identity to employees, supplying unwritten guidelines as to how to behave.

It represents the 'collective programming of mind which distinguishes the members of one organization from another' (Hofstede, 1991). For Marshall and McClean (1988), cultures represent 'the collection of traditions, values, policies, beliefs and attitudes that constitute a pervasive context for everything we do and think in an organisation'. For Edgar Schein (1993), too, cultures are 'a pattern of basic assumptions invented, discovered or developed by a given group as it learns to cope with its problems of external adaptation and internal integration'.

Every organizational culture is different – what works for one organization may not work for another, so assumptions are different. In order to understand or predict how an organization will behave under varying circumstances, one must know and understand the organization's pattern of basic assumptions. In every organization there will be some (or many) subcultures, often based on shared interest. The culture within these subgroups may vary, but at some level most share some common values and behaviours which are recognizably 'corporate'.

Culture blinds...

Culture represents the pervasive values, underlying assumptions, behaviours and norms that become taken-for-granted and largely invisible to those who are working within the culture. As the Chinese proverb says, 'the fish in the pond does not see water'. Louis (1983) claimed that culture determines what will be noticed and what will be hidden from perception. What is perceived, and the way it is perceived, becomes reality for the individual or group. It is through interactions with others that people create meaning, and this process is something individuals are generally unaware of as it is happening.

Culture is more often 'felt', most markedly by new employees as they enter an organization. The process of acculturation, by which new recruits become so integrated into the organization's way of doing things that they cease to be aware of what initially struck them as different about their new organization's culture, is thought to take as little as three weeks. Similarly, an organization's culture tends to be inferred from the outside, for instance by customers, based on perceptions created by the brand promise and customers' experience of the organization.

While a strong external brand can be a source of competitive advantage, it has to be matched by the company's culture or it can also become a company's 'weakest link'. For instance, if a company boasts of its excellent customer service through its advertising, but the reality of the service provided and of what is considered acceptable behaviour by employees are different, customers become dissatisfied and go elsewhere, as some once proud corporate giants have found to their cost in recent years. Similarly if, in the quest to recruit the best available employees, employers describe available roles and the organization in glowing and desirable terms, rather than describing the role context as it really is, new recruits soon become disillusioned and leave when they find the organizational experience to be very different from what they had been led to believe. As several major companies have learnt to their cost, poor cultural practice can damage their reputations.

Whether described as 'excellent', 'living', 'built to last' or 'great', high performance organizations generally have very strong and cohesive cultures, where the gap between espoused and real values is small.

Corporate cultures

Some organizations have strong unified pervasive cultures while others have weaker ones. Most have subcultures existing in different functional or geographical areas. These may form based, for instance, on gender, ethnicity, functional specialism and age group. In many organizations, the beleaguered 'smokers group' represents a cross-functional and cross-hierarchy subgroup in its own right. Each subgroup develops its own language, symbols, values, rules and behaviours. Some organizations positively encourage functional subgroups to play to their strengths, providing different physical environments, décor and management practices to enable people to give of their best.

Corporate culture often represents the contested arena where conflicting forces vie for supremacy. The differences between subgroups may lead to tension or conflict, such as the stereotypical differences between marketing functions and production departments. However, the dominant corporate culture still acts as a form of glue that usually holds business units together. If aspects of culture represent a barrier to what the organization is trying to achieve strategically, they may need to be changed. Cultural differences are usually seen most sharply in customer–supplier relationships and when two organizations are brought together, as in a merger, or when people from different organizations are required to collaborate, as in partnerships of various sorts.

To varying extents, corporate cultures will be influenced by national cultures, as described by Hofstede (1991) and Trompenaars (1993). In international organizations employing large numbers of local staff, the national culture will act as a moderator of the corporate culture – such as in recruitment practices, dress, management styles and subordinate behaviours. However, it is probable that the corporate culture will predominate over national culture, making local offices of the company have a familiar feel, atmosphere and shared values to some degree, wherever they are based.

According to Kotter (1995a), a unified culture offers advantages:

> *Corporate cultures can have a significant impact on a firm's long-term economic performance. We found that firms with cultures that emphasized all the key managerial constituencies outperformed firms that did not by a huge margin.*

Conversely, a strong corporate culture has its downsides. Since a strong organizational culture controls behaviour, it can block organizations from making changes that are needed to adapt to new market dynamics or new information technologies. As Baron and Walters (1994) suggest: 'Corporate cultures can either facilitate performance – maximising strategies – or be the instrument of their downfall'.

The difficulties of managing corporate culture

Pettigrew (1990) highlights a number of reasons why corporate culture is difficult to manage, and even more difficult to change. He points out that culture is not only deep but also broad. It refers not only to people, their relationships and beliefs, but also to products, structures, modes of recruitment and reward. Most firms do not have just a single corporate culture but a variety – in effect, a series of subcultures. Corporate culture is deeply imprinted, having a heavy historical impact on present and future management. The link between culture and the power distribution in the firm usually means that power groups with vested interests within the organization as it is may be unwilling to abandon those beliefs and assumptions without persistent and consistent challenge. Culture is interconnected not just with the politics of the firm but also with the structure, systems, people and priorities of the firm. The fact that so much of what is corporate culture is taken for granted makes it difficult to bring out into the open for people to consider.

Understanding cultures

Many theorists suggest that culture exists on several levels, with different features attached to each level. Knowledge of an organization's structure, information systems, strategic planning processes, markets, technology, goals etc. can offer clues about its culture, but not accurately. Typically, at the lowest layer are *assumptions* – the 'taken for granteds' – which are difficult to identify and explain, the real 'core' of culture. Above that are *beliefs*, which drive behaviour; these are more specific, are usually overt and talked about. On the next layer are *values*, which are often written down, include statements about purpose, mission and objectives, and are usually rather vague.

Overt phenomena

On the top layer are the visible manifestations of the culture – the way people dress and behave, the look of the offices, the customer service practices, operational characteristics and management styles. Edgar Schein (1993) has identified the following overt phenomena associated with culture:

1. Observed behavioural regularities when people interact, including the language they use
2. Group norms – the implicit standards and values that evolve in working groups
3. Espoused values – the articulated principles that the group claims to be trying to achieve
4. Formal philosophy – the broad policies and ideological principles
5. Rules of the game – the implicit rules for getting along in the organization that a newcomer must learn

6. Climate – the feeling that is conveyed in a group by the way group members interact
7. Embedded skills – the special competencies members display in accomplishing certain tasks
8. Habits of thinking, mental models and/or linguistic paradigms
9. Shared meanings – the emergent understandings that are created by group members as they interact with one another
10. 'Root metaphors' or integrating symbols – the ideas, feelings and images groups develop to characterize themselves, that become embodied in buildings, office layout etc.

Values

Beneath this overt layer are values. Here we are talking about the beliefs people hold about what is important and the way to go about things in the organization. They include justifications, goals, philosophies, slogans and strategies. For example, this way of doing things is valued over that because traditionally it has worked and has solved some organizational problems, of internal functioning or of response to the demands of the environment. The value 'It is best to communicate through the chain of command' is a value commonly found in the civil service, which arose originally from the military model of organization.

According to Deal and Kennedy (1982), values are the bedrock of organizational culture. They are the 'essence of organization's philosophy' for attaining success. They are the organization's 'essential and enduring tenets' (Collins and Porras, 1994). Organizations have gained great strength from shared values. For those who hold them, shared values create great certainty at a time of ambiguity. Dearlove and Coomber (2000) too place great emphasis on alignment or congruence between personal values and organizational values and the importance of emotional commitment. Peters and Waterman (1982) also claim that it was the sharing of values that made the difference between the 'excellent' versus the merely successful corporations in their study. They noted that these values are not always conveyed through formal documents.

Nadler and Tushman (1989) make the link between values, culture and norms of behaviour. They point out that values can sometimes be described in vague terms, whereas norms are a set of expected behaviours that are shaped by values. Where clear values and norms do not exist there is the danger of deviant forms of behaviour developing, together with chaotic evolution of the norms.

While it would be easy for organizations simply to adopt a made-up list of values – a typical list might include values such as integrity, teamworking, putting customers first, autonomy, personal growth – most writers agree that a vital part of making values meaningful is teasing them out in discussion and debate. Senge (1990) refers to the development of values as 'co-creating'. Defining the values is only one part of the process. Integrating them into day-to-day practice is the real challenge.

People are usually reasonably aware of and can articulate these values – indeed, new recruits to an organization are usually taught them formally or

informally – and they may be incorporated in statements of corporate philosophy. It is essential to distinguish between the *actual values* of an organization (i.e. those working principles that are the result of accumulated cultural
learning) and any *espoused values* (which may be written into company charters and may correspond to what people say happens or may want to happen,
but does not bear much relation to what people actually do). Too large a gap
between espoused and actual values can only generate cynicism.

Underlying assumptions

Beneath this layer are the basic underlying assumptions about the organization.
When some organizational values that were originally open to debate are seen
to work successfully for long enough, they tend to lose their subjective feel and
seem to become facts of life which are essentially 'right'. They become taken
for granted and drop out of awareness, just as habits become unconscious and
automatic. People lose a sense that certain ways of responding to situations
may be one choice amongst many possibilities. They assume that their behaviour reflects an accurate picture of reality, and that behaviour based on any
other premise is almost inconceivable. This fundamental level of organizational
culture is elusive, since the assumptions are, by definition, rarely debated.

Major change often brings to the surface assumptions that have long been
taken for granted but which employees may seek to preserve, and therefore
they oppose the change. Conversely, when artefacts and espoused values remain
on the 'wish list' rather than being a reflection of the true culture (i.e. a reflection of the basic underlying assumptions about the organization), cultural mis-
alignment and employee cynicism tend to occur. Then organizational leaders
often attempt to change or to realign the cultural elements. Changing the manifestations of the culture will be much easier than changing the core beliefs
which lie at the heart of the culture.

The 'shadow system'

Another characteristic of culture in human organizations is that they have both
formal and informal systems. The formal system (i.e. the legitimate hierarchy
of role and responsibilities) represents the espoused organizational culture and
values. However, systems of formal rules, authority and norms of rational
behaviour do not restrain the personal preferences of organizational members.
Instead these are controlled by the norms, values, beliefs and assumptions that
are shared by organizational members and define an organization's view of
itself and its environment. These less visible patterns of alliance, rivalry and
unofficial culture and values represent the informal or 'shadow' system.

Organizational networks

From complexity theory comes the notion that human organizations operate as
complex adaptive systems. As human systems, organizations are made up of

networks through which the culture operates. People use networks to deal with the highly ambiguous and unpredictable, inconsistent, conflicting, alienating aspects of organizational life. According to Stacey (1999), these networks are not established by some central prior intention or design. They are in effect self-organizing groups. They are neither formal nor legitimate – they have received no official seal of approval from the formal organization. Networks cannot be managed or controlled; one can only participate in them. They may be long-lasting social groups, or very short lived. They have a fluid, shifting quality.

For Deal and Kennedy (2000), networks exert a very powerful influence over organizational life:

> *The real business of a business gets done by the cultural network. In robust cultures, this informal group of players can reinforce the basic beliefs of the organization, enhance the symbolic value of heroic exploits by passing on stories of their deeds and accomplishments, set a new climate for change and provide a tight structure of influence for the CEO. In toxic cultures, the network becomes a formidable barrier to change.*

Power and organizational politics

Organizations are subject to organizational politics because of the fact that they are made up of coalitions of various individuals and interest groups. Drory and Romm (1990) suggest that the common features of many definitions of organizational politics are as follows:

- There is general recognition that to understand organizational politics involves breaking away from the realm of rational managerialism and being able to embrace a pluralistic perspective, including a study of human emotions, motivations and meaning-making
- Most definitions suggest that micropolitics involve protecting or advancing self-interest in the face of opposition
- There is recognition that an understanding of micropolitics is central to our understanding of the organization.

Many of the definitions of politics centre on notions of power and conflict resolution. According to Bolman and Deal (1997), there are enduring differences among coalition members regarding values, beliefs, information, interests and perceptions of reality. Micropolitics take place when organizational members use power to pursue their own interests. Power represents an individual's ability to influence or control their destiny, while interests represent the individual's end or goals, which may or may not coincide with those of the organization.

Hoyle (1982) defined micropolitics as the 'dark side of organizational life', embracing 'those strategies by which individuals and groups in organizational contexts seek to use their resources of power and influence to further their interests'. McCalman and Paton (2000) define politics as 'the use of power and influencing techniques and tactics (sanctioned or unsanctioned) aimed at accomplishing personal and/or organizational goals'. Pfeffer (1981) suggests that organizational politics 'involves those activities taken within organizations to acquire, develop, and use power and other resources to obtain one's preferred outcomes in a situation in which there is uncertainty or dissensus'. Ball (1987) considers micropolitics in relation to three key and interrelated areas of organizational activity – the interests of 'actors', the maintenance of organizational control and conflict over policy.

Butcher and Clarke (2002) are critical of advice given to managers contemplating change to take a rational and logical approach to dealing with politics. This advice typically involves combating political behaviour with a clear and objective plan of action that will be understood by all. This in turn has spawned what Buchanan and Boddy (1992) have christened the 'truth, trust, love and collaboration' approach to implementing change. The 'pursuit of excellence' fad of the 1980s extolled the need for honest and open communication, of the need to empower people to make decisions for themselves in the interests of the customer. Participation and involvement were seen as the way of overcoming self-interest and turf wars. Whilst this approach clearly has value, our data suggest that relying on such techniques is far from logical or rational.

Change, conflict and political activity

The study of change is a central feature of the approach of conflict theorists since change, or the possibility of change, brings to the surface subterranean conflicts and differences which are otherwise glossed over or obscured in the daily routines of organizational life. Micropolitics is most likely to occur when there is a crisis, uncertainty, change, differentiation of interests, or conflict. Most important decisions involve the allocation of scarce resources. These scarce resources, together with the enduring differences between coalition members, mean that conflict plays a central role in organizational dynamics and makes power the most important resource. Conflict typically occurs when there is competition for power, where the key issue is bound up with who is in control.

Moreover, according to Baldridge (1971), if the social system is fragmented by divergent values and conflicting interest groups, change is to be expected. Conflict theorists emphasize the fragmentation of social systems into interest groups, each with its own particular goals. They study the interaction between these different interest groups and the conflict processes by which one group tries to gain advantage over another. Interest groups cluster around divergent values, and the study of conflicting interests is a key part of the analysis.

Goals and decisions emerge from bargaining, negotiation and jockeying for position among different stakeholders. Shortage of resource, shifting allegiances as a result of mergers and acquisitions, global competition and the resulting emphasis on influence and negotiation have contributed to the reported increased importance of micropolitical skills in today's workplace. This is evident in the 2004 *Management Agenda* findings, where 60 per cent of respondents reported increased levels of political activity compared with the recent past.

Even though politics comes to the fore during times of change, the essentially political nature of organizational life is evident in these findings. People reported that engaging in political behaviour was essential for getting things done in their organization, since it is the norm. Political behaviour is often accompanied by breakdowns in trust, and increased risk avoidance by people who feel they need to 'watch their backs'. This often causes change efforts to become derailed by the behaviours of both political activists and avoiders.

Other writers, such as Thomas Kilmann, have explored sources of conflict from the point of view of potential conflict resolution (Kilmann, 1996). While differences in objectives, both explicit and implicit, can lend themselves to resolution by being brought into the open through skilled questioning, listening, negotiated agreement or arbitration, competition for power can be very difficult to resolve and the objectives, methods and factual detail may be irrelevant.

Change can also challenge the core values held by organizational members. More recent management literature has focused on issues such as the role of organizations in their communities, corporate social responsibility and corporate ethics. The focus on acting ethically is reflected in some of the literature on micropolitics, where the issue of whether political behaviour can be seen as ethical is debated. Maclagan (1998), for instance, argues that the assumption that political activities are motivated by pure self-interest may be incorrect – that people may have more balanced motivations between the self and the wider good.

Organizational climate

Culture should be distinguished from climate. The climate of the organization is the psychological atmosphere that surrounds the way the organization's structure works. It represents the 'feel of the place' at a given moment in time, and is evident, for instance, in the state of staff morale, in the degree of urgency people bring to their tasks, and in the levels of trust that exist between people. An organizational climate is a system composed of interrelated parts. A change in one part of the system impacts on all the others.

In contrast to culture, climate is more 'local' and more likely to be shaped by leaders at different levels of the organization. While culture is regarded as an enduring set of values, beliefs and assumptions that characterize an organization and its employees, climate refers to more temporary attitudes, feelings and behaviours. Culture is slow to change, whereas climate, because it is affected by attitudes towards events, can change quickly.

Climate is both the result of and the shaper of people's behaviour. In much current theory, climate is considered to have a greater bearing on an organization's ability to stimulate high performance than the broader culture. According to Cannon (2003), the three primary effects of organizational climate are on employee motivation, employee development and retention, and employee performance. Motivation is a direct result of the organizational unit's climate. It is the creation of specific psychological states that predispose an individual to behave in certain ways. Climate creates expectations; expectations arouse and reinforce certain kinds of motivation while inhibiting others.

The combination of aroused motivation and the skills of individuals, plus the effectiveness of the team, result in productive behaviour. The desired balance between various motivational states is dependent on the purpose and nature of the organizational tasks. Hence, motivation that is appropriate to the task at hand will result in high performance, whereas inappropriate motivation may negatively affect performance. The three primary influences affecting organizational climate include leadership practices; organizational culture; and structure, systems and procedures.

Many aspects of climate can be measured – through staff attitude surveys, for instance. As such, aspects of climate can sometimes be used as a short-term indicator of organizational health and likely performance. At the start of a period of change it is useful to assess the different aspects of the organization's climate, such as trust levels, morale and stress. Problems in the climate often appear to have their roots in the structure, and may produce a drag on productivity or on people's willingness to change. However, the organizational climate and employee attitudes cannot be controlled directly. To make changes in the climate, change should be targeted at the way work gets done.

How do cultures form?

Culture is shaped by many factors, including the societal culture in which an organization resides, its technologies, markets and competition, and the personality of its founding fathers. Culture develops during the course of social interaction. In organizations there are many different and competing value systems that create a range of organization realities and subcultures, rather than a uniform corporate culture.

Cultures are slow to form and, of course, developing a high performance culture does not happen overnight. Some theorists argue that organizational cultures evolve 'naturally' through a series of phases that reflect their strategic business needs. According to Harung and Dahl (1995), there are four stages of organizational development that lead through to breakthrough improvements of individual and organizational performance:

1. *Task-oriented*. Workers perform single or a few tasks which, when seen in isolation, are often meaningless. Coordination is achieved through an extensive vertical command and control hierarchy. Initiative and decision-making are concentrated at the top. This type of organization is often characterized by internal competition, where the priority may be more on pleasing superiors than, for instance, customers.
2. *Process-oriented*. Work is performed by teams and centred on holistic processes that encompass a number of tasks. Jobs are multi-skilled. Teams are, to a large extent, autonomous, and there is a flatter organizational structure. Emphasis is more on performance and contribution than on seniority.

3. *Value-*or *culture-driven*. The main focus is on making sure that all employees have sound and healthy values – i.e. that the culture is advanced. There
is a higher degree of empowerment and self-management than in process-
oriented organizations. Emphasis tends to be on mutual support and coaching.
4. *Development-oriented*. In later stages of human development, the individual automatically exhibits sound values, high creativity and effectiveness.
Therefore, the focus in this type of organization is on realizing that which is
most important – i.e. development of consciousness.

Culture's patterns are also enduring and provide employees with a sense of
continuity. As one CEO said of her organization: 'Managers may come and
managers may go, yet this organization goes on for ever – it's in the walls!'.
Many organizational behaviours and decisions are predetermined by the patterns of basic assumptions that are held by members of an organization. These
patterns continue to exist and to influence behaviours in an organization long
after the practices no longer serve a purpose, because they have led people to
make decisions that 'worked in the past'.

Cultural elements

Many analysts see organizational culture elements as part of a web of interconnected systems. These cultural elements have a significant symbolic role,
creating a shared understanding amongst organizational members about what
is important, what is valued and how it is appropriate to behave. Pettigrew (1990),
for instance, suggests that, at the deepest level, culture is represented as a complex set of values, beliefs, myths and patterns of reward inside the organization.

Johnson (1990) argues that these cultural elements have the role of reinforcing both the *status quo* and the past, even while they are being reproduced
and co-created through the use of ritual, symbolism, metaphor and shared values.
These reflect, and shape, the behaviour of organizational members. So important
is 'the centrality of organizational symbols in both preserving existing strategies
and helping achieve strategic change' that it 'suggests that more explicit attention
should be paid to the auditing of the symbolic artefacts of organizations'.

Managers who want to bring about major culture change need to develop
and cause to be absorbed distinctive sets of ideologies and cultural forms that
will suit the organization and its members. This involves changing many
cultural elements so that 'together they reflect a new pattern of values, norms
and expectations' (Kanter, 1983). To achieve significant culture change in this
way is thought to take several years. However, small-scale changes can be
achieved through 'tinkering' with some of the cultural elements, gradually producing a domino effect on the way things are done. Almost without those
involved being consciously aware of what is happening, a 'tipping point' is
reached in terms of changed attitudes and behaviours.

A cultural web of interconnected elements

Johnson and Scholes's (2002) cultural web model (see Figure 2.1) identifies a
number of symbolic elements that help to create meaning for organizational

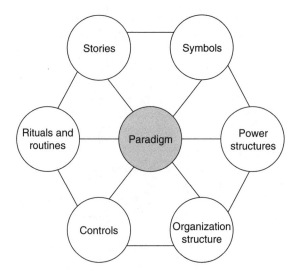

Figure 2.1 The cultural web.
Source: Johnson, G. and Scholes, K. (2002) *Exploring Corporate Strategy*
(6th edn), FT Prentice Hall, New York (Pearson)

members. Embedding new cultural practices involves changing the meaning
that is shared.

The paradigm

In the cultural web model, the paradigm at the heart of the model is the set of
core beliefs that result from the multiplicity of conversations, which maintain
the unity of the culture. When organizations remain firmly embedded within
their own paradigm, they may cease to adapt to changes in the environment. In
such circumstances, 'second-order' change will be required. If not, deteriorat-
ing performance will force change due to external pressure. Yet if change programmes are focused on the outer elements of the cultural web, a lot of effort
usually produces limited success.

Rituals and routines

Johnson suggests that myths, rituals and other symbolic aspects of organization do not merely endow and encapsulate meaning on a transitory basis. They
are enduring and can be resistant to change: 'In effect they are mechanisms
which help preserve the assumptions and beliefs within which the strategy is
rooted'.

Trice and Beyer (1984) view cultures as made up of two components: the
network of meaning contained in ideologies, norms and values, and the culture's forms; and the practices through which meanings are affirmed and communicated to organizational members. They emphasize the importance of

ritual, language and ceremony in heightening the expression of shared meaning. They identify specific rites for different functions, such as rites of enhancement, of renewal and of conflict reduction. Trice and Beyer (1984) show the importance of organizational rituals and ceremonies in providing organizational coherence.

Managers learn to rely on routines that have evolved in the organization. If new ways of doing things move outside established norms, affecting social systems and working relationships, such change is likely to be perceived as threatening. Indeed there may be solidarity among groups to protect current norms, evident in political opposition. Change agents have to face executives and others – agents of 'strategic momentum' – whose power is based on the existing organizational paradigm. The change agent has to challenge that which is taken for granted and create commitment to a new vision.

Symbols

Symbols are objects, actions, events, images, rituals and metaphors that rise out of, and help to create culture. Symbolism expresses the value system of an organization. This symbolic dimension is evident, for instance, in the design of physical space, with company facades and buildings projecting the organization's values to both employees and the external world. Corporate branding, made visible in logos, company colours and typefaces, tends to project the aspired-to culture. These symbols reinforce shared meaning among organizational members and are frequently used to influence meaning, and therefore behaviour.

When companies are attempting to change their culture, they often embark on a rebranding exercise, resulting in a new corporate identity. However, unless the new identity is forged onto the beginnings of changed behaviour, there can often be too great a mismatch between what customers and employees experience versus the promise implicit in the symbolic shift of identity. Such gaps tend to give rise to greater employee disaffection and cynicism, making real change more difficult.

Stories

Other significant secondary mechanisms in transmitting culture include the stories, legends, myths and parables about important events and people. These exaggerate and simplify key messages about how to behave and what is valued. Formal statements of organizational philosophy, creeds and charters are also important transmitters of the culture if they are consistent with what is actually valued and rewarded.

Wilkins (1989) suggests that stories used, for example by the leader in communicating the organization's vision, provide energy and integrate various units of the organization toward the vision. They act as 'third-order' controls because they facilitate memory, tend to generate belief, and seem to encourage attitudinal commitment by appealing to legitimate values. Wilkins examined the commonest types of story, which revolve around culture, appropriate work processes, general managerial philosophy, or the histories of visionary heroes and the 'glory days'. The stories reinforce the basic values of the culture by making success attainable, by motivating employees and by setting a standard for performance. Wilkins found a positive correlation between the number and type of organizational stories told and employee commitment to the organization.

Metaphor

Meyer (1982) suggests that 'organizational ideologies are manifested and sustained by beliefs, stories, language and ceremonial acts'. Pfeffer (1981, in Johnson, 1990) also argues that 'language, symbolism and ritual are important elements in the process of developing shared systems of belief and meaning' and 'it is the symbolic identification with organization or decisions, as much as real choice and participation, that produces commitment and action'.

Many theorists have examined the role of metaphor as an organizational control of the third order. Metaphor is a way of seeing things as if they were something else. In many organizations, the use of military metaphor is still evident in the 'chain of command', implying clear demarcations of rank, access to information, role responsibilities, and which actions represent compliance or insubordination. While metaphor can be enriching in some ways, since it moves people's perceptions along the path of the dominant beliefs and values, it can also be limiting, since the language used may draw employees' attention towards a particular set of things and cause them completely to overlook other things.

Power structures

Watson and Crossley (2001) suggest that organizational power relationships are intrinsic to managerial roles. Organizations, and often organizational units and various managerial levels within one organization, differ as regards the way power is distributed in them. The creation, implementation and management of strategy has political implications, and managers may need to utilize, influence and shape power relationships to cope with new learning and possible resistance. Similarly, Hardy (1996) suggests that 'actions that are crucial to the realization of strategic goals do not just "happen" – power is needed to orchestrate and direct them'. Hardy sees power as an integral part of the strategy process, whether there is general support for common goals or 'political cauldrons' of conflict or resistance.

Influencing cultural elements

Even though these elements of the cultural web reinforce and lend coherence to the existing culture, at the same time they lend themselves to new messages. For example, some organizations use positive stories which they want new recruits to learn in induction processes, so that new behaviours can 'virtuously contaminate' less positive behaviours. Creating new symbols of success – such as replacing awards for numbers of sales achieved, regardless of how they were achieved, with awards that also give honour to the method by which sales were achieved – helps to shift behaviours. Using rewards differently – for example, not promoting the most political manager to a senior position but favouring those who are effective without being unscrupulous – can send powerful signals that change for the better is possible. We shall look in more detail at the role of reward in high performance in Chapter 11.

Who are the culture builders?

It could be argued that everyone who works in an organization is building culture – everyday. Some of the 'taken for granteds' are gradually challenged within individual work groups, new ideas are spread through networks, and external influences start to take the blinkers away from the eyes of people who have long been blind to other possibilities because of the strength of their own culture.

However, some people have a disproportionate impact on culture acting as agents of change, simply because of the nature of their roles and responsibilities as much as by the strength of their personalities. 'Change agent' here refers to the executives, line managers, transition teams, human resources professionals, external and internal consultants and others who have a part to play in designed change processes. Connor (1988) argues that no substantive change can occur without effective sponsorship at senior-level. He suggests that in any change effort there are four key roles: 'sponsors', who legitimize the change; 'agents', who carry out the change; 'targets', who receive and accommodate the change; and 'advocates', who want the change but do not have the power to sponsor it themselves. It could be argued that everyone in a changing organization becomes a change agent at some level – even if simply by having conversations with colleagues about what is going on, individuals contribute to the corporate 'reframing'.

In transformational change, a change agent's role can be that of an architect designing and facilitating the change process. For Bunker and Alban (1997), this is about getting 'the whole system involved, knowledgeable, aligned around a set of goals, and moving in a concerted direction'. For Tichy and Devanna (1990), the change agent may be involved in structural and other changes.

The role of leaders in leading culture change

The impact of top leader attitudes on building an organization's capacity for culture change should not be underestimated.

Top managers generally have the 'sponsor' role in bringing about change, but they are also active agents of culture shifts in more subtle ways. While theories about different kinds of leadership abound, most share certain common elements. For David Weidman (2002), change leadership involves a radical shift in attitudes and style, moving away from:

- Optimizing the business model to creating the business model
- People leadership skills to change leadership skills
- Managing through turbulent seas to forcing change as a competitive advantage
- Avoiding change to embracing change
- Multinational to multicultural
- Master delegator to 'hands on' and 'minds on'
- Reducing uncertainty to leveraging uncertainty
- Change = chaos to change = progress
- Leading evolution to leading revolution.

The task of a change leader involves more than bringing about change. According to Moran and Brightman (2002):

> The job of a change leader in an organization is to challenge people to align their purpose, identity and mastery with necessary organization change. This type of critical questioning can only take place in a safe environment. Change leaders help create this safe environment for this type of critical questioning to take place. They encourage people to collaborate, take risks, take responsibility and be accountable for the change process the organization must continually undergo to maintain a leadership position in its industry.

Whether or not the organization is undergoing radical change, all leaders (whether they are sponsors, agents or influencers) must act as role models, tackling resistance, creating readiness for change and building commitment at every level of the organization. Leaders must prepare people for ongoing change to provide long-term growth and viability. They have to create a constructive change process, getting people positively involved in the change process so that resistance to change can give way to new development. They must provide clear change goals and targets, and help to develop a culture that is supportive of learning and experimentation.

At the same time, a leader's challenge is to balance the drive for change and progress with preserving the core of the organization. Collins and Porras (1994) quote Thomas J. Watson Junior of IBM, as follows:

> If an organization is to meet the challenges of the changing world, it must be prepared to change everything about itself except its basic beliefs as it moves through corporate life…. The only sacred cow in an organization should be its basic philosophy of doing business.

Paradoxically, leaders need to be able to both create a sense of stability, so that employees can have feelings of security, while promoting ongoing change to secure the future. Beaudan (2002) argues that in turbulent times, managers should forget about talking about change and concentrate on motivating, energizing and focusing employees on the present. For Beaudan, this is about acknowledging the facts, being visible, reasserting purpose and fostering new leaders.

Distinguishing leadership from management

Theorists have for years attempted to distinguish between management and leadership. John Kotter (1990) suggests that leadership is about establishing the direction, aligning people, motivating and inspiring, and producing long-lasting change. Management, by contrast, is about planning/budgeting, organizing/ staffing, controlling/problem-solving, and producing predictable results expected by shareholders. For Warren Bennis (1989), the manager administers, maintains, focuses on systems and standards, has a short-range view, has an eye on the bottom line, and initiates yet accepts the *status quo*. For Bennis, the distinction between the two is summarized as follows: 'Management is about doing things right; leadership is about doing the right things'.

A simple but effective way of thinking about the processes involved in change leadership is drawn from the work of Professor John Morris of Salford University. According to Morris's model, all managers are involved in three basic activities – keeping things going, putting things right and doing new things. It is the blend and emphasis of these three elements in how managers spend their time which will suggest whether they have primarily a management or a leadership focus.

For example, if the focus of 'doing new things' is in order to 'put things right' so that things can be 'kept going', this is more likely to be a management focus. On the other hand, a greater emphasis on doing new things which are likely to create a new way forward for the organization is more of a leadership focus. However, a leader whose focus is exclusively on doing new things needs a team of people who can translate the strategic direction into implementation activities so that the new direction can be realized. Similarly, the leader needs to be fully aware of the level of readiness of the organization for the new things that are to be introduced. If the organization is on a different axis from the leader, the implementation of new plans will be difficult to realize. The leader has to remain in touch with the organization and be able, as a result, to work out how best to bring about necessary change.

This leads Morris to consider that four processes are essential for effective leadership. The first is in providing answers to the question: what are we going to do? This is the process of *visioning*, creating a sense of direction and purpose. In practice, this involves developing a vision, mission, strategy, tactics, goals, measures etc. The next involves answering the question: how are we going to do this? The process involved is *designing* (organizational design) – creating the structures, processes, procedures, patterns of working and resources to make the strategy realizable.

The third involves answering the question: who is going to do this? The process involved is *enabling* people. This is not just about selection, training and development, but also about providing people with the right kind of management support they need to do the job. The final process, and perhaps the least practised, involves answering the question: why are we doing this? The process involved is *valuing*. This is thought to be the key process through which employee commitment can be obtained, and it entails creating a sense of community with strong and honest values.

The latter process highlights the almost symbolic role of leaders. Their greater visibility within organizations makes any slippage from practising what they preach all the more evident, and can lead to increased employee cynicism. Leadership involves setting the direction at the 'big picture' level, inspiring people to embark on the journey, because unless people are committed to what needs to be done, the organization will fail in its mission. For Warren Bennis, the leader innovates, develops, inspires trust, has a long-range perspective, originates, challenges the *status quo* and focuses on people.

In effect, leaders at all levels are involved in bringing about change, whether they are in top management roles, developing new strategic directions, or in more junior leadership positions charged with finding new, smarter, cheaper, faster ways of getting the core business done. Given that nothing stays the same, change is an inherent part of keeping things stable (first-order change). A second-order change involves changing the way things are changed – from taking the organization in a fundamentally new direction, to changing the way in which employees approach their work. Management, on the other hand, is about devising the means to implement the plan and making sure that the journey is completed. This somewhat artificial split tends to lead to debates about whether anyone can lead, whether the responsibilities of management and leadership can be carried out by the same person, etc.

Much recent theorizing suggests that both management and leadership are needed at all times, but that sometimes one is needed more than the other; and that management skills are not solely about maintaining the *status quo* but also involve providing the dynamic stability required by continuously modifying a firm's production processes. Similarly, that leadership is not solely restricted to those in senior positions but should be shared and nurtured at all levels (distributed leadership).

There is a heavy emphasis in leadership literature on alignment – i.e. ensuring that all aspects of an organization's system, especially employees, are pulling in the same direction, preferably that suggested by its strategy. Also, in contemporary thinking, leaders are expected to lead by winning over hearts and minds and gaining commitment from employees, rather than through dictat, bullying and contractual controls. This is attunement, or the almost spiritual attachment of people to the organization and their tasks within it.

Vogues in leadership theory of the past twenty years have typically focused on the attributes of leaders and the tasks of leaders in providing direction, in developing the organization and in championing change. Other functions include ensuring alignment, building commitment and facing adaptive challenges. Many theorists have seen the primary roles of leaders as being to enact change, which by definition requires creating a new system and then institutionalizing the new approaches (John Kotter, 1995b). Other theorists have focused on what it means to exercise change-oriented leadership, while not necessarily bringing about dramatic forms of change. Aligning aspects of the organization's culture with the change agenda by eliminating barriers to change is another key leadership task.

Another key theme is the role of leaders in maximizing the organization's capabilities. For Peters and Waterman (1982), 'Leadership denotes unleashing energy, building, freeing and growing'. Sir Raymond Lygo, Chief Executive of British Aerospace, was quoted as saying, 'Leadership is the art of getting from people more than they think they are capable of giving'.

More recent theories have focused on the results that leaders need to deliver and the tailoring of leader attributes and style to required outputs. Many studies highlight the various perceived deficiencies of real-life leaders, which are sometimes caused by the goals of the strategy and leadership going off at different tangents. Most theories focus on the role of top management; few focus on the role of middle management in bringing about change. However, Gabel (2002) points out the importance of this tier. Indeed, he suggests that success for many managers and leaders at all levels depends on their ability to manage a variety of situations from a position that is commonly experienced as being 'caught in the middle':

> *They inevitably act (or should act) with knowledge that there are those below them and those above them who have different or conflicting views on a given position facing the organization. The successful leader or manager understands these different perspectives and, while having to follow a specific direction or broad outlines of those above himself or herself, must lead those below in a manner that ensures organizational morale and success.*

According to research into leadership conducted for the UK's Chartered Management Institute (CMI), in today's workplace the emphasis has moved away from a style of leadership that focuses on a remote individual and toward a team approach and shared responsibilities. Most executives prefer a 'relational' model of leadership, in which the leader's main role is to create a sense of purpose and a central vision, then help to bring out the potential of others around them to achieve these goals. A growing scepticism in the power of a top executive such as Jack Welch (see Welch, 2001) to bring about lasting change is evident in the new focus is on 'non-heroic' leadership, which is an enabling form of leadership, practised by people at all levels. 'Servant leader' theories emphasize the ability of leaders to create a constructive climate.

Jim Collins, author of *From Good to Great* (2001), suggests that leadership at each of five levels is needed for corporate success. Level 1, the highly capable individual, makes productive contributions through talent, knowledge, skills and good work habits. Level 2, the contributing team member, contributes individual capabilities to the achievement of group objectives and works effectively with others in a group setting. Level 3, the competent manager, organizes people and resources toward the effective and efficient pursuit of pre-determined objectives. Level 4, the leader, catalyses commitment to, and vigorous pursuit of, predetermined objectives. Level 5, the executive, builds enduring greatness through a paradoxical blend of personal humility and professional will, and is totally committed to furthering the organization's interests. Level 5 leadership is the first of eight key traits of companies that have transformed themselves from good to 'great'.

How leaders embed and transmit culture

Leaders have been found to exert a profound influence on the creation and maintenance of corporate culture. Edgar Schein (1993) made a lengthy study of how leaders embed and transmit culture. He found that mechanisms for embedding culture vary according to how powerful their effects are, how implicit or explicit the messages are, and how intentional they are. The primary mechanisms include what leaders pay attention to, measure, and control. Waterman (1994) too found that top leaders' attitudes and attention can produce change: 'Visible management attention, rather than exhortation, gets things done'. Similarly, how leaders react to critical incidents and organizational crises, where the heightened emotional involvement increases the intensity of learning, is a powerful means of creating 'blame' or 'learning' cultures.

Deliberate role modelling, teaching and coaching by leaders is also disproportionately effective in teaching people what is really valued in the organization. This can be either potentially helpful or very damaging to the development of high performance. If leaders are conflicted, for instance, conflicts become a powerful part of the culture.

Leaders have a particularly strong role in crafting meaning in organizations. They control the formal communications processes which, through the way these are used rather than the content, can send powerful messages to employees – keeping them in the dark, overloading them with data, inviting involvement and ideas, being strictly one-way etc. Leaders can shape and influence the 'way we do things around here' through the language that they use and by their own behaviour. As Schein (1993) suggests:

> The bottom line for leaders is that if they do not become conscious of the cultures in which they are embedded, those cultures will manage them. Cultural understanding is desirable for all of us, but it is essential for those who lead.

Providing direction

Leaders are responsible for creating the organization's direction, usually in line with its core purpose. The strategies they use usually reflect leaders' perceptions about power – their own and that of other people. They will have a sense of how the process of decision-making should happen, about what should be delegated and what should be rigidly controlled. They may, for instance, have consulted (or not) a wide range of stakeholders, including front-line staff. Decisions taken by top management teach employees how much they are 'empowered', how positive top management is about the future of the organization, how confident and courageous top managers are about points of principle, which stakeholder groups count in decision-making, and whether or not top management are to be trusted.

Various studies (Pettigrew, 1985; Johnson, 1987) suggest that when top managers fully embrace the symbolic aspects of the leadership role, they can play a key part in guiding the organization through culture change.

Leadership by top managers seems to be an essential ingredient of major cultural change, because to change cultures generally requires power at a level usually only found at the top of organizations. Top managers control resources, around which there is usually much political positioning and conflict. If leaders want change to succeed, they tend to ensure that most of the needed resources are made available; if not, they will starve the change project of funds and procrastinate on decision-making so that the project becomes redundant. While Whipp *et al.* (1989) found that no single leadership style is the optimum, since leadership is highly context-sensitive, leaders at all levels need to communicate values and organizational direction, champion the longer-term perspective, and oversee but not manage the translation of strategic intentions into operational changes. The leadership role in revitalizing organizations is explored in more detail in Chapter 7.

The role of line managers as change agents

Line managers are usually the real leaders of change on a day-to-day basis. They are required to translate the strategic imperative into operational implementation. It is often the demands of the task, for example for teamworking, that drives culture change at this level. Middle managers in particular need to be able to create a climate appropriate to the desired change outcomes, such as improved customer service, by focusing people's energies on the practices and procedures that enable service, while providing management reward and support to those involved. They have a key role to play in releasing employee potential in the workplace, by designing roles that provide a positive and motivating stretch for employees, by coaching and developing their teams and by managing performance effectively.

They are the organization's 'gatekeepers', acting as conduits of information, opportunity and resource. However, they are sometimes described by top managers as 'the problem layer', they are often perceived to be resistant to change; likely to absorb but not pass on information they should be communicating to their teams. They are also caught in the 'coronary sandwich', in which much is expected of them both by their own managers and by direct reports. Unless they are appropriately delegated to, involved in decision-making and/or given relevant information, they are unlikely to be able to manage change very well and will feel under pressure. Often expected to manage 'business as usual' against a fast-changing backdrop, managers frequently do not receive the help – training, for instance – they need to support others through change.

Human resource professionals as change agents

What will be evident from the high performance input model is that HR, as the people specialist function, arguably more than other business functions, has potentially *the* key role in helping organizations to achieve sustainable high performance. This is because what is involved is essentially about culture-building, for which HR has at its disposal many of the necessary levers, including:

- Working with leadership teams to help shape thinking about the people implications of business strategy
- Developing people strategies which serve both short-term and longer-term needs
- Shaping policies that go beyond compliance to enable the application of best practice and imaginative treatment of employees
- Working with the organization's 'gatekeepers' – managers at all levels – and helping them build the skills required for effective team-building, performance management and leadership
- Building a leadership cadre whose values and approaches will reinforce high performance practices.

In addition, HR can use its tools – such as reward systems, organization design, and recruitment practices – to ensure that their organization is able to attract and retain the talent it needs.

The challenge for HR is to make choices about how best to use these levers and where to focus energies both to address short-term business needs and to build strategic capability for the future. Given the heavy workloads of most HR teams, this will not be about adding to the 'to do' list; it is more likely to involve reconfiguring objectives to meet a broader strategic agenda. This will involve finding quicker, easier, more customer-focused ways of delivering HR infrastructure, such as administration, in order to free up time for 'employee champion' and change agent roles. Similarly, aligning HR strategies to business strategy will involve addressing short-term resourcing and other requirements, while using HR planning, leadership development and other tools to support the development of a flexible, change-able culture. The role of HR as culture-builder is explored in more detail in Chapter 12.

Other change agents

Many specialist groups are involved in leading planned change. IT and Finance specialists are often at the forefront of change initiatives, for example the introduction of an integrated system such as SAP. What has become evident in many organizations is that it is helpful if all change agents act in a coordinated way, thinking through the related implications of what they are proposing so that greater consistency and efficiency can be achieved. Some of the more effective groupings of change agents involve functional specialists – HR, Finance and IT – with business managers, stakeholder representatives and external consultants, under the sponsorship of a top-level champion who maintains support for, and an active focus on, the progress of the change initiative.

Conclusion

Culture can change and is changing all the time. People working within a human system can and do produce change simply by interacting. Some individuals, particularly those in senior leadership positions, have greater potential to influence what happens than others simply because of their greater access to power and resources and their higher visibility, which amplifies the effect of what they do. Yet even leaders can more obviously impact the more transitory climate of the organization than its underlying culture, because culture is essentially longer lasting.

In later chapters we shall look at how the chances of building a high performance culture can be maximized by involving others in the process as actors in, rather than as subjects of, the change process. This is creating the context for 'virtuous' emergence. However, planning and designing do have a legitimate part to play in creating the foundations for a high performance culture. In the next two chapters we shall look at aspects of planned approaches to culture-building and change; in particular, how to analyse organizational cultures and (re)design organizations with high performance principles in mind.

Key points

- Shared meaning, or culture, is continuously created and recreated by individuals through their interactions with one another. Some of what is created becomes taken for granted and affects people's perception, especially of the need for change.
- The process of creating shared meaning is influenced to a large extent by people in organizations who hold power. These people are in a position to manipulate various symbols, such as what gets rewarded, which causes people to change their behaviour.
- Cultures can cause organizational members to ignore vital messages from elsewhere.
- Cultures are enduring, and can be difficult to change.
- Deliberate attempts to change culture are likely to meet opposition.
- A high performing organization is likely to be characterized by strong, shared values.

3

Can culture be deliberately changed?

Many managers have found from bitter experience that attempts to manage culture can result in frustration and confusion.
(Baron and Walters, 1994)

Introduction

While most of the 'excellent', 'visionary', 'living' and 'great' companies previously mentioned attribute their sustainable success in large part to their robust cultures, there are situations in which a company's culture (or elements of it) can become an impediment to further success. It is in this context that management teams call for cultural change and change projects proliferate. In this chapter we shall look at some of the challenges involved in bringing about culture change and consider if, and in what sense, culture can be deliberately changed. In particular, we shall look at where and how change efforts might be directed to close the gap between strategic intent and implementation.

Can cultures be changed?

This topic is much debated. Culture change is implicit in any form of organizational change. Organizational cultures, through their structures, visible artefacts, management practices and work processes, are the arena in which the change effort gets acted out. What is commonly understood as culture change usually involves a break with the past in a fundamental way, though sometimes this involves merely incorporating a few new cultural elements. Even to maintain a culture may require some adjustments as the environment changes. Culture is both an input and an output: employees and senior managers are as much the product of the culture as the creators of culture. Attempting to change the organization's culture is therefore a significant challenge.

However, deliberate culture change can be costly and difficult to achieve, as Kotter (1995a) states:

Such change is complex, takes time and requires leadership, which is something quite different from even excellent management. That leadership must be guided by a realistic vision of what kinds of cultures enhance performance.

Kotter and Heskett (1992) argue that the difficulties involved in managing culture change are underestimated by leaders. Changes are not only disruptive to organizational processes and procedures; they are also disruptive to individual members of the organization. Culture is the space where organizations hang on to what has been, and is. Any form of organizational change will cause shifts or tensions within the organization's culture at some level. The shadow (or informal) side of the organization is not rational, but is charged with emotions, affiliations, vested interests. It is here where resistance to change is likely to be most active.

Managers who want to bring about major culture change need to develop and cause to be absorbed distinctive sets of ideologies and cultural forms that will suit the organization and its members. This involves changing many cultural elements so that 'together they reflect a new pattern of values, norms and expectations' (Kanter, 1983). To achieve significant culture change in this way may take several years. Change leaders at any level will need to be able to understand the elements at work in any change process, and to use judgement about the style of leadership required to give the change effort the best chance of success. Since leading change is not just a rational process but is also a highly political, intuitive and emotional process, it requires 'emotional intelligence' on the part of leaders.

Given the difficulties, Richard Seel (2000) suggests 'we should move away from trying to change organizations and instead look at how we might help them become ready for change – to move to a state of self-organized criticality' (where even the smallest stimulus may cause major changes). Surfacing and critiquing the 'taken for granteds' is important if the organization is not to find itself out of tune with its environment. Organizations and individuals need to be able to cope with frequent change in order to secure long-term business success. In Roffey Park's model of high performance, the organization's ability to respond quickly and efficiently to changing circumstances is fundamental to sustainable success. Creating readiness for change is explored in Chapter 6.

Employee reactions

In *Management Agenda* surveys, we ask organizational employees to identify from their own experience what leads to successful change. Many respondents highlight the importance of having the right business strategy – good marketing, effective financial controls, sound product market posture, tightly controlled costs and high quality. However, these business factors are not the primary cause of successful change as far as our respondents are concerned. The ingredients of successful change for employees include being involved, understanding the vision and the rationale, and having opportunities for personal growth.

Organizational change imposed from above, by definition, violates the 'psychological contract' – the unwritten mutual expectations that employers and employees have of each other. Change can become self-defeating if the consequent disenchantment and loss of commitment leads people to under-perform or to leave the organization. To accept and respond positively to change, employees need to feel that they have some influence over it and can see benefits in it for themselves. However, the benefits of change for an employee may not be immediately obvious. In many cases, the harsh reality is that the business and the individual's job will not survive unless there is radical change. In this situation it is particularly important for the business to fully mobilize the energies and talents of all its employees by re-negotiating their original 'psychological contracts', even if the new version includes elements that some will not like (Boddy and Macbeth, 2000).

Whatever the trigger for change, different types of organizational change will have varying degrees of impact on employees and provoke emotional and other reactions. While incremental change can be challenging enough for some employees to cope with, 'step' changes such as mergers, acquisitions and re-engineering initiatives usually have a far greater personal impact on employees than incremental change. The human dimension of change is explored in more detail in *Change and Organizational Theory: towards the high performance organization* (Holbeche, 2005a).

What triggers resistance to change?

Employee resistance to change is frequently cited as a key reason why planned change does not work. Indeed, when change threatens something that employees hold dear, resistance can be a reasonable response, and there can sometimes be good justification for people digging in their heels, actively or passively. Change can, after all, have a detrimental impact on an individual's job and aspirations, even while it is carried out to benefit the organization. Transformational change in particular is a highly political process, which may threaten different interest groups and tends to be characterized by conflict. Resources (material and social) are at stake when policies are agreed and decisions taken.

Ball (1987) argues that the people who initiate change will need to anticipate political opposition and develop sources of power and influence of their own in order to bring about desired changes. Managers need to respond to resistance and understand different interests. They need to connect with what people have to win or lose by changing. Change leaders have to be able to reconcile different sets of interest within the change initiative.

Some of the typical reasons why employee resistance mounts and change gets 'blocked' are highlighted by respondents to Roffey Park's annual *Management Agenda* surveys:

- *Confusion and change-weariness*. There may be many change initiatives going on at the same time, the purposes of which are not always clear to employees. In the frenzy of activity linked with the change projects, managers and employees take their eye off the ball and neglect 'business as usual'. Competing activities and crises distract attention from the customer. The end result is lots of activity, but employees have little sense of progress. 'Change-weariness' sets in. Employees become disheartened and cynical about management.

- *Lack of inspiring purpose.* Change efforts are usually focused on cost-cutting rather than revenue enhancement. When shareholder interests are put first, employees resent paying the price in terms of job security or increased workloads and the future can seem bleak. When goals are set for the distant future, or left as vague vision statements, they tend not to motivate people to go the extra mile.

- *Lack of leadership.* Senior managers are often reluctant to take ownership of change, or lose interest in a change effort when it is under way. They become invisible, or behave in ways that contradict organizational value statements. Indeed, leaders' credibility can be undermined if they 'over-promise and under-deliver'. When leaders assume that, having launched a change initiative, change is under way, they may fail to follow up or reinforce change. Similarly, when executives act as if change is for everyone else, rather than themselves, employees doubt their motives and integrity. Employees then tend to wonder whether the extra effort was worthwhile. At a local level, too, leadership and direction provided by departmental managers often prove inadequate.

- *Tokenism.* When organizations appoint a 'Director of Change', this is often a symptom of lack of real ownership from the top. When change is officially driven by someone with 'change' in their job title, change ceases to be everybody's responsibility. As soon as a change effort ceases to be a high-profile, strategic imperative, people's behaviour, especially that of senior managers, backslides, and the Director of Change takes the blame.

- *Legacy of failure.* When most previous change efforts have failed, or there is poor monitoring of policies and implementation, employees learn to passively resist change. People, often already overwhelmed by their workload, became cynical about the likelihood of the change effort succeeding. They develop the ability to let change pass them by without really modifying their behaviour.

- *Lack of support.* Change tends to generate heavy workloads and uncertainties. Employees may become insecure and anxious. When there is little practical support for managers and employees to help them cope with the effects of change, and employees often appear to lose out and their stress levels increase. They may take on unsustainable challenges in their desire to keep their jobs. Health, well-being and safety may be compromised. Managers in particular may be vulnerable. They may be expected to provide support for others but have no help for themselves.

- *Poor communication.* When lots of money is spent on publicizing the change programme but employees never hear about the results, or the 'mushroom principle' of communications is applied (i.e. keep them in the dark), employee resistance is likely to increase.

In many cases there is little attempt to get employees on board with the change before systems and structure changes are introduced. It is generally assumed that employee behaviours will adapt automatically. Instead, more often than not, major change leads to confusion, resistance and sabotage, initially at least. When people do not understand *why* a change initiative is happening, *what* the impact on their role is and *what* is required of them, they may feel less willing to commit to the change effort.

> *Example 2.1   Change-weariness*
> One major institution had just successfully completed the integration of two departments. The move had been planned and implemented meticulously, with high levels of consultation and involvement. Team-building had taken place, and the newly merged department was working well. Less than two months after integration, the new CEO decided to carry out a more radical realignment of the organization, leading to the new department being split up and redistributed without consultation. The Department Head, who had overseen the integration, was left wondering how he would get people on board with the new move and 'put the genie back in the bottle'.

What do employees perceive to be the main reasons for change not working?

The above and other factors appear to influence the amounts of resistance that might be anticipated. Employees also suggest a number of common factors that contribute to change being unsuccessful:

- *Short-termism*. When managers are only concerned about the short-term needs of the business the approach they take to change is usually one of cost-cutting. Typically, spending cuts affect areas such as training and development where the organizational investment may not have an immediate payback. The key casualty of this approach is innovation – the source of future revenue growth and organizations often have subsequent problems retaining and recruiting the skilled people they need.
- *Business suffers*. When the sheer volume of activity generated by change causes organizations to become inward-looking and neglect 'business as usual', or hours are spent in meetings where nothing gets done, customers become fed up and take their business elsewhere. Competitors spot their opportunity and move in to grab the market and/or poach the best talent.
- *Poor implementation*. Typical symptoms are when implementation takes longer than originally allocated, only releases benefits in certain areas or is never completed. Implementation problems are often the result of poor planning, when major problems that have not been identified beforehand surface during implementation. Uncontrollable factors in the external environment can also have an adverse impact on implementation. These can be hard to

manage, especially if there are insufficient contingencies. Poor coordination is another threat to effective implementation. This occurs when project management is weak, and when managers treat change efforts as if they are unrelated, never see a change project through to conclusion, or fail to ensure adequate handovers between project teams and line managers who are meant to make the change work.

- *Inappropriate skill levels.* Change can offer unparalleled opportunities for staff development, with new technologies requiring new ways of working. However, implementation can fail if employees lack the necessary capabilities, or if training and instruction given to managers and front-line employees is inadequate. This tends to occur if human resource planning is not closely linked to the broad strategic drivers for the organization. Consequently, parts of the business can end up with skills shortages while others have an overload of non-transferable skills. Another typical lost opportunity occurs when limited genuine sharing of organizational and individual learning takes place. This tends to lead to an over-reliance on external support.

Assumptions about change

Change can arise both from the external environment and from within the organization. It can be undertaken in either a proactive or reactive manner. In other words, managers can either foresee the necessity for change and take the necessary steps, or ignore the need for change and be forced into an organizational transformation to survive.

Conventionally, managers are trained to approach change from a planned perspective. This assumes that culture can be deliberately changed, and this assumption is widely shared. Indeed, many of the UK Labour Government's aspirations to see 'joined-up' outcomes in public services are based on the assumption that organizational cultures can be changed. A CIPD survey revealed that more than 250 of a sample of 1000 of the largest UK public and private sector organizations claimed to have been involved in programmes of culture change in the preceding five years.

Typical types of culture change evident in management literature and practice include:

1. Revolutionary, non-incremental attempts to change the cultures of whole organizations
2. Radical attempts to change the cultures of sub-units or groups
3. Non-radical variances
4. Gradual and incremental shifts that eventually result in a comprehensive reframing of the culture of the organization
5. Changes of identity
6. Changes in terms of scale
7. Changes to organizational processes
8. Changes in organizational functions; their organization, coordination and control

9. Changes in values, beliefs and human behaviour in terms of relationships, social rules and practices
10. Changes in power distribution and the way organizational issues are influenced.

'Designed' or planned approaches to change assume that the future can be known, predicted and created – that is, that managers can control the long-term future of the human system. Such approaches are based on linear thinking (i.e. response is proportional to stimulus, and cause and effect can be traced). The emphasis is on looking for specific links between cause and effect. Success depends on extensive planning and design, precise assessment of the current situation, accurate anticipation of resistance to change, and skill at overcoming this resistance. The emphasis is on intention, stability and return to equilibrium for business success. The new order is designed rather than accidental.

Planned approaches favour the use of analytical tools (such as the culture assessment tools described in the next chapter) and hard data. Based on mechanistic models of organization, planned approaches assume that the system is characterized by an innate resistance to change, which needs to be overcome. They imply that, following effective analysis and appropriate action, cultures can be made to change; that by assessing your existing culture and deciding where you want to go you can work out a way to get there. They focus on rational processes and see change as a staged process. Following the changes in structure or work process, 'sheep dip' training is used to inculcate new behaviours.

Typically, three stages are involved:

1. *Preparing the ground (scanning and choosing).* This involves identifying the need and deciding on desired outcomes. It is important to be clear about the reasons for change. Usually, identifying the driving forces in the external and internal environments is the first stage, followed by choosing desired outcomes and briefing those involved.
2. *Diagnosing the situation (planning).* This involves identifying and evaluating options. Activities will include consulting others, determining resource and timescales, and getting commitment for action.
3. *Bringing about change (implementing and reviewing).* This involves implementing change and evaluating the outcomes. Activities will include deciding on the change strategy, taking action, being open to change, reminding others of their commitments, reviewing and learning, and recognizing and rewarding those involved.

Rosemary Stewart (1995) found that the following were helpful factors when trying to implement change through a designed change process: clarity/ rationale, preparation, and involvement and training. She also found several unhelpful or hindering factors, such as continual changes, change of mind, speed of changes, unpredictability of changes, lack of clarity/rationale, lack of involvement, indirectness, incompetence, inhumanity, contrary to norms, slighting/underestimating, inadequate training, workload, and bureaucracy.

Usually designed processes emphasize the creation of formal planning documents controlled by senior executives, since the underlying assumption of such approaches is that change is a hierarchically driven process. The manager is there to engineer change and impose order.

This can seem attractive in that the approach appears clear, unambiguous and 'fact-based', or at least supported by the use of strategic analysis tools. However, a planned approach to strategy and change assumes a relatively predictable or stable environment where economic conditions, competitors or government actions are unlikely to significantly affect an organization's ability to achieve its plan. It implies that there is a consistent adherence to the vision and plan within the organization over a long time, and that a 'critical mass' of the organization is aligned and working to create the same future state.

In practice, many plans stay on the shelf because the pace of change exceeds the organization's capacity to implement them. Often the desired changes prove much more complex than was originally envisaged. Similarly, successful implementation often depends on middle managers, who, being mostly excluded from the planning process, tend to lack understanding of what is required.

While most managers recognize that achieving the helpful conditions for planned change can be extremely problematic, if not impossible, they see the only alternatives to planning to be random action, 'wait and see' passivity or haphazard opportunism.

An alternative view...

Some theorists argue that top-down, planned change tends not to work well in our global networked economy, except for relatively simple problems. More recent thinking on strategy and management is drawing heavily on the 'new science' of chaos, complexity theory and systems dynamics. These theories bring into question current methods of planning and control within organizations, and our assumptions about the stability and predictability of the environments in which they operate.

Emergence can be defined as the *unpredictable/unintended outcome(s)* of intentional actions within complex environments. It is only by looking back, with hindsight, that managers are able to discover how they got to be where they are. It can be seen as the result of the interplay of actions, the consequences of which cannot be predicted beforehand. Emergence can be understood in terms of oxymorons such as 'intended opportunism' or 'purposive drift', where the individual or the organization both has a broad purpose and is responsive to the opportunities and threats in the environment. In contrast to planned strategy, which is 'moving towards' an objective, emergence is 'moving away from' where we are now – it implies open-ended change.

Emergence can be framed as the reconciliation of the polarity between conscious intention versus random action, where the mediating factor is the nature of the environment. The greater the degree of change, instability, complexity and lack of structure (e.g. rules, procedures, boundaries) in the environment, the more likely it is that strategies will be emergent rather than planned, because no plan will survive long enough to be delivered. The more stable the environment, the more likely it is that conscious intentions will be realized. Creativity, instability, experiment, valuing difference, empowerment, paradox and learning will be the skills and values that will provide growth and survival in the future. This is powerfully counter to values that operate in most organizations today.

Complexity theorists, drawing on the life sciences, suggest that organizations, like organisms, are dynamic entities. They are in a constant low-level state of flux and evolution, and naturally give rise to all kinds of incremental changes. Deal and Kennedy (2000) suggest that the notion that cultures are resistant to change is a myth, since:

> cultures are always adapting to the changes around them. Failure to adapt would be threatening since it would be seen as a sign that the culture is falling behind. Where cultures resist is when long standing core values or widely accepted rituals or practices are endangered.

From a complexity perspective, a complex adaptive system cannot be changed, only disturbed. Complex adaptive systems have the capacity for self-organization and emergent complexity. Like organisms, organizational cultures have an innate ability to create their own breakthroughs. It is usually the way organizations are designed and their cultural practices that tend to inhibit their natural adaptive tendencies. Organizational change can be an emergent phenomenon, a continuous and evolving process.

Emergent change

The basis of more emergent approaches to change is non-linear thinking (i.e. response is non-proportional to cause). They take account of irrational processes within organizations, such as political processes and unconscious group dynamics. Everything is in flux the whole time. Change is a cyclical process, and new order emerges; it is self-organized, not intended, not designed, not hierarchically controlled, and not externally driven. Self-organization occurs when a system is in far-from-equilibrium conditions. There is an emphasis on intuition, emotion, power and learning through trial and error. Change results from the utilization of random, unexpected and accidental events.

Moreover, widespread changes to a culture tend not to happen in a predictable way, even though they may be planned and consciously implemented, usually at the request of top management. Culture is systemic. It is an organizational view of the world, which helps interpret the changes the organization and the individual within it meet. Individuals are influenced by organizational culture even as they seek to influence it. Even small changes may have unforeseen consequences and produce much wider effects within the system due to the 'amplification effect' – akin to throwing a pebble into a pond. While the impact of the stone is felt first where it falls, the knock-on effect is different as the ripples gradually reach other parts of the pond at different speeds and with a different intensity.

More incremental culture change appears to take place in fits and starts as some of the cultural blockages are removed. Old practices become constraints. The 'old guard' retires. Sometimes the culture appears to move swiftly in a new direction, when a cultural 'tipping point' has been reached. This can occur when sufficient new people enter the system over time and, through strength of numbers, they avoid being fully acculturated into the existing system. Somehow, their collective influence brings about a new climate and starts to modify the underlying culture. Similarly, a new Chief Executive, for a short time, has the chance to make a mark and embed different ways of thinking about things.

For Ralph Stacey (1999), change in some form is happening constantly through organizational networks. Though some change occurs as part of a planned framework of change activities, organizations are changing anyway all the time, imperceptibly, often at local team level. The network promotes innovation and change through dialogue and disagreement that creates and disperses new knowledge. Dialogue between individuals and groups can subtly shift attitudes, beliefs and behaviours over time. Self-organization, then, arises out of conversations between people. Such conversations enable learning to be generated and intelligence shared within the network. Simple structures help to generate novel patterns, and the sum is often greater than the parts.

However, the network is in tension with, and subverts, the existing formal system, and aspects of it will eventually replace the existing system. Everyone is simultaneously member of both the formal and the informal organizational systems, and is therefore working, paradoxically, to both sustain and destabilize the existing system. The local activity in the network gives rise to unpredictable global outcomes as it is amplified through the feedback processes of the system.

Unlike in planned change, where the role of the manager is to impose order, under emergent change the role of the manager is to create the conditions in which change may happen. Since the future is inherently unknowable, there is an emphasis on pattern, circular causality. For Henry Mintzberg *et al.* (1995), emergent strategy involves working out how best to make use of patterns in the organization and the environment. It also involves spotting and reinforcing 'strategies' that are already developing inside the organization.

An underlying assumption of emerging change is that human systems are so complex that no individual or small group of individuals can understand them fully enough. Organizations are seen as networks of multiple feedback loops, and change is the activation of a system's inherent potential for transformation.

Implications of emergence: emergent strategy

Newer approaches tend to favour multiplicity and diversity of approach, with the use of 'hot spot' interventions around specific areas or issues. Tensions tend to be worked out rather than suppressed. Solutions tend to be emergent and fit for purpose, and ways of managing change emphasize agility and openness rather than fit and closure. Culture-building involves creating a process that can be owned and renewed by the people who work within the culture, ensuring that there is minimum discrepancy between what is needed and what exists.

The implications for managers and organizations of working in an emergent way are considerable, and have yet to be fully articulated (so great is our need to rely on the myth that we can plan and control our future). They include the following:

- Managers should pay as much attention to their environments and the threats and opportunities they contain as they do to their own plans
- Managers should raise their awareness of how they interpret events in the environment – particularly the assumptions and categories they use – as a key feature of both their own and organizational learning
- Managers should pay attention to creating fluid, adaptive organizations (e.g. in terms of structures, skills, processes and information flows) so that the best strategies can emerge.

Accepting emergence, and the uncertain future that it implies, creates anxiety within people and organizations. Managers need to develop ways of openly examining their individual and collective responses to anxiety as a way of avoiding decisions or actions that may be superficial, ineffective or counter-productive for the purpose of the organization. Senior management will have to let go of their traditional roles of planning, control and strategy formation. Under emergence, the role of senior management will be to create favourable conditions within the organization for learning, creativity and positive politics.

In the same way, managers should be sensitive to the people processes they use – for example to make decisions, involve and motivate people, run groups and meetings, and delegate work. Particularly important are managers' attitudes to and ability to handle conflict, debate and tension within the organization: Because the outcomes of such activities are likely to be emergent and unpredictable, then the way things are done will affect the chances of the best decisions and actions emerging.

One best way?

That is not to say that either planned or emergent approaches have a monopoly of virtues. Indeed it is likely that combinations of planning and emergence will be needed to reconcile some of the paradoxes of change, such as enabling organizations to gain the benefits of clarity (planned) as well as of employee ownership of the change effort (emergent).

According to conventional wisdom, the power dynamics in organizations mean that there can be no such thing as 'bottom-up' change. For Connor (1988), no substantive change can occur without effective sponsorship at senior level. Conversely, other theorists (Butcher and Atkinson, 2000) argue that, since much top-down change does not work, creating bottom-up 'pockets of good practice' is more effective. These work because they harness the creativity and diversity of individuals. Dialogue rather than through formal systems, is the means by which ideas spread, harnessing the creativity and diversity of individuals. A bottom-up change model incorporates the power of the political processes in today's flatter, more flexible companies.

Conversely, emergence without planning can lead to chaos. The late 1990s boom in dotcoms seemed to herald the era when emergence was the way forward. Set up in the main by young entrepreneurs with little or no management experience, many of these companies operated on a combination of brilliant market concept and the ability to win financial support for the dream, but little ability to bring to consolidate processes and then change them as needed by the evolving marketplace. Without effective planning, many of these companies fell by the wayside when the bubble burst.

Each approach on its own may be inadequate to the needs of specific situations and may need modification by tempering factors. Indeed, both approaches may be needed to different degrees according to the circumstances. For example, when a market threat or opportunity calls for urgent action, the common assumption is that the approach to strategic decision-making should be planned, managed and top-down, and that tight control should be exercised over the change process. Ironically, the lived experience of such emergencies is that even in apparently urgent situations, some degree of involvement and engagement with those who are expected to implement the change is required if people are to 'go the extra mile'.

Contingency theory

Contingency theory explores 'fit' at both a macro- and a micro-level. In the former (socio-economic) perspective, performance improvement flows from improved decision-making, which in turn flows from having the kind of differentiation and integration required to obtain and use appropriate data from the environment (Lawrence and Lorsch, 1969). A micro, psychological version suggests that individuals experience an inner feeling of competence when there is a three-way fit between uncertainty (the environment), organizational arrangements and individual predispositions. 'Fit' tends to suggest equilibrium and order, and encourages us to value order over disorder. 'Fit' implies congruence, and there is a tendency to equate fit with effectiveness. However, achieving perfect congruence within real organizations is difficult to achieve in practice.

Example 2.2 The value of listening
One major College of Further Education received a poor Ofsted inspection rating. For the College this was disappointing and serious, since it would make recruitment of new students more difficult, and with the fall-off in student numbers would come a reduction in College funding. Moreover, failure to have achieved improved grades would almost certainly result in a change of Principal and perhaps closure of the College. The Ofsted re-inspection would take place within two years, giving the

College a short, focused timeframe in which to make substantial change to its curriculum and standards.

The Principal and top team took responsibility for devising the post-inspection action plan and looked to senior managers at the next level down to implement it. The plan in itself was excellent and looked achievable to the Principal. Top management became increasingly frustrated by the apparent passivity of the next level of management, who seemed to be waiting to receive 'orders' rather than proactively seeking to improve standards in their own areas of responsibility. There seemed to be a vicious circle at work – the more the Principal 'pushed' and penalized those who were slow to respond to his dictats, the more managers complied only with his dictats. In frustration, the Principal issued even more orders, causing senior managers to consider that the only way to keep their jobs was to meet the Principal's deadlines. Their jobs became a serious game of compliance. More was required if the organization was going to improve.

The turning point came when senior managers spent time off-site considering what needed to be done, and how they needed to work together with the top team. With renewed confidence in their own abilities and right to exercise some discretion, senior managers started to work more skilfully with their own teams and as a cross-College group. Their own ability to engage others was enhanced by the use of some large-scale techniques such as open space technology (see Chapter 5) with the help of a facilitator. As lecturers in their turn felt that they had been listened to rather than simply being told what the plan was, they started to show greater willingness to apply new and improved teaching methods. This in turn started to produce a positive effect on student achievement.

In this case, it was only when planning was allied to a new approach from top management leading to greater opportunities for staff and student involvement, that the situation started to improve. Ironically, in order to make more speed, less haste was necessarily.

Logical incrementalism

Quinn (1978) describes logical incrementalism as 'the normative model for strategic decision-making'. This theory suggests that many managers have a view of where they want the organization to be in years to come, but try to move towards this position in an evolutionary way. They do this by attempting to ensure the success and development of a strong, secure, but flexible core business, and also by experimenting with 'side bet' ventures. In common with Abrahamson's 'dynamic stability' approach (see Abrahamson, 2000), managers seek to become highly sensitive to environmental signals through constant environmental scanning. They manage uncertainty by testing changes in strategy in small-scale steps. They also try to encourage experimentation in the organization; moreover, there is a reluctance to specify precise objectives too early as this might stifle ideas and prevent the sort of experimentation that is desired. The logical incremental approach will take account of the political nature of organizational life since smaller changes are less likely to face the same amount of resistance as major changes.

Approaches to changing culture

Culture change does not lend itself to an approach that develops only managers and staff as individuals, but rather to one that develops the organization as an interdependent system.

Culture change is a paradoxical phenomenon. Because culture is embedded in the organization's deepest assumptions, there is a limit to the usefulness of simply demanding that 'from next Monday we will have empowerment'. Lasting change emerges from a heightened appreciation of how things really work *now*, how people may be acting in the grip of 'taken for granted' assumptions. This loosens current cultural patterns and releases energy for exploring fresh options.

Culture change involves employees changing their behaviour. In planned culture change, desired behaviour is reinforced and undesired behaviour is penalized. Some theorists question the morality of attempting culture change: 'Not only are attempts to script culture change doomed to failure, the attempt to manage culture tends to be seen as unethical, a threat to individual liberty' (Barratt, 1992).

Stokes and Harrison (1992) consider that the concept of 'changing' organizational cultures is limiting. They suggest that it is important to think in terms of strengthening and balancing an organization's culture as much as changing it. The principle is to take pragmatic account of the difficulties of bringing about change, and to intervene no more deeply than is necessary to achieve your purpose.

The easiest approach to implementing change is by strengthening a culture. This takes place by intensifying the culture's expression, especially its higher aspects, and doing the same things, only better. This is appropriate when the organization does the right things but not well enough; when the basic culture fits but has too many drawbacks; or when you have little freedom and power to effect change. It is also appropriate when the organization has few resources to invest in change, and when members of the organization are satisfied with the current culture.

Strengthening a power culture, for instance, would involve setting an example for others to follow in terms of courage, fairness, integrity and responsibility. Strengthening a role culture could involve inventing information systems that allow people to track their results in 'real time'. Strengthening an achievement culture could involve pushing a decision to a lower level, while strengthening a support culture could involve asking for help; acknowledging uncertainty. Change methodologies such as Appreciative Inquiry (see Chapter 6) reflect a similar philosophy, operating on the basis of helping people to identify and maximize sources of outstanding organizational practice and capability.

Balancing a culture is the approach to use if you want to preserve the culture's benefits, add countervailing elements or encourage cultural differentiation. This is appropriate when the organization culture is narrow and homogeneous; when cultural patterns fit the organization's business; and when necessary checks and balances are missing. It is also the appropriate approach to use when you have substantial influence and freedom to act, when the organization can provide resources for change efforts, and when higher management is aware of the need for change and willing to support it.

Balancing a culture involves counteracting a limitation of the culture with a positive. In a power culture, for instance, the insecurity of subordinates could be balanced out by deliberate attempts to build trust. In a role culture, a cold, impersonal climate could be balanced by a deliberate attempt to nurture people and use more open communication. In an achievement culture, the tendency for individuals to drive themselves so hard that they reach burnout and disillusionment can be balanced by a deliberate attempt to focus energy and build cooperation between individuals and teams. In a support culture, the typically long decision cycles and conflict avoidance characteristics can be balanced out by decisive, value-based leadership, and the creation of a climate in which conflict is tolerated.

Generally, the approach that provokes most reaction from those affected is when you attempt to change the culture – whether by softening the dominant culture, introducing new values and beliefs, or changing structures, systems, work and leadership styles. This, the most difficult means of modifying a culture, is the approach to use when needed improvements are blocked by limitations of the current culture. The preconditions of this approach are that you have substantial influence and freedom to act in the organization; that the organization can provide resources for change efforts; and that top managers are pro-change and will participate personally in the process. It is also important to be sure that the organization can afford to suffer performance deterioration during change.

From a complexity perspective, once change appears to be happening the organization's immune response is likely to kick in. People who feel that they may be losing power will try to reassert it. This is where senior managers have a key role to play in damping down resistance and nurturing new behaviours until a critical mass has been achieved.

Embedding mechanisms

Bringing about culture change does not automatically involve making dramatic shifts. Edgar Schein (1993) suggests that much behavioural and cultural change occurs because of the effect of so-called 'embedding mechanisms', which vary in how powerful their effects on culture are; how implicit or explicit the messages are; and how intentional they are. Schein distinguished between primary and secondary embedding mechanisms. Primary embedding mechanisms include the criteria used for allocation of rewards and status (or punishment). These teach employees what is really valued, regardless of company rhetoric. Reward in particular is a powerful conditioner of people's behaviour. As Hawk (1995) suggests, reward systems must be aligned to the chosen direction because 'by changing their cultures without changing their reward system, companies run the risk of sending their employees terribly mixed signals'.

Measurement systems also play an important part in changing behaviour. Through measurement, the organization incentivizes or brings pressure to bear on people to change their behaviour. Typically this behaviour change is performed reluctantly, if what is being measured is in collision with existing custom and practice, or individual 'comfort zones'. Schein points out that 'secondary' mechanisms only work if they are consistent with primary mechanisms. Among the secondary articulation and reinforcement mechanisms, the organization's design, structure, systems and procedures reinforce the underlying attitudes and behaviours reflective of the organization's values.

Effective change leadership

Much current change theory focuses on transformational leadership. This is about changing behaviours (i.e. the human relations aspects of change) *before* institutionalizing through systems changes. Transformational change in particular needs strong leadership to identify new directions for the organization and to build momentum for change even though the future state of the organization remains undefined. It requires the creation of a 'vision which stretches the organization beyond its current limits and capabilities, a holistic perspective, an implementation process that is sustained by organizational learning and the creation of resources to support the change' (Miles, 1997).

Change has a strong psychological/emotional dimension. Every change process unleashes human emotions as people come to terms with what the change means to them. Effective change involves the psychological process of 'reframing', whereby people become willing to see new possibilities and stop hanging on to the past. If reframing is to occur, it is not enough for change activity to be introduced as simply a strategic initiative, on the back of the corporate plan. Change also has to take place at the symbolic/cultural and individual work levels. Therefore, in transformational change the management of organizational culture has to run alongside activities of a more rational, planning nature.

Leaders have to establish understanding and create commitment among organizational members to share the vision, and the actions required to achieve it. Leaders have a particular role to play in:

- Challenging the original frame, by symbolically separating from the past
- Stimulating the organization for change by creating a sense of urgency to enact the vision
- Leading the change effort
- Developing enabling structures
- Communicating
- Involving people and being honest

- Reinforcing change through recognition
- Institutionalizing the change through reward and other systems.

A top-down, bottom-up process

For change to succeed, the new direction has to be reflected in the behaviours and attitudes of all concerned. Whether the change initiative is driven top-down, bottom-up or some combination of the two, the key challenge is to create buy-in to, and preferably engagement with, the need for change. The whole organization needs to end up pulling in the same direction. Stakeholders, internal and external, have to be able to sense and experience the change.

Pettigrew (1990) argues that the sequencing of the pattern of change according to conventional wisdom (i.e. structure changes should follow strategy changes) may not be in line with what happens in practice. Using the example of culture change at ICI, Pettigrew highlights how first came a complex mixture of adjustments to core beliefs of top decision-makers, followed by changes of beliefs, and out of those changes of beliefs and structure began to emerge the new business strategy of the firm. For Pettigrew, there is need for persistence and patience in breaking down the core beliefs of the 'old guard', getting new problems sensed and articulated in the organization, developing a sense of concern that those problems are worthy of analytical and political attention, and then articulating the new order, often through highly inarticulate and impressive visions of the future.

The Department of Trade and Industry consultation paper on High Performance Workplaces advocates a high-involvement, bottom-up approach to change as the most effective. This approach is also reflected in work by Beer *et al.* (1990). For these authors, the process of galvanizing the organization to initiate change consists of six steps. These are:

1. Mobilize commitment to change through joint diagnosis of business problems
2. Develop a shared vision of how to organize for competitiveness
3. Foster consensus for the new vision, competence to enact it, and cohesion to move it along
4. Spread revitalization to all departments, without pushing it from the top
5. Institutionalize revitalization through formal policies, systems and structures
6. Monitor and adjust strategies in response to problems in the revitalization process.

Incorporating some 'top-down' elements, and building on the Beer *et al.* model, I have incorporated detail of some of the change process success factors that have come to light through various research and consultancy projects. I highlight here what employees tell us they find effective in the change process.

1. Create a climate for change to occur

Based on his studies at ICI, Jaguar and other companies, Pettigrew identifies the importance of a receptive outer context, together with managerial skill in mobilizing that context, in order to create an overall climate for change to occur. This may involve leadership behaviour either from individuals recently brought into the organization from outside, or from individuals who have been pushing for change from a powerful internal position for some time. In most cases, there is a very clear and consistent drive from the top. Pettigrew found that discrepant action by key figures in the new guard was used in order to raise the level of tension in the organization for change. He also found 'deviants' and 'heretics' were used, both external and internal to the organization, in order to think the unthinkable and say the unsayable. In many change programmes, external consultants are used for this purpose.

Mobilize commitment to change through joint diagnosis of business problems

By helping people develop a shared diagnosis of what is wrong in an organization and what can and must be improved, a general manager (of a unit) mobilizes the initial commitment that is necessary to begin the change process. Pettigrew recommends creating new meetings and other arenas where problems can be articulated and energy focused around the need for change.

Clarify what kind of change is required

The amount of change to be achieved will depend on a range of factors, one of which will be the organization's stage in its life cycle. The nature of change required at each of the different stages – emergence, growth, maturity, decline, decay – will vary. Bringing about significant change to an organization requires attention to three main areas (although within each of these areas there are likely to be many subdivisions):

- Skills and resources
- Structure and systems
- Culture, style and values.

The extent of the gap between the current organization and the 'ideal' as defined by senior management's vision can have an impact on the success of the change initiative. If the gap is too large, change efforts are likely to be frustrating because employees will believe them to be impossible to achieve. Change can make people question their competencies and ability to cope. Senior management therefore need to ensure that the gap between the current and desired organization is wide enough to be challenging to employees but not so wide as to demoralize people.

Manage the pace of change

Both major and incremental change should be phased, over the medium to long term, in order to help employees absorb the new ways of working. As employees become better able to cope and see the fruits of their labours, the more they become open to change.

2. Develop a shared vision of how to organize for competitiveness

For Pettigrew, the existence of inarticulate and imprecise visions from the agents of change at the top is a powerful means of engaging the imagination and energy of others. Once a core group of people is committed to a particular analysis of the problem, the general manager can lead employees toward a task-aligned vision of the organization that defines new roles and responsibilities. According to Javidan (2001), 'a vision is not a set of goals; it is a set of ambitions that, once internalized by subordinates, create powerful intrinsic motivation to work in that direction'.

Successful leaders' commitment to their vision is evident and credible to their subordinates. Such managers believe in managing by example. They take initiatives to achieve their goals, even if this involves risks to career, status or position. Their employees believe in the sincerity of their vision. On the whole, employees agree that change works best in the context of:

- A clear, agreed vision that creates unity and purpose
- A strong sense of what's happening in the market
- Benchmarking
- Leaders with clear understanding of the vision in line with the changing business need
- Clear agreement on the values and behaviours that are key to the vision
- Strategies to achieve the vision.

While the development of strategy is usually regarded as the task of senior managers, the implementation of strategy requires the understanding and commitment of employees at all levels. Frequently, change efforts stall once they are under way because there is no shared understanding of the task to be done and poor handovers between key groups on whom the success of the change effort depends. According to Atkinson (2000), in order to gain maximum commitment to any proposed change it is important to include those affected as much as possible in the specification stage, and to have an appropriate blend of effective leadership and followership.

Employees suggest the following:

- Allow affected employees to participate in creating and installing the change; control of change by those most affected can reduce resistance
- Find methods of analysing the situation
- Use genuine consultation.

3. Foster consensus for the new vision, competence to enact it, and cohesion to move it along

At this stage it is useful to engage a wider group of people in the vision, using cross-functional/cross-business, multilevel focus groups. In particular, it is vital to involve people who are affected by the change in the decision-making process. Use processes that capture the input of people who are likely to be critical to effective implementation. Good communication will be needed to ensure that all those who will be affected by the change understand why the change is taking place. Increasingly, organizations are using large-scale engagement techniques such as real-time strategic change and future search to involve wider groups of staff in the option-generation and decision-making processes. Pettigrew suggests releasing avenues and energy for change by moving people and portfolios.

Employees suggest that change works best when there are:

- Inspirational team members and leaders to share, encourage and lead
- Effective planning and meaningful communication processes.

Planning

Once a strategic choice has been made, a plan must be developed to guide the actions and behaviour of those involved in its execution and to enable progress to be monitored.

For Rowden (2001), planning should be as open a process as possible, with an emphasis on establishing general goals and direction, using pilot programmes to build commitment within the organization.

Employees consider the following to be effective:

Programme management:

- Make a plan
- Decide to implement the plan
- Announce the plan and secure commitment to it of those involved
- Set milestones
- Provide as much lead time as possible.

Fair and transparent processes:

- Facilitators help teams develop effective change processes
- Senior managers are not only lead change but also role model new behaviours.

Create broader 'buy-in' to change

When developing formal 'top-down' communication about change:

- Change leaders should anticipate three forms of resistance – logical, non-logical and group-based
- Communicate a vision for change
- Provide the context, and rationale, for change
- Provide details of the consequences of the proposed change effort.

For employees, buy-in is more likely to occur when managers:

- Explain the reason for change
- Help people understand the importance of the change

- Make it clear what people will gain/why it is an attractive proposition to help with change
- Address the negative aspects
- Get people to understand why they are needed on board
- Explain the consequences of not 'getting on the bus'/changing
- Help people understand why and how each individual plays an important part in the change
- Work with champions at all levels
- Set up working groups at all levels-gain involvement
- Break the change project down into bite-size chunks
- Integrate the change into personal objectives
- See it/touch it (not just statistics)
- Demonstrate the future
- Sell the positives with enthusiasm
- Seek ideas from all concerned
- Identifying existing cohesive groups and, when possible, use them as pilots for change (the grapevine will then work for, rather than against, the manager)
- Move from a one-way selling exercise to genuine two-way communication.

Manage resistance to change

- Identify the reasons why people are resisting the proposed change
- Understand people's fears and concerns
- Reassure people where possible, making them aware of the fact that the organization will aim to support them with the changes taking place.

Deal with organizational politics

- Assess the power base of the person or groups responsible for leading the change effort
- Identify key stakeholders and their interest in the proposed change
- Assess the power bases of key stakeholders
- Aim to get broad-based support in order to minimize the risk that one group will block change
- Work round the serious obstacles to change by using social networks.

Manage the transition

The literature suggests:

- Implement with a concern for engaging frontline employees, as well as suppliers, customers and other key stakeholders, in working out how plans should be executed (Barger and Kirby, 1995, in Rowden, 2001).

Employees suggest the following:

- Explain new roles and responsibilities
- Set measures – what's expected
- Communicate expected positive results of the change to the people making it.

- Report progress to date
- Train in new methods and skills to secure effective changed behaviour
- Monitor and adjust of strategies in response to problems in the implementation process
- Expect an initial dip in satisfaction and productivity as change is introduced.

4. Spread revitalization to all departments, without pushing it from the top

The temptation to force new approaches on the rest of the organization can be great, particularly when rapid change is needed, but this is a mistake that senior managers make if they try to push programmatic change throughout a company. It short-circuits the change process. It is better to let each department 'reinvent the wheel' – that is, to find its own way to the new organization, within broad parameters. People need to be 'connected' through internal networks, knowledge management systems and teamworking, so as to avoid unnecessary duplication of effort and to maximize the spread of good ideas.

The literature suggests the following:

- Define the behaviours, values and expectations of the new workplace
- Create a climate that is supportive of the desired change by realigning organizational culture, rewards, policies, procedures, systems and norms to support such change – in particular, management styles should become participative and facilitative, and employees should focus on continuous improvement and being accountable
- Equip people throughout the organization with the skills needed to participate meaningfully in planning and implementing strategic change through training in quality improvement philosophies, skills and techniques.

Employees find the following effective:

- Ensure a clear line of sight to the customer.
- Leaders and employees must have the requisite skills in leadership, creativity, problem-solving, continuous improvement, team effectiveness and customer service.

5. Institutionalize revitalization through formal policies, systems and structures

Only when it has become the new 'way we do things around here' should the new approach become institutionalized. Altering the management process at the very top is a key way of embedding positive change. A key aspect of this changing top management processes from being highly divisive to being more coherent and cohesive.

Pettigrew recommends reinforcing any embryonic shifts through closely matched structural changes, then strengthening such cultural and structural changes through the public use of the organization's reward systems. Finding and using 'role models' at all levels who can display key aspects of the new culture through their own behaviour helps continue the reinforcement of change. Similarly, revamping employee communication mechanisms carries the message deep into the organization.

Leaders need to reinforce change by actively discouraging political behaviour, by practising inspirational leadership and by developing it in others.

The literature suggests the following:

- As change takes place, new 'rules of the game' must be developed. Beer *et al.* (1990) emphasize that it is important to spread the new approach to all departments, without pushing it from the top
- There should be a constant supply of timely and useful information, enabling customer-focused and cost-effective decision-making to take place at all levels of the organization on a daily basis
- Update roles and responsibilities to reflect new performance demands
- The new performance requirements have to be clearly stated and understood by employees who are expected to make a change in behaviour and in the way they conduct business; these changes must be broadly aligned with the purpose, identity, and mastery of the majority of people working in the organization (Moran and Brightman (2001))
- Strengthen the performance management system to meet the needs for personal and organizational development
- Reward changed behaviour – positive change in behaviour is more likely when correct performance is rewarded than it is when incorrect performance is punished
- Institutionalize the new approach through formal policies, systems and structures.

Monitor and adjust strategies in response to problems in the revitalization process

For Calori *et al.* (2001), designing and controlling the change process over time allows the destructive aspects of change (such as redundancies) to be balanced by the new (growing) aspects. The key objective should be to create a learning organization capable of adapting to a changing environment. While designing the change process may be the general manager's responsibility, monitoring of the change process needs to be more widely shared.

Employees find the following effective:

Ongoing communication:
- Two-way communication vehicles
- Large-scale involvement

- Ongoing reinforcement – restate the 'why?'
- Celebrate successes along the way.

Continuous alignment:

- Align core work processes with organizational goals
- Align systems and/or incentives to reinforce the plan.

Remotivating and energizing people

Whether the changes they face are radical or incremental, people within organizations need to be able and willing to adapt to new ways of doing things as well as keep business going. So often, employees perceive themselves to have been bombarded with change to the point that they develop tactics for stalling yet more change efforts. When the overall culture becomes 'change-weary', approaches aimed at revitalization are called for. Often this is about helping people see what their previous change efforts have achieved, and celebrating milestones so that people gain a sense of progress (see the checklist at the end of this chapter for tips on how to revitalize organizations).

Successful leaders find ways of remotivating people to new change efforts, creating a culture of continuous improvement and re-energizing people involved in existing change projects. They provide a sense of continuity by linking current projects to the future with predictable intervals and choreographed transition procedures. They create explicit links in time to describe organizational practices that address past, present and future time horizons. Rhythms are created that allow people to pace their work and collaborate across the organization. Ideally, according to Gersick (1991), the rhythm of the transition process is synchronized with the rhythm of change in the environment.

Example 2.3   Revitalizing the BMW Group Plant at Oxford, UK
One example of successful culture change is that of the BMW Group Plant at Oxford, the 2003 winner of the CIPD People Management Award for its relatively rapid culture change away from 'blame culture' and 'people leaving their brains at the gate' to a success culture which is already bearing fruit in terms of the number of ideas (8000) from employees and the volume of savings generated in a single year. When BMW acquired the Rover Group in 1994, it inherited the Mini – one of the most 'British' products and a British car manufacturing culture, dogged for decades by industrial relations disputes and poor productivity. Six years later, BMW sold off much of the Rover Group but retained the Mini brand, revamping the product and investing more than £230 million in refitting the Cowley plant. The company launched a major change programme called the 'New Oxford Way'.

The programme focused on achieving three key challenges – upgrading the site and processes to world-class standard, integrating the different

BMW and Rover cultures, and launching a completely new vehicle. The change programme was planned around nine subprojects. The central element of these was 'Wings', a contraction of 'Working in Groups'. It involved the creation of 'self-steered' teams within the manufacturing areas that were given increased responsibility for production processes.

A culture of involvement and team-development is emerging. The teams have the power to tackle most problems themselves, and the group members rotate around tasks within their area to break up the monotony of production-line work; rather than being management-led, the focus is very much on employees. Representatives from the production lines are involved in management discussions about processes, and they are encouraged to raise suggestions – something that did not happen at Rover. The firm has halved the day-to-day duties of one person from each Wings team so that he or she can concentrate on developing the team. Every fortnight, each of the three shifts at the plant downs tools for a 45-minute team talk. Problems are now solved at ground-floor level (*People Management*, 23 October 2003).

Conclusion

Building a high performance organization requires organizational leaders to manage change beyond the short term. If they are taking a planned approach, they should carefully craft twin objectives for any change initiative – using change activity to achieve 'wins' in the here-and-now and to support the development of a high performing culture which offers the potential of high revenue returns in the medium and longer term.

Given the pressures for change from the environment, an organization's culture needs to equip it for change while valuing the best from the past. In any organization there will be some areas of cultural strength, which can be supportive of high performance, and other cultural practices that are potentially limiting and may block high performance. The commonest approaches to culture change are linked with identifying and addressing the areas of blockage. Whether or not the resulting planned culture change occurs in the way planners may hope is a different matter. Given the essential unpredictability of events in human systems, the culture-change process itself can sometimes, perversely, lead to greater confusion and resistance.

The challenge for those looking to change aspects of culture is to maximize the chances of change being 'virtuous'. Akin to the Pareto Principle, which suggests that, no matter what the area of activity, 80 per cent of the rewards come from just 20 per cent of what we do, the principle underpinning effective culture-building is to identify, and play to, areas of unique cultural strength which can be used to balance out areas in which the culture is weak. By playing to strengths, areas of weakness may become unblocked or less significant.

This is not intended to be a recipe for complacency, and there may be some aspects of culture that absolutely must be changed. In such a case, the way the change process is handled becomes of paramount importance. The most effective forms of change occur when the people most likely to be affected by change are themselves largely in the driving seat of making change happen.

Checklist: Revitalizing the organization

To re-energize people in an organization experiencing constant change:

1. Carry out an occasional emotional audit (sometimes the grapevine is best). How are people feeling, what are the issues that bother them? Identify blockages to change and high performance – and deal with them.
2. Use communications to revitalize people, give them chance to feed in ideas, and provide feedback on organizational progress.
3. Paint roadmaps for people, which include both the future direction and some of the past. Help employees feel that what they have contributed in the past has made sense and produced worthwhile results – give people cause to celebrate and be heartened about the future.
4. Create and sustain 'pockets of good practice'.
5. Provide feedback and challenge, but not blame.
6. Give people the chance to take stock of their skills and capabilities – both what they have developed in recent years, and what the organization needs them to develop for the future. Make sure that the individual's own aspirations are taken into account in development planning.
7. Bring some – just enough – fresh blood into the organization. 'If you can't change the people, change the people' may be true up to a point.
8. Reward people who are innovative, flexible and deliver outstanding results – and be prepared to welcome them back if they walk away.

4

Analysing cultures

*A cultural audit can be used to discover the nature of an organization
in cultural terms, the way it impacts on the strategy ... and the
difficulties of changing it.*

(*Faulkner and Johnson, 1992*)

Introduction

A planned, deliberate approach to culture change assumes that managers have
a clear understanding of which aspects of culture need to change to produce
greater business effectiveness. A culture audit is one of the ways in which managers attempt to identify those aspects of culture they wish to make the target
of change efforts.

In this chapter we will look at some of the ways in which organizational
cultures can be analysed. Whilst William Bridges (1995) is correct in stating that
'There is no generally agreed-upon way to inventory an organization's culture';
nor is there any shortage of theorists and consultancies who have developed
ways of mapping key elements of culture from many different perspectives.

Gaining a clear understanding of the nature of an organization's culture can
be complex, not only because there are many aspects of corporate cultures
to take into account, but also because organizational subcultures will share
similarities and differences from each other and the dominant culture.

The challenges

Perhaps because of these difficulties, taking stock of organizational culture is
not a universal pursuit, as reported in Roffey Park's *Management Agenda* 2003
survey. Only 41 per cent of respondents stated that their organization takes a
serious look at organizational culture on an ongoing basis or annually (31 per cent).
The majority suggested that looking at culture tends to happen only at times
of crisis or before a major change effort. Then culture analysis is often
assumed to involve external consultants and to be an expensive prelude to
major restructuring.

One possible explanation why many organizations tend not to take a serious look at their culture may be that the importance of culture in enabling change is little understood, with line managers often thought to be dismissive of the significance of culture in achieving high performance. In the survey, respondents were split over the question of senior management's view of culture change issues. A slight majority (46 per cent) felt that senior management took such issues seriously; however, a substantial part of the sample (41 per cent) said the reverse. Many senior managers fear that using any form of culture inventory is akin to letting the genie out of the bottle, raising employees' expectations that things will be different/better.

The benefits

Yet, ironically, as long as the method used to audit the culture is appropriate and the process is well managed, the information gathered can provide managers with useful 'evidence' about specific cultural barriers to high performance and about what might need to change. Some commercially available culture audits enable organizations to benchmark aspects of their culture against those of other organizations. Whilst each organization's culture is (and should be) unique, gaining this external perspective can often persuade senior managers of the value of undertaking a culture analysis since they are generally interested in finding out how their organization's results and approaches compare with those of other well-reputed organizations.

In the Roffey Park survey, some of the reported uses of culture audits are as a general managerial tool (63 per cent), for targeting major change initiatives (37 per cent), as a development opportunity (34 per cent), and for building organizational strength (34 per cent). Culture audits also allow managers to gain insights into how employees view the organization currently, versus how they would like it to be. This information provides managers with choices: while they can choose to ignore it, the positive effect on employee morale of acting on even the smallest aspects of culture where there is a broad consensus that change would be desirable can make the effort worthwhile. In addition, managers can gain a greater understanding of the commonly perceived strengths of the culture and compare these with what they believe will make for the basis of a high performance culture for their organization.

Culture audits can also be used for a range of more specific purposes. For example, they can be used to sample how robustly the culture is supportive of innovation, or of employee well-being. They can be used to identify how much the 'shadow side' or political aspects of culture are predominating. Climate surveys enable managers to explore more transitory aspects of organizations, such as morale and motivation levels.

Moreover, analysing a culture can prove an effective change intervention in its own right, leading to a greater awareness amongst organizational members of what they can do for themselves to change aspects of the culture that are damaging performance and to strengthen aspects of culture that offer opportunities for business success.

Alignment

One key objective of auditing an organization's culture is to test degrees of alignment. Alignment occurs when the changing environment and an organization's strategy, systems and culture all flow in the same direction. The circularity of the relationship between an organization's culture and its external environment is described by Weick (1977). He noted that rather than reacting to their environments, organizations create or act upon their environment – which later acts on the organization! People in organizations invest their settings with meaning and then come to understand them. Weick called this the 'creation of reality'. Analysts suggest that for organizations to be able to achieve high performance, gaps between intent, delivery mechanism and infrastructure should be minimal or non-existent.

If an organization's goals are about achieving high performance and the organization's culture is not conducive to high performance practice, change is likely to be necessary to produce closer alignment. Classical Organization Development (OD) theories tend to assume that organizations exist in one state that can then be subject to an 'unfreeze–change–refreeze' process. However, complexity theorists suggest that culture is not a static thing that readily lends itself to remodelling. They would argue that, at best, managers can hope to provide the conditions within which emergence is likely to occur.

This raises the question: Is there an ideal cultural condition which is likely to give rise to high performance?

'Bounded instability'

While there are limitations to thinking about a single ideal state from which sustainable high performance is likely to emerge, complexity theory suggests that if there were such a thing as an ideal state, it would be in 'bounded instability' – somewhere between chaos and stability. According to Jeffrey Goldstein (1994), this occurs when a non-linear system is placed in far-from-equilibrium conditions. When this happens, rather than resisting change, organizations and work groups tend toward change and development.

Bounded instability is more conducive to evolution than either stable equilibrium, which may lead to stagnation, or explosive instability, which may lead to chaos. Employees experience creative tension as they deal with unpredictable business challenges, but have just about enough process that they do not have to reinvent wheels.

This so-called 'edge of chaos', between chaos and order, where self-organization takes place, is considered to be the state most conducive to sustainable organizational performance because it is thought that in these conditions innovation, energetic performance and emergence are most likely to take place. Organizations may find themselves at the edge of chaos due to circumstance, such as when a crisis forces people to abandon old practices in order to find new ways forward to save the organization. Instead of hierarchically imposing change, the potential for change is unleashed and activated. Instead of 'unfreezing' and 'refreezing', a spontaneous reorganization emerges, representing a more effective way to accomplish the organization's objectives. Instead of large-scale changes requiring large efforts, small-scale efforts can facilitate large-scale changes. Instead of emphasizing planning, change is an evolving strategy utilizing chance and accidental events.

Paradox abounds in the self-organization approach. Instead of focusing only on what is internal to the organization, this approach includes the challenge of firming up and traversing the boundaries between a work group or organization and its environment. Instead of relying only on a rational and cognitive perspective, change needs to incorporate elements of play and the absurd. Instead of consensus – seeking as the means toward participation – non-consensus-seeking can lead to participatory structures.

To bring an organization to the edge of chaos requires a number of factors to be in balance – just enough to achieve the creative tension conducive to high performance. Speed is a critical element. If what happens in an organization is too rapid, it will tend towards chaos – there will be too few procedures, and little follow-through or consolidation. Conversely, if things happen too slowly, or if decision-making takes place at the wrong levels, the organization may stagnate. Similarly, the flow of information around the organization needs to be sufficient that it informs people but not so much that it becomes an information nightmare where people are deluged with data.

Diversity is another prerequisite for high performance. Without sufficient difference, an organization clones itself and is in danger of losing touch with its customers and the way the world is changing. Power also has to be in balance. If power is exercised too directly by some, it disempowers other people. On the other hand, with general empowerment there may be under-maximization of the organization's strategic potential since there may be duplication of effort and too much consensus-seeking, which can slow down decision-making.

Theorists of emergence would suggest that the role of leaders is to create the circumstances in which people will learn, adapt and stabilize what is working. Other theorists suggest that creative tension can be designed into an organization so that it is more likely than not to operate in the way described (see Chapter 5). From an organization design perspective, if the organization is ready for a structural/design solution, employee behaviour will adapt to the new arrangements.

Core competency theory

Another aspect of alignment relates to an organization's capability. According to core competency theory, specific aspects of culture and strategy together represent an organization's core competency. Playing to the strengths of an organization's core competency should be a major source of competitive advantage, so it is important to be able to identify these elements, especially if they are somewhat intangible. A cultural analysis can therefore be helpful in crystallizing some of these less easily defined competencies.

Developed by Hamel and Prahalad (1990), core competency theory has been highly influential in causing a rethink about organizations. The initial thinking was to restructure organizations around clusters of competence that feed into the production of products and services. Core competencies were identified by systematically focusing in on the 'success factors' that have achieved past results, and distinguishing these from the capabilities needed to compete in the same markets in the future. Since many companies had trouble defining their core competence, which is often a complex mix of technology and know-how, some of the attempts to acquire further core competency through acquisition came unstuck.

The more recent focus of core competency theory is on building the competencies that will make a disproportionate contribution to future customer value. Hamel and Prahalad argue that core competencies are the highest-level, longest-lasting units for strategy-making. Strategic decisions need to be taken about which core competencies to build for the future in order to be world class, together with developing strategies for building those competencies. This strategic view should dominate decisions about which businesses to acquire or divest, and what needs to be strengthened within an organization.

Core competency theory has fuelled the debate about the appropriate way of structuring an organization in order to build, and profit from, its core competency. The debate has centred on how durable horizontal, process-driven structures really are, even though business processes rather than functional 'silos' are considered key components of organization design for the future. In horizontal structures, new managerial roles emerge. The 'process owner' sets overall performance targets and has overall responsibility for the team's performance. The 'process team' itself may be made up of people at different levels in the hierarchy, and is accountable to the process owner for the day-to-day operating performance. The 'coach' role is usually part of the team rather than outside it, and supports the team's performance, while the product manager contributes technical expertise on product standards.

The argument is that horizontal organizations, which facilitate a focus on core processes, undermine an equally important element of an organization's competitive advantage: its core disciplines such as outstanding engineering, IT and other vertical knowledge sources. It is suggested that focusing on processes benefits today's customer, while focusing on disciplines will benefit the customers of tomorrow. Similarly, decentralizing can lead to a weakening of a company's core competency through loss of talent. Employees tend to associate more with the specific business unit to which they are attached than with the organization as a whole. Consequently, decentralization can reduce the employee mobility and flexibility needed in changing environments. Similarly, the mechanisms for moving people around the organization – such as career management functions – tend to operate less well, so that key employees can become 'hidden from view' in the broader organization.

Mapping an organization's culture(s) – an overview

Mapping an organization's culture(s) typically involves:

- Data-gathering and diagnosis, which is usually (but not always) carried out by internal consultants (such as HR) or external specialists.
- Agreeing a future culture profile, showing what the culture should be in the future to achieve high performance. This is usually prepared by participants from a range of different subgroups.
- Determining what needs to be modified (the leadership team determines which aspects of organizational culture may need to be modified).
- Participants in the process discussing and achieving consensus on what the discrepancies between current and future profiles mean. It is important that people are clear about the cultural trade-offs that may be needed, and about which aspects of the culture should be retained and strengthened. Typically, people use the formula of the aspects of culture that they wish to have more of, less of, or in the same amount as currently. Ideally, participants should illustrate through two or three stories the key values they want to percolate through the future culture. We will return to the diagnostic process in a little more detail below.
- Generating options. Having identified the areas to be strengthened or changed in order to achieve the desired future culture profile, the next stage involves generating options about how to achieve these. This involves using techniques such as brainstorming and attribute analysis.
- Evaluating options, which can involve techniques such as cost-benefit analyses, weighting and ranking.
- Making decisions and planning.
- Designing interventions, which involves being creative and purposeful, not relying on packaged, favourite interventions; being willing to redesign on the spot; and designing at the level of content and process simultaneously (Shaw and Phillips, 1998).
- Finally, implementing change.

Diagnosis

Often carried out by internal consultants – from HR, operations groups, process specialists – diagnosis involves collecting and making sense of data. Most internal consultancy work is related to first-order, transactional change, where elements of the organization are changed but the organization as a whole remains fundamentally unaltered. Identifying what needs to be changed can be quite straightforward. For example, to analyse organizational climate in a work unit:

- Observe work in progress
- Carry out interviews with key members of the workforce
- Conduct a survey of staff members using questionnaires or culture/climate audits.

The change agent then chooses how to intervene to improve the climate.

Data-gathering is likely to give rise to access issues, such as whether the consultant will have limited or more wide-ranging access to people and sources of data relating to the situation. The question of objectivity can arise, since in a very real way the consultant is in essence bringing about change simply by data-gathering. It is therefore very important that the consultant models the desired change as the consultancy process gets under way. Typically, participants in data-gathering include representatives from different parts of the organization or the whole organization. They are asked to describe the current organization's culture using, for instance, one or several of the culture analysis tools and methods described below. The data so gathered are enriched if participants in the process also include external stakeholders, such as customers.

The success of change is driven both by the accuracy of diagnosis and by the client's (usually senior management's) acceptance of the analysis. This requires the consultant (external or internal) to have a range of frameworks and models to draw on for understanding individuals, groups and organizations; to maintain a critical approach to models; to be able to construct his or her own models; and to encourage joint diagnosis with clients. Then consensus should be reached on an agreed profile of the current culture.

Once there is a degree of mutual understanding and trust between the client and consultant, other process issues are likely to come to the forefront – e.g. confidentiality, authority and power. Often these 'process' issues are raised at the 'content' level by third parties within the client organization, and the consultant may want to make them explicit – e.g. 'What you tell me will remain confidential to us'. The main concern is to define the 'felt' need, and explore boundaries with a view to identifying options for change. The more explicit the consultant is in showing how this will be done, the more unlikely the chance of ambiguity and eventual 'bad feeling' resulting from unfulfilled expectations.

Tools for taking stock

Any diagnosis of a culture is a change intervention in itself. At the very least it will cause people to ask themselves questions about how they would like things to be, which may be very different from how things are. This may cause some people to want to change things, while others may become more, not less, dissatisfied. Equally, becoming aware of how culture operates can make people want to understand better how to maintain something about the culture that works well. One approach that lends itself to the latter is Appreciative Inquiry, which causes people to focus in on the positive aspects of the organization so as better to understand the processes at work in success.

Part of the art of diagnosis lies in selecting appropriate methods of data collection, asking pertinent questions and encouraging client ownership of data. Knowledge of which technique is most appropriate in a particular context represents part of the change agent's expertise. In the *Management Agenda*, cultural analysis tools used include questionnaires (63 per cent), focus groups (41 per cent) and facilitated workshops (39 per cent).

There is a wide range of well-established tools and methods available, including:

- Observation
- Company documents, marketing materials, website
- Interviews (structured, semi-structured, open-ended)
- Process mapping
- Flow charts
- Cause and effect diagrams
- Pareto analysis
- Brainstorming
- Team Management Styles (TMS)
- The GROW model (goals, reality, options, wrap-up)
- McKinsey 7S method
- Nominal Group method
- Repertory Grid technique
- Resource maps
- SWOT analyses (strengths, weaknesses, opportunities, threats)
- Critical Incident interviews
- Questionnaires
- Needs analyses
- Cultural/climate audits (see below)
- Role evaluations
- Employee attitude survey data
- Customer survey data
- Focus groups
- 360-degree feedback data
- Organizational Effectiveness Inventory
- Organizational Culture Inventory (human synergistics)
- Performance management data
- Turnover statistics
- Exit interview data.

Newer approaches include:

- Appreciative Inquiry
- Clean Language – a questioning technique that helps questioner and interviewee to gain an in-depth understanding of the way in which culture and cultural issues are reflected in the language used to describe them
- Graphical Interpretation
- Network Maps
- Logical Levels (Robert Dilts)
- Four Levels of Need (business, performance, learning, process)
- Storytelling (see Chapter 7).

Some of the above are commercially available tools for mapping cultures and most tend to focus on the overarching elements of culture and climate. Questionnaires and inventories usually require respondents to describe the culture as they perceive it currently versus an ideal culture, which they define. Cultural differences are often represented as polar opposites. Management styles, for example, may be represented as Theory X or Theory Y, and climates may be described as 'closed and secretive' or 'open and trusting'. Such polarization can lead to dilemmas which produce either/or responses based on the assumption that one approach is superior to another.

Herb Stokes and Roger Harrison (1992) developed an *Organizational Culture Diagnosis*. This is based on their definition of four types of organizational culture. These are:

1. *Achievement* – based on competence, whose dominant values are growth, success and distinction
2. *Support* – based on relationships, whose values are mutuality, service and integration
3. *Power* – based on strength, whose values are direction, decisiveness and determination
4. *Role* – based on strength, structures and systems whose values are order, stability and control.

Each of the four cultures has its ideal state, strengths, limitations and so-called 'dark sides', which may not be obvious but can be damaging to individuals and the organization. So, for instance, in an ideal power culture the leader is strong and charismatic, bringing courage to the faint-hearted and clarity to the confused. A strength of a power culture is that individual effort is unified behind the vision of the leader, enabling the organization to move quickly as the market changes. However, a limitation may be that constructive change is limited by the vision and flexibility of the leader, and what is not openly acknowledged is that people give the boss's wishes the highest priority, even when it interferes with important work.

Any organizational culture will be made up of many different elements of such culture types, though there may be one recognizable culture type that predominates. Subcultures may have their own cultural types reflecting the particular nature of the group, but overall these are likely to coexist happily with the broader corporate culture, recognizably part of the culture but different from it.

Stokes and Harrison (1992) looked at how these culture types empower and disempower people. The Achievement culture empowers through identification with the values and ideals of a vision; through the liberation of creativity; and through freedom to act. It disempowers through burnout and stress; through treating the individual as an instrument of the task; and through inhibiting dissent through goals and values. The Support culture empowers through the power of cooperation and trust; through providing understanding, acceptance and assistance. It disempowers through suppressing conflict; through preoccupation with process; and through conformity to group norms.

The Power culture empowers through identification with a strong leader. It disempowers through fear, and through inability to act without permission. The Role culture empowers through systems that serve the people and the task, reducing conflict and confusion. It disempowers through restricting autonomy and creativity, and through erecting barriers to cooperation.

The ideal is where excellence can be achieved through dynamic tension between the four types of culture. In such a scenario, the stereotypical committed, idealistic and energetic employees of an achievement culture receive the decisive, strong, focused leadership of the power culture. At the same time they are supported by cooperative, caring, responsive characteristics of the support culture, and the role culture's reliable, rational, systematic processes, which help them to achieve more, without reaching burnout.

Similar four-box cultural classifications are by Charles Handy (1995a), who defined cultures as 'club', 'role', 'task' or 'existential', and Cameron and Quinn's *Competing Values Framework* (1998). According to the latter, cultures can be divided along a vertical dimension according to values such as flexibility and discretion versus control and stability. On the horizontal axis, values are around internal maintenance and integration versus external positioning and differentiation. The four cultural 'types' that emerge are the clan, adhocracy, hierarchy and market cultures.

In the clan culture, the leader acts as mentor and facilitator; effectiveness criteria are cohesion, morale and development of human resource; and the management theory is that participation fosters commitment. In the adhocracy culture, the leader is an innovator, entrepreneur and visionary; effectiveness criteria are cutting-edge output, creativity and growth; and the management theory is innovativeness fosters new resources. In the hierarchy, the leader is coordinator, monitor and organizer; effectiveness criteria are timeliness and smooth functioning; and the management theory is that control fosters efficiency. In the market culture, the leader is a hard-driver, competitor and producer; effectiveness criteria are market share, goal achievement and beating competitors, while the management theory is that competition fosters productivity.

In Cameron and Quinn's model, new or small organizations tend to progress through a predictable pattern of culture changes as they progress through the organizational life cycle. In the earliest stages they tend to have an adhocracy culture, characterized by entrepreneurship. They then develop a clan culture, which generates a sense of belonging and personal identification with the organization. As the organization grows, order and predictability are needed and a hierarchy orientation is introduced. This in turn is replaced by a market orientation, where the focus is on achieving results and on external market relationships.

The *Organizational Culture Assessment Instrument* (OCAI) by Cameron and Quinn (1998) is based on the Competing Values framework. It explains the underlying value orientations that characterize organizations. The value orientations are usually competing or contradicting each other. Organizational profiles identify ways in which an organization's culture is likely to change as values change over time.

The *Organizational Culture Inventory* (OCI), by Cook and Lafferty (1987), is widely used, and allows organizations to compare their cultural map with norm groups of other organizations. There are twelve OCI constructs, as follows:

- Satisfaction styles – achievement, self-actualizing, humanistic-encouraging, affiliative

- People/security styles – avoidance, dependent, conventional, approval
- Task/security styles – oppositional, power, competitive, perfectionistic.

The Organizational Character Index by Bridges uses a questionnaire to identify one of sixteen organizational character types. Based on the Myers Briggs Type Indicator, the archetypes are mapped along four dimensions:

Extraverted (E)	↔	Introverted (I)
Sensing (S)	↔	Intuitive (N)
Thinking (T)	↔	Feeling (F)
Judging (J)	↔	Perceiving (P)

Schein (1984) and Kotter and Heskett (1992) have identified cultural dimensions based on cultural strength and congruence. Norman Chorn, from the Centre for Corporate Strategy, has developed the *Strategic Alignment* or *PADI Model*. This is based on the degree of alignment between key dimensions such as performance, administration, development and intimacy and the organization's environment, strategy, culture and leadership. This model explores where the centre of gravity exists at each level of the model (environment, strategy, culture and leadership) and examines the trade-offs working at each level. So in demanding market conditions, is performance being achieved at the expense of intimacy? When there is need of innovation, do administrative requirements, including standardization, support or disable breakthroughs?

Qualitative methods

Other approaches to diagnosing organizational culture rely more on qualitative methods, such as storytelling and critical incident analysis, than on quantitative methods. Some would argue that because culture is based on underlying values and assumptions, it is only by using in-depth qualitative methods in which artefacts, stories and myths are studied over time that a real understanding of the culture's attributes can be gained. Quinn and Cameron advocate use of scenarios which can provide clues to unearth aspects of culture that may have become invisible to people working within the culture. Others argue that breadth is sacrificed by the exclusive use of qualitative methods. Most analysts use a combination of both qualitative and quantitative methods.

Cross-cultural analyses

In international organizations, different national characteristics or cultural practices (for instance with regard to timekeeping, or expectations of hierarchy) can cause misunderstanding. Hofstede and Trompenaars have each developed questionnaires as part of their own research into national cultural differences. In Trompenaars' model (1993), national differences exist among countries on a number of dimensions: universalism versus particularism, individualism versus collectivism, neutrality versus emotionality, focus on past versus present versus future, and an internal versus external focus.

In *The Seven Cultures of Capitalism*, Hampden-Turner and Trompenaars (1993) highlight several valuing processes necessary to wealth creation and show how the leading world economies each operate according to a unique set of values, which can be mapped along the following dimensions:

1. *Universalism vs Particularism*. When no code, rule or law seems to cover an exceptional case, should the most relevant rules be imposed, or should the case be considered on its unique merits, regardless of the rule? For example, in a universalist culture, the community shares a predominant belief that the 'rights' of the abstract society (or organization) prevail over the 'rights' of a special friend. In other words, the rules apply equally to everybody. Conversely, in a predominantly particularistic society, the 'rights' of a friend are taken to be more important than the 'rights' of the larger community. This does not mean that a particularistic society has no general or formal rules or laws; it only means that they are likely to be broken for the sake of friendship, even at the cost of 'order' within the larger society.
2. *Analysing vs Integrating*. Are we more effective as managers when we analyse phenomena into parts (e.g. facts, items, tasks, numbers, units etc.) or when we integrate such details into whole patterns, relationships and wider contexts?
3. *Individualism vs Communitarianism*. Is it more important to focus on enhancement of each individual, his or her rights, motivations, capacities etc., or should more attention be paid to the advancement of the corporation as a community, which all its members commit to serve?
4. *Achieved vs Ascribed status*. Should the status of employees depend on what they have achieved or how they have performed, or on some other characteristic important to the corporation – e.g. age, seniority, gender, education etc.?

Organizational cultures, especially in cross-national merger situations, often reflect different value tendencies. When cultural misunderstandings occur, they can create dilemmas that often provoke an either/or response. Charles Hampden-Turner (1994) has mapped organization-specific dilemmas and identified the importance of reconciling those dilemmas, rather than allowing cultural differences to divide, or lead to mediocre compromise. Reconciling apparently conflicting cultural approaches involves creating a process in which ideas can be generated around how to avoid the limitations of each culture while capitalizing on the strengths of both.

Making sense of the data gathered

Methods of data analysis include:

- Frequency counts
- Content analysis
- Linkage analysis
- 'Fishbone' diagrams
- Descriptive analysis.

Force field analysis

This commonly used analytical technique is based on Lewin's Force Field Theory, which examines the driving and restraining forces for change. It involves:

1. Defining the problem
   - Describe your current situation
   - Describe your ideal situation
2. Analysing the problem
   - List the restraining forces
   - List the driving forces
   - Rank the restraining/driving forces in order of importance
3. Developing solutions
   - Brainstorm possible action steps for key restraining forces
   - Brainstorm possible action steps for key driving forces
   - Select most promising action steps
4. Developing a plan
   - List the action steps and, for each step, list the resources required/available
   - Draft an overall action plan
   - Review the plan with a colleague
   - Complete the plan.

Assessing alignment

Another important use of cultural audits is to test the degree of alignment between different facets of the organization and its strategy and environment. The aim is usually to close the gaps that are most problematic to the achievement of business. One of the best-known models for assessing the degree of internal alignment between an organization and its strategy is the McKinsey 7S formula, devised by Tom Peters and Robert Waterman (1982; see Chapter 1).

Developed in the late 1970s, the McKinsey 7S model is useful for understanding the dynamics of organizational change and developing goals for a change programme. It emphasizes the importance of achieving consistency and balance between the seven descriptive elements (7Ss). The seven Ss are:

1. *Strategy* – a coherent set of actions aimed at gaining a sustainable competitive advantage (and as such, the approach to allocating resources)
2. *Structure* – the organization chart and related concepts that indicate who reports to whom and how tasks are divided up and integrated (reporting relations and management responsibilities)
3. *Systems* – the processes and procedures through which things get done.
4. *Staff* – the people in the organization, considered in terms of corporate demographics, i.e. their skills and abilities.
5. *Skills* – distinctive capabilities possessed by the organization as a whole, as distinct from those of an individual.
6. *Style* – the way managers collectively behave with respect to the use of time, attention and symbolic actions.

7. *Shared values* – ideas of what is right and desirable (in corporate and/or individual behaviour) as well as fundamental principles and concepts, which are typical of the organization and common to most of its members.

The first three Ss represent the so-called 'hard triangle,' which has been the conventional focus for change consultancy. However, in recent years there has been growing recognition that effective implementation does not flow automatically from close alignment between the first three factors. It has been interesting to note how many strategy specialists have developed consultancy offerings around the four remaining 'soft square' factors.

These elements represent the real keys to success or failure of change efforts since they represent the key variables affecting the successful implementation of the change strategy. The 'soft square' is in fact the 'hard' bit to do! The growth industry in 'talent management', culture change and attempts to quantify 'human capital' reflect the significance of the people dimension to business success and continuity.

Typical cultural barriers to high performance

In practice, alignment is difficult to achieve, and alignment gaps may become barriers or 'blockers' to high performance.

The following examples of cultural misalignments with business strategy come from the *Management Agenda* survey:

- Many companies aim to compete in the global marketplace, yet they often appear to focus mainly on their local market, rather than seeking to understand their international markets.
- Many organizations share the aspiration to develop a flexible, networked and innovative culture that will equip them to thrive in turbulent times. However, the picture emerges of many organizations being so internally focused that they are unable to collaborate easily internally, let alone with other organizations!
- While many organizational strategies call for innovation, in practice management styles and heavy workloads tend to militate against risk-taking and creativity.
- Despite organizations' aspiring to operate across organizational boundaries, relatively few people appear to be involved in forms of partnership working and there appears to be little sharing of the evolving knowledge and expertise.

Other common cultural barriers to high performance evident in the *Management Agenda* findings include:

- *Lack of shared values.* There is a lack of trust at all levels, reflected in political climates; lack of clear strategic direction; inappropriate management styles; harassment; conflict; values espoused but not practised; lack of role modelling by senior management; lack of openness to change; merger situations, which undermine trust levels.

- *Lack of leadership.* This includes not taking culture change or employee needs seriously; being out of touch with new working practices; having little time to coach and develop others; permitting politics and conflict; senior managers being the main perpetrators of harassment; failing to address the workload issue; managing innovation as if it is *status quo*; managers finding difficulties managing flexible workers; managers not walking the talk on values; lack of support to others; overly controlling management styles; only 41 per cent of sample believe that their top management act as leaders.
- *Staff.* Symptoms include lack of diversity; recruiting in own image; skills shortages; lack of shared learning; heavy workloads and high stress levels – 50 per cent of sample still believe their organizations make excessive demands – especially to do more with less; difficulties in working in global teams.
- *Inappropriate systems.* These include performance management processes that are out-of-date or meaningless to employees; reward systems that contradict espoused values; few processes that enable learning to be shared; email creating communication overload; poorly run meetings which waste time; 86 per cent of sample would like to see different working patterns, especially more flexibility; knowledge management is now being treated a little more seriously than in the past, but organizations still lack the means to share learning; change agents, such as HR, not adding value; and working on low-priority issues.

The picture emerges of somewhat rigid, inward-looking organizations, which are slow to change and where employees put as much effort into preserving their position as to achieving high performance. Complexity theory suggests that complex adaptive systems are at risk when they are in equilibrium. In an over-stable state, the organization will be characterized by too many rules, too much rigidity, and risk aversion. There will be too few connections between people, except through vertical hierarchy. Management styles will tend to be command and control, and contacts will be formal rather than informal. Individuals will tend to work alone rather than as members of teams. Conversely, in chaos, employees experience too little procedure, leading to anarchy and confusion. If anything, there are too many interconnections between people, creating a sense of free-for-all, lack of accountability and informal rather than formal contacts. Risk-taking can err on the reckless side, and gossip can be rife.

Not surprisingly, many respondents consider that a 'culture change' is needed. Edge-of-chaos, characterized by learning, rather than chaos, becomes the desired state.

Conclusion

No two organizations are alike, and developing the 'right' cultural mix, which is conducive to high performance and sustainable success, is therefore situational. Given the pressures for change coming from the external and internal environment, an organization's culture needs to equip it for change, while valuing the best from the past. Taking stock of how people perceive the culture at any point in time is a means of taking an organizational 'health-check'. Management teams gain not only a greater understanding of the culture's current strengths and weaknesses, but also insights into what might need to change for innovation and other elements of high performance to be stimulated. In this way, managers can develop a greater understanding of how culture's strengths can become potential sources of competitive advantage.

Having taken stock of current and future cultural profiles, organization design can be used to build the structures and organizational processes that are likely to reinforce the desired culture. In the next chapter, we will look at processes of organization (re)design which are geared to enabling high performance.

Checklist: Organizational assessment and alignment

- What is the identity of the firm we are trying to create with target customers?
- How is this identity unique to us, rather than our competitors?
- What management actions are we taking to reinforce that identity?
- What is our firm's culture overall?
- How do our customers feel about our identity and culture?
- How do employees feel about the culture?
- What are the key tasks, outcomes and outputs the organization is to deliver?
- What are the values of the firm?
- To what extent are these translated into leadership behaviours?
- To what extent are managers assessed on the way they demonstrate these values?
- What are the commonest management styles?
- How and where is power distributed?
- Are our models of capability robust enough for today's changing environment?
- How flexible are the skills we have?
- Where are they located?
- Are our staffing practices aligned to culture?
- Where physically do people work in relation to others?
- What is the physical environment like?
- Where are there differences in levels of employee satisfaction and motivation?
- How well are training and development practices aligned to culture?
- How well do employees feel supported by their managers?
- Do technology and systems support a flexible structure?
- Are technology and systems developed to enable future modifications?
- What are the work flows and information flows?

- Is decision-making happening at the right level?
- Do our processes cover functional requirements while also being designed to be cross-functional?
- How well are the various tasks and functions coordinated and integrated?
- Do our task-planning and strategy processes build in change-readiness?
- How well do our practices enable effective knowledge management and innovation?
- How do our role design and structure recognize both business as usual and change?
- What balance of hierarchy/matrix and functional organization do we have?
- How well are our performance management practices aligned?
- How well do our meetings practices support the need for speedy decision-making and ethical behaviour?
- Are information systems meeting current and likely future needs?
- How effective are our information systems in simplifying organizational processes?
- Do our formal reward mechanisms support change or steady state?
- Who gets promoted and why?
- How well are communication practices aligned to our culture?
- What balance of formal and informal practices happens, and in what direction?
- How much do employees feel involved in what is happening?
- How engaged are employees in the work they do?

5

Designing the high performance organization

With the number and complexity of changes increasing, it's time to rethink how we design organizations.

(McLagan, 2003)

Introduction

In this chapter, we shall look at how elements of high performance can be planned into the design of organizations. We will also explore some of the interconnected elements of organization design that can help or hinder an organization's effective operation.

Of course, any organization design tends to be time-bound and planning is no guarantee that what is intended will happen. Events and developments can and do affect the usefulness of a design over time, causing gradual adjustments to be made to keep it fit for purpose. Designs often become associated with particular events, such as when a new CEO arrives and kicks off a major restructuring exercise. When the next CEO arrives, the process begins again. The challenge is to move beyond the tactical to a more strategic approach, creating an organization design that is robust and clear yet has change-ability, flexibility and opportunities for emergence built in.

To be effective in today's changing context, an organization's design has to take into account the fact that, in the light of non-evolutionary and evolutionary change and the global technological revolution, concepts of organization, of the workplace and of work itself are being reviewed and changed. Through technology work can be done anywhere, any time, challenging the notion that work will be carried out in a 'workplace'. Will the large, impressive corporate headquarters buildings of yesteryear continue into the future when a major part of the workforce works from home? Designs also have to reflect the nature of the work to be done and the sources of competitive advantage. Increasingly, a company's assets are likely to be valued less in terms of existing plant and patents and more in relation to future intellectual capital and the means by which this can be secured. How can designs enable better knowledge creation and sharing, support empowerment and accountability? What forms of leadership and management are appropriate in a knowledge-based environment?

Similarly, the nature of the workforce is changing as 'knowledge work' increasingly becomes the basis of competitive advantage. Many organizations are experiencing the challenge of attracting, recruiting and retaining the talented employees they require. The needs and aspirations of 'knowledge workers' therefore have to be taken into account when redesigning organizations. In the light of these shifts, the rigid management practices, employment policies and bureaucratic processes of the past are under review, and what employees want and need in order to work effectively are becoming key considerations.

Changing too are design success criteria, as organizations look to achieve more effective asset utilization; greater flexibility and speed; innovation and high product quality; better organizational structures; and better work processes and practices. In many organizations, putting the customer at the heart of operations is the key to business success. Finding ways to give all employees a clear line of sight to the customer, external or internal, is the prime objective of organization redesign.

What is organization (re)design?

When thinking of organization design, many people think of structures. In practice, organization design consists of decisions about formal structures, processes, systems, roles and relationships (Walton and Nadler, 1994). In designing an organization, one must consider its purpose and philosophy, aims and how goals will be implemented or operationalized. Through the structure are established reporting lines, methods of communication, procedures for making decisions and solving system problems, rules or guidelines for the conduct of employees, and a system of rewarding goal attainment.

Typical elements of conventional organization design include:

- Formalization, or the presence of written rules, procedures and policies
- Specialization, or the subdivision of indirect labour
- Decentralization, or the vertical locus of decision-making authority.

These are context specific. For example, larger firms typically have formalized, specialized and decentralized structures. More organic firms are less formalized, more specialized and decentralized. Formalization is thought to be in inverse association with quality management, while technical specialization and decentralization associate positively. With regard to product dynamism, there is a positive association with specialization and decentralization, but a negative association with formalization (Germain and Spears, 1999). According to Miles and Snow (1986), organizational forms arise to cope with new environmental conditions, and result from a variety of experimental actions taken by innovative companies.

Flexible organizations are not those of a particular design, such as team-based or matrix organizations, but rather organizations that can move from one design archetype to another, or mix archetypes. Typical archetypes include highly centralized, moderately centralized/moderately autonomous, and highly autonomous and decentralized structures. These three archetypes are points on a continuum, ranging from 'highly centralized' at one extreme to 'highly autonomous and decentralized' at the other. Each archetype has different member-ship, operating philosophy, hierarchy, control systems, information flows, technology, work processes, behavioural latitude, decision-making processes, management style, informal networks, leaders, use of the grapevine, status, involvement and dress codes.

Structures therefore do not work in isolation from other cultural elements. In earlier chapters we considered how corporate cultures can be slow to evolve, and tend to do so in fits and starts. In many organizations, change initiatives tend to be piecemeal, resulting in an organization design containing complica-tions and paradox. Old management practices work uneasily within physical environments that are intended to give rise to greater creativity and empower-ment. What McLagan calls a 'transformational approach' – a structural and mental redesign of organizations – is needed.

Organizational redesign is defined as the set of managerial actions used to change an organization's technologies, processes and structures (Huber and Glick, 1993). According to Kanter *et al.* (1992):

> *The success of organizational change ... depends on the extent to which every aspect of the system {design} – formal structure, information flows, rewards, recruitment etc. – support the new definition of what the organiza-tion is to be and how it is to operate. More specifically, the aspects of organ-ization which will be affected by a change in mission and strategy include the organizational form (functional, divisional, matrix), its size, the group-ing of business units (function, product/service, target market), hierarchical levels (many, few), planning and control systems, job specialization, train-ing and education programmes, degree of centralization, delegation and participation.*
>
> *(Volberda, 1992)*

Strategic alignment

Organization designs now have to take account of the current level and growth rate of turbulence in the external environment, the use of information systems to increase the availability of operational information (Parker, 1995), the role of organizational culture as a powerful influence on organizational structure and individual performance, and the organization's strategic intent. Designs therefore have to be both permeable and robust, clear and simple, yet enable complex activity to be carried out and 'fuzzy logic' to be deployed.

According to contingency theory, following Chandler's (1962) dictum, struc-ture follows strategy. Yet the link between structures and strategy is not always clear in practice. Often organizational structure changes reflect changes in the overall corporate structure, rather than business unit strategy. Similarly, structures may fail to achieve their strategic purpose if management styles remain out of step with the strategy. So, employees working in a heavily layered hierarchy may find themselves being exhorted to use their initiative to serve the customer, but may have to go through an extensive checking process before they can act.

In redesigning organizations, it is important to understand the driving forces behind the need for change, as well as shifts in corporate culture. The degree to which organizations are responsive to changes in their strategic objectives will reflect the flexibility of their structural design. The purpose of redesign efforts is to improve organizational effectiveness, problem solving, and the ability to adapt to a constantly changing environment. The overall goal of redesign efforts, according to Douglas (1999), is to therefore increase flexibility, improve responsiveness and increase information flow. Another common key goal of restructuring is to save costs and improve profitability through greater efficiencies. Whether changing structures actually results in higher productivity is a different matter. In today's organizations, three core design criteria are becoming the yardstick by which organization designs are assessed:

1. To reduce unit costs
2. To respond quickly to environmental changes
3. To meet the demands of the 'new' knowledge workforce.

Sometimes, the three success criteria may seem irreconcilable and require trade-offs. For example, introducing a disciplined process to improve efficiency and drive down cost may limit employees' scope for innovation and individual ownership of the work they do. If the process is so rigid that it becomes a strait-jacket of compliance, it may be cost-effective in the short term but limit organizational adaptability and lead to employee turnover.

One acid test of what is valued is to look at the organization's decision-making processes. For example, which business issue absorbs more senior management attention? Is it (a) re-engineering core processes, or (b) regenerating core strategies? Similarly, what is the company's strength? Is it (a) operational efficiency, or (b) innovation and growth? If the focus is generally on (a) and less on (b), the tendency will be to 'milk the cash cow' in terms of short-term returns, at the expense of longer-term revenue growth.

Ideally, of course, (a) and (b) should be mutually reinforcing, but frequently (b) destroys (a). Today's organization designs need to reconcile such mutual exclusivities. The focus is therefore shifting to building an organization structure that can enable high performance working *and* improve efficiencies *and* produce greater innovation. By making tactical design changes in the light of a longer-term strategic aim of high performance, such as enabling better knowledge sharing between team members, designers (usually a combination of line managers and HR) should accelerate the journey towards achieving both great results in the short term and sustainable high performance in the longer term.

Taking people into account

Organizational design is also about creating an overall context for high performance, in which systems, processes and objectives mesh with employees' motivations and values. Major change requires employees to become good at critical new behaviours and skills. According to Michael Colenso (1998), these are generic competencies which no serious organization can afford to ignore. They include things like continuous quality improvement, continuous process improvement, continuous customer satisfaction improvement, the ability to change fast and the ability to learn fast.

While flexibility can be designed into systems, processes and structures to some extent, it is people who make these elements work. Redesign activities involve both structural and functional change, and therefore a wider range of factors has to be taken into account. These include not only the cost savings to be achieved in the short-term, but also how people can become more productive over time, how the organization can be designed to assist their efforts rather than get in the way, and how people can be supported to generate greater value in their new roles, using new systems and processes.

Organization design today is placing a greater emphasis than in the past on designing an organization that people actually want to work in and where the styles of management are appropriate to a high performance culture. According to Block (in Hosking and Morley, 1991), there is a growing realization that strict controls, greater work pressure, more clearly defined jobs and tighter supervision 'have run their course in terms of their ability to give organizations productivity gains'. Individuals and groups are becoming the building blocks of organizational control (Kiedel, 1995). The best organization designs will address issues relating to employee motivation (the 'want to do' factor), their knowledge of what is required (the 'know what to do' factor) and their ability to do what is required (the 'can do' factor).

In practice, the 'want to do' factor is reflected in formal and informal systems such as compensation for time and effort, rewards for suggestions and motivational messages as in structures. The 'know what to do' factor is given flesh through direction and goal-setting, the way information and knowledge are created and shared, and through employees learning the job as they go along. The best way of ensuring that people are willing and able to work in a redesigned organization is to involve them in the process of design. Front-line staff in particular usually have a clear understanding of how work processes can be improved in ways that benefit the customer and the organization. However, a common complaint from front-line employees is that nobody asks them or listens to their suggestions.

The 'can do' factor is evident in the resources made available to employees, including time and facilities, and in the skills, tools and techniques that employees are able to deploy. A new organizational design needs to be supported by the appropriate technologies, in terms of hardware, software (knowledge, techniques and skills) and the configuration of the technologies. Trahant and Burke (1996) advocate the use of a change readiness assessment to identify which people in the organization are ready to adopt and use the new technology, and also those people who lack the necessary skills to evolve with the organization.

Culture and design

The list of elements to consider in redesigning organizations to create sustainable high performance does not stop there. According to the CBI/TUC submission to the UK Productivity Initiative (2001):

> *Research evidence suggests that new forms of work organization, effective management and leadership, a culture that encourages innovation, employee involvement and employee development tailored to organizational needs, are all necessary conditions for adaptable, high performance workplaces. Commitment to equal opportunities and managing diversity are also key issues. A central feature in the mix is the adoption of an inclusive management style that encourages workers at all levels of the organization to contribute. Management leadership and employee involvement are complementary features of the high performance/high commitment model.*

Culture is a major influence on the structure of the organization because it provides consistency, order and structure for activity, establishes communication patterns and determines the nature and use of power (Schneider, 1994). Since culture can derail strategic intentions, some theorists argue that the key concern in redesigning organizations should be to bring about cultural change more obviously linked with strategic planning. Cultural change then becomes driven by business demands and involves linking the change in the culture of the organization with organizational goals, for example building new team structures and information systems to enable greater effectiveness.

However, culture is a factor in the redesign process over which managers have little or no control. As discussed in the previous chapter, organizations can exist in a variety of states which can support or harm their objectives, or do both simultaneously. The existence and development of a strong culture is essential to ensure the fit of culture and strategy and to increase the commitment by employees to the organization. Theorists such as Kiedel (1995) suggest that cultures can be strengthened, with the new organizational forms focusing on the use of two variables – autonomy and cooperation – which may lead to increased job satisfaction of individuals and greater employee commitment. Such forms are more likely to give rise to emergent innovation and collaboration.

Comparing organizations along two dimensions – the complexity of the product/service and rate of change/speed of change in the organization's environment – produces four quadrants of organization design state. In relatively slow-moving market conditions for relatively simple products, production-line processes, supported by continuous process improvement, can be very suitable. However, such conditions can engender a degree of routine and 'job's worth' thinking, which can lead to stagnation.

In environments where people are working on highly complex products with relatively long lead times, such as the large defence or pharmaceutical companies used to enjoy, roles tend to be highly specialist, with the role of management being to provide the maximum support and minimum interruption to specialists at work. The challenge in such organizations comes when the pace of change accelerates, leading to pressure to get products to market faster. Individuals may then be encouraged to try new work processes, such as teamworking, which feel unfamiliar. They may feel under pressure to cut corners in ways that perhaps offend professional sensibilities, leading to demotivation and disaffection.

In fast-moving environments, with simple products, production-line processes can be rapidly improved with the use of skilled teamworking and self-managing environments, leading to greater innovation and product breakthroughs. However, such organizations can become very concerned with capturing and institutionalizing processes in such a way as to limit the real opportunities for experimentation. In fast-moving environments with highly complex products, the rapidity of change may mean that little gets standardized, that learning is not shared and that little gets achieved, except with heroic effort. This is the classic 'chaos' state which few organizations survive for long, yet which often becomes the stuff of corporate folklore if a turnaround is achieved. Such a state can also be a powerful galvanizer towards a new culture more conducive to effective production.

While contingency theory suggests 'fit' as the key criterion, complexity theory suggests that the state which borders chaos, 'bounded instability', may be a desirable condition for organizations which aim to survive and thrive over time. This 'edge of chaos', also known as the 'learning organization', is considered conducive to creative tension, in which people have to collaborate to make things happen and where learning is shared and co-created. However, since human organizations are characterized by anxiety and power, which can cause organizations and individuals to turn inwards and take their eye off the marketplace, such a state is unlikely to last for long without deliberate interventions.

Success criteria for organization design

Organization designs both institutionalize and enable positive aspects of culture and frustrate other aspects of culture. If the underlying culture is at odds with a new design, it is likely that the culture will win out, with new practices sabotaged before they become fully embedded. The challenge is to identify broad criteria for redesign efforts which appear conducive to creating contexts where high performance is more likely to occur. For example, drawing some organizational design criteria from complexity theory, it would seem that an organization's ability to remain at the 'edge of chaos,' characterized by enough standard procedures and systems that people know what is meant to happen but also enough flexibility and space for people to operate autonomously so empowerment can result, depends on having an appropriate balance of the following:

- Information flow – there should be enough information, of the right quality and timeliness, to ensure that people know what is happening, but not so much that people feel bombarded and stop paying attention to messages
- Diversity – there should be enough difference in ideas, approaches and people that fresh perspectives can be incorporated, but not so little coherence that fragmentation results due to lack of common purpose
- Power – there should be enough freedom from direct control that people can use their initiative, but not so much freedom that chaos ensues.

Design success criteria are changing. According to Ashkenas *et al.* (1998), for much of the twentieth century four critical factors influenced organizational success:

1. *Size*. The larger a company became, the more it was able to attain production or service efficiencies, leverage its capital and put pressure on customers and suppliers.
2. *Role clarity*. In a larger organization tasks were divided, clear distinctions made between manager and worker, and levels of authority clearly spelt out. This had the advantage that everyone knew his or her place and performed to specification.
3. *Specialization*. As tasks were subdivided, specialisms were created and expertise developed. Disciplines such as human resources, finance, information technology etc. came into being.
4. *Control*. Large organizations created controls to ensure that all parts of the organization performed as needed to produce the products or services. The manager's role was to ensure that others were doing the right things at the right time.

Organizational structure was seen as the primary vehicle for achieving effectiveness. Typical questions relating to structures included:

- How many layers of management do we need?
- What signing authority will different levels have?
- What is the proper span of control?
- What is the best balance between centralization and decentralization?
- How do we describe and classify each job and set pay levels?
- How do we organize field locations and international operations?

The aim was to create a structure which came as close as possible to meeting the four success factors.

The rapid pace of change due to technology and the arrival of the global economy have caused a radical shift in the basis of competitive success. To a large extent, the old success factors have become liabilities. Sustainable success in the medium to longer term comes from an organization's ability to leverage its resources in a changing economic context. In *The Boundaryless Organization*

(Ashkenas *et al.*, 1998), the authors suggest that there are four key themes that are critical to such leverage. These are:

1. *Speed* (not size). This is the ability to reduce bureaucracy, speed up cycle times and create increased capabilities for change. It is the ability to bring new products to market faster, and change strategies more rapidly than ever before. Speed implies that there is enough pace that people are stimulated to respond and increase their output year-on-year, but not so much unremitting pace that people become 'burned out'. Smaller firms tend to have advantages over larger firms in the time they take to change direction because there are fewer people to mobilize towards change. Large companies need to act like small companies, while retaining access to the large company's resources. The US company Gore, manufacturers of Goretex, restricts the size of any business unit to a maximum of 150 employees. As units grow larger, they are subdivided into other units. Gore recognizes that size can inhibit speed, ownership and innovation.

2. *Flexibility* (not rigidity). Role clarity constrains flexibility. People in flexible organizations do multiple jobs, and constantly learn new skills while the organization pursues multiple paths, experiments and makes shifts. Flexible organizations thrive on ambiguity, throw out job descriptions, and encourage *ad hoc* teams which form and reform as tasks shift.

3. *Integration* (not specialization). Integrated organizations create mechanisms to pull task activities together as they are needed rather than assigning specialists to tasks. Specialists are still needed, but it is often the ability of specialists to collaborate with others to create an integrated whole that is more valuable than having management pull tasks together. Concepts of change are built into processes, enabling the rapid dissemination of new initiatives and mobilizing the right resources to make things happen.

4. *Innovation* (not control). Boundaryless organizations create innovative processes and environments that encourage and reward creativity, rather than allowing a focus on control to stifle innovation. Innovative organizations are more likely to take one of the new organizational forms, such as a network organization. Internal and external networks enrich the knowledge flow. Human resource management is sophisticated, and team processes are integrated into the business process.

The 'fashion element' in organization design

While organizations may need to adjust their structures to suit changing requirements, some organization designs may have been introduced because they have been popular, rather than appropriate in every case, as the following quotation suggests:

> *If nothing else, believing that flattened organizations are the answer to survival is a cultural trap. Americans are creating flattened organizations which meet their unspoken cultural assumptions about relationships, authority and creativity. Flattened organizations resemble the American*

> *cultural dream of equality and fairness, creating a society in which anyone, regardless of background, can succeed and find happiness. Many other cultures, however, do not share these values and find flattened organizations a chaotic, non-productive way to work.*
>
> *(Carroll* et al., *1990)*

Nevertheless, some of the commonest forms of structure change do tend to flow from the theory in vogue at the corporate centre, as much as from business and cultural considerations. Yet because an idea is popular, this does not make it inappropriate. It might, however, need adapting to the particular circumstances. There is also the danger that when an idea falls out of fashion, what was useful about it also gets jettisoned. For instance, a key concept behind *Thriving on Chaos* was the need to move from a hierarchical management pyramid to a horizontal, fast, cross-functional, cooperative one. Tom Peters elaborated 45 precepts for managers, which included:

- Over-invest in people, front-line sales, service, distribution
- Use multifunction teams for all development activities
- Achieve total customer responsiveness
- Measure innovation
- Organize as much as possible around teams
- Radically reduce layers of management
- Reconceive middle managers as facilitators instead of guardians
- Develop simple systems to encourage participation and understanding
- Share information with everyone.

These principles would appear to be as relevant now as when they were first identified in the 1980s. They are echoed in the studies carried out into what creates sustained success over time, and featured in works such as *Built to Last* by Collins and Porras (1994) and *The Living Company* by Arie de Geus (1997).

High performance structures

Structural redesign is the commonest form of organizational change. The organization structure consists of interdependent systems, each of which has informal and formal elements. Structures are at the heart of organizational change, since they are at the operating core of any business. A major structural change is defined as any move away from one of the primary forms – centralized, decentralized and hybrid.

Structural change usually occurs to address problems within existing structures. In conventional hierarchies, vertical inter-group problems (e.g. top versus middle management) often result from unclear reporting lines, actual authority levels and communication difficulties. Horizontal inter-group conflict (e.g. operations versus sales) can occur when there are ineffective accountability and reward systems. Decision-making procedures which are biased in favour of particular groups can often strain diagonal group relations, such as male/female.

As in many aspects of change, paradox is a feature of organizational design. This is often evident in internal structures. A business organizes to have internal support for coping with current market conditions, yet it also has to attempt to change outside conditions for its own competitive advantage. Resilient organizations aim to build unity from diversity. They have stabilizing mechanisms that hold everything together, and at the same time contain destabilizing activities that encourage change.

Strategizing organization design

When redesigning an organization's structures, it is important to translate the organization's medium-term strategic aims into structure plans and test to see how aligned they are. One test of alignment between strategy and vertical structure is to read the organization's mission statement and ask: Does it mention how the organization must act/behave in order to meet business objectives?

The following questions will reveal the logic of alignment in your organization:

- What are the future goals of our business over the next two years and onwards? (Include markets served, financial objectives, products delivered and technology required as well as the unique competitive advantages you wish to exploit.)
- What capabilities will be required to meet the organization's goals? (Include both the processes – such as monitoring and controlling costs – and the people skills – such as functional/technical skills and general capabilities such as dependability, predictability, speed, responsiveness, and ability to learn.)
- What organizational initiatives will ensure that the capabilities are in place?

The answers to these questions should help managers to determine and select the organization design that best matches the corporate strategy, taking into account the company's market needs, host country's culture, competitors, nature of the industry and core competencies. The next phases are:

- Assess whether the organization's employees can work well in the preferred design
- Develop an action plan on how to rebalance (creating a new congruence) the organization from the current configuration to the new.

Organization design methodology

There are few systematic organization design methodologies openly available. However, Naomi Stanford gives an overview of one such methodology, which has been used in British Airways since 1998. Known as OD Lite, the methodology and its application are explored in her book, *Organization Design* (2004). The start-to-end process aims to take twelve weeks, with formal review points four weeks subsequent to launch and again six months later. It consists of five phases:

1. *Preparing for change* – this involves making the decision on whether an organization redesign is the right way to proceed; doing diagnostic exercises; ascertaining what is working well currently and where things could be improved; and assessing whether the manager has the skills, resources and staying power to opt for a redesign and keep his or her operation running
2. *Choosing to redesign* – involvement and collaboration with the people who do the work is central to design/redesign. Therefore a series of workshops takes place, the outputs of which are the high-level 'frame' which creates the context, meaning and direction for the redesign, including its purpose and objectives, boundaries, principles for redesigning (e.g. no job losses), a stakeholder analysis and a risk analysis, and appointment of project manager to work on the key elements of a project plan
3. *Creating the high-level and detailed design* – the local management team decides the overall structure and appoints small design teams, comprising a diagonal slice of the organization, to do detailed work on a specific aspect of design (e.g. ways of working, the marketing proposition or risk factors); detailed elements are coordinated by the project manager and consultant
4. *Handling the transition* – sometimes called the implementation phase, this includes role-modelling the desired behaviours and changes in performance; managing resistance to changes; providing the means to move from current systems and processes to newly designed ones; tracking and recording changes as they happen to ensure planned milestones are achieved
5. *Review phase* – within four weeks after going live there is a review and evaluation of the project to identify the progress of the design in terms of its success measures (e.g. employee satisfaction, customer satisfaction, operational effectiveness and innovation/learning), and also to capture and consolidate project teams' learning to make it available for future work.

Selecting a structure

Complex organizations must frequently redesign operating or support units to realign them in the event of acquisitions, for example. In redesigning structures, it is important to take stock of the structural changes that have taken place over the last several years. How have the structural changes affected managers' spans of control? Is this effect similar across the hierarchical levels? Have these changes resulted in a more horizontal or vertical organization chart? Are these structural changes a transition to a new organizational structure, or a modification of the existing structure? How has the degree to which jobs are standardized changed? To what extent have these changes in job standardization and decision-making flexibility led to changes in job descriptions? If so, what is the nature of these changes?

Selecting a structure should be based on the requirements of the business. Centralization, for instance, means that labour can be specialized, that greater efficiency exists in policy-making, and that better control and evaluation systems should be possible. However, centralization can stifle innovation, distance the organization from its customers and lead to over-standardization. Decentralization allows for greater autonomy and accountability, but can lead to duplication and failure to maximize synergies. In practice, many firms find that environmental trends, such as competitive pressures, global influences and technology and the requirement for continuous improvement, make the primary forms of structure – centralized, decentralized and hybrid – seem inadequate to cope with the external forces to reduce costs.

Structural variables

Key structural variables are organizational size, technology, or environmental complexity, and the degree of organizational formalization. Factors such as task specialization, spans of control, size and responsibility of the administrative function, levels of hierarchy and integration must be balanced against each other. Each of these aspects of structure begins as a formal system, but its operation almost invariably generates a parallel informal system. Often these informal systems become more powerful in shaping behaviour than the formal systems. Reporting relationships comprise a formal system of status and authority, though there is often a major discrepancy in reality between what the organization chart implies and the actual distribution of power.

Decision-making procedures

These are the way problems are solved within the system. Practices reflect time-honoured or approved methods of resolving problems, and suggest how a problem is supposed to be solved. Organizational policies must reflect external requirements, such as health and safety legislation, which organizations must comply with. However, where non-compliance does not carry heavy penalties, many organizations ignore in practice legislation that is perceived to have negative financial implications for them, such as the Working Time Directive.

Similarly, since these formal systems are often frustrating to individuals, they are often subverted or ignored. People revert to political behaviour in order to influence decisions that are satisfactory to them, and tensions can arise between the formal and informal systems.

Norms and accountabilities

These are the behaviours expected of people working in the system. The formal norms include explicit codes of conduct, such as whether employees are allowed to smoke at their desks, dress code etc., and informal norms include unwritten codes, such as the number of hours employees are really expected to work, despite any work–life balance policies. The formal accountability system includes elements such as the annual performance review, measures and a financial reporting model. Formal methods of accountability are often undercut in practice by inadequate confrontation, such as when a poor performer is simply passed from department to department without managers honestly appraising his or her performance. In some cases, at senior levels, poor performance is actually rewarded by promotion!

Functions

The goal of redesign efforts should be to increase flexibility and improve responsiveness, while functional change focuses on the greater utilization of individual skills and ability. By expanding the ways in which individuals can apply their skills, organizations can increase their ability to improvise. Improvisation allows individuals to interact freely, develop relationships and use their initiative to meet organizational needs. Formal structures, such as cross-functional teams and self-managing groups, are enablers of unstructured interaction and improvisation. They are also likely to increase individual job satisfaction of employees.

Spans of control

Spans of control should reflect the nature of the work to be done. In the past, received wisdom suggested that managers should manage no more than six people in a work group. In a conventional hierarchy, managers were often seen primarily as 'the best of the rest' or the lead technician. Responsibilities for people were largely seen to be about achieving the right level of output in a timely way. Relationships, though important, were not seen as key to employee commitment, since labour turnover in many organizations was low.

During the 1990s, the organizational paradigm shifted dramatically as organizations restructured, downsized and became 'lean and mean'. Flatter structures became relatively widespread, and spans of control increased dramatically. At the same time, the idea that the newly empowered workforce would need training to carry out the responsibilities that had previously been carried out by the manager took hold. Managers now were expected to manage their team's development as well as performance. They were required to be the 'glue' that binds employees to the company, and contact with the manager was considered important. This also meant that appraisals had to become more meaningful and support employees in taking responsibility for their own career development. Having large spans of control (up to 30 in some cases) made life impossible for many managers, who were being encouraged to become coaches and enablers of others while at the same time getting the 'day job' done.

The current trend is to revert once more to spans of six to eight, and the manager's role becomes more that of coach and peer expert. Appraisals, staff development and corporate teamworking become more obvious elements of the manager's role. At the same time, many managers are clearly unhappy with the people aspects of their role, or feel ill-equipped for them. Roffey Park's annual survey suggests that while employees may have adjusted to greater degrees of empowerment many managers have not, and have a tendency to 'micro-manage' – which is seen as interference.

In establishing appropriate spans of control, those responsible for the organization design need to consider carefully the range of requirements of the respective roles of managers and employees. Consultation is critical to ensure that appropriate spans of control are established which meet the design criteria yet allow for some 'stretch'.

Reward system

This is the most powerful means of shaping people's behaviour. Formal rewards include salary, benefits and recognition programmes. Informal rewards can include opportunities for greater access to power, interesting projects, a pleasant office – or any office. Expectancy theory (Nadler *et al.*, 1979) states that people will behave in ways which help them achieve outcomes which they value. In many cases, pay is the least motivating part of the reward system. An individual may be much more motivated by recognition of a job well done than by a small bonus awarded through a complex performance-related scheme.

Common structural forms

In Roffey Park surveys, examples of common forms of structure change include the following.

Flatter structures

The move towards flatter structures has been a consistently strong trend since 1998, when the first Roffey Park *Management Agenda* research was published. In the 2002–2004 surveys this trend was maintained, since a massive 83 per cent of respondents reported experiencing structural change, with 38 per cent of respondents reporting that their organization had cut out management layers in the previous year in an attempt to attain ever-flatter structures. Benefits of a newly flattened structure included the facilitation of more open thinking, clear accountability, clear goals, and clarity of roles and functions. Disadvantages of the new system were reported as a lack of leadership, increased workloads, significant amounts of fear and suspicion, and disjointed management.

Relayering

In addition, this research includes a higher percentage of respondents reporting that their organizations are reintroducing layers of management – up to 29 per cent from 19 per cent the previous year. Benefits reported by respondents working within a structure that had begun to reintroduce layers of management included the increase of effective performance, the greater use of initiative and clarity on accountabilities, better communication, less status orientation, and increased development opportunities and job satisfaction. The main drawbacks appear to be that unnecessary layering restricts decision-making, and that the people being promoted appear to be those who excel at organizational politics.

Matrix structures

The years 2002–2004 also saw a significant rise in organizations introducing a matrix structure, up from 22 per cent to 28 per cent. Respondents were asked what they felt the benefits of the new structure were (if they had responded that the structure was working effectively) and what the problems were (if it was not perceived to be effective). Benefits reported by respondents working within a new matrix structure included better qualified people being recruited, improved accountability, cost savings, and more strategic direction. Disadvantages of the new system were reported as additional bureaucracy, and duplication of management.

All of these structure changes have taken place within the context of conventional hierarchies. They are different attempts to overcome some of the limitations of traditional organizations. However, Klein suggests that conventional organizations are designed to fail. He states that the motivation of organizational members is to follow their own self-interest rather than the good of the organization. Klein feels that the corporate model requires too much specialization, which dwarfs decision-makers' capabilities. This specialization and limited knowledge and information of the whole can lead to problems for the total organization.

Teamworking cultures

'Team working is an organizational intervention around which companies can re-engineer for competitive advantage' (Parry et al., 1998). Teamworking can sustain functional innovation, while facilitating the business. Good process discipline and control needs to be combined with a redesigned social system. Teamworking becomes the key organizational unit on which to base such a redesign, offering the benefits of flexibility and responsiveness. Involvement and commitment from senior managers is essential, since teamworking will lead to different methods of coordinating work through new organizational routines. More recent interest in team working cultures focuses on improved task processes. Teams develop their own values, norms and rules, and can become a more powerful source of control than managerial/bureaucratic conventions.

Parry et al. (1998) suggest that teamworking is best understood in terms of overall organizational patterns rather than through sets of team properties. They have identified key dimensions of organization design with regard to teamworking. First is the 'prescribed framework' in which are found the formal attributes of the organization structure; then they describe teams as mini-organizations in themselves, each with purpose, levels of autonomy, operating procedures, decision-making and task design. They distinguish the 'self directed team', whose purpose is to create greater flexibility and innovation in permanent work groups. Empowerment is generally used as a means to improve levels of local commitment and accountability.

The 'lean team' is found in organizations operating a lean production system, with total emphasis on quality, continuous improvement and productivity. A tightly coupled production system demands teamworking to ensure maximum waste reduction. The purpose of the 'project team' is to sustain cross-functional teamworking across internal organizational boundaries with the objective of integrating and compressing development timescales.

Where are structures going?

Hierarchy is still the dominant form of organization. Hierarchies in themselves are not inappropriate, according to Ashkenas *et al.* (1998), but they needed to be checked for 'health.' Warning signs of an unhealthy hierarchy are:

- A slow response time
- Rigidity towards change
- Underground activity
- Internal frustration
- Customer alienation.

A healthy hierarchy has an appropriate two-way flow of information, widely distributed competencies, authority to act settled close to where decisions need to be made, and rewards that reinforce performance. When these conditions are met, to the appropriate degrees, organizations can achieve significant gains in speed, flexibility, integration and innovation.

Flexible organizations versus traditional organizations

The concept of flexible organization avoids the current bias that one organization design is better than another. It uses bottom-line measures such as market share, profitability, key operating ratios and customer satisfaction measures to decide which design works better, making performance the key issue for the organization. The question is: which organization design works better in a particular market and location, and which design best enhances the company's core competencies – the employees' intellectual and physical capabilities that the company uses for competitive advantage?

The key focus should be on congruence – the fit between all the organization's components consistent to the chosen organization design so that the organization is the most efficient. In a traditional organization, executives associate organization design with management style. Organizations tend to be viewed mechanistically, focusing on pieces rather than the whole. In a flexible organization, design is an internal business strategy issue, equally important to developing the corporate strategy. The question to be answered is 'what is the best organization design to align the workforce with the corporate strategy?' Organization design is a strategic initiative that must be revisited regularly to ensure that it is contributing maximum value to the corporation's performance.

New organizational configurations

These reflect the shift away from more traditional bureaucratic organizations. The impetus now is towards 'flexible and agile organizational forms' (Bahrami, 1992) in which boundaries are 'fluid and permeable' (Kanter *et al.*, 1992). The Roffey Park *Management Agenda* findings reflect this. Examples of some of the emerging forms are described below.

Cluster organizations

Robert Waterman (1993), in his book *Adhocracy: The Power to Change*, advocates a concept pioneered by Drucker and Mintzberg to have innovative project teams operating across a company's departmental boundaries. A radical structure example is the 'cluster' organization advocated by Quinn–Mills. This is a group of people drawn from different disciplines and undifferentiated by job title who work together on a semi-permanent basis. A cluster develops its own expertise, and demonstrates a strong customer orientation. Pure cluster organizations have:

- Groups undifferentiated by job title, working together on a semi-permanent basis
- A group size of 30–50, or subclusters of 5 or 7
- Residual or no hierarchy
- No direct reporting relationships
- Decision-making delegated to the lowest level possible (i.e. to those who do the work)
- Leadership that rotates to task competence
- Members of the group who are responsible to the group for performance and quality and are therefore accountable
- Groups linked by contacts among members, and interface with the company through residual hierarchy.

Benefits of cluster organizations are said to be:

- Lower administrative overheads
- More entrepreneurial behaviour
- Greater flexibility
- More openness to technology
- Better retention of employees
- Fewer risks of promoting people into roles for which they are unsuited.

Such organizational forms, while offering these many benefits, are relatively rare outside consultancies.

Less radical structures include the 'integrative cluster structure', a hybrid form that builds on the most important elements of the pure cluster form, but where reporting relationships remain in place and the hierarchy is slimmed down rather than replaced. Layers of middle management are eliminated, and team-based work introduced. Teams are overlaid on the downsized hierarchy. Consequently, it represents a more gradual approach to restructuring.

High performance work design and practice

For a competitive strategy to be successful, speed, innovation, quality and flexibility are essential organizational characteristics. Underpinning these practices is a continuous improvement approach, ensuring that ways of working, products and services are revitalized and produced more effectively. Consolidating such approaches requires a total quality management (TQM) environment and high performance work structuring. While TQM did not catch on in the UK to the same extent as elsewhere, its underlying philosophy and many of its practices are highly relevant to the creation of an adaptable, high performing organization.

High performance work structuring

The structuring of work can focus on an individualistic approach, making individual jobs more motivating, and a group approach. From a high performance perspective, the basic unit is the work group. There is a shift from emphasis on 'vertical tasks' within functional units to emphasis on 'horizontal tasks', hand-offs and collaboration across units. The theory behind high performance work structuring is that in order to achieve higher commitment from employees, there should be system and value changes resulting in a complete value shift, along with job content and actual system changes.

Work is organized around the basic transformations in the process to form complete tasks. Each work group is capable of evaluating its performance against standards. Work therefore moves from 'content'-specific tools and techniques to 'process', using a holistic synthesis of techniques. Jobs are structured so that work group members can individually control at least one transformation. The role of the supervisor or facilitator is to plan and organize the work with the team.

Lean production techniques

Lean production was developed in Japan in the 1950s, and was extensively practised initially by the Toyota Motor Co. Lean production is a disciplined process-focused production system, the objective of which is to minimize the consumption of resources that add no value to a product. The originators, Eiji Toyoda and Taiichi Ohno, determined that there are seven major wastes in production: defects, transportation, overproduction, waiting, processing, movement and inventory. Lean production uses the process of continuous improvement applied to products, processes and services with the goal of improving performance and reducing waste over time. The fundamental tool is *Kaizen*, in which cross-functional teams systematically analyse processes to eliminate waste and achieve improvement.

A key concept in lean production is to understand value from the customer's point of view. The five fundamental concepts to achieve this are as follows (Womack *et al.*, 1991).

1. Specify value – see the value as defined by the end-user
2. Identify the value stream – understand all the activities required to produce a product, then optimize the whole process from the view of the end-user
3. Flow – get the activities that add value to flow without interruption
4. Pull – respond to the demand of the customer
5. Perfection – systematically identify and eliminate waste in production.

Lean production cannot succeed without the disciplined use of effective tools to identify the root cause of variations/problems. Support tools for this approach include the 5Ss (sort, straighten, shine, standardize and sustain – in other words, a clean and well-organized workplace is conducive to being able to find things when you need them). Extensive use is made of Pareto charts, scatter diagrams, fishbone diagrams and similar tools to determine the root cause of variation and identify corrective action. Another tool, the '5 Whys', involves asking 'why?' five or more times until the root cause has been found.

At its most effective, lean production is accompanied by 'lean behaviour'. This is 'the application of lean production techniques to the management of personal and organizational behaviours with the goal of eliminating behavioural waste' (Owen, 2000) – in other words, a means of improving 'soft' skills using the 'hard' skills practised in production processes. As in lean production, a key element of lean behaviours is to understand value as seen from the end-user's point of view. According to Owen (2000), the five fundamental concepts become:

1. Specify value – understand the wants and expectations of the people we interact with
2. Identify the value stream – understand what people do and why they do it
3. Flow – behave in a manner that minimizes or eliminates delays or stoppages in the work performed by others
4. Pull – recognize that people operate under many different mental models which require us to adjust our styles or approach often
5. Perfection – systematically identify and eliminate behavioural waste.

Lean behaviours apply the process of continuous improvement to an individual or an organization with the aim of improving performance over time. This approach rigorously aligns the production work carried out in lean factories with the development of leadership and management skills.

Companies operating such approaches include Levi-Strauss, Motorola and Honeywell. What is common about so-called 'high performing' companies is their agenda to create relationships with employees which support their business objectives. Employee relations are therefore a priority, to be clear about the kind of relationship the business strategy requires, and 'to push the execution of employee relations policies down to the lowest level possible, compatible with the corporation's overall values' (Tyson, 1995). Corporate values are most clearly visible in reward policies, which are sometimes used to instil specific values. Profit-related pay and share ownership are obvious manifestations of value statements about the worth of people to an organization. Similarly, communications transmit values, although usually more is understood by the behaviour of the people conveying the message than by the words used.

Continuous improvement

Continuous improvement (CI) is an essential part of TQM, and it derives from classical management theory, such as the learning curve and product differentiation. CI is defined as 'a purposeful and explicit set of principles, mechanisms and activities within an organization adopted to generate ongoing, systematic and cumulative improvement in deliverables, operating procedures and systems' (Lillrank, 1995). Saab, for example, introduced lean production-type manufacturing principles, including just-in-time (JIT) logistics, standardization, elimination of waste, team-based structures and CI in the late 1980s as part of its business turnaround.

Quality Control Circles (QCC) were the original Japanese vehicles for promoting CI. The QCC is a group of employees from the same work unit who gather regularly to study, discuss and solve work-related problems using a set of statistical tools (the Seven Tools) and following a problem-solving format (the QC story). QCCs should be self-governing, and activity should be voluntary but simultaneously work towards goals set by management. They are neither part of the formal command and control structure nor of the informal organization, but represent a hybrid form of organization that incorporates elements from both.

CI is seen as an environmental response to conditions that call for organizations to develop methods for adaptation. It offers the possibility of flexible adaptation to changing requirements and a vehicle for employee participation.

Basic design requirements for continuous improvement

Literature suggests that a specific CI organization is not necessary for success, providing that the corporate culture is generally supportive of self-development. Training, continuous education and discussion forums are sufficient as supporting arrangements.

However, if continuous improvement is to become an embedded part of an organization's philosophy and practice, certain general design requirements must be met. These address the motivation ('want to do'), skill development ('can do') and understanding ('know what to do') needs of employees. The 'want to do' factors include compensation for time and effort, rewards for suggestions, and motivational messages. The 'can do' factors include time and facilities, skills, and tools and techniques. The 'know what to do' factors include the setting of direction and goals, setting of the organizational arena, implementation, information and knowledge.

Design requirements are as follows:

1. *Pressure for improvement.* There must be competitive pressure that requires operational efficiency, such as improved quality, reduced error costs and more precise deliveries.
2. *Some fundamental conditions must be met.* The organization must have a basic ability to 'unfreeze' (Lewin, 1952) its existing principles and practices and envision better ways. Adequate resources must be invested in CI.
3. *Some basic design requirements must be met by the organization.* These include a minimum set of individual, group and organizational level conditions that any manager aiming at CI would have to achieve, such as the conditions necessary for an organization to move from a traditional hierarchical organization to a more participative one. Dobbs suggests the following are required to encourage empowerment: participation, innovation, access to information, and accountability.
4. *Design dimensions define the basic set of alternative solutions a manager can choose from.* Generic design requirements flow from the general task design criteria (Hackman and Oldham, 1980).

- Work structuring is designed to include the whole task, which produces greater flexibility and wider career paths, resulting in broader experience
- Reductions in the administrative hierarchy and less hierarchical control of power will be evident, with decisions being pushed further down the organization, which enhances autonomy and responsibility
- Teams will increasingly be cross-functional, cross-hierarchical and multi-disciplinary, giving rise to greater interaction, communication and information flows
- Individuals and teams must be motivated to invest time and energy in improvement activities
- Incentive systems designed round compensation for extra time and effort, and rewards for valuable suggestions, are required
- Individuals and groups must be equipped with relevant facilities, skills and equipment
- People must know what they are expected to do – the organizational area of activity must be defined, the intended direction communicated, and priorities and goals established
- Jobs that require flexible and innovative behaviour must be ingrained with a degree of constant change, which may provide some degree of job satisfaction.

Role of information systems

As early as 1960, Simon suggested that organizations need to resemble information-processing and decision-making systems rather than production systems. In today's complex environment, organizations must make timely, informed decisions, and the ability to process large amounts of information is essential. Organizational redesign efforts should emphasize improving the information flow, which will improve organizational responsiveness. The following questions are important to bear in mind when redesigning information flow:

- Has the changing information environment (internal and external usage and technology) had an impact on structural changes at this organization, or have the structural changes of the organization been the driver for changes in the use of information systems?
- What role has the information system played in simplifying organizational changes?
- Have information systems changed over the last one to three years to meet changing information requirements? If so, how?
- Are the current information systems installed at this organization adequate to our needs?
- What specific information subsystems do we use (i.e. decision support systems), and what jobs that previously were performed manually are now done by computer?

When information systems are used to share information widely and openly throughout the organization, decision-making can take place at lower levels than would be the case in conventional hierarchies, without a reduction in quality or an increase in risk, providing certain elements are in place. One of these elements is that all employees understand the nature of the organization they are in and what the organization's goals are. Another is that truly confidential information remains confidential, such as when preparations are under way for an acquisition. Guzzo and Klein (1991) suggest that information systems, by their presence or absence, affect organizational roles, interaction or communication patterns, skill requirements, career paths, strategy and culture.

One of the key issues appears to be not so much access to the hardware but more the increasing numbers of employees who are becoming an IT underclass as their skills have not kept pace with technological development. In some organizations the 'worst of both worlds' exists, where paper-based information, voice-mails and e-mails vie for attention, in some cases duplicating messages and in others being limited to only one medium. For people who prefer one medium over others, this can be a risk factor. Another challenging scenario is when only one medium is used, such as e-mail. This can disadvantage employees who prefer to communicate face to face. Any communication strategy has to take different preferences into account. The day-to-day management of information flows is usually left to the individual, although increasingly companies are adopting e-mail and voice-mail protocols which are usually intended to help employees – such as banning their use on a particular day of the week, or limiting the range of issues which can be communicated via these media.

The growth of employee monitoring via technology is becoming subject to increasing challenge in some organizations. While the use of monitoring of telephone calls in call-centre environments is seen as quality control, increasingly it is seen to be a means of increasing the pressure on employees to respond ever more quickly to customer enquiries. Interestingly, the backlash appears to be coming less from employees than from disgruntled customers, who resent the long call queues, the standard responses when they finally get through, and the difficulties of reaching a real solution to their problem. Some companies, such as BUPA, have managed to develop a more personalized form of call-centre service that reflects the need for tailoring responses to individual clients even while using standard procedures.

A more delicate area for monitoring is employee use of e-mails and the Internet to ensure that employees are complying with company procedures. If this is carried out in a heavy-handed way it can send the message that no employee is to be trusted, yet if it is not carried out at all the organization is perhaps neglecting its ethical responsibilities to the wider community.

Use of space

There is increasing awareness of the importance of configuring workspace to achieve maximum ergonomic benefit. Factors that are typically considered include comfort, and health and safety – do the workspace and furniture provide appropriate levels of lighting, PC screen size, back support etc.? Noise levels are also considered. Does an open plan or other configuration allow for the types of concentration required for particular types of activity? Companies such as Standard Life draw on the skills of experts in ergonomics to ensure that space is designed appropriately to the needs of the task and the employee.

The physical workplace is also subject to scrutiny for other reasons, most notably the capability of technology to enable work to be done away from the workplace. The growth of remote working is accelerating, enabling companies to close down and sell off offices and realize the asset. When employees work from home, the company does not in theory lose responsibility for their health and safety. In practice, company approaches vary tremendously, with some companies requiring their employees to make their home-working space open to inspection before they are allowed to base themselves at home. Companies also vary in how much they are willing to subsidize employees in furnishing their workspace appropriately, though usually the company provides computing equipment and relevant ISDN or other links. Companies such as BT Retail pride themselves on having a home-based staff, including the Managing Director.

Another key aspect of facilities is their ability to act as a powerful statement for the company. Headquarters buildings in particular send strong symbolic messages about what a company values and how it wishes to be perceived. While many such buildings convey the impression of power and status, some have been designed to facilitate knowledge-sharing and teamworking. Cafés and open meeting spaces are used to good effect to break down hierarchical and other barriers. Other companies whose business is all about creativity would of course be expected to model the way. One communications agency has designed its offices as a series of different spaces where use of colour and the style of furniture lends itself to different purposes – so there are quiet, comfortable spaces for reflection, stand-up meeting spaces, 'concentrate at desk' spaces, bean-bag creativity spaces etc.

Other companies have adopted similar approaches. The property consultancy Jones Lang LaSalle has devoted space in its main offices to particular kinds of activity. Colour is a key component of design here, with certain hues lending themselves to different kinds of mental activity. Since the refurbishment, employees have remarked on how differently they are able to achieve certain kinds of task, and managers have been pleased with the positive effect on performance of complex tasks.

Conclusion

Any organization design that aims to support sustainable high performance must have flexibility built into it. Flexibility will depend on the organization's ability to process information and make decisions quickly and well. Information technology systems are therefore an essential element of organizational redesign. Unless people are willing and able to share information and resources, the organization may lack the speed, responsiveness and flexibility required in today's markets. Designs therefore need to enable the maximum possibility for teamworking and cross-fertilization of ideas. New working practices need to be supported by appropriate training and other resources.

Next, organizational culture can help or hinder what the organization is aiming to achieve. Management behaviours in particular need to be in line with what the organization is trying to achieve and the values it espouses. Every aspect of organization design should reinforce what the organization believes is right. If an organization believes in putting the customer at the heart of its operations, work processes, communication strategies, leadership behaviours, rewards, management styles, training and development, and human resource planning will be in line with this objective and are as much part of organization design as structures and systems.

Fundamentally, organizational flexibility depends on people being willing to change. Therefore, an organizational redesign should attempt to balance the organization's requirements with employees' needs. Structural changes need to be designed and monitored with an eye to levels of job satisfaction or employee motivation. These include flexible working, work–life balance, and structures and processes that support career development and improve people's opportunities for job satisfaction. Redesigning organizations provides a real opportunity to take a fresh look at how business effectiveness can be improved and provide meaningful opportunities for learning and growth for employees, which should lead to greater engagement. When highly skilled, high performing and flexible employees are committed to their organization, great business results usually follow.

Checklist: Organizational redesign

Success factors and measures:

- What have we got to be good at to compete?
- What level of performance do we need to achieve?
- What key assumptions are we making now and for the future?
- What are the core competencies?
- What are we aiming to improve?
- Should we focus more on creativity management than on continuous improvement?
- What values and behaviours need to be operating to be successful?

Organizational outcomes:

- Speed
- Flexibility
- Level of service
- Unit cost improvement
- Engaged staff
- Innovation
- Continuous improvement.

Culture:

- What is the desired culture to support the business?
- What is the current culture?
- What is reinforcing it?
- How effectively do we implement and monitor equal opportunities/ diversity policy and practice?
- How do we reinforce effective performance, such as focusing on the customer and innovation?
- To what extent do we want employee involvement?
- What is the type and level of participation currently?
- How formal and effective are our collective relations?
- What systems do we have in place to maintain a focus on employee well-being?
- How and where will power be distributed?

Structure and role design:

- What structures would suit the business?
- Should the organizational configuration be parallel or integrated?
- How well do our governance structures work?

- What are the decision-making processes and where is the authority to make decisions?
- How effective are the decision-making processes?
- What are the barriers?
- What job, families and bargaining units exist?
- What knowledge and skills are required?
- How will the knowledge and skills be combined?
- How will tasks be organized?
- How can jobs be designed to maximize variety, skill, autonomy, identity, feedback?
- How much is competence specialized and focused vs widespread?
- How standardized is the work to be done? How much standardization is necessary?

Process:

- Is the customer at the beginning and end of every task?
- What are the main steps in achieving the task?
- What are the inputs and outputs?
- What are the workflows and information points?
- What are the decision points?
- How much control is required over the process?
- How can the process be improved?

Quality strategy:

- What continuous improvement mechanisms are in place?

Technology and systems:

- Do they support a flexible structure?
- Are they developed/written to enable future modifications?
- Are our operating systems project-based or production-based?
- How well do our communication processes work, and how do they need to be strengthened?

People, resourcing and skills:

- What does our future capability need to be?
- What are our long-term requirements?
- What contracts will be determined?
- How can resources best be matched to requirements?
- What do individuals want?
- What does the market demand?
- Do we need to transform or shed staff?
- How effective are our selection methods?
- How flexible are the skills in the organization?

- How will training and development needs be determined?
- What training and development will be required to build capabilities?
- How much do our arrangements enhance people's skills?
- How will people move through our organization – what are the career paths, and what are individuals' aspirations?

Performance management:

- How can we achieve effective performance management processes?
- What criteria will be used to manage performance?
- How effective is the current process?
- What would make it really effective?
- Should goal-setting and implementation be centralized or decentralized?

Rewards and recognition:

- How are people recognized and rewarded currently?
- Do our reward and recognition systems reinforce required behaviour?
- Is change needed?
- What reward processes are appropriate?
- What are the risks in changing?
- What are the benefits?
- What do we want to reward?

Leadership and management style:

- What should leaders and managers spend more/less time doing?
- Do managers display the behaviours required for effective leadership?
- How can consistency be achieved?

Succession planning:

- What type of talent do we need to bring in?
- What are the sources of candidates with the right capabilities?
- Where are we most at risk?

Overall design – check for alignment and coordination:

- How much does our organization design reinforce the *status quo*, and how much does it offer flexibility?
- What are the implications of our design for autonomy, responsibility, task complexity, job design, communication, establishment of priorities, innovation and accountability?
- How well are all the above aligned and consistent with the aims and tasks to be achieved?
- How will the various tasks and functions be coordinated and integrated?

Section 2: Creating Dynamic Stability

6

Creating a 'change-able' organization

To change successfully, organizations should stop changing all the time.
(Abrahamson, 2000)

Introduction

Organizations have to change just to stand still. As discussed earlier, increased competition in the global economy means that organizations in every sector are having to compete on the basis of speed, cost, quality, innovation, flexibility and customer responsiveness. Much of the change literature suggests that organizations must therefore expect major change to be ongoing. For instance, Moran and Brightman (2001) define change management as 'the process of continually renewing the organization's direction, structure and capabilities to serve the ever-changing needs of the marketplace, customers and employees'. They argue that: 'Change management activities must operate at a high level today since the rate of change is greater than ever'.

However, not everyone agrees. Abrahamson (2000) suggests that organizations should not see major ongoing change as their destiny. He argues that most organizations are not equipped to deal well with change, since they are usually set up to stabilize processes. Moreover, the way change tends to be managed can be so disruptive that it can tear organizations apart. He argues that, as CEOs take drastic measures to maximize economic growth, change often creates initiative overload, resulting in organizational chaos and employee resistance, rather than new ways forward for the organization.

Instead, Abrahamson advocates a more modulated approach to change – what he calls 'pacing'. Major change initiatives should be interspersed with 'carefully paced periods of smaller, organic change'. Since change is now a way of life, Abrahamson argues, a more reasonable way of thinking about change is to see it as 'dynamic stability', the norm to be embraced positively, rather than a painful add-on to 'business as usual'. This way of thinking may require a mindset shift for employees at all levels. After all, he suggests, though some change is management-led and occurs within a strategic framework, most change is really happening almost imperceptibly at team and local levels.

In this chapter we will explore what is involved in creating dynamic stability, or the basis of innovation, flexibility and change-ability. In particular we shall consider how organizations can build flexibility in to their structures, systems, processes and mindsets.

Dynamic stability

For Abrahamson, the goal should be change that can be sustained over both the short and the long term. As such, he is advocating strategic flexibility. This way, he argues, organizations can see the benefits of change without 'fatal pain'. He illustrates his argument with the example of GE under Jack Welch. During the 1980s, following a succession of major restructurings and divestitures, Welch learned the importance of stabilizing the organization for a time between major change initiatives, enabling the introduction of far-reaching cultural initiatives such as boundarylessness and six sigma quality, which have been far less disruptive. By protecting some stability, Welch made major changes more feasible.

This 'dynamic stability' approach, or ' the process of relatively small change efforts that involve the reconfiguration of existing practices and business models rather than the creation of new ones', is similar to that of Henri Bergson (1907, in Calori et al., 2001), who defined the concept of 'creative evolution'. For Bergson, everything endures – the past is prolonged in the present, time is duration, and duration, rather than being seen as a source of stagnation, is the source of creation. Creation springs from a vital impetus that drives us toward our desired future, transforming our identity. The challenge for managers is to exploit the natural creativity in the workforce to the full.

Becoming a change-able, learning organization

In Roffey Park's model of inputs for sustainable high performance, an organization's ability to respond quickly and efficiently to changing circumstances is fundamental to current and future success. Rowden (2001) has identified four models of strategic change, three of which are planned change, implementation-focused change, and readiness-focused change.

The fourth model of strategic change identified by Rowden describes organizational change as a process rather than an event. Since business contexts are chaotic, it can take time to recognize that a situation demands a change, and further time to develop a plan of change.

Organizational change-ability requires systems, processes and people to be flexible and versatile. More importantly, success rests on new behaviour patterns among those involved, and it can take considerable time to change working habits. Underpinning this flexibility is a learning culture that supports people as they work through change. Therefore, Rowden argues that:

> *the organization's capacity to learn as it goes may be the only true source of competitive advantage. No longer able to forecast the future, many leading organizations are constructing arks comprised of their inherent capacity to adapt to unforeseen situations, to learn from their experiences, to shift their shared mindsets, and to change more quickly, broadly and deeply than ever before.*

That which is taken for granted and which is the basis of strategy formulation is broken down and 'reframed'. This is the 'learning organization' model, which attempts to compensate for the limitations of earlier models and is to a great extent synonymous with organizational change-ability. Rowden argues that organizations which do not develop learning organization approaches will not be able to move swiftly enough to survive.

Since knowledge is becoming an increasingly important source of competitive advantage, organizations that can find, spread and manage knowledge well are able to respond and innovate faster. Change-able organizations learn how to manage knowledge well. Change, rather than being driven solely from the top, can be driven from the bottom up, and involve the middle of the firm and the periphery. Everyone is engaged in identifying and solving problems, enabling the organization to increase its capacity to grow, learn and achieve its purpose. Therefore, in a change-able, learning organization, front-line people are exposed to new ideas, through, for example, talking with customers and suppliers, being involved in purchasing decisions and visiting clients. When the pursuit of opportunity becomes a major driver, everything the organization does may need to change.

Change-ability – key principles

Many studies of change focus on why change is difficult, or tends not to work. Many of these failure factors are about people, and the perceived negative effects on employees of the way change is managed. Embracing change as a way of life therefore puts people in the spotlight. Many things can produce changes in people's behaviour. Theorists debate whether it is necessary to stimulate people to change – through articulating a crisis situation, or through creating some other 'burning platform' as a way of mobilizing an organization to change. Increasingly there is recognition that for major culture change to occur, employees need to feel a sense of ownership of the change effort. Change that is merely imposed tends not to motivate people to want to 'go the extra mile'.

Underpinning the creation of a change-able culture are several key principles relating to people. These are drawn from a variety of sources (Thomas, 1985; Lawrie, 1990; Schein, 1990), and are as follows:

- People need predictability (physical, psychological and social)
- People also need variety – new experiences, growth, breaks in routine and creative outlets

- Change that people initiate themselves is viewed as good, needed and valuable
- Change that is imposed is likely to be met with some form of resistance
- The greater the change, the greater the resistance that can be expected
- Change is not seen as threatening if the affected parties perceive the change as helpful
- Pressures for change can be established or increased by providing specific information
- Information-gathering and analysis are more useful if performed by a group rather than an individual
- When those people affected and those people who are pushing for the change feel that they are members of the same group, opposition to change is generally reduced
- When people are involved in driving or creating the change, they own what they create.

The learning organization approach to change

The learning organization approach to strategic organizational change embraces ongoing initiatives that are directed from the top to the bottom of the organization, and others that are generated from within the organization in response to environmental/customer needs. Rather than the creation of fixed plans by a few senior executives, the learning organization produces open, flexible plans that are fully shared and embraced by the whole organization.

In addition, key management variables, goals and strategies, technologies, job design, organizational structure and people (Johns, 1983) are factored in to the implementation of the proposed change. This has a profound effect on the depth of the change effort, such as when an organization transforms itself away from mass production towards lean production.

The learning organization approach has been recognized by the UK government as being key to sustainable high performance. The learning organization approach is characterized by:

- Constant readiness
- Continuous planning
- Improvised implementation
- Action learning.

Constant readiness

For Rowden (2001), implementation problems will continue to occur if the organization as a whole is not ready for change. Creating readiness for change is therefore a fundamental pre-condition for successful change. Rather than building readiness for a pre-determined change, the organization exists in a state of constant readiness for change in general. It is attuned to its environment, and is willing to question its ways of doing business.

When the pursuit of opportunity (rather than cost reduction) becomes a major driver, mindsets, reward systems and management practices may need to change. The purpose of the change is to create a learning organization capable of adapting to a changing environment.

A change-ready organization has a positive work climate characterized by:

- Decision-making and problem-solving based on participation of employees
- An open, problem-solving atmosphere
- Trust among employees and managers
- A sense of 'ownership' of work goals
- Self-control and self-direction of employees.

A 'change-ready' organization has built into its management system sufficient questioning and strategic thinking that it avoids the danger of strategic drift. It has managers who can work within the tradition of rational/analytic thought processes and can also stimulate creativity – their own and that of others. It has leaders who are able to provide a sufficient sense of direction so that people have clear parameters within which to experiment. It has enough permeability that new ideas can seep in from beyond those boundaries. Readiness for change is fostered by the provision of regular feedback on the performance of functions and business units. Some might say that this is the general manager's responsibility, but monitoring the change process needs to be shared. This keeps everyone aware of gaps that need to be filled between the current and desired levels of performance.

A change-ready organization has enough standardization that everyone knows how to make things work, but not so much that rigidity sets in and innovation and responsiveness are stifled. It has a sufficiently open management style that employees are encouraged to share information and market intelligence that can help keep the organization attuned to changing customer needs and ahead of its competitors. It also has mechanisms to capture and develop further that knowledge to the benefit of the organization and its stakeholders. Success stories are circulated, and there are regular and effective communication processes.

Developing change readiness may require a cultural shift. Indeed, as Caulkin (1995) suggests, management for innovation requires employees and employers to 'go the extra mile' to deliver something beyond the letter of the employment contract. It requires initiative, commitment and willingness to take risks on the part of the employee, and trust, support and tolerance of mistakes on the part of the employer. Assessing the need for, and the types of change required to bring about the culture shift, should happen after a revised vision and modification in an organization's strategy. It is only after these have been considered that the precise changes to be made should be identified.

Geoff Atkinson (2000) considers that a planned process to creating change-readiness is appropriate, and advocates four steps as follows:

1. Specify what your organization will look like when change-ready
2. Audit where you are against that in terms of the new, not the old

3. Prioritize gaps and plan
4. Implement the plan.

In specifying the desired state of the organization when 'change ready', or the kind of organizational culture to be created, models such as the EFQM Business Excellence Model, Peters and Waterman's McKinsey 7S Model or the Service–Profit Chain can be useful. According to Atkinson, in order to gain maximum commitment to any proposed change it is important to include those affected as much as possible in the specification stage and to have an appropriate blend of effective leadership and followership.

Flexible, continuous planning

Since business contexts are chaotic, conventional business planning processes can become increasingly restrictive. It can take time to recognize that a situation demands a change, and further time to develop a plan of change. Rather than the creation of fixed plans by a few senior executives, the learning organization produces open, flexible plans that are fully shared and embraced by the whole organization. Variables are likely to include goals and strategies, technologies, job design, organizational structure and people (Johns, 1983).

Flexible strategic planning, as opposed to a static form of planning, is called for in a turbulent environment. This is where the present and future are linked, by bringing the future into people's current work. People in learning organizations are continuously aware of, and interact with, their environment. They think about the world, markets, customers, suppliers and opportunities that may exist in the months and years ahead, and build them into today's decisions. Individual performance is directly linked to organizational performance. According to McLagan (2003), teams that consist of some people who are present-oriented and others who are future-oriented tend to perform better over time.

Improvised implementation

The learning organization fosters inquiry and dialogue, making it safe for people to share openly and take risks. It encourages experimentation and change within parameters.

According to Donald Sull (in Arkin, 2000):

> You don't have to worry so much about the future. Instead of a 10 year vision, you live for today. So suddenly the strategy process goes from being one of deep analysis to a more improvisational process where you are seizing opportunities as they arise.

In adaptive planning models of organizational change, managers should communicate their long-term intention in terms of broad purpose and principle rather than detailed plans, as only broad principles will stimulate the creativity, learning and adaptability of those in closest contact with the environment. This involves being clear about the context by asking 'where are we going?' and 'where are we not going?', and then analysing opportunities by asking 'what things in the business must I change?' and 'how do I change it/shut it down/ pull the plug?'. This is then followed by action, converting opportunities into results and developing an experimental mindset where the search is on for 'what can I try and when?'.

The role of managers and leaders in creating change-ability

A key task of leaders at all levels is to build the organization's adaptability in the context of ongoing change. Successful change occurs when people willingly change their behaviour to suit the circumstance. Most respondents to the Roffey Park survey felt that effective change, with people being willing to change their behaviours, was the result of good management, together with having an appropriate organization structure. In some cases, people were willing to change as a result of the influence of a particular manager or colleague whom they regarded as a role model.

Researchers have tried to describe the characteristics of managers who successfully manage people through continuous change. Whipp *et al.* (1989) suggest that managers in successful organizations see their role as managing ideas, and try to avoid being kept within strict functional boundaries. Executive committees become problem-focused, delegating operational decision-making downwards. Senior management functions as an interpreter of context and facilitator of change.

Brown and Eisenhardt (1997) suggest that such managers provide clear responsibility and priorities with extensive communication and freedom to improvise. They create an environment that supports extensive communication in real time, within a structure of a few, very specific and relevant rules. This limited structure prevents anarchy, and enables the maximum of empowerment. Bennis and Nanus (1985) suggest that effective change leaders have ideas that add value by building new perceptions on old practices.

Leadership at all levels

Butcher and Atkinson (2000) suggest that, as organizations fragment into smaller, more entrepreneurial units, 'bottom-up' models of change draw on the influence of individuals in leading new initiatives. They advocate a model of change that they call 'pockets of good practice' or 'leadership at all levels'. With this model, defined groups of people challenge the *status quo* by adopting certain practices and improving their performance as a result. Each pocket is inspired by an individual manager who selects himself or herself and gets noticed by his or her actions. These individuals develop a personal vision of what could be achieved in terms of business performance if practices were different from the norm; they then use their initiative to implement that vision within a small part of the company.

What is important is that they gain the enthusiastic buy-in of a small group of like-minded people who challenge corporate habits, goals and assumptions in an effort to improve performance. 'Pockets' may then appear systematically over the organization, each one representing the vision of a different individual but influenced by the success of the other pockets. Teams and individuals integrate practical context issues and approaches into the delivery of the strategic direction, and make the plans happen. The nature of the change gradually reveals itself through the spontaneous and creative actions of people throughout the organization. Over time achievements are institutionalised, and reward systems, formal structures and other systems are modified.

Leadership, rather than supervision

Any leader's actions are likely to have a strong effect on the beliefs and expectations of the work group. According to Cannon (2003), leaders build productive climates by shaping culture over the longer term while simultaneously impacting on climate through individual leadership practices. On the whole, innovation appears to thrive in a relatively egalitarian, status-free context, where participative styles of management are the order of the day and where teams develop their own processes without strong control by management. This means establishing dialogue between the different groups and individuals within the business, creating a shared vision and objectives based on the success of the enterprise, and committing to work together constructively to achieve that success.

Senior managers need to be able and willing to lead rather than supervise, according to *Management Agenda* respondents. They need to take a 'hands off' approach, letting go of power and giving staff the necessary breathing space to encourage creative thinking. They need to be worthy of trust and act in ways that are congruent with organizational values. Transformational leadership, particularly exercised by the board, is a key factor in whether organizations achieve a creative culture. Role-modelling by top management can give other people 'permission' to try out new approaches. Senior managers need to encourage risk-taking and innovation in others.

However, leaders who inspire workers through ideas and concepts, and who can create an environment where the latent talent of individuals can thrive, play a more important role than senior managers who lead by example or status alone.

The role of the leader is to communicate organizational values and direction. Executives develop a clear sense of direction for their organization over a period of time. Their views on the future direction should be based on some deeply held personal values and ideas. However, to be effective, their vision has to be shared. Involving others in the development of the vision achieves greater ownership and commitment. The leader champions the longer-term perspective and oversees, but does not manage the translation of strategic intentions into operational changes. The behaviours of top management have a major impact on organizational learning, positively or negatively, since employees soon work out whether a senior manager's support is genuine or otherwise.

Creating strategic flexibility

For Whipp *et al.* (1989), some of the key issues involved in creating and maintaining strategic flexibility are:

- The need for flexible employees who are able to cross over between functional specializations
- HR strategy and planning, which is required to mesh strategic needs with operational requirements.

In a change-ready organization, concepts of change are built into processes, enabling the rapid dissemination of new initiatives and mobilizing the right resources to make things happen. Therefore the focus is strategic – identifying key capabilities for future business growth and how these can be developed. This involves both building retention plans around key individuals and treating departing individuals with dignity and respect.

Building flexibility into organizational structures, practices and systems

In their seminal article of the 1980s, Whipp *et al.* (1989) argued that:

> *Organizations will have to remain flexible in the sense of responding not only to shifting market pressures, but also creating the required internal innovations. The basis for future strategic flexibility would appear to rest on the combined deployment of capital, human resources, structure and technology.*

Ghoshal and Bartlett (1989) too argue that aiming for control and predictability is no longer tenable in a world of increasing competition and technological change. Quite the reverse: in inhibiting the scope for creative and individual enterprise, an over-reliance on systems (part of a Taylorist legacy) has proved to be the undoing of once household-name companies like the former electronics giant, Westinghouse.

Indeed, a general lack of expectation of permanence pervades the culture of the post-bureaucratic organization. As Heckscher points out, because flexibility is critical to innovation and agility, the organizational form is dominated by tentative principles rather than by fixed rules (Heckscher and Donnellon, 1994). Building structural flexibility is likely to involve moves towards self-designing organizations and problem/opportunity-based temporary structures. A balance will be needed between 'business as usual' projects and change projects in parallel. Such organizations also have flexibility built in to their systems, processes and people. Decision-making needs to be devolved to the lowest point possible in the hierarchy. Processes need to cover functional requirements, but are also designed to be cross-functional. Strategy and task-planning processes build in change-readiness as a criterion. They will need to provide for internal innovation by building in some slack in terms of resources and providing rewards for innovation.

Philpott (2002) highlights some of the forms of organizational flexibility that are key to high performance/high productivity outcomes:

- Organizations must be numerically flexible so that working time adjusts to meet changing patterns of demand
- Organizations must be functionally flexible, by improving skill levels and developing working practices that utilize skills to the full so as to enhance product quality
- Organizations must be occupationally flexible, enabling workers to become mobile between different tasks
- Organizations must be wage flexible, enabling pay to vary in line with individual or team performance, as well as with fluctuations in external labour-market conditions, as an incentive to higher productivity
- Organizations must display flexibility of organizational mindset to tap into all available talent, embracing diversity and adopting patterns of working that enable employees to combine jobs with domestic responsibilities.

Currently, around 29 per cent of UK employees work part-time or in some other form of flexible working pattern. In most of the organizations in the Roffey Park *Management Agenda* surveys, flexible working accounts for up to 25 per cent of the workforce. Part-time and shift working is of course well established in the retail and leisure industries. The number of part-time jobs is increasing faster than the number of full-time jobs. By 2006, the number of individuals working part-time is set to increase to 31 per cent as a result of both organizational and individual needs (DfEE, 1997–8).

Ricardo Semler, majority owner of Semco, transformed this largely conventional business by creating a large number of 'satellites' – former employees working as freelances, by themselves or in groups, but with a high degree of support from Semco. They work under a variety of contracts, but many use company equipment and even work on the premises, although they may be working for competitors. While only 60 per cent of the satellites survived, 80 per cent of the people involved in the original satellites still work for Semco. The company's liberal policies seem to have inspired loyalty as well as the freedom to 'go into orbit' (Pickard, 1996).

Volberda (1998) emphasizes the paradoxical nature of flexibility. He suggests that the organization can move back up the natural path from the planned to the flexible if it adopts a more organic structure, and a more heterogeneous, open and externally orientated culture. If it fails to retain some stability, the organization becomes chaotic. Stability depends on having some of the existing characteristics alongside developing new characteristics.

The ways in which organizations are building in flexibility as reported in the *Management Agenda* include developing strategic alliances (58 per cent), mergers (15 per cent) and public/private partnerships (23 per cent); hot-desking (29 per cent); outsourcing (52 per cent); more flexible work processes (50 per cent); and centralization (40 per cent). Conversely, political and economic instability are leading to organizational practices that tend to limit flexibility. These include implementing spending restrictions and, in some cases, suspending recruitment. Not surprisingly, from a management perspective, some of the reported main challenges of managing change include retention, achieving buy-in, staying up to speed, embracing change, integrating teams and focusing energy on innovation.

Calori *et al.* (2001) suggest that flexibility in resources is one of four parameters that influence the speed of change. The other factors are the internal political forces, the degrees of latitude permitted in the chosen courses of action, and whether or not the organization can be offensive (or must it be defensive?). When these factors are all favourable, fast change is possible.

Empowerment

A key challenge for leaders of innovation is to develop a culture of empowerment, where individuals are able and willing to accept responsibility but also have the skills and resources to produce the results for which they are accountable. Many traditional views of empowerment are based around the notion of giving power to people, according to Rosemary Stewart (1995). This suggests that the manager is active in the process of handing power over to his or her direct reports. However, when asked 'what stops you from using your abilities to the full at work?', many people respond with comments such as ' If I got it wrong I'd be in trouble', and 'I don't have the time or the freedom to do my best'. It follows then that if an individual, or indeed a whole organization, is serious about empowering its workforce, a reframing of the nature of empowerment is required.

An alternative view, for Stewart, frames the process as one of taking restraints away as opposed to giving power – i.e. organizations and managers should focus on ceasing to disempower people by removing the inhibiting factors.

For this, it is important to ensure that employees have the information they need to do their jobs. Leaders need to establish an environment where some risks and mistakes are acceptable if learning takes place. An open, dynamic and egalitarian culture will have a reasonable chance of creating the right degree of empowerment for creativity to flourish.

Mavericks

McLagan (2003) argues that mavericks are essential to champion new directions that create an organization's future. They stand for radical, not evolutionary, change, and often provoke resistance to their ideas. For McLagan, the leadership challenge is to make it possible for mavericks to survive in an environment that does not evict them.

Meyerson (2001) suggests that in evolutionary change, which proceeds in a gentle, incremental, decentralized manner, something else is needed to produce broad and lasting shifts with less upheaval than more radical approaches. She describes leaders of incremental change efforts as 'tempered radicals'. These are internal change agents who take the low-key risks and do the early experimentation. They:

> *gently and continually push against prevailing norms, making a difference in small but steady ways and setting examples from which others can learn. The changes they inspire are so incremental that they barely merit notice – which is exactly why they work so well. Like drops of water, these approaches are innocuous enough in themselves. But over time, and in accumulation, they can erode granite.*

Meyerson suggests that the trick for organizations is to locate and nurture this subtle form of leadership.

Meyerson (2001) argues that 'tempered radicals' teach important lessons and inspire change. In so doing, they exercise a form of leadership that is less visible than traditional forms, but just as important. She describes four change tactics of 'tempered radicals', whether these are in leadership positions or not. These include disruptive self-expression, in which an individual simply acts in a way that personally feels right but that others notice; verbal jujitsu, which turns an insensitive statement, action or behaviour back on itself; variable term opportunism, which involves spotting, creating and capitalizing on short-term and long-term opportunities for change; and strategic alliance building, through which an individual can enlist the help of others, especially powerful people, and push through change with more force.

Experimental mindset

Without a culture of experimentation, organizations are likely to atrophy strategically. Equally, valuing only what is new can produce an endless round of relearning and unnecessary activity. For Whipp *et al.* (1989), organizations that tend to perform less well over time have an element of 'amnesia' about them. They forget what they knew, and do not learn from their experience anyway. Abrahamson finds two approaches useful to avoid this trap: tinkering and kludging. 'Tinkering' refers to the way in which companies can pull together inspired solutions to their problems from the 'corporate basement'. It involves pulling together existing expertise in production with marketing, and avoids the 'not-invented-here' syndrome. He cites Dow Chemical, who successfully aimed Saran Wrap, a product originally developed for industrial applications, at consumers, an entirely different market.

'Kludging' follows the same principle as tinkering but on a larger scale, and involves many more parts. Kludges can result in the creation of a new division or business. Abrahamson suggests that old economy companies can use kludging very effectively when adapting to new economy conditions. The mindset required is 'both/and' thinking (dialectical) rather than 'either/or' thinking (binary), so that both planned and emergent can comfortably coexist.

Figure 6.1 illustrates key elements of a change-able organization.

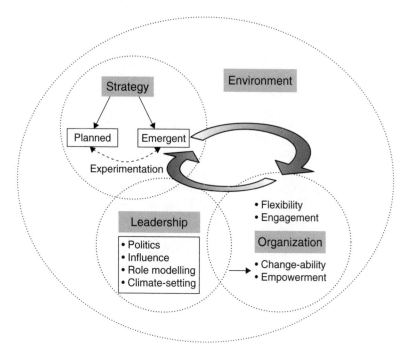

Figure 6.1 A change-able organization.

Using communications to create change-ability

Effective communications can not only help people to understand why change is needed, but also make them want to contribute to that change. Radical changes such as mergers tend to be characterized by project management approaches. A communication strategy designed to support the implementation of the change project ensures that employees and other stakeholders are at least kept informed about developments. Similarly, when an organization is trying to inculcate new cultural values, the communication of the change programme is often treated like a product launch, with whole staff get-togethers in football pitches and a good deal of razzmatazz. However, when changes large and small come to be seen as almost routine, there is a tendency for formalized communications to fall by the wayside. Indeed, such top-down approaches to communication are arguably inappropriate to the goal of creating a 'change-able' organization. This goal calls for a wider variety of processes to engage staff and help create emergent direction.

For Cameron and Quinn (1998), some of the most important challenges in enabling successful ongoing change include finding ways through which employees can become involved in fashioning and carrying out change strategies. In the context of new cultural values, employee involvement is essential in ensuring continuous communication. Friends Provident, a financial services company, is a case in point.

Example 6.1　Friends Provident
When Friends Provident changed from mutual status, it took the opportunity of the flotation to refocus the organization's culture. The approach taken was to deal with organizational changes slowly, clearly and quietly, rather than trumpeting new values and having a culture communications bandwagon.

First the executive committee drew up some guiding principles that would eventually underpin the activities of all 4300 employees. A series of workshops eventually produced five corporate values, which were launched without fanfare. The executive team agreed to cascade the concept down the line at three-monthly intervals, allowing tiers of managers to gain ownership of the values before passing them on. Workshops were designed to help teams translate the principles into action, and it was seven months later that the whole organization got to hear about them. The approach taken built employee involvement and ownership of the values in a way that was culturally sustainable (Littlefield, 2001).

Building engagement

When people are energized, motivated and performing, there is a good possibility that they are engaged with their organization and want to contribute to its success. 'Engagement' goes beyond 'satisfaction' and 'commitment'. It is the activating element of latent goodwill and tends to occur in certain conditions. First, a common cause is essential, with an aligned strategy that people can sign up to. Brand values need to be translated into meaningful experiences for customers and employees alike. Second, a strong culture is required, with an agreed and well communicated set of values that guide people's actions.

However, developing vision and values should not be considered a purely top-down prerogative, leading to the need to create employee 'buy-in' to the message being 'sold'; nor should finding solutions to problems as they arise. Two-way approaches are more likely to lead to effective engagement. According to a 2002 DTI consultation paper, high performance workplaces tend to be characterized by a joint approach to solving business problems involving everyone employed in the firm.

Developing a joint approach means establishing dialogue between the different groups and individuals within the business, creating a shared vision and objectives based on the success of the enterprise, and committing to work together constructively to achieve that success. Implementing change occurs through informing, consulting and involving all stakeholders in the business. This can only be achieved by building relationships of trust at the workplace which facilitate genuine employee involvement and influence through open and comprehensive communication and consultation. Developing trust requires that the different rights, responsibilities and interests of different groups and individuals within the business are recognized. Partnership working between management and staff representative bodies is often the subject of much scepticism. For real trust to be built requires a mutual understanding of and respect for one another's different needs and interests, and a genuine attempt at reconciliation and consensus-building.

Staff consultation

In the early years of the millennium there appears to be a changing employee relations climate in Europe, with work councils and trades union voices becoming stronger. European legislation is supporting better working conditions and employment contracts, often in the face of opposition from businesses. UK employers in particular have a poor historical record on consulting their staff, especially over redundancies. Only when consultation becomes a legal requirement, such as TUPE (Transfer of Undertakings – Protection of Employment), when organizations are obliged to consult employees about impending collective redundancies or transfer in the ownership of an undertaking, or under Health and Safety legislation, does it become part of the fabric of employee relations.

The Information and Consultation Directive, due to come into force in 2005, will place obligations on employers with over 150 employees to formalize staff consultation procedures. Employers may have consultation processes forced on them if they do not adopt voluntary processes. In the meantime, enlightened employers are increasing the variety of ways in which they can consult with and involve employees in decision-making. According to the proposed EU legislation, workers' representatives will have the right to consult management about any matter that will affect employment – such as redundancies, changes in ownership and a wide range of day-to-day management issues.

Trades unions have largely welcomed the proposal, claiming that a revolution to win hearts and minds will follow. Some business leaders, however, warn that consultation will affect business flexibility at a time when the global marketplace is changing so fast that change needs to be swift. While staff consultations can carry some risks for employers and staff alike, the key is 'to strike a balance between ensuring employees' views are taken on board and avoiding processes which could result in the delaying of business decisions', according to Noel O'Reilly (2001).

A study carried out by the IPA (2001) shows that some UK employers are starting to develop effective models of consultation, taking in mechanisms such as staff councils, joint union–employer taskforces and consultation arrangements at local and national level. Organizations such as British Bakeries, Blue Circle Cement and Asda have set up voluntary models, and are proving that strong staff consultation and involvement are essential to business effectiveness. Royal Sun Alliance has introduced policies to ensure that the large proportion of its staff who are based at home receive the same support and feedback as office-based staff.

Another study, the 1998 Workplace Employee Relations Survey (WERS98), suggests that most companies in the UK have some form of employee communication. It found that there is a wide range of direct communication practices: team-briefings, workplace-wide meetings, cascading of information and regular staff newsletters. Most of these communication practices reflect top-down approaches. Organizations that failed to use any of these methods were typically stand-alone sites. The WERS survey (Cully *et al.*, 1999) also found that 50 per cent of workplaces with 25 or more employees operate some sort of 'joint consultative committee' which typically addresses issues such as working practices, health and safety, welfare services and facilities, and future workplace plans. Interestingly, pay issues were among the least frequently mentioned.

Staff surveys are frequently mishandled. Employee expectations are often raised, only to be dashed when there is no further communication after the survey has taken place. Managing expectations is as important as taking the 'pulse' of the organization. Good practice suggests that employees should receive a minimum of feedback, if only a global summary of results. If action is going to be taken on some of the findings, this should be indicated, preferably with a report of some early actions that have already been taken. If the survey was for executive information purposes only, it should be badged as such. Some managers fear that surveying staff at critical times, such as when a takeover is looming, is likely to produce only negative reactions. In fact, surveys at such times can be very useful in pinpointing critical issues that will need to be managed during the transition, and for reminding people of some of the organization's strengths.

CIPD suggests five models for staff representation. These are:

1. Works council, or joint consultative committee, which typically exists in large organizations that have recognized trade unions for years, and looks at employment prospects, business issues, redundancies etc.
2. Employee forum, which is similar to a works council but not as historic, and exists where the organization does not recognize unions for negotiating purposes or where the union is not active
3. Mixed economy, where there is limited union involvement within a framework of elected representatives
4. Direct consultation, which means everything apart from representation, and typically focuses on job-related rather than strategic issues
5. Partnership, which should engage with the workforce representatives and regard them as complementary (Emmott, 2003).

Some leading companies are formalizing their new approach to workplace relations by means of partnership agreements usually involving the recognized trade unions. Partnership usually requires representative structures because they provide a means to have a dialogue about change in a focused and effective way, moving from the general policy intent to the specifics of implementation. In some cases these agreements entail agreement by employees to accept new working practices in return for assurances about future job security.

Example 6.2   Barclays Bank

Barclays Bank had a bad pay dispute in 1997, and industrial relations were at an all-time low. Barclays set up a Partnership agreement in early 2000, in conjunction with Unifi. This proved to be a turning point in employer–employee relations. The bank received funding from the Partnership Institute and the Department of Trade and Industry (DTI). Union officials and lay members are elected on a 50/50 basis, and are consulted over changes in policy at an early stage. One of the areas the Partnership has focused on is setting up generic policies on things such as flexible working, pay deals, maternity policies and career break options, which Barclays hopes will make it an Employer of Choice (DTI, 2002).

In order to mobilize commitment to change through joint diagnosis of business problems, it is essential that managers recognize the different rights, responsibilities and interests of different groups and individuals within the business. There needs to be strong management resolve to implement change through informing, consulting and involving all stakeholders in the business. This can only be achieved by building relationships of trust at the workplace which facilitate genuine employee involvement and influence through open and comprehensive communication and consultation. This requires a mutual understanding of, and respect for, one another's different needs and interests, and a genuine attempt to reconcile them and build consensus. By helping people develop a shared diagnosis of what is wrong in an organization and what can and must be improved, a general manager (of a unit) mobilizes the initial commitment that is necessary to begin the change process.

Example 6.3   Volkswagen UK

A well-known success story of involvement is that of Volkswagen UK. Its culture has been specially designed to demonstrate and promote a belief in the role of individuals. In order to maintain this ethos and encourage equality, Volkswagen Group introduced an initiative called 'New Retail' three years ago. Under this, everyone – employees and clients alike – is treated as a valued customer. Volkswagen Group management believes that this has enabled the group to develop into an organization where employees value and respect one another and each staff member strives for improvement. Focus groups are called to discuss new policies, including a current proposal for flexible working and job sharing (DTI, 2002).

Employee involvement and the role of the manager

A common characteristic of high performing organizations is high levels of employee involvement, since individuals are more likely to give of their best if they feel valued and are given the opportunity to contribute their ideas.

Increasingly, the role of the manager is being redefined as that of innovator or nurturer of ideas. Coherence between strategic and operational issues is a hallmark of high performance. Managers below executive level have to be able to understand the need for changes, and be in a position to create appropriate responses. Successful firms pay close attention to improving communication flows concerning objectives, constraints and opportunities in order to develop managers' wider strategic awareness.

Gaining 'buy-in'?

On many of the change projects in which Roffey Park is involved on a consultancy basis, the key challenge for management teams is not so much deciding on a course of action leading to change, but gaining buy-in to the proposed change. Some of the commonest approaches to increasing employee involvement and achieving 'buy-in' to change, include:

- Joint problem-solving teams
- Employee feedback
- Project teams
- Joint consultation and collective representation
- The use of electronic media
- Focus groups
- Attitude surveys.

The problem with adopting the approach of looking for 'buy-in' is that managers are in essence having to sell the message that change is necessary, whether or not the message is palatable to those who are likely to be most affected by it. This is a difficult task at the best of times, but all the more challenging when people are being required radically to alter the way they work, or when some aspect of their job security is likely to be threatened by the change.

An alternative approach is reflected in the principle 'people own what they help create'. Rather than having to sell a message, this philosophy suggests that engaging people may be a better option. Rather than being solely one-way, the communication of objectives involves employee engagement on a large scale, using some of the intervention techniques outlined in this chapter. Such techniques flatten hierarchies, at least temporarily, and allow a free flow of ideas informed by greater understanding of the business and its strategic challenges. One level of involvement is where employees are encouraged to make suggestions about improvements and ideas for new products and services. They may also be invited to share their views about how a specific strategic initiative should be implemented. They may in some cases be offered the opportunity to share thinking about possible strategic choices facing the organization. This can produce dilemmas for management teams who, in matters of strategy, usually expect (and are expected) to determine an overall direction for the organization. Engaging a wider group in participative decision-making can seem a far-fetched notion. Many managers fear that they will look weak to staff by not having all the answers. Some managers think that by listening to staff ideas they are letting the genie out of the bottle and raising false expectations. Other managers are open to the idea, but have no idea how to go about doing this.

Large-scale interventions

A wide variety of techniques is available for engaging large numbers of staff in visioning and decision-making. A prerequisite for success is that senior managers genuinely endorse their use, are prepared to be flexible about how change should be implemented, and are willing to experiment with releasing staff potential. Some large-scale intervention techniques bring together all, or as many as possible, of an organization's staff under one roof at the same time. Such visioning/planning events can help an organization's divergent stakeholders discover that they have common ground. The idea is to collapse hierarchy as much as possible so that people feel encouraged to contribute their ideas without fear of stepping on toes.

Usually the issues discussed relate to implementation, although a number of organizations use such methods to gain employee ownership of organizational values, planning and improvement processes. The outcome of any such engagement exercise should be that staff feel they have had a chance to contribute to the development of the organization, and that they take responsibility for actions which result from discussions.

Open Space Technology (OST)

Popularized by Harrison Owen, this approach enables high levels of group interaction and productivity, providing a basis for enhanced organizational function over time. It is used in critical situations requiring high resolution characterized by high levels of complexity, diversity (of participants) and conflict (potential or actual), and with a decision time of yesterday. For OST to work, it must focus on a real business issue that is of passionate concern to those who will be involved. It should not be used when specific predetermined outcomes are desired, such as when installing a new financial system, but it can be extremely effective in designing such a system, providing for the full involvement of all concerned parties.

It works by a group of people sitting in a circle, where they can see one another. Participants are invited to identify any issue for which they have a passion and are willing to take responsibility. They write their issue on a piece of paper, go into the centre of the circle, announce it to the group and post the paper on the wall. When all the issues have been announced, the group signs up for the issues they want to deal with. The proposer designates a time and place to convene the session and record the proceedings if necessary. The group then becomes self-managing.

The process is underpinned by the following principles:

- Whoever comes are the right people
- Whatever happens is the only thing that could have happened

- When it starts is the right time
- When it's over, it's over.

The 'Law of Two Feet' implies that people should stand up for what they believe, and if people feel that they are neither contributing nor learning where they are, they should use their feet and go elsewhere.

The job of the facilitator is to create time and space in which the group can realize its potential, whether that potential be a new product, a strategic plan or a redesigned organization. The ultimate facilitator will do nothing and remain totally invisible.

The people taking part can be anybody who cares about the issues under consideration; diversity is a plus. Gatherings can be for up to 1000 people, although theoretically there is no limit, assuming that multi-site, simultaneous events are computer-connected. Preparation is not an issue, since the space opens with the first conversation. The event can last between one and three days.

Example 6.4   Novotel

One organization that has used OST to develop new ways of operating is Novotel, one of the world's major hotel chains. From its earliest days in the 1960s, Novotel, operating in the 3-star hotel market, had emphasized standardization. In the 1980s it joined the Accor group, where a sister company, Formula One, was launched at the no-frills end of the market. Changes in demand in the marketplace meant that Novotel was going to have to compete in the more customized end of the market. As the marketplace shifted, occupancy rates started to fall at Novotel as the standardized offering became less acceptable to customers.

Novotel management recognized that something had to be done, even though there was no crisis. Rather than believing the signs that things were going well, and being lulled into complacency, they saw and amplified the danger signals they thought mattered.

Against this backdrop, an Open Space meeting of hotel managers took place in Fontainebleau, France, in 1992. Managers said that they wanted the freedom to take decisions and try out new ideas. The output from the Open Space informed subsequent decision-making. In 1993, the company's two co-presidents chose eighteen members of the new top management team, and reduced the superstructure by two layers. This group started to work together with two consultants to define three work systems: communication, management and commercial. The quality control system was abolished. A new profile of hotel general managers was outlined, and new performance measures were defined. Each director of operations organized three-day meetings with their hotel managers and the two co-presidents to refine the project.

Later that year, the number of layers in hotel management was reduced by one. Hotel general managers went through a new assessment centre, and personal development plans were designed. A three-day convention (with 300 participants) was held to launch 'progress groups' and 'clubs'. Personal development plans (PDPs) for hotel managers started.

In the first quarter of 1994, 'Progres Novotel' was launched and the competencies of all employees were assessed. New marketing initiatives were taken, and propositions made by the progress groups and clubs were implemented. Occupancy rates improved thereafter. The name of the change project – 'Back to the Future' – surfaced from within the change initiative itself rather than being imposed top-down, and reflected both/and thinking (Calori et al., 2001).

Real-time strategic change (RTSC)

The purpose of this technique, developed by Jacobs (1994), is to rapidly create an organization's preferred future and sustain it over time. It can be used when any sort of fundamental change is required and lasting change is the goal. Similarly, it can be very useful when the issues involved are complex or ill-defined, when strategic direction is lacking, when new competencies are needed by people or when new technologies are being introduced. It is also sometimes used when organizations are merging or forming alliances, when a business process redesign is being implemented, and when labour and management need to be aligned.

It should not be used when the issues are not fundamental, or where there is a preference for staged, incremental change. Nor should it be used if leadership does not believe in sharing power and is not really open to input about the organization's future and how to achieve it, or where there is a poor fit between the principles of real-time strategic change and the organization's preferred ways of doing business.

The people taking part can include external stakeholders, such as customers, suppliers, regulators and subject matter experts, as well as employees. There is no upper limit on participant numbers, although typically events involve numbers anywhere between 10 and 1000.

Preparation for the event can be time-consuming (one to three months) and laborious. Each event may be run several times within the transition period. If the desired ways of doing business are applied immediately, the transition period can last up to eighteen months, though typically it is between three and nine months.

There are three phases to RTSC: scoping possibilities, developing and aligning leadership, and creating organizational congruence. Scoping possibilities involves crafting a clear, considered plan for a change effort. Developing and aligning leadership is about building leadership commitment and the competencies required for a successful change effort and for congruent leadership in the future. Leaders align around the case for change and when and how to engage other members in this work. Creating organizational congruence involves engaging the whole organization in aligning the external realities, the preferred future, strategy and plans, systems, structures and processes, and daily work.

Future search

A future search (Weisbord and Janoff, 2000) is a large group planning meeting that brings a 'whole system' into the room to work on a task-focused agenda. According to the authors, 'Future Search conferences often enable people to experience and accept polarities. They help participants bridge barriers of culture, class, age, gender, ethnicity, power, status and hierarchy by working as peers on tasks of mutual concern'. Such events help people to recognize that bringing different points of view to bear constructively on a situation only makes a culture stronger, rather than the opposite.

This method is typically used to evolve a common-ground future for an organization or community, and develop self-managed plans to move towards it. It can be used when a shared vision is desired, an action plan is needed, when other efforts have stalled or when new leadership is taking over. It can be used to help people implement a shared vision that already exists. It is also useful when a key transition is at hand, such as changing markets or new technology, or when opposing parties need to meet and they have no good forum. It is particularly valuable when time is short.

Conditions for success using this method are that the whole system is in the room (full attendance). The people taking part can be a broad cross-section of stakeholders, organizations, multilevel or multifunctional communities – any sector that the sponsors consider relevant. Everybody is invited to share leadership as peers. Gatherings are typically for between 60 and 80 people, although the optimum number is no more than 64. Parallel or sequential conferences can be used to increase numbers. Typically, future search events last three days.

The focus should be on common ground and the future, not on problems and conflict. However, it should not be used when leadership is reluctant to engage in conversations about change; when conditions for success are not met; when nobody but the initiator wants the process, or when it is force-fitted into a planned meeting. Similarly, if the agenda is preconceived or no planning time is available, it should not be used.

Future search typically involves five tasks of two to four hours each, spread over three days. It works by reviewing the past, exploring the present, creating ideal future scenarios, identifying common ground from which action plans can be built. Work on the present is done by stakeholder groups whose members have some shared perspective on the task. Action planning employs both stakeholder and self-selected groups. Every task concludes with a group dialogue. The spirit of future search is self-management and discovery. Preparation for the process typically takes between three and six months.

Appreciative Inquiry (AI)

Organization development tools tend to reflect humanistic values. David Cooperrider and others developed Appreciative Inquiry, which is a new way of looking at human social systems and how they evolve. The idea of AI began with the professorial staff at Case Western Reserve University's Weatherhead

School of Management in the late 1980s. The basic assumption behind conventional OD approaches is that organizing is a problem to be solved. AI works on the understanding that paying attention to what works well and valuing the best of what is, rather than on solving problems, contributes to the development of a positive culture. In AI, the basic assumption is that organizing is a miracle to be embraced.

This is a very different perspective from the way managers in the West typically approach their work. Holman and Devane (1999) describe Appreciative Inquiry as:

> *The cooperative search for the best in people, their organizations, and the world around them. It involves systematic discovery of what gives a system 'life' when it is most effective and capable in economic, ecological and human terms. AI involves the art and practice of asking questions that strengthen a system's capacity to heighten positive potential. It mobilizes inquiry through crafting an 'unconditional positive question', often involving hundreds or even thousands of people. In AI, intervention gives way to imagination and innovation; instead of negation, criticism and spiralling diagnosis, there is discovery, dream and design. AI assumes that every living system has untapped, rich and inspiring accounts of the positive. Link this 'positive change core' directly to any change agenda and changes never thought possible are suddenly and democratically mobilised.*

AI begins with the choice of topic. Either everyone with some stake in the future needs to have a say in the focus of the inquiry, or a truly representative group should be tasked with the choice. The topic should be expressed in the affirmative. The AI process follows the 4-D cycle, that is:

1. *Discovery* – appreciating what gives life to the organization, valuing the best of 'what is'. The aim is to capture all that is best about the whole system and to include as many people's stories as possible.
2. *Dream* – envisioning the impact of shared dreams collected during interviews about 'what might be'. Participants are asked to identify what made previous achievements possible, and to use the information to envisage a desired future.
3. *Design* – dialoguing and co-constructing the ideal organization design, 'what should be'. This is not merely about reproducing past successes, but about envisioning a future that will go beyond everything that has happened before.
4. *Destiny/Delivery* – innovating, sustaining, empowering, learning and action-intention, 'what will be'. The essential idea of the delivery phase is to commit to action and to come good on that commitment.

Hammond (1998) lists eight assumptions that characterize the Appreciative Inquiry approach:

1. In every society, organization or group something works
2. What we focus on becomes our reality
3. Reality is created in the moment, and there are multiple realities
4. The act of asking questions of an organization or group influences the group in some way

5. People have more confidence and comfort to journey to the future (the unknown) when they carry forward parts of the past (the known)
6. If we carry parts of the past forward, they should be what is best about the past
7. It is important to value differences
8. The language we use creates our reality.

The choice of topic and how it is framed are important – for example, enquire into retention rather than turnover. The next phase is to create or ask questions that explore the best of what is. After this, people listen to one another's stories of the system at its best. They then have the energy to develop an ideal future state – the 'dream' phase. This should be something beyond what has happened before. AI articulates this vision of the future through provocative propositions that stretch the boundaries of what is possible. For example, if the discovery phase found that extraordinary customer service happened when front-line staff felt confident, the organization would support their initiative and a provocative proposition might read: *Front-line staff will have maximum discretion to delight our customers* (Hammond, 1998).

The final stage is the 'delivery' phase, where everyone commits to action that they carry out. AI works best where there is a good match between what the group or organization is trying to do and how it goes about achieving this. For example, if a group wants greater cross-functional working, ensure that people engage in the process across functional lines.

> *Example 6.5   NHS Trusts merger*
> Two NHS hospital Trusts were embarking on a merger, with a view to pooling resources and serving the dispersed community better. After widespread consultation in the community, the merger went ahead, with the perception amongst staff in both institutions that they were being taken over and that the other Trust was going to have the lion's share of the best departments. An Appreciative Inquiry process was chosen as a means of creating greater understanding between staff in each hospital. First, 40 members of staff in each hospital were trained up to carry out an Inquiry in the other Trust. These people in turn trained up others, so that most members of staff were interviewed as part of the process. As each group learned what the other valued about their culture, they gained respect and trust toward each other. The outputs of the various phases of the AI process were then incorporated into the vision for the merged Trust by its new Chief Executive. In a very real way, top-down and bottom-up change came together, to positive effect.

Celebrating success

Reward and recognition schemes play a special role in creating change-ability. Valuing different forms of contribution is important to staff motivation. While achieving good financial results is critical, paying attention only to the bottom-line can be counterproductive. Managers should also pay attention to and reward employee commitment, new ideas, smarter ways of working and customer feedback. Celebrating individuals and teams, even the small successes, can unlock employee motivation and lead to greater things.

The role of HR in creating organizational change-ability

A key role for HR in creating a change-able culture is working with line managers to achieve greater empowerment and accountability. This involves making sure that decisions are taken at the right level, and that managers have the skills to coach and delegate effectively.

Flexibility of mindset tends to come when people are able to see the bigger picture. This can be achieved when people understand the rationale for change. HR can proactively shape communication strategies and encourage the use of large-scale interventions described above to allow people to develop a shared understanding of the business challenges and a joint approach to finding practical ways of addressing these. People become more flexible as they learn, having the opportunity to take on new roles, work in cross-functional teams and develop new skills. HR can provide access to training and development, which can provide people with the knowledge and skills required for new roles within the changing organization. They can provide development tools that put employees in command of their own learning.

HR can also help create a change-able culture by unblocking some of the organizational barriers, such as misaligned reward systems, conflict within and between teams which causes the organization to focus internally, and managers who will not release people for development. They can work closely with managers, helping them to lead and manage performance more effectively. They can also act as a 'knowledge hub', spreading good practice across the organization and importing fresh ideas from outside the organization.

Conclusion

Although creativity can coexist with change, the impact of large-scale change is often damaging to the creative process and to continuity of ideas. Therefore, wherever possible change leaders should choose manage change in ways that are less disruptive. Large-scale change should be interspersed with small-scale change projects, many of which should build on employee initiatives and be given coherence because every employee understands what the organization is trying to do.

If organizations want to encourage people to be flexible, innovative and willing to use their initiative, the culture has to be 'right'. There needs to be a genuine belief in empowerment, and good teamworking – especially cross-boundary. People need to be given time to generate and work through good ideas. People's work should be stimulating and provide real scope for creative solutions. Visionary leadership is essential to creating these conditions. Clear communication and parameters for experimentation mean that people can put their creative energies into things that matter to the business. Good systems and flexible working can help people gear their work to the nature of the task in hand.

Building a robust and change-able culture creates the platform for successful change and also for the development of successful future products and services. Fundamentally, strategic flexibility depends on flexible mindsets, the ready flow of ideas and the speed with which the organization can adapt and refocus its energies. In conditions such as these, stability can be truly dynamic.

Checklist: Building dynamic stability

- Link changes in the culture of the organization with organizational goals and effectiveness.
- Develop organizational forms which focus on autonomy and cooperation (such as flat, simple matrix, or network organization).
- Link individual performance to organizational performance.
- Ensure that people are recognized and rewarded for flexibility and learning.
- Ensure that power distribution works for the organization, rather than against it – there should be enough freedom from direct control that people can use their initiative but not so much freedom that chaos ensues.
- Use soft, informal controls (e.g. role models) rather than hard, formal controls.
- Ensure that risk-taking and experimentation are encouraged rather than penalized.
- People in flexible organizations do multiple jobs, constantly learning new skills while the organization pursues multiple paths, experiments and makes shifts. Flexible organizations thrive on ambiguity, throw out job descriptions and encourage *ad hoc* teams which form and reform as tasks shift.
- Build slack into the system to allow for flexibility and the unexpected.
- Draw a distinction between learning which focuses people on current best practice and that which produces a wide and diverse range of capability.
- Ensure that there is enough freedom from direct control that people can use their initiative, but not so much freedom that chaos ensues.
- Jobs that require flexible and innovative behaviour must be ingrained with a degree of constant change, which may provide some degree of job satisfaction.
- Strike a careful balance between resources needed for today's work environment and the need for innovation to protect the organization's long-term future.
- Provide a range of communication vehicles through which employees can become involved in decision-making.

7

Creating a knowledge-rich context for innovation

Introduction

For many organizations, achieving competitive advantage through strategic flexibility is the 'Holy Grail'. They look for cheaper, more efficient structural arrangements and working practices. For example, they outsource work to call centres, often in parts of the developing world. Operations can, and do, take place round the clock. However, structural flexibility alone is not enough to achieve sustainable success. Nor are efficient processes and higher productivity enough to secure an organization's ongoing leading edge. In today's global marketplace, where competition is rife, organizations are only as competitive as they are innovative and get new products to market quickly. To be dynamically stable, therefore, organizations need to build their sources of future revenue by maximizing the generation and flow of ideas and knowledge.

Innovation is the driving force behind the modern economy, underpinning economic growth, forcing the pace of business competitiveness and providing improvements to the quality of life. If a dynamically stable culture is a prerequisite for high performance, innovation is the cornerstone of dynamic stability. Innovation enables organizations to prosper, react quickly, learn from others and create options for the future. Even industries with traditionally long lead times, such as pharmaceuticals and defence, are under pressure to speed up their research and development processes. Innovation applies to products – what is offered; process – how it is created or delivered; and service. An innovation strategy is only successful set in the context of other goals:

- Growth – generating a new stream of orders
- Diversity – finding new areas of business
- Initiative – motivating people to solve problems and seek new opportunities
- Focus – maintaining organizational cohesion.

In his report about the competitive economy agenda for the UK's Department of Trade and Industry (2003), Michael Porter of Harvard Business School suggests that the UK economy needs to move from 'competing on low costs of doing business to competing on unique value and innovation'. Innovation is what gives organizations the edge over their competitors. Proctor and Gamble, for instance, are said to have 28 000 patents, only some of which will prove to be worth a fortune. Regardless of sector, organizations that focus on research and development while also improving current operations and milking the 'cash cow' of existing products are likely to achieve a sustainable pipeline of revenue-generating possibilities.

In Chapter 6 we looked at how change-ability is a key characteristic of learning organizations. The most successful organizations are likely to be those where innovation occurs fluently, that have flexibility and adaptability built into their work processes, and that have a skilled, motivated and customer-focused workforce. Employees at all levels need to be able and willing to help find new ways forward for their business, while continuously improving the *status quo*. In other words, an organization that aims at optimizing its human capital, and whose employees are going to be enriched by the process, needs to operate as a learning organization. In this chapter we will explore how organizations can enable innovation, creativity and knowledge-sharing.

The strategic issues relating to innovation, knowledge and learning

Today's organizations run on knowledge, and most would like to capitalize on that fact. Strategic goals linked to knowledge may include, for instance:

- Generating a reputation for (technical) expertise
- Translating expertise into new projects
- Gaining new experience in specific areas at lowest cost to the organization
- Gaining new business without over-stretching internal resources.

Organizations that take the generation and management of knowledge seriously use a variety of organizational forms, such as cross-functional teams, product or customer-focused business units and work groups, to develop and spread ideas and information. Other key strategic issues relating to knowledge and research and development include:

- Managing internal competition for resources between different project teams
- Ensuring the resource base is in touch and appropriately funded
- Developing coherence and shape in technical resources (keep teams intact)
- Developing capability for learning across the business
- Selling resources as 'technical reputation' to new clients.

What blocks strategic flexibility, innovation and learning?

In practice, many organizations experience distinct barriers to flexibility, innovation and knowledge management. In the *Management Agenda* survey (2003), only 22 per cent of respondents describe their organizations as 'successful' at fostering creativity; 55 per cent perceived an unsupportive culture as limiting creativity. A closed and hierarchical company with an oppressive blame culture is not going to breed creativity and bright ideas. Rather, according to the *Management*

Agenda 2004 respondents, many organizations are showing all the signs of rigidity and introspection.

Barriers to creative thinking and innovation

Blockages to creative thinking and innovation fall into several categories:

- *Perceptual blocks*, such as having too narrow a definition of the problem
- *Cultural blocks*, such as tradition being preferred to change, and beliefs that reason, logic and practicality are good while feeling, intuition and qualitative judgements are bad
- *Environmental blocks*, such as distractions like telephones or activities that keep people so busy they have no time to think
- *Emotional blocks*, such as the fear of making a mistake, or of taking a risk.

According to Bill Tate (1997), many of the blockages occur in the 'shadow side' of organizations, the non-rational aspects of culture such as interdepartmental rivalry, which Tate suggests are more powerful than the logical hoped-for results expected from job descriptions, policy manuals and other logical aspects of organization. All of these blockages need to be released in order for creativity and innovation to flow through. Tate also suggests that the informal systems, processes and relationships are more likely to prove the springboard for innovation than the more formal aspects, which are 'inherently weak at change and innovation'.

The main barriers to knowledge co-creation and sharing appear to lie within organizational cultures and individual behaviours. In times of change and potential job insecurity, organizational politics become more evident. Organizational politics are increasingly recognized as damaging to trust, which in turn leads people to become risk-averse rather than keen to push back boundaries. When management practice creates a 'blame culture', in which people are penalized for making mistakes as they learn, employees become reluctant to step out of the comfort zone. They prefer to stick to 'safe', established procedures, whether or not these are still relevant. To compound this, when employees stick to procedures without taking broader accountability for their work, managers often become impatient and end up 'micro-managing' – doing other people's jobs instead of their own. The resulting low morale and reduced performance complete the vicious circle.

Many employees lack trust in their organization's leaders at all levels. People simply do not believe that their leaders mean what they say, because chronic problems, such as poor performance management and large amounts of political behaviour, are not tackled.

Not surprisingly, according to managers in the *Management Agenda* survey, some of the main challenges of managing change include retention, achieving buy-in, staying up to speed, embracing change, integrating teams and focusing energy on innovation.

Some important barriers to the co-creation and sharing of new knowledge relate to people's careers and other concerns. In a society where many organizations in recent years have treated employees as dispensable, few employees rely on their employers to safeguard their interests. Developing 'intellectual capital' should be in both the organization's interest and the employees', to further their career advancement. However, these two interests may not always coincide. Employees are often unwilling to spread their good ideas more widely within their organization if it may be at the expense of their own 'uniqueness' and reduce their value as a knowledge expert. Organizations therefore have to recognize employees' legitimate concerns, build more equitable means of sharing the rewards of employees' ideas, protect their career interests, and at the same time facilitate the sharing of good ideas through simple and effective mechanisms. Employees who work with others to develop and share good ideas usually end up with better ideas, from which they too can benefit.

For many people, the main barriers to creativity lie not in their own ability to develop new ideas but in lack of time to reflect and be meditative – often because of over-heavy workloads. Usually there are few or no rewards for innovation. In the knowledge economy, where ideas and expertise represent intellectual capital, organizations that take a short-sighted view about sharing the rewards of creativity risk seeing employees saving their best ideas for other parts of their lives. Conversely, there can be built-in incentives for maintaining the status quo. Ideas imply new ways of doing things, and they may provoke negative reactions from colleagues. For example, a groundbreaking idea for a new product may cause jealousy, while an idea for a new internal process may threaten individual or group vested interests.

Some of the other perceived barriers to innovation and knowledge management are reported by *Management Agenda* respondents:

- Insecurity
- No parameters for experimentation/empowerment
- Weak strategic oversight
- No rewards for knowledge management
- HR is reactive rather than proactive
- There is a general lack of clarity of direction and purpose
- Even if people are initially clear, they lose sight of the goals as things change
- Crisis mentality
- Employees experience work overload
- Stress is commonplace
- There is too much focus on unrealistic targets
- Employees are resistant to change
- Decision-making is slow
- Overload of data, not enough of the right kinds of information
- Risk-averse senior managers
- Employees are told, rather than genuinely consulted
- Difficult to develop and sustain organizational 'glue'.

If an organization wishes radically to galvanize knowledge creation and learning, it must first tackle some of the main cultural obstacles to innovation. In organizations where employees are recognized as 'volunteers' rather than 'wage-slaves', leaders develop policies and organizational arrangements that promote good practice and support employees to do their jobs. They proactively tackle the symptoms of a poor work climate, such as the lack of a teamworking ethos, an ageist culture, lack of diversity, bullying/harassment, political manoeuvring, and lack of quality leadership.

Managers can help reshape organizational culture by identifying the small changes – what Gareth Morgan (1986) calls the 'fifteen per cent' that can unblock the organization. For example, some barriers to creativity occur when a hierarchy operates too rigidly. To break through this barrier, some organizations use 'skip-level' meetings while others bring groups of employees together informally to discuss business challenges and develop ideas for addressing them. Suggestions schemes are also used to help break through managerial layers and enable all employees to share their ideas directly, without a hierarchical filter. Leaders then need to create a sense of urgency, orienting employees to customers and suppliers, and giving autonomy and space to its employees while setting stretch targets.

Enablers of creativity, innovation and learning

According to the CBI/TUC submission to the UK Productivity Initiative (2001):

> Research evidence suggests that new forms of work organisation, effective management and leadership, a culture that encourages innovation, employee involvement and employee development tailored to organisational needs, are all necessary conditions for adaptable, high performance workplaces. Management, leadership and employee involvement are complementary features of the high performance/high commitment model.

The key to fostering creativity in the workplace is a supportive culture that encourages creativity to flourish. Some of the 'small things' that can make a difference to releasing creativity and performance are evident in the *Management Agenda* surveys. Employees are calling for wider availability of flexible work processes, effective teamworking, open and democratic leadership at all levels, the deliberate curbing of political behaviours, innovative career tracks, manageable workloads, and training and development opportunities. In high performance organizations, diversity is not left to chance but is 'mainstreamed' and teamworking is actively encouraged.

People need to be clear about where the organization is going so that they are able to prioritize well. Clear, two-way communications are therefore essential. Employees want effective performance management to take place and managers to have a focus on both people and results. They want managers who can support staff and are trained to coach and enable others by providing structured feedback on a regular basis. They want managers to be rewarded for how well they develop and use the skills of their teams. Developing a 'project' mentality alongside the 'day job' enables fresh ideas to enrich employees' output.

When employees have the opportunity to stretch themselves beyond their comfort zone, working on projects that are of importance to the organization, they enhance their knowledge of the business and their ability to learn.

Innovation cannot be forced out of people; the process is more one of 'happenstance' or emergence, with much depending on chance meetings or social networks. Managers can, however, help create the conditions within which emergent ideas are more likely to appear. This requires leaders at all levels to display a learning orientation. Learning makes it possible for leaders to anticipate the future and even create it, according to Brown and Eisenhardt (1997).

Guidelines for dynamic stability and stimulating innovation

With a learning orientation, innovation is not necessarily the result of expensive projects but can be more low key. Successful managers explore the future by experimenting with a wide variety of low-cost 'probes', which, according to Abrahamson, enhance learning about future possibilities. Abrahamson suggests the following operating guidelines for creating dynamic stability:

1. *Reward shameless borrowing.* By 'shameless borrowing', Abrahamson argues in favour of 'creative imitation'. Unearthing interesting practice within the organization or applying ideas from other organizations, especially when knowledge management systems enable knowledge to be captured, shared and imitated, makes more sense than simply invention for its own sake.
2. *Appoint a Chief Memory Officer.* Abrahamson suggests that companies which forget the past are condemned to relive it (what Kransdorff, 1995, terms 'corporate amnesia'). Successful organizations try to create an atmosphere of learning from both success and failure. By remembering the past but avoiding the mistakes, organizations can get the best out of the present. A Chief Memory Officer can review past projects, successful or unsuccessful, before any 'innovation' is launched.
3. *Tinker and kludge internally first.* Abrahamson refers to Southwest Airlines, which replicates parts of its existing business formula, such as human resource management practices, in new regions, so that other mini-airlines are created and added to the portfolio.
4. *Hire generalists.* Let generalists combine the broad array of different skills, techniques and ideas needed to create dynamic stability. They are 'boundary-spanners', who are likely to have a wide network internally and externally and are able to develop fresh ideas from a range of different sources. In his study of 'great' companies, Jim Collins (2001) points out that companies need to 'get the right people on the bus (and the wrong people off the bus) before you figure out where to drive it'. The old adage 'people are our greatest asset' is wrong; 'the right people are your greatest asset' is more accurate.
5. *Retain key personnel.* This is in order to provide 'organizational memory'. Providing employees with a sense of security can be a mainspring for creativity. Amongst several examples, Collins and Porras (1994) describe how Hewlett and Packard focused on creating an environment conducive to

the creation of great products. They quote Bill Hewlett of Hewlett Packard in an early speech saying:

Before we hired an engineer we made sure he would be operating in a stable and secure climate. We made sure that each of our engineers had a long-range opportunity with the company and suitable projects to work on. Another thing, we made certain that we had adequate supervision so that our engineers would be happy and would be productive to the maximum extent.

Interestingly, the DTI Consultation Paper on High Performance Workplaces (2002) also highlights job security as a key feature of organizations that operate high performance work practices.

6. *Use continual re-evaluation.* There should be continual re-evaluation of progress and future plans throughout the organization. Giving people a sense of progress, so that what is new is not presented as an implied criticism of what went before, helps employees to see the value of new approaches and understand where innovation is needed.

Stimulating creativity

A great deal of creativity occurs spontaneously, is linked with problem-solving and focused on productivity. According to psychologist Alex Osborn, writing in the 1960s, informal conversations with colleagues, contacts or friends provide the most significant source of inspiration for new ideas. Indeed, in the *Management Agenda* surveys, respondents repeatedly report that their best ideas come when they are working in successful, high performing teams.

However, creativity can also be deliberately stimulated. Some companies, such as Shell, create fast-track processes that capture new ideas from employees and progress them through an incubator. In the 1980s, 'skunkworks' were the popular way of legitimizing creative activity within the corporate context, for a few people at least. In the 1990s, many companies created spin-offs around potential innovations, allowing the idea and its originator the chance to flourish.

Senior managers can stimulate creativity in other practical ways. They can recognize and champion knowledge management as a business process, provide some resource for experimentation, make sure that everyone's views are heard, and encourage and praise new ideas. They can reward innovation. Managers often fear that by encouraging creativity they are letting the genie out of the bottle, and that every new idea is likely to undermine well-founded procedures. Where there are no parameters for experimentation and empowerment, this is a reasonable risk. Obviously a shared vision and clear role definitions and areas of responsibility help provide some clarity about where innovation is needed and scope for creativity at the same time, but more precise areas where new ideas would be useful should be specified.

Targeting innovation in areas where it is required makes the creative process controllable and can help managers and teams. The first task is to state clearly the problem requiring a creative solution, such as 'how can we reduce the high cost of production?'. What people find most helpful is, when they have understood the parameters within which innovation is required, that they need some resources (especially time), and be left to 'come up with the goods'. Finally, creative ideas should be screened and evaluated. Some ideas may need an internal 'hard sell' to gain support within the organization; others may be implemented immediately.

Leaders need to encourage employees to initiate tasks they think are important, and give teams, in particular, freedom to find their own solutions to problems. They can create project champions who coordinate the work of teams exploring particular themes. Other useful practices include allowing people to spend some of their time on projects of their own choosing, and letting people spend some of the training budget on learning at their own discretion. Similarly, processes for project evaluation and methods of decision-making should be quick and effective.

Techniques for stimulating creativity and knowledge-sharing

Techniques for stimulating creativity do not of themselves need to be groundbreaking. Indeed, some conventional techniques are most helpful in generating ideas. Brainstorming, where free-flow group discussion can stimulate a significant number of ideas, is one of the standard techniques. Metaphor is at the heart of many creative techniques. Working on disguised problems, because they are represented differently through metaphor, can lead to new and innovative approaches to the situation. Various tools to prompt creative thinking are widely available on the market, such as Oech's 'Creative Whack Pack'.

The 'Lotus Blossom' technique is another way of generating ideas in a group. This method takes a central theme and finds ideas for it. Ideas then flow quickly from one theme to another, with each idea becoming a central theme in its turn – hence the name of the technique. With 'Perspectives', the group generates a list of frameworks to stimulate idea generation. By searching through different perspectives, the group can find similar situations to the present one or a problem parallel to its own challenge. Alternative perspectives can be transferred to a solution for the original problem.

'Mind mapping' can be used by individuals and groups. Developed by Tony Buzan in the 1970s, this is a process that encourages you to let go of boundaries and think expansively. It uses association to make connections between ideas and create a visual network. Brainwriting is a technique in which participants write down several ideas on different pieces of paper, then regularly exchange papers, keying in new ideas from ideas already on the list. No talking is allowed during this process. Another technique involves restating the problem, which often leads to new perspectives on the problem and new approaches that might be more effective in developing a solution. In some cases the best prompt for creative thinking is a field trip or social event, where people's usual ways of thinking and acting are freed up.

Humour can help. Latin cultures in particular deliberately nurture a fun environment at the workplace to override the dead weight of bureaucracy. Ekvall, researching in the 1970s into the ideal context for creativity, lists ten required factors, including a positive climate, freedom, support for ideas, time for experimentation, dynamism, trust and humour. He found that teamworking is vastly enabled if team members share a strong sense of humour.

Rewarding creativity and knowledge creation

In the *Management Agenda* survey (2003), 89 per cent of respondents reported that their organizations have no specific rewards for knowledge management activity or for creative output. Clear performance management systems that provide feedback to front-line teams, and meaningful rewards for knowledge-sharing, knowledge creation and innovation, will stimulate creativity, as will effective review processes. Managers may need training in how to support people in their learning, and be encouraged to create capacity/time to coach people. Non-financial rewards such praise and encouragement of new ideas and giving credit where it is due can be very motivating. An expensive but potentially very productive way of developing profitable ideas is to employ more people and build some slack into the system.

Many people appreciate financial and other rewards for knowledge-sharing, knowledge creation and innovation/creativity, with gain-sharing being a particular favourite. One hi-tech company offers its employees part-ownership of spin-off companies set up to exploit their inventions. Many of its employees are now millionaires, but choose to remain employed because they like being part of a highly profitable 'group' that treats its people well. In Richer Sounds, Britain's largest hi-fi retailer, the suggestion scheme, with a cash bonus of at least £5 for each idea and quirky incentives for the best, has been remarkably successful, producing on average twenty suggestions a year from each employee.

Speed up the flow of ideas

Speed is of the essence in innovation. Information must be timely delivered as lead times for information acquisition among competitors shorten. Information flow needs to be at the right level – enough information of the right quality and timeliness to ensure that people know what is happening, but not so much that people feel bombarded and stop paying attention to messages. Some organizations have institutionally phased out jargon, encouraging plain language so that both their customers and their employees have the information they need.

Effective governance, with appropriate decision-making at the right level, is a vital area where organizations can speed up innovation. Developing effective review processes of task, process and learning can help teams acquire sophisticated skills and knowledge, which can be spread throughout the organization as team members move to work on other projects.

Suggestions schemes

Employee suggestion schemes are standard means of soliciting ideas that can save money, improve processes and boost profits. Organizations that genuinely want to encourage and enable innovation put time and energy into creating multiple ways of involving employees in the development of the organization and its products and services. Upward communication flows are typically provided through employee attitude surveys and staff suggestion schemes. Though somewhat conventional, a good suggestion scheme, implemented within a positive company culture, will enhance communication and be beneficial to all parties. The WERS survey found that problem-solving groups and staff surveys were more likely to be found in workplaces with a personnel specialist in the organization, those with an integrated employee development plan, and those with a recognized union.

> *Example 7.1   The Co-operative Bank*
> The Co-operative Bank introduced a suggestions scheme in 1995 that aimed to fulfil the company objectives to use the skills of the individual for the benefit of the organization. Building on an earlier scheme, the Star Scheme was introduced as part of a wider programme aimed at improving company communication, internal process management and customer service. The first step was to separate the ideas into those that were useful for a particular department and those that had a positive impact on the whole bank. The latter could enter the Star Scheme.
>
> Crucially, the person who comes up with the idea sees it through to completion, taking complete ownership. Suggestions are submitted in writing and then discussed with a line manager, who has to take time to consider the suggestion before making comments. If the suggestion is not considered viable, people are given the rationale immediately. If the idea goes forward, the initiator gets support from his or her divisional administrator, and a Key Contact – a recognized expert in the field in which the suggestion is made. The initiator takes on a quasi-project management role, and has control over the implementation of the suggestion. The team works together to implement the idea and evaluate its success. The initiator is awarded 5 per cent of the first year's proven savings from their suggestion, up to a maximum of £25 000. Successful suggestions have included a money-saving scheme in the fraud department, to reduce waste paper by replacing notepaper with wipe-off cards. About a dozen ideas are seen through the scheme every year, and countless other ideas are successfully implemented within departments (Holt, 2000).

> *Example 7.2   British Telecom*
> BT's suggestion scheme has saved the company £100 million over a four-year period by harnessing employees' ideas. BT ideas provides a formal framework for encouraging staff to be creative, and rewards them for any ideas it uses. If a good idea saves money or generates income, the

originator receives 10 per cent of the savings or additional income up to £30 000. The company also runs an incubator website to allow people to get in touch with other staff for help in developing their ideas.

Training for creativity

Training in creative thinking processes is relevant at different levels in any hierarchy. Managers increasingly see their roles as being about managing ideas, and try to avoid being kept within strict functional boundaries. Indeed, functional boundaries tend to disappear at more senior levels. A key role for managers is supporting people in their learning – having a 'no blame' culture. For this they need to make capacity/time to coach people and offer informal feedback. They can learn how to run effective review processes which enable ideas and learning to be shared amongst work groups.

Executives usually tend to focus on problems, delegating operational decision-making downwards. Senior managers act as interpreters of context and facilitators of change. At senior levels, the ability to sense where innovation is needed and to think strategically is critical. Research into where directors get their ideas from was carried out by Roffey Park in the late 1990s. While team 'Awaydays' can be useful, Roffey Park research found that, at work, directors and senior managers prefer to exchange ideas through professional and industrial networks or private clubs rather than in formal or facilitated events such as boardroom meetings or benchmarking groups, where they might have less control over the agenda and choice of people they share ideas with. Because they tend to shy away from formal programmes, it is likely that their best ideas are rarely captured.

If these informal events are to reach their full potential, participants must be encouraged to suspend their judgement so that a full flow of ideas develops. A skilled facilitator can assist this process. In some companies, executives use facilitators to help manage large-scale interventions such as those described in Chapter 6, which engage large numbers of employees in a strategic/creative activity. Others use arts-based training provided by artists, musicians, storytellers and other professional performers, for example exploring how music and poetry can change moods and unlock creative thinking. The BBC sees leadership development as key to improving the quality of management and boosting creativity across the organization. Anyone responsible for managing more than three people is required to take part, and the leadership programme incorporates BBC values.

Use of space

The connection between the impact of physical space on employees' morale and their creative ability is well known. A number of companies are deliberately designing office space to reflect the nature of the work in hand and to suit the preferences of employees. They are adapting ideas from the outside world, such as cafés, streets, palm trees and ponds, to the enclosed world of the office. They are introducing a new design language of colours and open-plan vistas, specially designed fit-for-purpose spaces, designed to enable creative and productive working.

A multi-national company has incorporated into its UK headquarters rooms of different sizes and shapes, with furniture of different styles and strongly coloured décor to stimulate different creative thinking modes (such as ideas generation, reflection and concentrated/writing), alongside other spaces which are designed to encourage interaction and 'chance' conversations.

Recognizing that some of the best ideas occur when people have the chance to meet, architects are now designing buildings that can engineer such opportunities. British Airways' famous Waterside development, with its 'street' and cafés, is designed to act as a social hub, a place for informal gatherings, and to signal that work can also be pleasurable. Other companies have followed suit, building large atriums filled with plants, water features and other pleasant details intended to create a calm ambience. Even relatively conventional buildings now commonly boast a breakout space on corridors. St Lukes, a London-based advertising agency, has adorned its warehouse-style workplace with signs bearing slogans such as 'Profit is like health – necessary, but not the reason why we live'. St Lukes' cooperative culture is expressed in many ways, including an all-day refectory and a totally silent 'chill-out' room. Brand rooms dedicated to each of the clients of the agency take on the character of the product or service being advertised.

Within the physical space, norms and practices can also be geared to stimulating creativity. At Allied Domecq, one senior brand manager introduced a 'dress appropriately' policy, which means that people can wear casual clothes when it is sensible to do so – especially when this can enhance creativity. An open office policy, where people feel free to share their ideas and receive feedback, is actively practised.

Building knowledge

Knowledge is multifaceted and complex, being both situated and abstract, implicit and explicit, distributed and individual, physical and mental, developing and static, verbal and encoded. For Davenport and Prusak (2003), knowledge is a fluid mix of framed experience, values, contextual information and expert insight that provides a framework for evaluating and incorporating new experiences and information. It originates and is applied in the minds of the knowers. In organizations, it is embedded not only in documents or repositories but also in organizational routines, processes, practices and norms. For Davis and Botkin (1994), knowledge is the application and productive use of information. Knowledge management is the 'systematic and active development of ways to create, use, learn and share knowledge for a strategic purpose' (Funes and Johnson, 1998).

Processes to support knowledge-sharing

Successful firms are aware of the time value of acquiring new skills and knowledge. They strive to create an environment that nurtures and supports innovation, and maximizes knowledge which has been acquired.

Information flow

Whipp *et al.* (1989) suggest that information must be timely delivered as lead times for information acquisition among competitors shorten. Information is shared through a variety of media, such as departmental meetings, conferences, interdepartmental meetings, in-house magazines, company newsletters, and videos. Two-way and effective communication processes are essential to knowledge-sharing. Good chairing of meetings, especially by facilitators, is helpful. Circulating success stories about the use of knowledge to win more business, for example, can motivate others to follow suit.

Most organizations now actively encourage employee use of the Internet, intranet, bulletin boards, e-mail and shared databases. Increasing take-up of a 'knowledge web' so that it is first port of call can be achieved through training and incentives. While good systems are useful where they exist, there is sometimes little buy-in to updating information on the system. One company rectified this problem by penalizing employees who did not put customer information onto the intranet. They restricted access to people who did, causing sales staff (who were dependent on the latest customer data) to be very keen to share what they knew with their colleagues, for fear of losing access to valuable information!

A clear, communicated knowledge management strategy is required to make the most of intellectual capital. HR and other functions can act as 'corporate glue', sharing good practice they have encountered in different parts of the business. Christina Evans (2003) suggests the following tips for HR, IT and Information Management professionals:

1. Understand the value of the information you have – technology has made information more freely available, but the true value of that information is often hidden because of the sheer volume of data
2. Get a better handle on managing information – locate some of the sources of information that people need to do their jobs, such as supplier information, and ensure ease of access to that information
3. Keep it simple – work with real needs
4. Treat managing knowledge as a task that has a deliverable and therefore requires an allocation of time
5. Provide basic tools and train people in how to use them
6. Learn from other people's mistakes
7. Ensure that new knowledge management systems interface with existing systems.

Create and maintain a knowledge base

As knowledge is generated, it needs to be captured and made accessible to others. A flexible organization needs to create and maintain a flexible knowledge base within the organization. For Whipp *et al.* (1989), building this environment involves movement away from functional adherence towards greater identification with organizational goals. In such a context, cross-functional groups and project teams spread good practice around the organization. Such organizations tend to have flat structures, fewer middle managers, a delegated style and limited support functions.

Organizations that are successful at managing for knowledge ensure that they have processes by which different creative initiatives can be joined up. Increasingly, this is achieved through IT systems, many of which evolve in stages and do not always provide a single source of information which all staff can access. Often this is because the original investment decisions were taken at a time when the technology was less fit for purpose, but usually the main reason is a lack of understanding by senior managers of the potential uses of the system, or they have delegated choice of system to IT specialists who may have less of an understanding of overall business requirements, present and future.

If IT is to be used strategically as a flexible knowledge base, senior management must become familiar with the use of technology and how it fits into the development of the organization. There also needs to be a move towards strategy-led technology, rather than abdicating technology decisions to functional specialists. It is important to examine the feasibility of adapting existing systems to provide just-in-time knowledge, making sure that any new knowledge management systems address a real need. When introducing new systems in a complex organization, it is also vital to pilot them with a small but representative user-group. As the system goes live, appropriate information requires 'information-literate' managers to access and organize data. Training is usually essential for all users to ensure that the system is used effectively.

Example 7.3   PPP Healthcare

PPP Healthcare has been keen to use the corporate intranet as springboard for knowledge-enhancing practices. All staff within Customer Services work on a shift system, in teams of about fifteen, including a team manager. Given the size of the department and the shift patterns operated within it, staff operate a hot-desking arrangement. Before the introduction of the intranet, staff had to gather together all the (copious) documentation needed to do their job and take this to whatever desk they were using.

Since its introduction, not only does the intranet act as a central filing cabinet for key information, but this information is also available in a more accessible and up-to-date format. As the intranet's main purpose was to enable communication across the organization, the intranet project team wanted to create a system that would provide a knowledge-sharing tool that cuts across formal boundaries. It also wanted to create a sense of community across PPP Healthcare's 2000-plus employees.

To encourage usage, the project team created a 'free-time' area containing social information, to complement information that staff needed to access for their work. The 'free-time' area initially contained information such as menus for the staff restaurant, horoscopes, local and national weather reports etc., as well as information about the company's staff discount scheme. In addition to the 'free-time' area, department-specific information is held on the intranet. Customer Service, for example, has an area that contains pictures of colleagues who are based in India. This has enabled UK staff to get a better sense of their culture and enhanced teamworking across organizational boundaries (Evans, 2003).

Storytelling

In order for knowledge and learning to be shared and re-used, it first has to be surfaced. Storytelling, amongst oral history techniques, is gaining popularity. English Nature, for instance, has used storytelling techniques to complete 'lessons learnt' projects. One concerned a Public Inquiry. The storytelling project revealed some important insights into how the project team, set up to represent English Nature, had been formed (i.e. the team selection process). It also explored how the team organized themselves for the task they had to do, how they identified the knowledge gaps within the team and how they then filled those gaps. It also detailed valuable insights into the sensitive issues faced by the team and how the team resolved these. The material unearthed by the project included many previously unrecorded tips and techniques which have provided fruitful learning materials that are now a resource on the organization's media and public inquiry training courses (Evans, 2002).

Deal and Kennedy (2000) distinguish between 'robust' and 'toxic' cultures. Storytelling and the role of networks in transmitting culture through the stories they tell differ in their impact. In robust cultures, informal networks can reinforce the basic beliefs of the organization, enhance the symbolic value of heroic exploits by passing on stories of their deeds and accomplishments, set a new climate for change, and provide a tight structure of influence for the CEO. In toxic cultures, the network becomes a formidable barrier to change. The tales storytellers tell, like myths in a tribal setting, give meaning to the workaday world. For the corporation, storytellers maintain cohesion and provide guidelines for people to follow. Storytelling is one of the most powerful ways to convey information and shape behaviour.

Build in some slack

Organizational systems and processes send out powerful signals about what the company stands for and values. These should encourage behaviour that the company really wants rather than leaving good practice to chance. If innovation and knowledge management are important, they should receive some time and priority. Some of the more innovative companies do this. A well-known 3M policy is to enable all technical staff to spend 15 per cent of their time on projects of their own. In practice, take-up varies, with some people taking less and others more time working on their own projects. What is important is the message that the organization has some slack built in, which enables some freedom of movement.

Managers need to help people manage the ever-increasing workloads of today. Regular reviews of workloads enable employees to stop doing some things, so that other things can be developed. At the same time, individuals need to develop a disciplined action plan that helps them to focus on the things that will make a difference to their organization's success.

Team Awaydays provide the opportunity to share ideas about how to work 'smarter not harder', and some organizations experiment with 'e-mail free' days and other protocols which restrict the use of e-mail to essential purposes. Of course, one solution that seems a little unlikely but may be the best answer is simply to employ more people!

Reduce bureaucracy

Management-led initiatives to reduce unnecessary bureaucracy, such as KPMG's 'Darwin' project, can result in employee time being freed up for client work, building business ideas and profitability. This innovative approach focuses on eliminating unnecessary administrative processes which get in the way of client work. In large organizations, the demands of bureaucracy can almost kill off teams' ability to be creative. John Whatmore's (1993) research into the leadership of creative groups found that managers who were able to act as a 'shield', protecting their team from the organizational pressure to conform, were most likely to see teams producing creative results.

When MTV, Viacom's music channel, was launched, the idea was that the company would recruit inexperienced people and engage them in creative projects. The company tried to clear away all forms of bureaucracy to let them focus on the creative process. The business managers who were attached to creative departments were authorized to make large capital purchases, to prevent lots of form-filling and lengthy authorization procedures slowing down the creative process. This resulted not only in high generation of creative outputs, but also the lowest staff turnover rate in the industry.

Creating a learning community

Companies that are better at creating, acquiring and spreading knowledge help employees put that knowledge into action. If organizations are to create and support a learning and information-sharing orientation, certain conditions need to be in place. First there needs to be a knowledge-friendly culture. Then there has to be a reward system for sharing knowledge, otherwise employees would have little incentive for sharing their ideas, especially in a context where 'knowledge is power'. Finally, there need to be multiple channels for knowledge transfer, especially encouragement of personal contact across work groups. There are many business advantages to be gained. One study of 158 global companies in North America, Europe and Asia found that those which had designed organizations to manage knowledge more systematically and effectively had major benefits in terms of product improvements, faster speed to market, increased market share, improved sales volume and cost reductions and avoidance (McLagan, 2003).

Action learning

Learning organizations use learning to reach their goals. Learning is happening continuously through action learning processes rather than being limited to re-evaluating change efforts once a year. First championed by Revens (1983), action learning has become widespread, with variations like self-managed learning stemming from this source. Based on the relatively simple principle that learning is about recognizing what we don't know rather than what we do know, action learning involves participants meeting in small groups, with or without a facilitator. Group members ask each other questions about how they see the problems that are being considered – the idea is that each participant acts as a mirror to help the group recognize what it doesn't know. The learning should be self-managed, is usually project-based, and focuses on finding a solution internally rather than seeking external help from 'experts'.

At an organizational level, benefits of active learning approaches are:

- Retention of key personnel to provide 'organizational memory'
- Management development that is used to communicate core values as well as develop skills
- Continual re-evaluation of progress and future plans throughout the organization.

Teams are encouraged to learn from experience by reviewing what has worked or not, and why. The organization is then able to regulate its course as it goes, adjusting the speed and effectiveness as it learns how to change. Cross-functional team or group-based projects allow people with different disciplines to learn from each other and spread good practice across the organization. Reflection becomes part of the 'way we do things around here', and is built into the implementation of strategic change. Through this process, according to Rowden (2001), people question the original assumptions and search for deep, system ('double-loop') solutions to problems.

Cross-functional teams

It is often said that breakthrough discoveries are more likely to arise in circumstances where different elements are brought together than when the elements are the same or similar. Similarly, in human organizations, bringing together people with different skills and backgrounds can enrich the creative process, and encourage new ideas and the transfer of good practice across the organization.

For Whipp *et al.* (1989), the key to achieving and sustaining strategic flexibility is the active management of the internal and external relations involved. This requires managers to create cross-disciplinary teams that maximize the strengths the business needs. The cultivation of internal networks is a key means of integrating functions and operating units.

It is becoming evident that teams will increasingly be cross-functional, cross-hierarchical and multidisciplinary, giving rise to greater interaction, communication and information flows. Flexible employees, able to cross over between functional specializations, will move away from functional adherence towards greater identification with organizational goals.

Communities of practice

Some companies already encourage the development of communities of practice, which transcend organizational boundaries and cause an effective interplay of new thinking between professional colleagues.

Communities of practice (CoPs) are 'groups of people informally bound together by shared expertise and passion for a joint enterprise – engineers engaged in deep-water drilling, for example' (Wenger and Snyder, 2000). According to these authors, CoPs can drive strategy, generate new lines of business, solve problems, promote the spread of best practice, develop people's professional skills, and help companies recruit and retain talent. Communities of practice are informal – they organize themselves, set their own agendas and membership is self-selected.

Typically, such communities are cross-organizational, although some can exist within single business units. Each has a core of participants whose passion for the topic energizes the community and provides intellectual and social leadership. In Daimler-Chrysler, 'tech clubs' composed of experts from different car platforms helped the company move successfully to platforms of change that cut R&D costs and car development cycle times by more than half.

The organic, spontaneous nature of such communities makes them resistant to supervision or interference. Instead, 'successful managers bring the right people together, provide an infrastructure in which communities can thrive, and measure the communities' value in non-traditional ways'. One way to strengthen communities of practice is to provide them with official sponsors and support teams to provide resources and coordination. Non-traditional ways of measuring value include collecting members' stories, which can clarify the complex relationship among activities, knowledge and performance. At Shell, such stories are published in newsletters and reports. As communities generate knowledge they renew themselves, especially as, through learning together, members can make their own work easier or more effective.

Use of e-learning and online communities

E-learning is gradually gaining currency as a preferred means of delivering just-in-time development which can be tailored to individual needs. Often used in conjunction with other methods, 'blended' learning should enable people with different learning preferences and work pressures to learn in the way most suited to their needs. In addition, such approaches can be very cost-effective.

A learning community is an online environment supporting and facilitating a community of learners as they go through specific programmes and connect and network thereafter. Typically they consist of many people engaged in a common learning process, with access to relevant resources and facilitation by 'experts' who moderate discussions or provide answers. They are often supported by news and other forms of learning events, and have little or no direction on the part of members. International organizations often prefer to support classroom development of high flyers with, between modules, interactive online elements that further and embed learning and workplace application. Many universities and business schools have adopted use of online communities to support their qualification programmes, and they are increasingly being adopted to support corporate leadership development programmes.

Networks

As organizational boundaries become more permeable, greater value is placed on the sharing of information vital to competitive performance. Successful organizations encourage the development of networks – internal and external – as a means of stimulating 'connectivity' and intra- and inter-organizational learning. Such learning contributes to strategic thinking and to changing behaviour.

Example 7.4   Allied Domecq
In the drinks company Allied Domecq, a high-level think tank known as 'Adventure' was dreamt up in 1994 by Paul Wielgus, a manager at the company. Adventure consists of a small group of 'innovation zealots' who network with other like-minded individuals within the company. The network can put people in touch with people with different or related views. It also supports people who have good ideas that are not making progress. The network idea has now spread within the company, and has helped spark many of the product innovations that have benefited the business (Pickard, 1996).

Example 7.5   The City Leadership Forum
In the City of Brighton and Hove in the UK, a variety of networks exist within the local council and beyond it. The City Leadership Forum is a voluntary development partnership that has sprung up in a self-organizing way. It provides management and leadership briefings for managers in most social service and voluntary organizations, as well as for other public sector bodies such as the NHS, the police, the probationary service and the law courts who serve the local community. One of the Forum's initiatives was the development of a successful inter-organizational mentoring scheme.

Diversity

Many research studies suggest that organizations with a diverse and multicultural workforce are more likely to generate innovative solutions to problems than monocultural organizations, since diversity should give organizations access to different ideas, approaches and fresh perspectives. Equal opportunities and managing for diversity are therefore key business issues. A central feature in the mix is the adoption of an inclusive management style that encourages workers at all levels of the organization to contribute.

Diversity is reported in the *Management Agenda* as noticeable for its absence in many organizations. While diversity policies may exist, management and HR practices often perpetuate monocultural identities. When asked how long their organization had treated equality and diversity seriously as a business priority, *Management Agenda's* replies were as follows:

- Those reporting 'ten years or longer' included 22 per cent from the public sector, 19 per cent from the private sector, and 24 per cent from the not-for-profit sector
- Those reporting that their organization does not treat diversity seriously included 9 per cent from the public sector, 22 per cent from the private sector and 17 per cent from not-for-profit organizations.

Ironically, though the public sector is expected to role-model good employment practice to other sectors, it would seem that policies alone are not enough to ensure more than compliance with the letter of the law. Embracing the spirit of the law is something else. For instance, when people were asked to say if they thought that barriers existed to inhibit women's progress into senior management in their organizations, 51 per cent of public sector respondents said 'yes', while 35 per cent of private sector and 27 per cent of not-for-profit respondents agreed. With regard to ethnic minorities, barriers to inhibit progress into senior management were perceived to be strong in 48 per cent of public sector organizations, compared with 24 per cent of private sector and 40 per cent of not-for-profit organizations.

The *Management Agenda*, and Roffey Park focus groups, suggest that many of the real barriers to equality and diversity are to be found in HR practices, such as recruitment, promotion and succession planning, where the tendency to 'clone' and perpetuate the existing cultural and gender mix at senior levels is commonplace. Similarly, 'unfriendly' cultures with fixed working arrangements, long hours and inflexibility, lack of cross-cultural awareness and vested interests tend to work against diversity. Often described as 'the permafrost layer', manager attitudes can also effectively work against diversity.

Managing for diversity

A healthy workplace has a culture where individuals are valued. Diversity is essentially about valuing different offerings. *Management Agenda* respondents suggest that in such organizations:

- Diversity is actively managed, not left to chance
- Existing promotion and appointment practices are challenged to ensure that they are fair.

Executives and HR need to make and communicate the business case for diversity. They need to set and sell goals and targets, hold managers accountable for these, and change the organizational culture to embrace diversity. Ingham (2003) suggests that when implementing a diversity policy, it is important first to analyse your business environment, internally and externally, to see how diverse your employee base is, and whether it reflects the customer base. Then it is important to define diversity and its possible organizational benefits, such as an improved external image and becoming an employer of choice through the development of its employee value proposition (EVP). The diversity policy should be integrated into the corporate strategy and woven into the organization's values. Staff at all levels need to be involved in diversity, through initiatives such as setting up diversity councils and diversity action groups. The policy needs to be communicated internally and externally, with regular updates, and through a variety of media.

Diversity should be embedded into core HR processes and systems. Some external help may be required to kick-start the process. Examples of approaches used by a variety of public and private sector organizations to achieve greater diversity include:

- Policy development
- Equalities monitoring, including turnover and the reasons why people leave
- Levelling up the workforce through positive action, active recruitment and development of relationships, and investing in the under-represented groups within the current workforce at low levels
- Ensuring that Diversity/Equal Opportunities are integrated across the whole range of activities, from business planning to induction and performance management
- Management development for the whole workforce and for disadvantaged groups
- Recruiting high flyers from under-represented groups
- Supporting people so that they do not feel isolated
- Diversity sessions which raise awareness of the interpersonal and organizational processes that may promote or undermine equality
- Printing business cards in large print and Braille
- Encouraging members of under-represented groups into senior positions, using mentors and shadowing
- Use of diversity 'champions'
- Bringing 'success stories' to the forefront
- Introducing remote working
- Evaluation, including benchmarking progress at regular intervals, which should enable progress to be measured and success stories circulated.

The HR role in creating a knowledge-rich context for innovation

HR can help develop working practices and management approaches that are conducive to breakthrough ideas, as well as continuous improvement. It is in the nature of innovation that there is a high degree of failure, risk, uncertainty and complexity. Developing new behaviour patterns among those involved can take time. Weak strategic oversight, organizational politics, a blame culture and risk-averse senior managers are only some of the blockers of innovation and learning. Leaders in particular have a key role to play in leading rather than supervising, providing clarity of direction and parameters within which experimentation is encouraged.

HR can champion good practice by stimulating teamworking, acting as 'corporate glue' and sharing good practice. HR can also play a pivotal role in building the foundations for innovation through developing effective policies for diversity. HR can work with line management and IT specialists to develop effective systems for capturing and disseminating knowledge. HR specialists can use their knowledge of ergonomics to influence the design of physical space to support knowledge working, a classic example of which was the Waterside development for British Airways, with its central 'street' layout and café-style meeting spaces designed to encourage informal interaction and knowledge-sharing.

HR specialists can role model good practice and contribute to reducing bureaucracy by making HR processes simpler and encouraging line managers to review workloads to make them more manageable. They can train people in creative thinking processes, and ensure that work is structured to include the whole task – resulting is greater flexibility, broader experience and wider career paths. HR can build financial and other rewards for knowledge-sharing, and link individual performance to organizational performance.

Conclusion

The leader's actions have a strong effect on the beliefs and expectations of the work group. According to Cannon (2003), leaders build productive climates by shaping culture over the longer term while simultaneously impacting on climate through individual leadership practices. On the whole, innovation appears to thrive in a relatively egalitarian, status-free context, where participative styles of management are the order of the day and where teams develop their own processes without strong control by management. This means establishing dialogue between the different groups and individuals within the business, creating a shared vision and objectives based on the success of the enterprise, and committing to work together constructively to achieve that success.

Innovation is likely to thrive in a context where diversity is enabled and people feel valued. Managing for diversity should be seen as a business issue. HR can work at ensuring that diversity is not left to chance by building the business case for diversity, selling and setting goals and targets, and holding managers accountable for these. Leaders, especially those at the top of organizations, need to really understand and provide long-term commitment to the implementation of diversity policies. They need to measure the impact of diversity on business performance. The diversity policy should be integrated into the corporate strategy and woven into the organization's values. Unless organizations are able to embrace and make the most of the creative potential of a diverse workforce, they are likely to be left out in the cold in an ever-harsher economic landscape.

Checklist: Developing new routines

- Does our culture support innovative ideas?
- What do we need to do more of?
- What do we need to do less of, or stop?
- What new behaviours do we need?
- What enablers can we use?
- How can we share experiences and learn fast?
- What things do we do well, which core capabilities are we good at, that can be strengthened further through continuous improvement?
- Which problem areas and failure points do we wish we could eliminate?
- How can we align our innovation strategy with overall business strategy?
- How can we embed new routines into the organization?
- How can we acquire external sources of knowledge?
- How can we generate our own (technical) competence in-house?
- Are systems and controls used for checking people's work accuracy kept to the minimum?
- Does our reward strategy encourage equally both those who generate fresh ideas and those who develop them into products?
- Do we have slack built into the system?
- Have we actively reduced the amount of bureaucracy to the minimum?

Section 3: The Boundaryless Organization

8

Working across boundaries

Introduction

Are the days of the stand-alone organization numbered? With global competition, technological advances and the demands of the customer for better, cheaper, faster solutions delivered around the clock, few organizations can maintain competitive advantage without acquiring new means of production, distribution or access to talent. High performance requires cross-boundary working.

Strategic alliances, virtual working and e-enablement are only some of the ways in which work boundaries are being traversed. As corporate and geographical boundaries are crossed, so employees are exposed to different cultures and values and need to be able to develop new ways of working. This is also the case when functional and other workplace boundaries are crossed with the help of technology. In the following chapter we shall explore how work can effectively cross geographic and technological boundaries.

The increasing fluidity of organizational forms provides many opportunities for employees to work with people in ways that can unleash potential, creativity and learning. In a very real sense, working across boundaries leads to a rich diversity of experience for those involved and can be the source of new ideas and practices. Ashkenas *et al.* (1998) have identified a number of the boundaries – functional, corporate, cultural, geographic and mindset – across which work can take place. In the UK, crossing sector boundaries is becoming increasingly commonplace.

Crossing corporate boundaries

In some organizations, employees work across internal boundaries as a matter of course – in cross-functional teams tackling major projects, for example. With the growth of global teams, many employees find themselves working with people who they may rarely or never see because of geographical separation. As strategic needs change, project teams may migrate to an entirely separate business unit. Employees may join teams made up of people working on various forms of contract and flexible working arrangements, and have to learn how to share information effectively. Managers then have the challenge of managing teams of people, only some of whom are physically co-located or working during the same period.

One of the commonest ways of fuelling growth in the last two decades has been through merger and acquisition. Mergers push back organizational boundaries in a significant way, and control is relatively clear-cut. For employees in acquired companies, who are usually required to make the more major adjustments to a new corporate culture, the nature of the boundaries being crossed is in high profile. In the early years of this millennium, general merger activity appeared to slow down in many sectors, with a 26 per cent reported reduction in global merger and acquisition activity in 2002. Nevertheless, cross-border merger activity appears to be on the increase, with international direct investment expanding fast.

However, an even more significant workplace trend is the increase in the numbers of organizations engaged in some form of strategic alliance with other organizations. In this chapter we shall look more particularly at this fastest growing form of cross-boundary working.

The growth of strategic alliances

Strategic alliances are shaping the landscape of the twenty-first century and are becoming a strategy of choice because they can be quicker to set up than mergers and are more flexible. Strategic alliances are relationships between two or more organizations to meet shared goals. They are created to meet a common need, whether this is to learn from each other or to fulfil a specific market requirement. They can be short-lived, or last for many years.

The growth of this trend is reflected in Roffey Park's *Management Agenda* surveys. In recent years respondents have reported strategic alliances to be the fastest growing trend for their organization, with 86 per cent of respondents' organizations involved in strategic alliances to varying degrees in 2004. Of these, 93 per cent are working with a significant number of alliances – anything between two and ten partners. The commonest form of alliance is joint venture (64 per cent). In joint ventures, employees generally remain employed by their parent company. Sometimes they are transferred to the new entity whether they like it or not.

Types of strategic alliance

As organizational boundaries become more permeable, various forms of partnering replace old customer–supplier relationships. Whatever the sector, few businesses will remain untouched by alliance activity as corporate boundaries become less distinct and stable. Companies are increasingly operating within a cluster of partner companies, with different sides of the core business becoming a shared boundary with another business. The buzzword is 'partnering' – a tough concept for employees who have been expected to compete with companies they are now expected to partner.

Alliances can be formal arrangements (e.g. legally constituted joint ventures, public–private partnerships, strategic outsourcing) or more informal agreements to work together (e.g. cross-boundary working between government departments, informal collaboration between communities of practice, small firms' networks, community groups etc.).

In the public sector, employees may be working in partnering arrangements with outsourced suppliers, or collaborating with other public and voluntary sector bodies to achieve a common task. For example, it is increasingly common for NHS Trusts to work in partnership with local authorities and social care providers to combine efforts in providing care for the elderly.

Alliances cross sectors. They can bring together public and private sector bodies through public–private partnerships (PPPs) or private finance initiatives (PFIs) in major infrastructure projects such as roads and transport systems. In the survey, 55 per cent of respondents' organizations were involved in public–private partnerships to some extent.

Given this backdrop, employees will increasingly have to navigate their working life through different forms of alliance. Some of these will be with competitors, while others will be with customers or suppliers. Some will be highly structured, while others will be informal, yet important. Some may be tightly coupled to the core business and others more loosely. Some will have clearly defined goals and outcomes. Others might focus on less tangible outcomes, such as acquiring new managerial or strategic capabilities.

Why alliances can be difficult to manage

Alliances can be vulnerable because, against a backdrop of competition, they require an extra degree of commitment and cooperation from a wide range of individuals and groups of employees. They operate on the basis of shared governance or ownership. Unlike a merger, where the ownership is usually clear, alliances often call for constant bargaining, managing expectations, handling conflict and building consensus. For many managers whose experience has been within more conventional forms of organization, these skills may be underdeveloped.

As Knell and Harding (2000) argue:

The partnership agenda is only loosely embedded in UK workplaces, and is far from a ubiquitous feature of UK industrial relations. The relations between the social partners – trade unions, government and employers – are central to productivity and performance. But at present they display the classic symptoms of networked animosity, with the government acting as referee between unpredictable, unchanging positions on both sides.

Similarly, though workers in alliances may be drawn from different organizations, management responsibilities and accountabilities cross organizational boundaries. In construction and civil engineering projects, for instance, specialists such as quantity surveyors, architects, designers and construction engineers work alongside the people who actually construct the building, who may be employed directly by the main contractor, or may be employed by subcontractors. Nevertheless, the main contractor supervising the project remains responsible for health and safety on the project, and the manager in charge at site level carries personal responsibility for ensuring that safe working practices are used.

For employees, these cross-boundary ways of working are not always straightforward. People involved in cross-boundary working experience a shift away from familiar ways of working, with clear lines of authority and loyalties, to something much more ambiguous and potentially contested. Outsourced public sector employees often find themselves working for a private sector employer, with different modes of operation and, perhaps, value-sets. Alliances call for a whole different way of thinking about the workplace – where collaboration and competition need to coexist. Alliances need to develop their own cultures, which are often different from either of the parent cultures.

Alliances involve ambiguous and complex lines of control. In a joint venture (JV), employees from the partner companies may remain employed by their respective organizations and be on very different terms and conditions. Their reporting lines and loyalties may be to their parent organization, rather than the joint venture. In one joint venture we studied, employees working in the JV shared the same building but were given different rights of access to information, systems and even the canteen. Developing a common identity and purpose in such a situation can be difficult. Not surprisingly, 42 per cent of alliance employees in our Agenda survey considered lack of trust to be an area of difficulty.

Management practices and employee attitudes and behaviours may adjust relatively slowly to these more fluid arrangements. Since a single company will increasingly operate around a set of strategies that govern its various alliances, that company will become defined more by its single over-arching strategic intent than by its structures and operations. Executive teams will need to acquire skills in Strategic Alliance strategy, formation and management so that the 'right' partners and approach are chosen. Individuals working in alliances will need to understand how alliance strategy feeds into their company's strategy. As yet, there appears to be little training available to equip employees for working in partnering arrangements.

Because alliances are more fluid than other organizational forms, employees are usually working under greater uncertainty than in more fixed organizational forms. Consequently, key individuals working in a joint venture may seek to return to the parent company if they feel their career interests are better served elsewhere. At a business level, alliances are based on a shared commitment between partners. Roffey Park's annual *Management Agenda* survey found that maintained partner commitment was the single biggest factor affecting success. If one partner loses interest or faith in the alliance, the whole venture can be in jeopardy.

That alliances are difficult to manage well is evident in the comment of one (successful) joint venture manager:

> *You wouldn't do a joint venture if you could avoid it. It complicates things, slows things down. Organizations have different objectives, as do individuals.*

An individual's own objectives will overcome loyalty to a joint venture. The biggest single impediment to a joint venture going forward is individual egos. Getting consensus is time-consuming and it's difficult to deliver shareholder value to two sets of shareholders.

The reality for many organizations and employees is that genuine partnering is difficult to achieve, for a host of reasons, and that many strategic alliances, however sensible their objective, fail within a short period.

Most problems or causes of failure seem to stem from the neglect of the alliance relationship and from inappropriate behaviours of people. Alliance partners inevitably bring their own longer-term agenda to the relationship, so a degree of conflict is inherent in the relationship. Rather than hoping such conflict can be avoided, the aim should be to build the alliance around common ground and develop good processes for resolving differences. Perhaps because of the inevitable tensions in an alliance, it is the relationships between individuals that make this organizational form function.

The importance of the alliance relationship

The importance of relationships to the success of alliances is underlined by Spekeman *et al.* (1996):

It would be a mistake to view an alliance as only a business relationship which moves through its life cycle. Without exception, our findings show clearly that an alliance is a complex interaction of business and interpersonal activities whose purpose is to achieve mutually beneficial goals. Both the business and interpersonal activities are essential ingredients and both must be attended to. Focus on one activity to the exclusion of the other is to cause the alliance to unravel.

Individual behaviours and actions have a direct influence on the alliance relationship and the success of the alliance. Roffey Park's research into the human implications of strategic alliances discovered that if the alliance is to succeed, commitment and good personal relationships at a variety of levels are needed to fill the gaps where formal processes and structures may not exist. Commitment depends on the building and maintenance of mutual trust.

Two of the key roles in making alliances successful are the 'champion' and the 'alliance manager'. Senior champions are vital at an early stage, but also in sustaining corporate commitment to the alliance. Top managers set the tone. For example, if top managers adopt a 'not invented here' attitude, this will be echoed by staff in general. Conversely, if top managers are determined to enable people to work together effectively, they can role-model trust and collaboration. The alliance manager is operationally responsible, providing the 'glue' for the alliance, working between partners and representing all interests.

One chief executive of a joint venture whose employees remained employed by their respective parent companies hosted monthly social get-togethers for all staff. These informal gatherings allowed employees from the two organizations to get to know each other, share ideas and be updated on the progress of the alliance. The sharing of relevant information is critical to partners' ability to deliver their part of the alliance. The more information is shared, the higher the level of trust. However, people also need to be clear about information that they need to protect.

The alliance relationship should receive as much attention as the business process during the formation stage. The nature of the relationship should be explored, and strategies and processes put in place for managing and monitoring the relationship during implementation.

The role of the alliance manager is often pivotal in helping an alliance to succeed. Alliance managers need to be capable of juggling different and potentially competing interests – both managing the alliance itself and relationships with all stakeholders; both working within the formal structure and going beyond it.

Alliances bring employees face to face with cultural differences between the partner organizations. One organization's approach may be to build trust, while the other's may be to control through tight governance and managerial mechanisms. One partner may have formal, clear structures, while the other may have informal, *ad hoc* arrangements for achieving collaboration. One may prescribe goals explicitly, while the other may let goals emerge implicitly. One partner may exchange information in a generous way, or bargain, while the other may be withholding. In one organization the dominant discourse may be consensus, while in the other it is 'creative conflict'. One parent may have a very dominant, 'one-way' culture, while the other may tolerate subcultures. Whatever the differences, successful alliances demonstrate an alliance 'spirit' – key interpersonal relationships reflecting trust, communication, perspective taking, rapport-building and commitment.

The ability to partner

Employees working in alliances will need to have (or develop) 'partnering' skills which enable them to thrive in situations that straddle the competitive/collaborative divide. As they start to work in alliances, employees have to be prepared to shed old certainties and to embrace ambiguity. What can help cross-boundary teams to work is where team members are optimistic about the opportunities implicit in new ways of working, rather than focusing mainly on the problems, and where they have the desire to make something positive happen, whatever the difficulties. According to Butler (2000), 'they must "get it" and believe passionately that the world is changing and that they want to be part of it'.

Team members will need to have the ability to build and extend their own expertise by working with people who see the world differently from the way they do. They need to enjoy experimenting, working with ambiguity and at great speed. In establishing such teams it is important to ensure that each individual, as well as the team as a whole, has a strong sense of urgency and a shared purpose, together with clear goals. Roles should be clear and communicated to the team and people who will be interacting with it. Levels of decision-making and communication need to be agreed. New ways of working, new approaches and monitoring systems need to be established.

When cross-boundary teams work together, they learn rapidly and acquire a wide array of highly valuable and sophisticated skills and knowledge. In many cases, when teams are dispersed after their task has been completed, the rich learning evaporates as team members revert to their former roles. A real significant business challenge is to provide opportunities for employees with expertise in cross-boundary working to share their knowledge with the broader organization. This not only minimizes the cost of having to continuously reinvent the wheel but also enables the organization and its employees to grow strategic capability.

Managers need to make fine judgements about how to behave, what style of management to adopt and when, and decide whether, and to what extent, to share information with partners. They also need a sound grasp of their company's strategic priorities in order to help them to deal effectively with key issues. However, this commercial understanding alone is not enough. At an organizational and personal level, alliance players have to work hard at establishing cooperation and rapport, yet always be mindful that an alliance is, at its core, a temporary business agreement between two separate commercial ventures with their own interests and priorities. They therefore need flexibility, sensitivity and clarity of purpose to help them overcome innumerable tensions and differences with their alliance counterparts.

In the Roffey Park research, we found that the more successful alliance managers were willing to build trust by, amongst other things, taking judicious risks in sharing privileged information with managers from the other partner company (we called this 'gifting'). This seemed to lead to reciprocal sharing and a common sense of purpose.

Key elements in making strategic alliances work

Roffey Park research looking at a range of case study alliances (Garrow *et al.*, 2000) focused on the set-up phase and its impact on subsequent working relationships. Sorting out the contractual and mechanical aspects of an alliance can cause tensions in the emerging alliance relationship, and may even be better done by different managers from those who will actually be making the alliance work. The research found several sets of factors that were important in influencing the effectiveness of alliance working, as shown in Figure 8.1.

This model highlights the importance of:

- Establishing some early behavioural and process ground rules so the alliance can begin to operate
- The part played by senior sponsors or champions of the alliance in setting the tone during the set-up phase

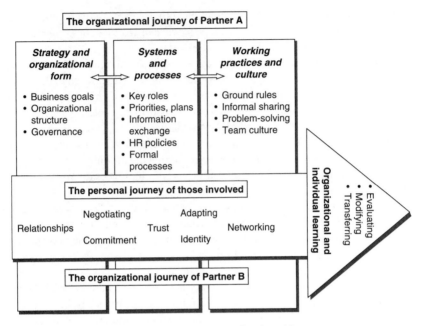

Figure 8.1 Strategic alliances – the organizational journey.

- The interaction of organizational forms and management processes (often 'top down') with the emergent working culture of the alliance (often established in a 'bottom up' way)
- The ability of alliances which involve close working to evolve a culture of their own – different from those of the parent organizations
- The 'personal journeys' of those involved and the skills needed by alliance managers and alliance teamworkers, including a consciousness of their own learning.

Alliance partners need to understand each others' objectives and pursue 'win–win' solutions, which often involve compromise. High-level objectives need to be translated into clear, short-term goals at team and individual level. If clear objectives have been set, alliance partners should then have criteria by which they will measure success. A balance is required between formal management processes and the emerging 'spirit' of the alliance. Too much bureaucracy at an early stage signals a lack of trust and stifles innovation. Unexpected synergy can occur if people remain open to new opportunities. A good way of working towards a shared culture is to establish behavioural 'ground rules' which describe how people will deal with each other.

Key behaviours and actions for effective alliance working

Alliance working seems to require a more informal and open personal style of leadership than the conventional model in large, hierarchical organizations.

This is one way of showing that problems will not be hidden and that individuals are encouraged to use their initiative to act. According to HR Development Manager, Colin Brown (Pickard, 2001), key lessons from Abbey National's partnering experience include picking the right partners, having a very open style of communication, ensuring proper training and resources for managers, recruiting managers who can establish and maintain relationships with new groups of people, and learning how to get the right balance between close working relationships and looser ties. According to Morrison and Mezentseff (1997), the leader acts as teacher, designer, steward and coordinator.

Key behaviours for effective alliance working include: building personal relationships, understanding the partner's needs, negotiating for success, managing differences, operational effectiveness, communication, and information-sharing. Most of the skills needed in alliances are those increasingly required for teamworking within organizations. They include broad business understanding, and managing complexity. Alliance workers, especially alliance managers, also require a high level of emotional resilience. They can feel they are giving a lot of emotional energy to the alliance, which their own organization may or may not see.

Drawing on the Roffey Park research into many types of strategic alliance suggests that the following behaviours are helpful:

1. *Show serious commitment to the alliance at the highest level.*
   - Senior managers giving up the 'trappings of power' – formality, positional power, 'my budget' etc.
   - Minimize blame, maximize problem-solving, use political discretion
   - 'Don't be pompous, be patient'
   - Be open to new ideas
   - Be personally accessible if needed by others
   - Have no hidden agendas
   - Trust each other to tell it how it is
   - Act on your best judgement and initiative, and be prepared to justify decisions to the parent organization
   - Show staff that the two partners are regularly talking and agreeing on policy issues
   - Convey positive attitudes through problem-solving, improving, moving forward.
2. *Understand your partner's needs.* To work with another organization, you have to really understand where they are coming from and show that you understand. Without this level of business and cultural understanding, negotiation and problem-solving are almost impossible.
   - Listen to the partner's needs and understand their business situation and goals
   - Put the alliance in the context of a wider understanding of your partner's business
   - Understand the partner's weaknesses and where these present risks for you

- Know what is important to everyone else and what their agenda is (e.g. profit, risk, responsibility)
- Appreciate each other's need to look after number one
- Use set-up time to understand your partner's culture
- Watch out for shifts that may signal the alliance is going to be less important for your partner in the future.

3. *Goal focus.* Each partner needs a clear view of what the alliance is for and how much resource it is worth. Perhaps because alliances can be ambiguous, people need to work harder to identify shared interim goals.
   - Clarify purpose of partnership, its goals and how much effort it merits
   - Maintain a strategic perspective, and understand the repercussions of key decisions
   - Understand the organizational and personal benefits of partnership working
   - Use strategic planning disciplines
   - Have a clear and shared understanding of key tasks, functions and objectives
   - Focus on tangible benefits of collaboration and go for some early wins
   - Use good chairing skills in meetings to keep focus on objectives and not allow trivial issues to dominate.

4. *Negotiate for success.* Your needs and those of your partner will probably conflict. By driving too hard a bargain you can make the alliance fail. The most successful alliance workers know when to stand firm and when to concede.
   - Aim for a win–win: 'you can get too good a deal', which will not work for them
   - Use 'positive challenge' – an approach that is both tough and conciliatory
   - Bring 'gifts' (i.e. things they need which you can give)
   - Be happy to compromise over things that do not threaten your long-term needs
   - Accept that progress is made through allowing members to negotiate and bargain with each other, including how much information they are willing to share
   - Use informal networks and relationships to influence decisions.

5. *Manage differences.* Differences and tensions are bound to arise. Successful alliance working requires that these be raised and resolved with the minimum of damage to the underlying relationships. Keeping differences out in the open where they can be dealt with is better than letting trouble fester.
   - Accommodate differences in culture/style by adjusting your own behaviour
   - Have explicit discussions with your partner about ground rules for behaviour
   - Deal promptly with day-to-day tensions/problems, resolving conflict through constructive and honest debate
   - Try to keep serious disputes within the senior management team – i.e. don't let them damage the morale of other staff
   - Never be the first to cheat

- Get things out into the open, let differences be seen and heard (Deering and Murphy, 1998)
- Empathize with the difficulty you have caused and apologize personally (Uddin, 1998)
- If there are deep-seated areas of difference, continue to seek common ground and work on the things you can agree on
- Pause to review, especially at ends of meetings, how well people are working together.

6. *Operational effectiveness.* Work needs to be clearly managed, and processes are needed to ensure delivery within a complex and shifting environment. Good day-to-day process is more important in an alliance than in conventional business.

- Use project and contract management approaches to clarify deliverables and timeframes and share these at meetings, and use meetings to review progress
- Use active performance management
- Don't leave too many loose ends – complete one thing before moving on to the next
- Alliance managers need to manage a host of detailed and complex tasks.

7. *Communication and information.* Communication is critical to avoid misunderstandings and reinforce trust.

- Both formal and informal communication is important
- Communication needs to be honest and open, but recognize that alliance partners need to judge what information they will share
- Don't spring surprises on your partners
- Improve your internal communication and minimize the internal barriers in your own organization
- Use networks to obtain and share information
- Spot issues of importance to your partner and volunteer information that will help them to see and deal with such issues. Do this informally – by telephone or e-mail – and between meetings
- Find a shared language if you have your own jargon – the alliance 'esperanto'
- Use informal communication to demonstrate trust – 'an informal telephone call works better than a formal tracking system of correspondence'
- Make sure those inside the alliance hear about things before the outside world does
- Build in feedback to all staff about how the alliance is going – the big picture
- Don't neglect upward feedback
- Assure grass roots teams of their value to the alliance
- Communicate success and give recognition.

Given that alliances are supposed to be close business relationships, perhaps the best description of effective alliance behaviour is to treat the alliance partner as a friend.

The role of learning and development specialists in making strategic alliances work

Given the challenges for people working in unfamiliar territory and the import-ance of relationships, training and development (T&D) professionals can play an important role in developing cross-boundary working. Developers can play a key role in shaping the culture of the alliance, as well as helping people build the skills and knowledge to be operationally effective in these more fluid contexts.

1. Assess the impact of people issues on success

Any alliance brings employees face to face with cultural differences.

- As the alliance is being formed, evaluate the issues relating to process/culture that may cause problems – what are the cultural 'hotspots' that may interfere with effectiveness? What will people need to know or do to help the alliance get off to a good start?
- Facilitate forums where people can understand their organizational differences and choose the most appropriate approaches to getting the job done, whether these are from one company or the other, the 'best of both', or a different way altogether.

2. Help to establish behavioural ground rules

While cultural differences need not automatically cause conflict, tensions are bound to arise. Successful alliance working involves surfacing and addressing these issues. Trainers can facilitate the explicit negotiation of ground rules in early meetings. Typical alliance agreements include:

- Help to keep differences out in the open where they can be dealt with
- Aim for win–win
- Some operating principles apply more specifically to leaders than to other employees – for example, provide vehicles for people to have constructive and honest debate, which can resolve conflict; use informal networks and relationships to influence decisions; facilitate resolution of disputes within the senior management team so that they do not damage the morale of staff.

3. Help to develop a new culture

An alliance gives the opportunity for entrepreneurial behaviour that may break the mould of the parent companies.

- Given that alliances tend to be new territory for many employers, T&D pro-fessionals can usefully challenge sacred cows before they become too firmly established; adaptability is a key cultural attribute to aim for, and trainers can help people tread the line between having clear and agreed processes, and being prepared to work with 'shades of grey'

- New approaches to risk and problem-solving may be needed; work directly with teams to help them think creatively and achieve business breakthroughs; some trainers develop specific tools for use in an alliance, while others achieve good results using a variety of conventional approaches
- Help to ensure that communications and information flow are working effectively; act as a sounding board to senior management, advising on how communications can be improved
- Help people to develop conflict-management skills
- Provide team-building for cross-functional and other teams, especially as they are set up; help teams learn how to review both work progress and team effectiveness so that they can manage their process effectively and capture learning.

4. Support an open style of leadership

Leaders need to demonstrate an open-door, problem-solving approach. They need to be goal-focused and able to manage difference. T&D professionals can help leaders to develop these approaches and create a climate where there are no hidden agendas.

- Coach leaders on being accessible and visible, and on aspects of their style that may be helping or hindering others; provide feedback mechanisms that enable leaders to fine-tune their style; in some cases, it may be useful to arrange access for senior managers to appropriate external executive coaches
- Keep leaders in touch with external business and organizational developments – in some alliances, managers meet with counterparts from other organizations for 'breakfast briefings' and other informal sharing opportunities; trainers can facilitate these, identifying people and organizations from whom the alliance leaders can learn.

5. Foster relationship building

Understanding the partner's needs is critical in relationship building. While any training intervention provides the opportunity for relationship building, T&D professionals can support relationship building in other ways too.

- Establish networks, with or without a specific topic focus
- Provide learning groups and other forums for people to understand each other's goals and business situation
- Create vehicles for 'peer coaching' which allow individuals to learn from a range of others who have a specific skill or approach
- Initially act as broker, if need be, by putting people in touch with relevant sources of expertise – this means, of course, that you have a good idea about who is able to offer what, and building a database of talent and know-how is a start; this can then form a 'self-help' tool for individuals to access.

6. Help alliance managers to create operational effectiveness

Work with the alliance manager, line managers and teams to ensure that business goals and priorities are clear and that appropriate approaches to meetings, goal setting and other key processes are chosen.

- Provide training for line managers in project management, performance management and relationship/contract management skills, as required
- Help managers to develop their ability to coach and develop others
- Work as consultant to line managers, helping them to manage others effectively and develop sound personal organizational skills – essential when they need to deal with a host of detailed and complex tasks.

7. Help people learn new skills and approaches

Working in alliances often requires people to work on projects or in teams, in partnership with people from other organizations who have different approaches to doing business. While project management and team-building can be learned, some of the most helpful behaviours stem from a partnering mindset. In particular, the ability to partner with other people requires people to use the following behaviours, skills and knowledge.

- Build open personal relationships
- An open leadership style
- Understand partner's needs
- Goal focus
- Negotiate for success
- Manage differences
- Operational effectiveness
- Build trust
- Manage their own career development, including maintaining links within the parent organization
- Be positive, enthusiastic and energetic
- Communicate and share information
- Broad organizational and business understanding
- Cultural agility
- Be friendly
- Negotiate
- Manage complexity
- Tolerate ambiguity
- Emotional resilience
- Take 'sensible' risks
- Think creatively
- Take a long-term view
- Have a broad business understanding (Garrow *et al.*, 2000).

While these relatively sophisticated skills may be developed through alliance working, in an ideal world it may be more helpful to select people who are already predisposed to new ways of working to work in an alliance.

Alliance managers in particular may need to act as visionary, strategic sponsor, advocate, networker, facilitator, manager and mediator. These multiple roles call for all of the above skills, plus:

- Political acumen and influencing skills
- Leadership ability
- Managerial acumen
- Willingness to push back the boundaries
- The ability to build teams who share the alliance spirit.

8. Use appropriate learning approaches

The processes used to support people in alliances should ideally be as innovative as the product of the alliance itself. T&D professionals should find relevant and timely ways to support people in their learning, whether this involves technological solutions or variations on face-to-face delivery. That does not mean that just-in-time interactive technologies should become the only way in which tailored training takes place. Trainers should develop a repertoire of approaches that mirror different learning preferences.

Since most development takes place on the job, trainers should understand enough about the different job roles in the alliance to be able to create appropriate solutions to training and development needs.

- Work in partnership with line managers and teams to develop excellent processes
- Train line managers how to coach so that team members receive the support they need when they need it
- Provide a focal point for 'needs and offers' on development – offering someone a development opportunity tailored to their specific needs can produce good returns for all concerned.

9. Provide a vehicle for people to share learning – both within the alliance and beyond

Of course successful alliances, with their 'can do' culture and exciting developments, can be stimulating to experience as an employee. They provide excellent opportunities for learning (itself a change process), and equip employees with approaches that will stand them in good stead wherever their career takes them. Individuals involved in alliances usually feel they develop rapidly through this experience, although this is learning is often kept private, little discussed with other people. The challenge is to help people become aware of how much they are learning, and to share improved processes and approaches quite explicitly. One way is to work with teams to help them create effective review and evaluation processes so that they and others can learn what works and what does not.

Sharing knowledge is important for people not only within the alliance but also within the parent organization. So often, people involved in alliances take their enhanced skills and valuable experience to other companies rather than back into the parent organization, which is then forced to reinvent wheels. Some organizations see capturing and sharing valuable learning as a business imperative. Hewlett-Packard, for instance, has alliance-making ground rules, which include: 'Once you have more than a few alliances, set up systems to ensure that alliance-making know-how is shared'. HP has a central department looking after alliances, and an alliance manual.

10. Model effective alliance behaviours

It would be somewhat bizarre if training and development professionals failed to walk the talk on partnering! Working as business partner means having a good understanding of the alliance and what it is designed to achieve, and providing bespoke solutions to development needs in that context. Acting as consultant to alliance managers involves being credible, building value-added relationships, using a range of diagnostic tools to identify what needs to be done, and implementing cost-effective and timely solutions. Acting as partner also means sharing learning and good practice with fellow training and development professionals from the different parent bodies so that the benefits of interesting new approaches can become more widespread.

As more and more organizations aspire to enter strategic alliances, and struggle to make them succeed, the chances are that more attention will be paid to the key success factor (i.e. the strength of the alliance relationship). For training and development professionals, alliances offer a major opportunity to contribute to business success by helping people build relationships and trust, providing people with the skills they need, and shaping a culture in which learning is shared and which provides a template for effective collaboration. They also offer the chance to break out of preconceived ways of operating to create a real business partnership.

Trainers can provide multiple vehicles for sharing learning about emerging good practice, and help to create genuine synergies. They can proactively help to reintegrate alliance workers back into the parent body, and disseminate good practice by documenting experience and recording stories. The link between training and development interventions and potential value to the bottom line should be obvious.

Conclusion

Indeed, the real challenge is not so much working within an alliance but in mainstreaming partnering skills and learning from alliances back into the parent body. Alliances provide a valid business focus for experimenting with 'learning organization' approaches. Assuming that the alliance works successfully, it is probable that new and improved systems will have been developed from which parent organizations can benefit.

The ability of organizations to learn from their alliance experiences is still relatively underdeveloped. Individuals involved in alliances gain valuable learning from their experience, although this is generally rarely discussed with others in their parent organization. This learning may be lost to the organization if good alliance managers carry their experience to another employer. Organizational learning can be improved by more thorough evaluation and documentation of learning experiences. Alliance workers can be debriefed so that generic learning can be carried forward from one alliance to the next, so that the wheel does not have to be reinvented each time. Individuals can enhance their skill acquisition by building personal learning goals into alliance working, and discussing learning more explicitly in performance reviews and team meetings. Often, their most important learning is in developing a wider view of business and in dealing with more complex personal relationships.

Maximizing the benefits of alliances, especially their potential to enhance organizational learning, will enable companies to dominate their sectors. For organizations who aspire to partner with others, knowing how to develop a cadre of employees, both specialists and managers, who are capable of working in various complex yet temporary assignments, will become a key source of competitive advantage and sustainable high performance.

9

Crossing boundaries of time and place

Introduction

Technology is so fundamentally altering the way work can be done that organizations are no longer restricted in the ways they conduct their business by fixed physical locations and working hours. Many organizations are reaping the financial benefits of internationalizing their operations by, for example, outsourcing call centres to parts of the developing world where labour costs are relatively low and skill levels high. Technology is also enabling better use of available time and space, through practices such as hot-desking and remote working, for instance.

Electronic communication is cheaper, easier and faster than face-to-face communication, and people have access to more sources of information than ever before. However, the communications revolution brings with it a new set of problems. With the growth of home-based working, mobile phones, laptops and other electronic means of keeping communication constant regardless of location, work can be carried out any time, anywhere. This is causing a redefinition of concepts such as 'work' 'the workplace', 'working hours' and 'leisure'.

In this chapter we will explore the organizational challenges of transcending boundaries of time, culture and geography through technology, and examine the practical implications for managers and employees.

Transforming organizations through technology

In many organizations, the process of becoming e-enabled appears well under way. This quiet revolution is evident in the numbers of companies involved in e-business in many sectors, operating virtual teams and making use of e-learning. The commonest reasons for embracing e-business are to improve services, modernize the business and develop new products and services. Technology is also enabling new ways of working, with virtual or remote working becoming more widespread. Of *Management Agenda* respondents, 80 per cent maintain that virtual management arrangements in their organizations have increased over the past five years, and 47 per cent manage a virtual team or are part of a virtual team.

Home-based working

US companies have been relatively fast to embrace home-based working, but one UK example of an organization that is now 'virtual' is Cambridge Electronics. The company decided that, since all employees wanted to work remotely from home or wherever they wanted to work, they would get rid of the office. They cancelled the lease, taking the rent out of the budget line, and stored the office furniture, just in case. Every client of the company, most of whom are in the USA, has a secure, dedicated website, and all the work that is done for the client, including all the administration, timesheets and quotations, is carried out by staff over the secure website. Now employees choose the most productive hours to work, rather than being forced into a nine-to-five regime that might not suit them.

For teleworking to be successful from a business point of view it needs a champion who is senior enough to be respected – but not necessarily the top executive. Ideally this champion should have a personal interest, because teleworking will directly benefit his or her department or division. There should be a long-term plan to ensure, for instance, that enough modem capacity is purchased and that there is employee agreement. Starting a teleworking programme costs money initially, so budgeting should be adequate. Best practice with regard to selecting teleworkers can ensure that people feel fairly treated.

Managing at a distance

Increasingly, managers are being called on to manage people at a distance. This may be because people are working flexibly, or because the manager is not co-located with staff. Managers may be leading international teams who rarely meet face to face. This enables organizations to reap the benefits of the cost and time savings that accrue when project teams of experts work together remotely across a split-site organization. Similarly, as workplaces become more flexible, more people are likely to find themselves working from home. Increasingly, virtual working is seen as a win–win phenomenon, yet many teleworkers report the challenge of balancing work and home life – especially if they have young children at home. Another reported challenge for the home-based worker is a sense of isolation from the rest of the team.

Managing remotely is difficult to do well, because building a sense of community can be tricky when there is reduced face-to-face contact and increased separation from co-workers. This can make it difficult to establish and maintain trust between the members of a virtual team.

Managing remotely requires specific skills for which managers commonly receive little or no preparation. Technology can be both an enabler and a barrier to communication. Sometimes it creates misunderstanding because you lose the nuances of facial expressions and body language that enhance face-to-face interactions.

Managers need well-honed interpersonal and communication skills, as well as integrity, clarity of direction and the ability to build trust. Emotionally intelligent behaviours, such as listening, demonstrating patience and sensitivity, are important. A Roffey Park study found that it is the way that managers use their interpersonal skills at the microlevel that differentiates the best virtual managers from the rest. For example, more effective managers:

- Build rapport and relationships quickly and then sustain them
- Ask precise questions
- Are excellent listeners who spot underlying meanings and process messages
- Test out meaning by summarizing and reflecting
- Trust their intuition.

Because remote teams, by their nature, require a less dominant style of management, managers need to be able to use a more participative, consensual management style. They also need good links with the wider organization. Managers also need to be willing to 'let go', focus on outputs, demonstrate political and cultural awareness, be flexible and consultative, and keep in touch.

Smith and Sinclair (2003) suggest that an excellent virtual manager has to:

- Be strong on time management
- Be a good planner
- Appreciate diversity
- Put effort into building relationships with co-workers
- Have systems for regular communication and feedback
- Have a significant commitment to coaching and developing others.

Managers in several companies that practise remote management helped to develop the following ideas on how to manage effectively at a distance. These include practical matters such as providing documentary repository access for all users and restructuring the performance management process to reflect the maximum shifts done with each manager. Databases that can communicate 'two-way' messages in a standard, clear and friendly way are useful. Guidelines and procedures should be clear and relevant to help staff become effectively self-managing. Ideally, they should be drawn up in consultation with staff.

Getting to know staff is important. With new starters, managers should spend time with them during their induction and get to know their strengths and weaknesses. Managers should explain how the staff member's role is affected by distance. Performance and time-keeping standards and measurement should be made clear from the outset, and the standards should be consistent across sites. Effective managers need to be well organized, making adequate time allowances for dealing with issues when visiting remote sites, spending most time on the critical issues but remaining flexible.

Promoting teamworking and letting groups get together is important. Typically, some form of initial face-to-face team building is essential, and organized contact meetings are required to maintain social continuity and reduce potential isolation. To ensure development of staff, one-to-one sessions should be agreed.

Developing potential

Effective remote managers take an active interest in team members' careers, often acting as a proactive 'gate-keeper' to opportunities. They delegate well, and ensure that training and development needs are met. They encourage team members to take responsibility for their own development, and have regular one-to-one coaching sessions with team members.

Communication

Communication is key to the effectiveness of remote management, even more than when a manager works alongside the team. Notice boards at each site should be kept up to date. Visibility issues are important. Even having a photo of someone can build trust. 'Mini' monthly team briefings should be provided. Managers advise ensuring that tasks are planned so that wherever possible the manager rotates locations to try and visit them as evenly as possible and provide consistency of contact. There should be regular discussion with all members of the team, including face to face. Communicating directly is not always easily achieved, but managers have found that site visits, going in early or staying late, to have a chat with staff they don't see often can help.

Similarly, 'time shift' conferencing groupware via discussion databases allows issues to be aired and information shared where all participants have different working patterns. Comments on the topics can be made hours or days apart, and from across many time zones, yet the thread remains as a coherent whole. The key to a productive conference is to nominate a moderator, who supervises the conference, catalyses discussions and keeps contributors to the topic. Using video conferencing at larger remote sites can be useful. Managers can also encourage employees to call and discuss problems with them and with their peers, in a sort of learning group.

Consistency of message and medium is important. It helps everyone if a regular time is set aside to communicate each day by telephone, or by e-mail if the manager is not available in person. This regular contact should provide an easy way of finding out what problems or issues the employee is facing. Also, using different modes of communication appropriately is important. For example, e-mails, rather than video conferences, should be used for agendas and action plans. In circumstances where the only contact is via e-mail, responsiveness is key. E-mail protocols such as receipting e-mails so that the sender knows they have been opened as a priority are helpful.

BT has pioneered virtual working in the UK. Being acutely aware of the need to offer attractive and innovative packages in order to win the 'war for talent', the organization focused on using technology to develop flexible working solutions and to ensure greater work–life balance for employees. This focus gained BT UK title of Employer of the Year in 2001, and has helped it to retain valued employees. This flexible approach has enabled people to move out of central London offices, thus achieving substantial savings for the organization. To date, BT has over 6000 employees working from home, with the overriding idea that 'work is what you do, not a place you go to'. IBM's transformation to e-business has also made home-working commonplace within the organization.

Developing virtual teams

Virtual teams – where two or more employees work together to achieve a common goal using technology as their primary means of communication – have similar needs, and tend to go through the same stages of storming, forming, norming and performing as conventional teams. Similarly, teams in global organizations can struggle with same kinds of issues as those experienced by teams in smaller, domestic organizations. For instance, cross-functional team working is often undercut by conflicting loyalties and time pressures.

However, when teams are composed of people of different national cultures, and working in different time zones, another layer of complexity is added, with issues of cultural diversity coming to the fore. Virtual teams face challenges in the areas of trust, attentiveness and communication. Psychologically, virtual workers are likely to be distanced from traditional symbols and artefacts of their organization and may feel metaphorically, as well as literally, distanced from the centre of the action. They may feel they do not 'belong' in the way that co-located workers may. Team leaders need to be able to work sensitively and flexibly to get the best out of international and virtual teams. Ideally, teams should meet for team-building to establish ways of working that are going to help them achieve their goals.

Bayer Pharmaceuticals uses remote teamworking for short-term projects to develop project education materials and sales excellence initiatives. The teams exist for up to ten months, and typically comprise seven or eight people across a range of Bayer's departments (such as products or medical specialists) and in different parts of the world. While time and cost savings are important, Bayer recognizes the need for some face-to-face meeting. Such meetings expose team members to the global rather than local nature of their project and force team members to network, increasing their visibility as well as enhancing teamworking (Kubicek, 2003).

For organizations looking to maximize international and virtual teamworking, it is preferable to recruit the right people in the first place and to provide an effective induction for new team members. Allocating an experienced mentor is helpful in training people how to work remotely. Getting new team members to capture their learning and then pass it on to the next person can be useful in consolidating learning.

Virtual team members need to be largely self-managing and enjoy working within broader freedoms. They need to be willing to use their initiative and take responsibility for decision-making, seeking advice only after exploring all possibilities. They need to be sufficiently 'plugged in' to what is happening that they can make sensible decisions, being aware of the impact of their choices on other parts of the organization. They need to be self-motivated and resilient, and able to think straight in crises. They also need to keep their manager informed of important developments and of their whereabouts. They should be effective team players, and willing to help other team members with their challenges and problems. They obviously need to be able to use new technology effectively.

Trust

The creation of trust between team members is vital. Javenpaa *et al.* (1998, cited in Smith and Sinclair, 2003) proposes that trust is 'a function of the team members' perceived ability, integrity and benevolence, as well as of the members' own propensity to trust'. They describe 'benevolence' as the extent to which team members show interpersonal care and concern and help others out without being transactional. 'Integrity' relates to behaving in line with clear principles, being dependable and reliable. They discovered that in virtual teams integrity is more important in the short term than benevolence, as this is more reliant on time and possibly social contact to develop.

Once a remote team is in place and operating effectively, the key challenge is to integrate learning across the whole team. Allocating specific time for learning during face-to-face meetings, getting together in one place and devoting time to celebration, recognition and learning are helpful for reinforcing team cohesion. Javenpaa *et al.* (1998) found that in high trust teams, feedback on proposals was 'specific, in-depth, and thoughtful indicating careful reading and a concern to contribute to the improvement of the material'. Teams were proactive, task-output driven and optimistic. Both team members and managers honoured their commitments and kept their promises. Leadership was dynamic, setting the parameters, but task-goal clarity was seen as the team's responsibility. Role division was left as emergent and interdependent. Time management was explicit and process-based. Interaction within the team was frequent, with few gaps. Managers were also willing to admit when they had made mistakes.

E-Transformation

Butler (2000) suggests that e-business success is the new world order in business today. However, transforming mature organizations through e-business is a major operational and leadership challenge. Although e-business is still relatively in its infancy, mature organizations appear to be taking too long to become e-enabled alongside conventional ways of doing business.

According to the Chairman and CEO of Oracle, Jeff Henley, e-commerce involves a great deal more than simply adding some technology to existing processes. It is a new way of thinking of doing business and of organizing. E-business offers the potential of major cost savings, but the e-business environment calls for entirely different ways of working – a faster pace, quicker decision-making, risk-taking, a greater customer focus, instant alliances, and even different financial metrics. According to Butler, strategy requires experimentation rather than months of analysis. In research conducted by Hewitt Associates (2000), the main concern of respondents in organizations undergoing e-transformation was 'What do we keep, and how do we change fast?'.

Strong leadership required

It is the speed of change required on all levels and the possibilities that new technologies provide that mark out corporate transformation into e-business. Butler (2000) argues that a company's commitment to an e-business initiative needs to be strong and clear in many vital aspects – e-business leadership, roles and responsibilities, cross-functional interdependencies, budget matters and management structure.

Active senior management support for e-business and a real will to invest in the right software and hardware are vital to the acceptance of 'e-transformation'. To become successfully e-enabled, organizations need to have effective communication and the right mindset. Most particularly, senior management backing is needed to develop a culture that is genuinely supportive of e-business. One of the main blockers of this transformation is when e-business operations are managed in the same way as conventional business, as traditional mechanisms for keeping leadership aligned are too slow. Suff (2000) maintains that the board has to be convinced that the Internet will alter how the company does business forever – and must lead accordingly.

McCartney (2002) describes the transformation of IBM under Lou Gerstner. The hiring of Gerstner was seen to be particularly important because, for the first time, IBM did not hire from within. Gerstner drove through a whole wave of organizational changes, including the shift to e-business and a focus on simplification. Similarly, influential leadership, coupled with previous experience of e-business, was helpful when BT launched their e-BT initiative in October 1999. The CEO delivered a clear and powerful message to the top 100 managers of one company – 'BT is an IP business. Any product or service launched that does not involve IP in any way is not a viable product or service'. The senior management team within BT is also seen to be driving the changes very strongly and supporting the implementation of new technology to improve services and efficiencies, both internally and externally, to BT's customers.

However, it is not enough for managers to support e-business and new processes; they have to be seen actively using the new technology. At IBM, e-learning technology such as web broadcasts and conference calls are used so that employees can communicate, debate and pose questions to senior management. Such technology ensures that senior managers are more visible and accessible to all staff, and are able to share their passion for the business. Similarly, the CEOs of BT's lines of business are far more accessible – they e-mail all employees on a regular basis, and many take part in online chat sessions (where they are online for one hour each week and anyone can ask a question).

Leadership skills

Managers are increasingly using information technology to help them achieve organizational goals. These new information resources call for new ways of thinking and acting. Self-managing work teams are increasingly accessing data in real time, making many types of role created during the industrial era redundant. According to Shafritz and Ott (2001), 'We are creating technical systems with machines that are programmable and methods that are mechanical . . . these hybrid technical systems must represent an unstable state', and 'At the cognitive level, understanding and operating programmable technology requires different reasoning skills than does mechanical technology'.

McCartney's research highlights the following as key leadership competencies for e-business:

- Passion and commitment
- Vision
- Strong communication
- Thought leadership
- Creativity and innovation
- Coaching
- Motivating
- Challenging
- Flexibility.

Managers will increasingly need to think inductively, rather than deductively as they have conventionally been trained. Itoi (2001) suggests that the new e-business chief is equal parts innovator, manager and counsellor. She maintains that e-business decision-makers routinely experiment with a variety of techniques to bring out the best in their staff, but are also treated as general managers and are held accountable for producing measurable, lasting results. In addition, e-business chiefs must possess patience for counselling staff through business upheavals. They have an important role to play in motivating staff, boosting morale and building internal confidence when there is a lot of uncertainty about the e-business market.

Gaining employee buy-in

E-business depends on staff support. McKeown (2000) maintains that employees entering the world of e-business worry about job security and diminished status. He argues that the best solution is to offer education before the change to e-business, and to focus on planning e-careers rather than e-jobs. This helps staff to visualize a positive future.

Training is vital to achieving buy-in. Jackson Batten achieves this by arranging regular staff meetings where the company identifies how it can improve customer service or efficiency. Even employees who are not directly involved in the 'e' part of e-business must constantly be retrained in order to keep up to date. It is important to involve employees in the system development, testing and implementation, and to provide equal access to opportunities and resources, such as support for employees in having PCs for home. In some cases, it may be necessary to demonstrate the advantages and bottom-line benefits and provide bite-size introduction to systems that work.

BT avoided 'throwing employees in at the deep end' by accompanying all online processes with written booklets to guide employees. This was particularly useful for employees who lacked either the confidence or the experience to use the system immediately. A development and training portal (the BT Academy) was also launched to improve and transition employee skills. At IBM, the collaborative computing team runs a series of non-traditional events in order to illustrate how people can make the best use of technology in the business environment. The events are designed to improve ways of working, and increase productivity and efficiency. Seminars and workshops encompass technology, knowledge management, creativity and consultancy.

The process of e-transformation

The process of e-transformation tends to occur around the development of new products and services. As a technology-based company already, Oracle learned that there are three things to address in transforming to e-business: technology, processes and structure. With regard to technology, Henley (in Williams and Hart, 1999) suggests that 'everyone will need a PC or something to access powerful databases and transaction capabilities sitting in the network somewhere and doing it with a simple browser. This is why people will have to reinvent and modernise their IT structures'. He argues that centralizing and consolidating data centres makes sense to enable global business practices, and share customer and supply information.

With regard to process change, simplification is the watchword, enabled by employee self-service. Everyone in Oracle is totally 'electronic', and the company now has Internet procurement applications. Oracle has developed online sales tools through the Internet – an e-business channel on the web, which runs like cable TV. This enables demonstrations on the web, in a variety of languages. With regard to structures, Henley asks: 'Do you want the same kind of organization in a global world that you had traditionally before?'. In Oracle, functions report up to the corporation and on a dotted line to the country, enabling change to be pushed through more quickly. At the same time, flexibility is required in the way in which local issues are dealt with.

Given the need for speed and flexibility, the process of e-transformation tends to follow project lines. Butler (2000) and others suggest the following tips to enable e-transformation:

- Have a clear, well-coordinated starting point – there needs to be agreement about what results to expect and in what timeframe. A clear corporate plan is helpful.
- Align and educate leadership and management teams – leaders need to be 'lead learners', challenging their own thinking and the thinking of those around them, looking for new business opportunities and alliances, and learning about their business world outside traditional boundaries. Executives need to have a solid understanding of the rapidly changing capabilities for technology.
- Establish a cross-functional team – project teams consolidate new ideas, manage pilots and full implementation and coordinate efforts between parts of the organization. Executive guidance and 'air cover' for the team are vital.

- Choose project leaders carefully – they need to understand how the business works and must constantly challenge the *status quo*. They need organizational credibility and an appreciation of the technical issues at hand.
- Choose team members wisely – select team members who are optimistic and enthusiastic about e-endeavours, who demonstrate leadership qualities, creativity, strong interpersonal skills and the ability to influence co-workers and bosses.
- Ensure that communication on the why, what and how is clear – let managers know their role in overcoming functional barriers, such as freeing up resources and making quick decisions to address problems within their areas. Create a sense of urgency from the chairman down. Know how the changes are likely to affect key groups such as customer service representatives, traditional sales people, distributors and customers, and have plans on how to communicate with, and involve, each group.
- Clarify budgets – infrastructure costs are significant for those who have to update legacy systems. Anticipate these, and plan how best to maximize value and use across the business.
- Consciously build a high performing team – establish clear roles and responsibilities, and use team-building to enable members to understand each other and what they bring to the task.
- Recognize and reward performance – establish strong links to the performance review process, ensuring that measures of performance count in the larger picture of career planning, leadership development, bonus systems and pay scales.
- Document lessons learned – build information links between different projects and document learning in easy-to-use formats; use coaches and mentors.
- Learn from previous change initiatives – so that the same mistakes are not repeated.
- Plan how to ease team members back into the organization – careful planning about team members' next career move prevents the loss of newly developed talent.

The cultural implications of e-transformation

McCartney's (2002) research into the human implications of e-transformation found that aligning the internal culture of an organization to the e-business context can be both time-consuming and difficult. Embedding changes requires managers and leaders in particular consistently to demonstrate specific behaviours and concerns.

Communication

Strong, consistent and frequent communication is a vital element of reinforcing the shift towards being a successful e-business organization. According to McCartney, communication within an e-business environment has to be more proactive than in a traditional organization. At BT, communication levels are high – press announcements are simultaneously published for everyone to see, and the online news channel, BT Today News Desk, is continuously updated. This effective communication system enables the leadership team to get clear messages across to its audience. The BT intranet also has a section called 'setting the record straight', to clarify stories about BT which appear in the press.

Sharing knowledge

Embedding change requires rapid spreading of knowledge so that employees become empowered to operate in new ways. Suff (2000) describes e-transformation at Iceland. The main staff challenge was changing the way employees thought about the business and their role within it. Suff concludes that it is vital that those involved in implementing e-business understand the business, and that the business understands e-business and its capabilities. In order to achieve this crossover of knowledge and understanding, Iceland conducted internal seminars, and functional departments worked together on a number of e-business projects. Staff were also seconded into the IS department, and this process was replicated with people from the stores. This allows those designing new systems to understand requirements better before the development takes place. Similarly, WH Smith set up a steering group of employees from across the organization's six core businesses to drive the e-business strategy forward. This enabled every division to feel involved and represented.

Measures

Employees working within an e-business environment need to be able to see how their performance contributes to the whole. Individual performance assessment can be difficult when employees may lack previous experience of working within an e-business environment. In some organizations, each employee has his or her own performance development plan which links in to the overall business plan, so employees are able to measure their progress against that. BT's HR department measures employee satisfaction, motivation levels and the Human Investment ratio, which measures productivity (the individual's contribution to the bottom line). Simple and relevant embedding mechanisms such as these can equip organizations to move with greater agility and speed than before.

Working across international boundaries

In a global marketplace, doing business across geographic boundaries is becoming commonplace. One company successfully operating across geographic boundaries is SABMiller, formed after a merger when South African Breweries acquired the Miller Brewing Company in July 2002. Human capital competitiveness is a strategic priority in any business that SABMiller operates, and the new organization is underpinned by a single, performance-based people management strategy. SAB began a rapid expansion in the 1990s in developing and underdeveloped countries by acquiring existing local brands and boosting their operations to higher performance levels. Therefore, the drive for success had to be based on the so-called 'people proposition'.

This business proposition depended on the quality of people being sent to manage these operations and the degree to which they were capable of transferring the SAB capability in terms of management, technical capability, brand-building, sales and distribution capability. The Company managed to develop local talent and skills in markets such as Russia, the Czech Republic and Poland, among others. By conducting business as it has in Eastern Europe, SAB is continually perfecting a strategy which is very difficult to emulate, as developing top-calibre people who are highly competitive needs a long-term philosophy and process (Doke, 2003).

In the *Management Agenda* survey, 50 per cent of organizations operate internationally, and most require employees to undertake international travel. The most commonly reported forms of international opportunities offered by organizations in our survey are short-term assignments and expatriate assignments. Similarly, a Mercer's International Assignments Survey (2003) found that nearly four in ten multinational companies (39 per cent) have increased their use of short-term business assignments.

Ironically, as organizations are realizing the importance of international leaders, so global companies appear to be struggling to maximize the benefits of multicultural, international working. Changes in the make-up of the workforce are creating increasing problems for organizations in the recruitment of individuals willing to work internationally. Adjusting to a new location and culture can be real challenge for expatriate families. In many cases, the main reasons why key employees refuse to take up expatriate and other long overseas assignments are the effect this will have on their work–life balance, and disruption to their personal/family arrangements. Other typical reasons for refusing an overseas assignment include concerns about language barriers and having no real role on re-entry to the UK after an overseas posting.

For those who do make the commitment to an overseas posting, knowing who is who at a local level, as well as back at headquarters, becomes difficult unless individuals make a continuous effort to build their networks and keep in touch with the home base. As many as 25 per cent of employees who come back from an overseas posting resign within a year, according to a survey by the Centre for International Briefing. After two years, the figure rises to a staggering 40 per cent. Some find that no new role has been defined for them and look in vain for appreciation of their new skills, which often include a second language (McLuhan, 1999).

Rather than being a corporate afterthought, international assignments are therefore moving to the forefront of management and organizational dynamics. Companies are slowly realizing that well-managed international assignments are a key element in developing global corporate competencies. International assignments are also gradually being regarded as logical and required steps in career paths – and not only for those on faster tracks. Expatriate postings are becoming interconnected with executive and leadership development, and with succession planning.

In a survey carried out by Panter (1995), 84 per cent of the sample agreed that their company saw a need to develop international managers. When asked what skills international managers needed, cross-cultural skills, leadership skills in an international context and strategic management skills were seen as most important, with leadership being slightly more important for the larger companies. Another study found that shortages of international managers were a particularly acute problem for British multinational companies. Two-thirds of the companies surveyed said that they had experienced shortages of international managers, and over 70 per cent indicated that future shortages were anticipated. Reasons suggested for this shortfall are that UK salary levels are uncompetitive, and also that managers are becoming less willing to be mobile. These are issues that require attention if organizations are to operate successfully on an international level.

To encourage greater employee mobility, organizations are increasingly including spouse support in their international assignments policy, with important elements being career counselling and language training for spouses. Most companies provide participants with home leave at least once a year, with many providing three trips home a year for those on short-term assignments. Many also provide additional return trips for employees with children in the home country, and paying for children to attend boarding school in the home country is another common benefit.

Identifying and developing international leaders

The definition of an international manager is also continuously shifting, to reflect the different forms of international organizations that are emerging in the global marketplace. International managers used to be thought of as people who could go from one country to another and manage in that country (Barham, 1993). With organizations trying new forms of international coordination and integration, the international manager is starting to become someone who can exercise leadership across a number of countries and cultures simultaneously, perhaps on a global or regional basis.

Selection of international leaders

The criteria on which successful international leaders should be selected is an important issue which hasn't yet been resolved (Kets de Vries and Mead, 1993). Although much more research is needed to refine the selection criteria, there are a number of factors that have been identified by research as being important in the selection decision. These include:

- Conflict resolution skills
- Leadership style
- Effective communication
- Social orientation
- Flexibility and open-mindedness
- Interest in and willingness to try new things
- Ability to cope with stress
- Tolerance for ambiguity.

There is, however, debate as to which of these criteria are the critical ones for international selection. It has been found that the greater the consideration paid during the selection process to adaptability and the ability to communicate, the higher the success rate in the assignment. Another survey found that in practice functional expertise was the most important criterion in selecting and preparing employees for international work. This reflects the fact that many companies select expatriates by focusing mainly on technical competence and willingness to go abroad, with little attention to other factors. Given the dominance of the more personal attributes highlighted above, it appears that there is a need for organizations to ensure that interpersonal and personal characteristics are also built into the process.

Organizations such as Colgate-Palmolive, a company with decades of international business experience, often hire entry-level marketing candidates who have already demonstrated such characteristics and capabilities. The company intentionally hires new graduates or MBAs who have lived or worked abroad, speak more than one language, or can demonstrate their pre-existing aptitude for global business.

Given the growing shortage of international managers, a number of firms are actively seeking to attract employees who will be willing to manage abroad. This highlights a growing concern, which is that not only do organizations have the difficulty of selecting the right person for the job but also they need to attract suitable and potentially successful individuals to the organization. Companies are therefore attempting to sell themselves more effectively to graduates through various types of marketing designed to highlight the international nature of their activities. The prospects of early international experience are emphasized to attract graduates who are specifically seeking an international career.

Example 9.1   BP Amoco

BP Amoco is committed to developing an internationally diverse leadership, and believes that one of the most direct ways of achieving an international management cadre is by deliberately recruiting people with an international perspective. BP Amoco has consciously attempted to develop a more multicultural management workforce in recent years. Recruitment takes place through the worldwide recruitment network. A common set of recruitment competencies are used, and these are as culturally 'neutral' as possible so as not to disadvantage candidates whose first language is other than English and whose experience of life does not include the UK, US or Europe. A genuine attempt has been made to devise culturally neutral selection procedures, with candidates tested and interviewed in their native language.

In addition, a number of international graduates are recruited each year. These are expected to be internationally mobile, to speak a minimum of three languages, and are typically high potential. There are over 60 alumni of the scheme, and over time it is anticipated that this more culturally diverse graduate intake should percolate through to senior management Holbeche (1999).

The skills of international leadership

A number of leadership development requirements which face a company as it moves towards a global perspective have been suggested (Rhinesmith, 1989). International leaders need to:

- Change their frame of reference from a local or national orientation to a truly global perspective. This involves understanding influences, trends, and directions in technology, financial resources, marketing and distribution practices, political and cultural influences and international economics.
- Understand and develop competitive strategies, plans and tactics that operate outside the confines of a domestic marketplace orientation.
- Understand how to organize and lead multinational teams; deal with issues of collaboration and cross-cultural variances; and develop processes for coaching, mentoring, and assessing performance across a variety of attitudes, beliefs and standards. The requirements of international leadership extend well beyond traditional management practices to reflect sensitivity to cultural diversity and perspective, and understanding of different – and sometimes conflicting – social forces without prejudice.
- Realize that continuous change is the dominant influence in global business activities today. The traditional role of making order out of chaos will shift to one of continually managing change and chaos in ways that are responsive to customers and competitive conditions.
- Speed up business development where possible by exploiting and adapting learning between different countries and markets.
- Be able to manage their own personal effectiveness. International leadership involves a considerable amount of travelling and stress. In a recent survey, managers reported spending a third of their life away from home. This makes it very difficult to achieve a satisfactory balance between work and home, and the costs to family life can be considerable.

There is therefore ample evidence of the skills and abilities needed by the successful international leader; what is less clear is how the individual can be helped to acquire and develop these skills.

Developing international managers

Assignments and secondments in other countries are still seen as the best way of developing international managers, but because of flatter organization structures these tend to be quite long term and some companies are finding them more difficult to organize. Most multinational companies agree that their managers need international expertise; but a survey revealed that more than half of the large European corporations participating in the study lacked a strategy for internationalizing their managers (Price Waterhouse/Cranfield Project, 1991; see Brewster et al., 1991). Responses to the survey showed that the most common method of 'internationalizing' managers was through the expatriation/repatriation process.

Many involved in the expatriation/repatriation process are junior managers being consciously trained for future positions in the company. Expatriation is part of their development as high-potential future executives. Companies commonly focus on young managers – aged 26 to 32 – for a number of practical reasons. First, these individuals are at early career stages and are assumed to be psychologically flexible. It is hoped that early exposure to diverse methods will help them to become and remain flexible throughout their management career.

Secondly, these younger managers are freer for international assignments. Often they are not married or, if they are partnered, they either have young children or no children and are therefore more mobile. Useful support is where employees on international assignments are given help in managing the culture change on arrival in the host country and on re-entry to their home country. The adaptable, culturally sensitive mindset required to be successful should be a prerequisite, and coaching and mentoring arrangements can remove the fear factor and help employees to adapt to new ways of operating as well as keep in touch with developments at the home base.

Despite the popularity of expatriation, the preparation provided for individuals is often surprisingly minimal. The research suggests that a successful training programme for international managers should focus on three aspects of development; pre-departure, on-site and repatriation orientation (Dunbar and Katcher, 1990). Ideally, preparation for an international assignment should begin a year or more in advance so that global awareness and thinking internationally about the business become part of a continuous process. Specific information inputs before departure can then be more readily absorbed and put into practice (Rothwell, 1992). A review of the relevant literature suggests that the areas of training that should be covered include:

Pre-departure
Language briefing
National or regional orientation: business issues
Personal and family orientation: customs and roles
Career management: succession planning

On-site
Language training
Local mentoring: customs and roles
Stress and adjustment training
Career assessment
National or regional orientation: business issues

Repatriation process
Life after the perks: financial management
Re-entry shock: customs and roles
Career management: options and plans

An alternative framework, suggested by Selmer *et al.* (1998), proposes that cross-cultural training should be designed around the psychological receptivity of the international manager in an attempt to develop the cognitive structures that are most suited to international working. Selmer argues that social interaction is influenced by the individual's 'world view', comprised of values, attitudes, opinion, ideas and knowledge that have been accumulated through personal experience. This 'world view' is subjected to considerable pressure in the initial stages of the assignment, when the appropriateness of various behaviours may not be consistent with local norms.

The uncertainty created by this corresponds to the symptoms and reactions of culture shock (Oberg, 1960). Gradually, over the course of the assignment, the individual reassesses his or her cognitive structures to suit the new social context. Selmer and colleagues believe that an individual's capacity for efficient learning ebbs and flows during the expatriate period. They therefore agree that cross-cultural training should be sequential, starting at pre-departure and continuing to the post-arrival phases.

In the pre-departure phase, programmes should focus on essential information on local conditions. In terms of cognitive restructuring, the individual's exposure to cultural differences is too transitory to encourage significant change to his or her frame of reference. Preparatory activities should, however, emphasize the initial adjustment problems that will develop from an inadequate frame of reference. Grove and Torbiorn (1985) reported that there were few premature returns or complaints from Swedish expatriates in Saudi Arabia who were told during pre-departure training that the cross-cultural experience would be deeply disturbing. Lowering the trainee's expectations of being able to cope therefore reduces future frustrations, as the expatriate will be aware that personal behaviour will be inconsistent with local practices.

Training immediately after arrival should enhance cultural awareness and lower ethnocentrism. In the culture-shocked phase, training should facilitate cognitive restructuring by providing explanations of actual cross-cultural experiences and encouraging expatriates to learn *how* to learn about the new culture. In the conformist phase, where managers have adjusted their frame of reference, culturally efficient skills would be efficiently learnt by actual practice on the job, which in turn would provide trainees with objective reactions from significant others. It is also suggested that training on assignment should involve a number of expatriates from different organizations operating within the same host culture in order that they can share and learn from one another's experiences.

The literature on expatriate training does therefore appear to reinforce the point that such training should be an ongoing process that continues throughout the assignment as opposed to being merely a short burst prior to departure. The training needs of expatriates will vary over the course of the assignment, and their receptiveness to different aspects of the training will also tend to fluctuate with the changing needs. This needs to be recognized and incorporated into any expatriate development programme.

Example 9.2   Honeywell Inc.

Honeywell Inc. believes in identifying and developing potential expatriates, usually years before a posting (Ettore, 1993). Each employee is made aware, via routine testing with specialists and consultants, of cross-cultural strengths and weaknesses. Managers use these tests as pools to identify potential expatriates, discussing career paths with them. The aim is for them to develop a cross-cultural intellect, or what they call 'strategic accountability'. A manager may suggest therefore that an employee begin studying a language or informally explore areas where an employee feels he or she might be flexible and inflexible in a foreign culture. Honeywell managers are encouraged to pick US employees for international task teams for one- to two-day meetings abroad. Some are sent on six-month foreign assignments with no home leave to see how they adjust to an overseas posting. Expatriates are made aware that they will experience cultural differences in problem-solving, motivation, leadership, use of power, consensus building and decision-making.

A few companies have begun to use repatriated employees to coach other employees who are about to be posted abroad. The briefing works particularly well if the returnee has had recent experience in the same host country. However, just the interaction with someone who has lived and worked in another country is invaluable for the soon-to-be expatriate, especially if it is a first posting abroad.

Example 9.3   Shell

Shell is one company that believes that there is no substitute for global experience. This belief is so strong that Shell employees can only refuse an international assignment once; two refusals mean the end of a career with the company (Trompenaars, 1998). Shell has 5000 expatriates world-wide, and puts a lot of effort into cross-cultural coaching. Those being sent to countries whose cultures are very different from the UK (about 35 per cent) undergo a week's residential training course in the UK or The Netherlands to give them knowledge and understanding of the social and business norms they will encounter. At least 95 per cent receive individual attention from one of the 'area desks' specializing in facts on every region of the world. About 1300 people receive briefings of one kind or another every year. Significantly, Shell intends that all graduate entrants will in future receive compulsory cross-cultural training, whether or not they have been earmarked for a foreign assignment (Barham, 1991).

Many companies conduct extensive international in-house seminars. These courses typically cover national culture differences, local politics and laws when conducting business abroad, family adaptation and international finance.

Due to the focus on the expatriation process for developing international managers, the development and training needs of host-country nationals often tend to take very much of a back seat. This is obviously one area that needs attention if companies are going to internationalize effectively. The small number of companies that have recognized this are increasingly seeking to develop their host-country nationals through transfers to corporate headquarters. This process exposes the managers to the headquarters culture, and helps them to develop a corporate perspective.

Example 9.4   Volvo
Volvo used a one-year long development programme based on learning sets to develop its high-potential international cadre. Participants would carry out international placements during the programme, meeting every few weeks at different locations in groups of six to eight. During these facilitated 'learning set' meetings, participants would explore both their work and development agendas. Exposure to different cultures and having an ongoing means of making sense of their experience proved invaluable to the individuals and extremely useful to the company, as a high performing international cadre formed through this process.

Conclusion

To maximize potential synergies, and provide greater 'reach' and flexibility for both employees and the organization, people are increasingly required to operate effectively across mindset, functional, corporate and geographic boundaries. In practice, many organizations struggle to maximize the potential of cross-boundary working, whether the context is merger integration, joint ventures, teleworking, international teamworking, or implementing diversity policies. Often employees find working in ambiguous or remote relationships difficult, and managers are challenged by managing 'new' forms of a team, made up of contractors and people working remotely or on various forms of flexible work pattern alongside full-time employees.

Managers and HR can use the opportunity afforded by cross-boundary working to introduce effective learning mechanisms, ensuring the mainstreaming of sophisticated knowledge and skills acquired by those working in various forms of strategic alliance or international placements. HR professionals can facilitate cross-boundary teamworking, help people to learn new skills and approaches, and develop new career tracks to support the broadening of experience. Managers can learn to support people working more flexibly by focusing more on work outputs and outcomes rather than on where work is carried out. Learning to manage people who are working across boundaries is about building trust in employees through appropriate selection, training and delegation, effective communication, and being willing to 'let go'.

These different and rapidly evolving ways of working are likely to be the mainspring of organizational performance in the future. In a Darwinian sense, cross-boundary working reflects the rapid evolution of the global marketplace, within which only the robustly flexible will thrive. This is where the need for high performance skills of the knowledge economy, such as speed, clarity, self-management and cultural flexibility, is most apparent. Employees who thrive in such contexts are able to acquire knowledge and deploy high-level skills, such as the ability to deal with ambiguity, resourcefulness, and effective decision-making. The challenge for organizations is to benefit more broadly from employee experiences by finding ways to mainstream individual learning. This organizational learning DNA is likely to be the key differentiator between organizations that merely survive and those which produce sustainably high performance.

Section 4: High Performance Management Practices

10

Stimulating people to sustainable levels of high performance

Your employees start every day with an extraordinary amount of energy, but the amount of 'discretionary effort' that people apply to their jobs varies tremendously. One study showed that even in relatively simple jobs the difference in discretionary performance between superior and average performers was 19 per cent.

(Hunter et al., 1990)

Introduction

A high performance organization employs people who are motivated to achieve ever-higher levels of performance. In a successful organization, high performance is achieved not only by its 'high flyers' but also by the people who make up the 'engine room' of the organization. In this chapter we shall look at what managers and HR professionals can do to enable people to produce 'good work'. This is about designing organizational structures and job roles that support high performance. Most of all, it is about building an organizational climate conducive to high performance.

Engaged performance

An economy's output depends on two things: how many people are working; and how much they produce, that is how productive they are.

(HM Treasury, 2000)

Why is that some people and organizations are more productive than others? Some people regularly 'go the extra mile' and are motivated to do so. They produce outstanding results. They release so-called 'discretionary effort', which organizations cannot command, however desirable it might be. On the other hand, many people work hard, fill their working time and beyond with large volumes of activity, but somehow productivity does not improve.

It could be argued that most employees want to do a good job, if only because work itself has a number of beneficial latent functions, according to Adrian Furnham (2003). Work is a source of activity, it keeps people occupied, it structures time and gives daily life reference points. The phenomenon of people feeling completely at a loss as to how to spend their time when they are newly made redundant or retire is well known. Amongst its other functions, some of which will be explored in the final chapters, work provides an opportunity for social interaction and a source of friendship.

Individuals tend to perform well when they are in 'flow', when they are so pleasurably immersed in challenging work that their brains work efficiently and they are energized and stimulated by what they are doing. Flow tends to occur when the work in which people are engaged is tightly linked to the individual's own goals.

This is what Gardner *et al.* (2001) describe as 'good work':

Doing good work feels good. Few things in life are as enjoyable as when we concentrate on a difficult task, using all our skills, knowing what has to be done. In flow we feel totally involved, lost in a seemingly effortless performance. Paradoxically, we feel 100 percent alive when we are so committed to the task in hand that we lose track of time, of our interests – even of our own existence. But it also happens surprisingly often at work – as long as the job provides clear goals, immediate feedback, and a level of challenges matching our skills. When these conditions are present, we have a chance to experience work as 'good' – that is, as something that allows full expression of what is best in us, something we experience as rewarding and enjoyable. Time and again, we have observed the rewards of flow bestowed on individuals who have become wholly engaged in activities that exhibit the highest sense of responsibility.

The challenge for managers is to produce the conditions in which people are doing, and believe they are doing, 'good work', for which they willingly release their discretionary effort and achieve satisfaction from a job well done.

Unlocking motivation

In a previous book (Holbeche, 1997), I explored some of the ways in which employee motivation can be affected by structure change. It is a complex subject, since what motivates one person in one work context may demotivate another person. Similarly, what motivates individuals may change at different stages of their lives. For example, employees who have young children may be more demotivated by the idea of working late than when their children have grown up and left home.

The challenge is not for managers to motivate employees, but to create the context where more people can be motivated for more of the time. Engaged performance involves recognizing and building to individual employees' motivations so that they release their discretionary effort. When people are engaged, they act in empowered ways – with autonomy, responsibility and a strong drive to deliver.

Despite the individual nature of motivation, several organizational elements are generally recognized as having an impact on employee motivation and performance. These include the organizational climate, how work is organized, the nature of the role, how people are rewarded and the way in which managers behave. Autonomy, including individual choice of project and enjoyment of work, are key elements of engaged performance. So too is personal connection to something larger, to the organization itself, especially when it is clear to the employee that his or her work directly contributes to the business strategy. The impact of reward on performance appears to be relatively small and short-term in its effect.

Within these different elements, it is recognized that high performing organizations have 'bundles' of HR practices which appear to stimulate people to higher performance without causing undue stress or harm to employee health and well-being. The underlying principle of these more effective HR practices is understanding and balancing employees' agendas with organizational needs as much as possible. Rather than being a process, engaged performance is the result of getting a number of things right for employees. Two of the ways in which managers, leaders and HR can directly influence high performance are by dealing with and 'unblocking' some of the main barriers to empowerment, and by developing appropriate management practices.

Barriers to empowerment

Many *Management Agenda* respondents report that they do not feel empowered to do their jobs. Some of the main barriers to empowerment fall into the category of lack of trust. They include cynicism and individualistic behaviours that damage teamwork. Company politics tend to make employees risk-averse and mistrustful of others, which is potentially undermining of both innovation and teamworking. Many employees lack trust in their organization's leaders at all levels. They comment negatively about risk-averse senior management who delay decisions, and abdication by managers. People simply do not believe that their leaders mean what they say because chronic problems, such as poor performance management and large amounts of political behaviour, are not tackled.

In practice, many employees lack parameters within which to be empowered; they are given unclear goals, receive little help in developing the skills they need to do the job, are inappropriately delegated to, and end up feeling aggrieved that what they have done receives no attention or – worse – that the only form of feedback they receive is criticism. In the public sector in particular, managers appear to feel they have little autonomy. Frequent changes in government policy tend to cause confusion and heavy workloads, with little progress to show for them.

Bullying at work is a recognized feature of organizational life, with 18 per cent of *Management Agenda* respondents experiencing harassment to some or a great extent. The commonest form of abuse is people being excluded or sidelined. Another common form of harassment is when people perceive that they have been prevented from having a work–life balance. The main perpetrators of harassment are reported to be senior managers. *Management Agenda* respondents suggest that a culture change will be necessary in many of their organizations if empowerment is to become a reality.

Micro-management

Sadly, various surveys suggest that one of the greatest sources of workplace stress is people's relationship with their bosses. For example, 75 per cent of respondents in the 2003 *Management Agenda* survey describe their boss as a major source of stress. Managers who fail to 'walk the talk', who hold staff back and who pursue personal rather than organizational agendas are described as being destructive of high performance. Many respondents report that there is too much focus on unrealistic targets in their organizations.

Managers are commonly described as being poor at delegating, and only too pleased to take back tasks if the employee gets something wrong. If there is also a blame culture, people will tend not to ask for help when they are struggling or get things wrong; instead they tend to keep their heads down until they are found out. This lack of accountability in turn tends to encourage managers to start micro-managing, which then causes employees to ask themselves why they should bother to take any initiative. This vicious circle is made worse when workloads are heavy, stress levels high and people play politics rather than getting on with the job. This context seems more likely to reduce employee motivation than to raise aspirations and skill levels.

Enablers of high performance working

In organizations where employees are recognized as 'volunteers' rather than 'wage-slaves', leaders develop policies, management approaches and organizational arrangements which promote good practice and support employees to do their jobs. When employees believe that what they do is worthwhile, they tend to 'go the extra mile' and produce engaged performance.

Focusing on the customer

Focusing on the customer seems to produce high levels of staff engagement. B&Q, the DIY retailer, for instance, use effective measurement as a means of managing performance and of assessing levels of employee engagement, with its knock-on effect on customer service. Every B&Q store is constrained by the number of customers it can serve in peak periods. B&Q is therefore examining the ways in which it can increase the average transaction value (or sales) per customer while keeping its existing cost base static – i.e. generate more revenue from the same number of customers. Store management therefore focuses on increasing the knowledge of shop-floor staff, training them to advise customers on the differences between cheaper and more expensive goods, and helping service-oriented customer advisers to develop sales techniques.

The store firm also encourages the use of employee-specific metrics. Employee engagement, for instance, is measured twice a year through a census using Gallup's B12 instrument. The outputs are then compared between stores and against other retailers and non-retail organizations in the UK and US.

Example 10.1   Bayer Diagnostics

Building a customer-focused culture pays dividends, as Bayer Diagnostics has also found. When chemical and pharmaceutical group Bayer bought Chiron Diagnostics in 1998, the Group chose to define a new approach to meet the future needs of the business rather than simply merge the two cultures. The new culture would be based on behaviours determined by customer expectations, and how employees met those expectations. The company worked with feedback to realize its new vision. It found the questions that are indicative of customer loyalty. Leaders were challenged to meet the answers head on, and to be prepared to be measured against them.

Once Bayer Diagnostics had determined customer demands through customer satisfaction surveys, the challenge was to create a close fit between customer expectations and employee behaviours. The company put in place an employee attitude survey for about 7000 of its employees, with a core of Gallup 'B12' questions. These are the key measures of employee attitudes that, for Bayer, drive customer loyalty. They include whether employees felt inspired by the business, and whether they felt that their job activity directly affected customers.

Managers and employees were challenged to create a more customer-focused culture that was more productive and used the skills of the workforce. Managers and supervisors took part in a separate 360-degree feedback programme, which has helped management to develop to meet the needs of the business. It has also created a common language of leadership across all the countries in which Bayer Diagnostics operates. All feedback processes are linked through the use of the Balanced Business Scorecard, measuring performance in four areas – financial, people, process and client. Ongoing surveys, conducted via the web or on paper, mean that Bayer can analyse trends and predict the changing behaviours of its workforce, allowing its leaders to make informed decisions about what actions to take to ensure the business performs. New hires and promotions are tested against the model, ensuring that the customer focus is perpetuated (Horn, 2002).

Customer-focused purpose

For Richard Ellsworth (2002), the most effective vision for change is customer-focused. Roffey Park's research confirms Ellsworth's findings. In the *Management Agenda* survey, respondents were generally positive about their collective sense of purpose and commitment. The highest commitment tended to be reported by people whose organization had a customer-focused purpose. People report that their own level of commitment is high, with three-quarters of the sample (75 per cent) maintaining that they often stretch themselves at work and 'go the extra mile', compared to just 3 per cent that rarely do.

In one organization, having a customer-focused purpose was about 'Staff who go beyond their job description to meet the needs of individual students'. In another, it was demonstrated in 'Greater awareness and concern being voiced regarding vulnerable members of our society (our clients)'. One respondent described how 'Our surveys show that people take pride in doing a good job and believe they are dealing well with customers, despite constraints and difficulties'.

We also found a number of interesting correlations in our data with 'having meaningful work'. It would appear that organizations with a primarily share-holder focus are relatively more likely to have employees who experience a lack of meaning and who are actively looking for more meaning. Employees are unlikely to feel involved in decision-making, and there is more likely to be a transactional psychological contract. There is likely to be more political behaviour, more risk-aversion and low trust. Employees are more likely to report low commitment, both towards the organization and from it to them. They are more likely to be cynical about their leaders and the organization itself. These organizations are also reported to be least likely to have high levels of creativity. In organizations with a broader stakeholder focus, employees are likely to be more neutral – lacking a clear sense of purpose yet not actively pursuing a strong sense of purpose.

Conversely, organizations with a strong customer focus are likely to have employees who feel better about what is going on. This customer focus is also likely to encompass high degrees of environmental responsibility, which employees consider a good thing. Typically, such organizations have high levels of recognition and employee development, and appropriate forms of reward. Employees are also likely to demonstrate higher levels of trust in their leaders, have higher morale, and experience less stress. They are more likely to feel that they are involved in decision-making and idea-sharing. They are also more likely to report that they have a satisfactory work–life balance. Such organizations are more likely to be considered supportive of creativity by employees.

Research carried out in the travel and tourism industry on behalf of the Best Practice Forum by Surrey University (2003) suggested that the seven most critical areas for a successful business in this growing sector of industry were:

- Setting goals based around a customer focus
- Planning and controlling the operation
- Partnering and networking
- Having a clear internal and external communication
- Setting and achieving consistent standards
- A strategic approach to workplace management
- Performance measurement and benchmarking.

In the *Management Agenda* survey, respondents reporting the closest alignment between organizational purpose and related systems and practices appear to experience a more meaningful work experience than where these links are less clear. In his book *Leading with Purpose*, Ellsworth (2002) suggests that companies with a customer-focused purpose:

- Found change easier to manage
- Had employees who experienced work as more meaningful
- Achieved higher shareholder returns over the long-term
- Had stronger cultures
- Had more internal alignment.

In one company, the integration of its customer-focused purpose with its working practices has been worked through to a fine degree. Values deriving from the core purpose include defending human rights, supporting community trade and activating self-esteem. Managers at all levels develop balanced objectives, which are then integrated into a customer plan as part of the scorecard approach, alongside plans for people, operations and finance. Competencies including 'think customer', 'drive results through people', 'managing change' and 'communicating effectively' guide employee behaviour. Ways of working are designed to be better for customers, simpler for staff and cheaper to use, while maintaining high quality.

However, having a customer-focused purpose goes beyond having a static insight into the customer's world, including the customer's end-user. Building a customer-focused vision invariably means that one change will lead to another as customers' needs change.

Example 10.2   Scottish Power

According to Paul Archer, MD of Scottish Power's customer service division in 2000, 'organizations should be designed around the needs of their customers'. To this end, Scottish Power set about improving systems and processes. However, it was recognized that these would be not benefit the customer if people were not trained and motivated and communication was poor. A programme of consultation at open forums with employees working in customer services established some key themes for a change programme:

- Overall customer service needed to be improved
- Training and development were an important part of making it happen
- Communication and teamworking had to be enhanced and a culture of trust established
- Quality had to be put above quantity.

Over 700 opportunities and ideas for improvement came from these open forums. Senior managers listened and decided to act quickly. In June 2000, the 'Wall of Pledges' was launched. It had nineteen bricks, each one representing a pledge from senior management to address key issues raised through the open forums. Each brick became the responsibility of a 'business champion', and the results started to come through quickly, with an overall improvement on many of the key performance indicators. For instance, the billing backlog, which had become a great barrier to customer service, was reduced by 80 per cent. Staffing issues were being addressed and communication was improving.

The change programme can be seen as four stages: review, reform, renew and reinvent. At a second round of open forums, Archer talked about the roles of everyone in the organization in creating change. Key themes were prioritized and cross-functional teams were set up with other divisions to encourage joined-up thinking. Scottish Power is aiming to move away from a management-led approach to decision-making taking place as near to the customer as possible. Some new managers have been appointed to help invigorate the organization. Training and development are being used as a strategic tool to embed the customer-focused culture (Sparrow, 2001).

Building a positive work climate

Some things that can make a difference to releasing creativity and high performance are evident in the *Management Agenda*. We ask employees to describe what in their organizations appears to enable high performance working. Employees mention as positive having access to a wider availability of flexible work processes; effective teamworking; open and democratic leadership at all levels; the deliberate curbing of political behaviours; innovative career tracks; manageable workloads; and training and development opportunities. In high performance organizations, diversity is not left to chance but is 'mainstreamed' and teamworking is actively encouraged. People are clear about where the organization is going so that they are able to prioritize well. Effective performance management takes place, and managers have a focus on both people and results. Managers support staff and are trained to coach and enable others. They provide structured feedback on a regular basis, and are rewarded for how well they develop and use the skills of their teams.

In organizations aiming for high performance, leaders and HR tackle the symptoms of a poor work climate, such as the lack of a teamworking ethos, an ageist culture, lack of diversity, bullying/harassment and political manoeuvring. Developing quality leadership at all levels becomes a priority. Organizational systems, processes and policies send out powerful signals about what the company stands for and values. These should encourage and reinforce behaviour that the company really values rather than leaving good practice to chance. For example, as a company, 3M is well-known for innovation. The company recognizes the nature of the creative task, and a 3M policy enables all technical staff to spend 15 per cent of their time on projects of their own. In practice, take-up varies, with some people taking less and others more time working on their own projects. What is important is the message that the organization has some slack built in, which enables some freedom of movement.

Empowerment

A positive climate is typified by empowerment. In a high performing organization, authority moves from decisions made only at the top to decisions made all along the line, at whatever points are appropriate. Moving decision-making authority down the organization requires managers to be willing to let go of power and to trust that employees at lower levels will make accurate, well-informed decisions. This trust is directly linked to the loosening of boundaries surrounding competence and information. There are no unnecessary rules, policies, procedures or practices. There are useful and effective systems, and good information flow.

A culture of empowerment is characterized as being 'no-blame'. There is an acceptance of risk-taking and learning. There is a deliberate focus on building trust. Challenging but achievable goals are set for the organization and its employees. Everyone within the organization knows what is expected of them. Roles provide enough 'stretch' that employees are stimulated to achieve and grow, but not so much that employees become 'burnt out'. Employees' responsibilities and accountabilities are matched with the correct level of authority, so employees can accomplish tasks without having constantly to seek approval, and people are neither under- nor over-managed (see Figure 10.1).

People are proud to belong to the organization. Empowerment thrives when there is clarity about what needs to be done as well as what can be stopped. It also thrives when there are not too many change projects under way at any one time. *Management Agenda* respondents suggest that it is only in such a culture that people are likely to be fully accountable for their performance. In order to shift authority to the right level, current decision-making assumptions should be challenged, large-scale interventions used to shift authority, management roles moved from controller to coach, and layers removed if necessary.

Organizational climate dimensions

Studies of organizational climate – how it feels to work in a particular environment – suggest that a positive work climate has a significant effect on organizational performance. For instance, Collins and Porras (1994) found that each of the eighteen 'visionary' companies they studied had dynamic, change-oriented climates, with employees sharing a strong sense of purpose. In the Litwin and Stringer model (Watkin, 2001), organizational climate is reflected in the following:

- *Responsibility* – how much people are held to account, combined with freedom to act. Employees tend to be more motivated when they are allowed to accomplish tasks without constantly seeking their managers' approval. To improve this, it is important to delegate as many tasks as possible to employees and hold them accountable for the outcomes. They should be encouraged to take calculated risks without fear of blame.

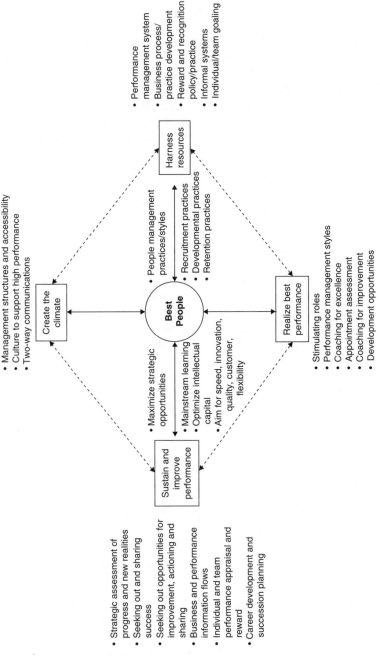

Figure 10.1 A model for performance management.

- *Flexibility* – the extent to which people are allowed to be innovative. In a positive climate, new ideas are accepted easily and unnecessary rules and red tape are kept to the minimum. Employees are encouraged to come up with new ideas, and there are minimum lines of authority.
- *Standards* – set to be stretching yet achievable, characterized by a drive to improve. Managers set challenging but realistic goals, give regular feedback and make sure that performance measures are adequate and clear. Individual employees should be given plenty of opportunity to take part in the goal-setting and planning process. Marriott Hotels has a list of 20 standards, known as 'The Daily List', which all Marriott employees should be aware of, wherever they are in the world. It covers such areas as appearance, cleanliness and telephone technique. A 20-day rolling programme encourages managers and team leaders to focus on each one separately. Marriott also has a major training initiative for all staff, known as 'Spirit to Serve'. While the 90-day 'new hire' induction deals with the technical side of working for Marriott, Spirit to Serve concentrates on how employees work with customers and with each other (Carrington, 2002).
- *Team commitment* – people tend to give of their best when they are committed to the organization and proud to belong to it. In most roles, employees need to be able to cooperate with others in order to get the job done. Managers should resolve conflicts quickly and foster cooperation between individuals.
- *Clarity* – of goals, purpose, levels of accountability, organizational values. It is important that employees know what exactly is expected of them and how they can contribute to the organization's goals. Policies, procedures and lines of authority should also be clear. Communication methods should be two-way and effective.
- *Rewards* – when people feel appropriately (i.e. differentially) rewarded for good performance. Pay needs to be equitable. Managers need to use encouragement more often than criticism. The promotion system should help the best people rise to the top, and development opportunities should be used to both reward and improve performance.
- *Leadership style* – when leadership/management style is out of step with the demands of the situation, effort falls away. Alignment can be checked by using multi-rater feedback questionnaires on style and climate dimensions. Leadership development should be used as appropriate.

How does climate affect performance?

Dimensions of climate directly affect employee motivation in different ways, according to Cannon (2003). Standards and clarity are strong stimulants of the power motivation, leading to concern with maintaining or increasing control. On the other hand, standards and clarity tend to induce high stress, while dimensions such as support and recognition tend to lower stress. A low-stress climate, characterized by high levels of support and recognition, is likely to lead to higher employee development and retention. Commitment and responsibility are strong stimulants of achievement motivation, developing a concern with excellence and goal achievement. Recognition and teamwork strongly stimulate the affiliative motivation, causing concern with the quality of human relationships and with feelings of trust, mutuality and teamwork among organizational members.

A culture of risk-taking, in which employees are encouraged and rewarded for taking risks, can improve an individual's performance by up to 39 per cent, leading people to want to put more into their jobs, be more committed to their organization and more closely matched with their jobs than in a risk-averse culture (source: Corporate Leadership Council 2002 Performance Management Survey). Similarly, a culture of internal communication, in which there is frequent and effective communication between peers, can make a significant difference to performance.

However, various studies have found that the climate factors that most positively affect short-term performance are in an inverse relationship with employee needs – i.e. the job structures and management pressure that most directly generate short-term productivity tend to result in negative conditions for employee development and retention.

Effective public sector leadership and management

In public sector bodies, organizational leaders have to create the conditions for high performance against a backdrop of high public expectation and politician-led targets. Organizationally, public sector bodies are complex, and their agendas are usually broad. The range of work carried out by local authorities, for example, is as diverse as maintaining roads, ensuring that the vulnerable in society are safe, protecting public health, helping high street businesses serve their customers better, managing the local education service and providing refuse collection.

Many surveys suggest that working in UK local government organizations is far from easy. Managers are frequently reported as being sources of pressure for employees. Other 'hotspots' include high public expectations, slimmed-down structures, poor inter-team relations, inability to handle heavy workloads, and lack of support from 'County Hall' or the corporate centre.

The most effective leaders are reported by *Management Agenda* respondents as being those who develop other people and are perceived to be empathetic to the people they lead. Ineffective leaders allow bureaucracy to overwhelm people and let low performers 'get away with it', leading to overall lower levels of performance. These two elements of leadership – developing others and holding people accountable – are thought to be key differentiators of the best leaders.

Leadership and performance in the education sector

In their studies of leadership practices in UK schools and colleges, the Hay Group found that good organizational performance, assessed in terms of examination results, financial management, staff development and student retention, is positively correlated with a good organizational climate. In particular, a college leader who is able to use a wide repertoire of leadership styles and who is 'emotionally intelligent' is more likely to help create a positive climate, which in turn leads to higher student retention. Drawing on the work of Litwin and Stringer (1984) at Harvard University, Hay's research indicates that a leader's behaviour is the biggest single variable affecting organizational climate, accounting for between 50 and 70 per cent of performance variations (Watkin, 2001).

Good leaders make good climates

In other words, good managers create good climates. However, there is no one single style that consistently produces high performance in others. The Hay Group suggest that leaders deliver business performance through a blend of role requirements, individual characteristics, leadership styles and the work climate they help to create. They suggest that a combination of leadership styles is required in order to enable the leader to match the needs of the organization at any given time. The styles they highlight include pace-setting, democratic, coaching, authoritative, affiliative, and coercive.

The role of leaders in building a high performance climate is more about tackling some of the main barriers to high performance, such as lack of time and bureaucracy, than increasing the pressure for results and producing grand-sounding vision statements.

Is good performance solely due to leaders?

On the other hand, the idea that achieving high performance is solely due to the leader is open to challenge. In fact, it can be argued that highly charismatic leaders can actually drain energy from the organization they lead. Collins and Porras (1994), for instance, suggest that charismatic leadership can actually damage a company's long-term prospects, and point to several 'visionary companies' (such as 3M) that focus on being a visionary company rather than having high-profile leaders.

In the somewhat beleaguered education sector, Hudson (2004), in a critique of the assumptions about the role of leaders (especially 'superheads' in turning around failing schools) points out that a missing element in this diagnosis is the prevailing culture of the institution and the interaction between leaders and followers, the relationships, the trust, the dialogue, the learning. For Sergiovanni (1984), too, cultural forces are at the top of his hierarchy of leadership forces. For him, 'cultural life in schools is constructed reality, and leaders play a part in constructing this reality', but such reality can only be jointly constructed with teachers and pupils.

Similarly, external forces and pressures can sometimes produce contradictory effects from those intended. A plethora of government targets mean that managers and staff working in the secondary and tertiary education sectors in the UK, at the leading edge of the 'Learning for Life' and 16–19 education initiatives which are designed to close skills gaps, face great pressure to attract and retain students and help them achieve success in their chosen qualifications. Constraints on resources, the demand for higher standards, new ways of working and growing bureaucracy make the task of meeting the demands of a wide variety of stakeholders, including the Department for Education and Skills, Learning and

Skills Councils, ALI, Local Education Authorities, OFSTED, governors, parents and pupils, all the more challenging. In addition there are often community and social issues to deal with, as well as constraints on reward systems and levels for staff. Far from motivating staff to achieve more, combined pressures for change could potentially lead to initiative overload and falling standards.

The leader's actions have a strong effect on the beliefs and expectations of the work group. According to Cannon (2003), leaders build productive climates by shaping culture over the longer term while simultaneously impacting on climate through individual leadership practices. On the whole, innovation appears to thrive in a relatively egalitarian, status-free context, where participative styles of management are the order of the day and where teams develop their own processes without strong control by management. Equally, leadership does not happen in a vacuum, and while a leader can democratically share power and leadership, he or she is dependent on a positive response from staff to act collegially, engage in professional dialogue and promote learning.

Research into nineteen US schools found that in learning organizations with high readiness for shared leadership, principals were 'proactive; chameleon-like it seemed – intuitively sensing where support was needed, when to stand back and when to take the lead, revealing the interactive nature between leadership and followership'. In these schools, principals 'took the risk of "letting go" and appeared to believe in the capability of their teachers' (Hipp and Huffman, 2000).

To achieve higher levels of performance, the old adage of 'smarter, not harder' should apply, together with giving people the means to target their efforts as constructively as possible. There also needs to be a focus on managing talent, so that directors and managers have a clear idea about the quality of talent available to them. A key enabler of a flexible high performing organization is the new role of the strategic middle manager. With shared information and authority, the manager must facilitate, coach and counsel, mentor, translate strategies into goals and design processes for joint assessment.

Improving the workplace climate

To create a winning environment, the first step is to take stock of the climate and compare the 'as is' with the sort of climate required for high performance. A diagnosis of how healthy the climate is can clarify whether the climate needs to be modified slightly, or is inadequate to support unit requirements and therefore needs major overhaul. Telltale signs of organizational 'ill-health' can be found in poor communication among staff members, long and unproductive meetings, and low staff morale. Conversely, a healthy climate may be evident in low rates of staff turnover amongst talented people.

Based on their diagnosis, managers then need to set priorities and goals to develop the required climate and formulate a strategy, together with action plan, to bring about changes. Specific activities should be targeted at climate dimensions where there is the greatest opportunity for influencing a unit's climate.

For those organizations that have been more successful at fostering creativity and innovation, the key enablers are to be found in the organizational culture. Initiatives aimed at improving climate and culture need to be made coherent.

Cross-stream groups and project teams can spread good practice around. Some of the many ways in which workplace climate can be improved include:

- Regular reviews of workloads
- E-mail protocols that restrict use to essential purposes
- Good chairing of meetings, especially by facilitators
- Encouraging employees to initiate tasks they think are important
- Having a realistic set of values that are evaluated
- Managers offering informal feedback
- HR acting as 'corporate glue'
- Managers encouraging risk-taking and innovation in others
- The extent to which the manager rewards innovation
- Honesty of communication during discussions of individual performance
- Quick and effective methods of decision-making
- People being allowed to spend some of their time on projects of their own choosing
- Letting people spend some of the training budget on learning of their own choosing
- Teams given freedom to make mistakes
- Using multi-rater feedback to raise self-awareness for development purposes.

(*Management Agenda* findings.)

Example 10.3   Hewlett Packard

Hewlett Packard is one of the companies described as 'visionary' by Collins and Porras (1994, in Sadler, 2003). The company defined how a corporation should treat employees and contribute to the community in which it operates. The principal features of the company's HR policies and systems reflect this culture, and include:

- An open-door management policy, together with 'management by walking around'
- Few status differentials – no management perks, an open office layout for managers, frequent informal social occasions at all levels, an open book approach to financial results
- Recruitment primarily directly from college – selection tests are not used, but teams of engineers and managers go to campuses and interview candidates, selecting those they feel will fit in with the HP culture
- An informal approach to talent identification and placement in the early years; at middle-level management and above, managers are reviewed regularly and assessed on technical, leadership and administrative skills
- Appraisals made on the basis of objectives that individuals set for themselves
- Generous financial rewards and openness in respect of them
- Extensive use of team rewards
- Layoffs only as a last resort
- Substantial provision of training and development opportunities.

High quality communication

In high performing organizations, a great value is placed on the quality, rather than the quantity, of communication. Organizational values are reflected in behaviours. People care about the organization and its reputation. Information moves from being closely held or integrated at the top to open information sharing throughout the organization. Owing to this shared understanding, all employees have a common sense of purpose and an understanding of organizational goals. They are therefore more understanding of organizational directives.

In order to share information effectively, the message and the channel need to be aligned, both good and bad news needs to be shared, messages need to be both simple and complex, and information should be used to encourage change. In the 2004 *Management Agenda* survey, respondents described the communication processes that they find most useful. An overwhelming majority (92 per cent) stressed the importance of having one-to-one sessions with their manager. Team briefings (77 per cent) and e-mails (69 per cent) were also considered useful, as were web chats, shared folders, floor briefings, voice mails, presentations, newsletters, text messages, team events, conference calls and staff survey feedback.

Meetings

Meetings are often described as a waste of time, especially if they involve large numbers of people who are present, whether or not they have anything to learn or contribute. Preparation and effective follow-up can make meetings more valuable. Meetings 'health checks' can be useful in establishing some planning and discipline regarding time spent in meetings. These can take the form of a prompt distributed amongst people planning to attend a specific meeting, to explore:

- What's the purpose of the meeting?
- Who needs to be there?
- What items need to be discussed and what is their nature (e.g. information sharing, decision required etc.)?
- What preparation is required?
- Time allocation for specific items
- Follow-up procedures and responsibilities.

Enabling physical environment

The physical environment must not only be safe and secure but also conducive to the nature of work to be carried out and to the needs of employees. Overheated or cramped conditions or too much exposure to VDUs, strobe lighting or noise may cause physical illness and sometimes psychiatric conditions such as depression. BP Amoco and Standard Life are just two of many organizations that take care to ensure that the ergonomics of the workplace are appropriate. People must have the tools they need to do the job, in particular access to information and efficient processes. IT systems especially need to be fit-for-purpose and help people do the job, rather than be an added difficulty. Equipment should be serviced and replaced before it becomes obsolete.

Similarly, the scope of employers' responsibility includes harassment, where it is recognized that medical problems may be caused by managers or fellow employees who bully or victimize individuals. Employers who fail to recognize, control or alleviate this may be culpable.

Fun

When people enjoy what they do, they tend to work hard and play hard. According to Pfeffer (1998a):

> *People work for money, but they work even more for meaning in their lives. In fact they work to have fun. Companies that ignore this fact are essentially bribing their employees and will pay the price in lack of loyalty and commitment.*

The workplace climate should encourage celebration of success and use opportunities when employees come together as a means of creating a sense of shared community. This is particularly challenging when people work remotely, but many managers address the problem by bringing groups of employees together at least once a month so that they can socialize while doing business. Various surveys suggest that giving staff time off to play football or go-karting results in better 'bonding' in the office, and a more productive workforce.

Example 10.4   Transformation and high performance at DARA
Effective people management and development have been important elements of the successful corporate transformation at the UK's Defence Aviation Repair Agency (DARA). Although at the time of writing the future of DARA has been put in doubt by a government review of defence contracts, the award-winning culture change that has been effected at DARA has been recognized at outstanding.

The Agency was created in April 1999 following the strategic defence review conducted by the government in the previous year. Born of a merger of existing parts of the Ministry of Defence, it was to offer a competitive alternative to the private sector by taking on trading-fund status. This meant that, although DARA remained a part of the MOD, the government would withdraw its financial backing and the agency would have to survive by competing on the open market for business.

The management only had two years to turn the organization into a commercially successful operation, winning business from the government and the private sector. DARA has not only achieved trading fund status; it has also consistently exceeded its own expectations, beating quality targets by 12 per cent. The increase in orders was exceeded by £8.3 million and the increase in commercial revenue was 2 per cent above target.

The path to transformation from a 'hierarchical and risk-averse' culture that would not survive in a commercial environment to one that emphasized the importance of the customer involved several important steps along the way:

- Developing a vision of high performance working
- Taking stock of what was working so that it could be retained
- Avoiding 'rubbishing' the past
- Cross-fertilization through multidisciplinary, multi-skilled teams
- Hands-off leadership
- Flat structures
- Open-door policies
- A 'New Ways of Working' change programme
- Behavioural competencies and a system of self-directed team working for staff on the shop floor
- Replacing the inflexible pay and grading system with broadbanding, with an upfront pay rise in return for commitment to accepting the new culture
- Training up internal facilitators to deliver the change programme to the rest of the workforce
- The introduction of new technology.

These various changes were introduced against a backdrop of 3000 job cuts, made to eliminate any duplication of work. Many staff did not see the reason for change, since a number of them had worked for the organization for over 20 years. A voluntary early-release scheme was introduced to allow those who could not make the change to leave with dignity.

Employee resistance was gradually overcome through the following:

- A 'multidirectional' communication strategy, which involved face-to-face group briefings by chief executive Steve Hill and other directors, a regular newsletter giving employees the chance to write in with their views, an annual staff attitude survey and a company intranet
- The chief executive and the board making it clear that *status quo* was not an option
- DARA became the first part of the MOD to sign a formal partnership agreement with its four recognized trades unions in May 2000, transforming the nature of union-management relations from 'traditional' to proactive; in return, DARA pledged the unions to respect and encourage the role of trade unions within the partnership
- As part of the leadership development programme, managers were required to spend three days on the shop floor doing some non-technical work to break down the barriers between themselves and their team and to find out what the real problems were
- Managers were helped to understand the need for change and given skills to train employees; managers also had to plan their own training routines with the help of the organization development specialists so

that they could better identify, prioritize and tackle problems that existed on the shop floor.

The effect of these various initiatives has been dramatic. Managers better understand the business they are in. The Agency is now engaging more actively with its customers and anticipating demands. Efficiency soared from 40 per cent to 70 per cent after only one session on team communications. Better customer service, including a saving of £14 million through faster turnaround times, has seen customer relationships improve tenfold.

Employees now have autonomy to solve their own problems, and this degree of ownership gives them more of a sense of pride in their work. They can even control their annual leave, as long as their team meets its targets. An employee development scheme has been introduced to give people the skills they need to help them progress through the organization. By developing its own consultants and change agents, DARA aims to become completely self-sufficient with regard to employee development (Rana, 2002).

Talent development

Speaking in 1998, Richard Brown, CEO of Cable and Wireless, suggested that, even in down times, organizations should 'train and develop your critical people, managerial and technical. Nothing is more important than growing your "A" players, which is conducive to better retention, and promptly dealing with "C" players. This is an opportunity for exercising leadership'.

Building competence

In a high performance organization, competence moves from leadership skills exercised at senior levels and technical skills exercised at lower levels to competencies distributed through all levels, regardless of title or position. When an individual has the skill to do a job, he or she is encouraged to pitch in and do it. Training, including strategic education, is given to all employees. Changes in staffing and recruiting philosophy support the aim of gaining competent employees. Job rotation, developmental assignments and performance management all aim to produce higher performance standards and build capability, commitment and retention among those who meet the standards. Diffusing all kinds of competency throughout the organization supports the aim of being able to improvise and to engage in speedy problem-solving and decision-making.

Challenging jobs

The quality of work that employees produce depends to a large extent on fitting the person to the role (through effective recruitment, selection and training).

It also involves fitting the job to the person (through job design; roles that are appropriate to employees' skills and interests and in which there is sufficient 'stretch' that they are stimulated to achieve more but not so much pressure that they are spread too thinly). Roles should be designed to ensure that individuals are not overloaded and that workloads are relevant and manageable.

Typically, people become energized and experience 'flow' when they are in interesting and challenging jobs. People investing the bulk of their energies in what they do best tend to have increased feelings of happiness and accomplishment. According to Howard Gardner, we would all benefit from paying less attention to our weaknesses and more respect to the unique collection of our strengths, idiosyncrasies and experience. Sadly, it would appear that this is not generally the situation many employees experience in their job roles. Since 1970, the Gallup Organization has interviewed 2 million 'top performers' in 60 countries about how and when they work their best. In their book *Now Discover Your Strengths*, Marcus Buckingham and Donald Clifton (2001) claim that as few as 20 per cent of employees in large organizations said that they got to play to their distinctive abilities each day.

For many people, having the chance to achieve something significant is very motivating. In my study of *High Flyers* (Holbeche, 1998), I asked respondents who were considered to have high potential to identify, unprompted, the one thing which most motivated them:

- 35 per cent reported that personal achievement was the main motivator for them
- 30 per cent noted challenge as the key motivator
- Other motivators mentioned were helping others, recognition, financial reward and power.

Jobs therefore should be designed to ensure that the jobholder is continuing to learn and have access to new opportunities to develop through challenge. The appropriate degree of challenge and stretch will depend on the individual and the circumstances. For people whose role has been relatively static, the level of challenge needed to have a motivating effect can be quite low. For others, challenge needs to be of a high order to be stimulating. Research by the Centre for Creative Leadership suggests that the level of challenge varies according to the difficulty of the task, the availability of resources required to do the task, the importance of the task, and the visibility of the results of performance to people whose opinions matter to the jobholder.

For high flyers in particular, it is important that the outcome of the task is not a foregone conclusion. People get a stronger sense of achievement if the chances of success or failure are finely balanced. People also want to know that their performance has been recognized and high performance appropriately rewarded. Many people place a high value on the quality of work relationships, in particular the opportunity for effective teamworking, which brings them into contact with people from other parts of the organization or elsewhere. Responsibility is a major motivator for many employees, especially if they develop knowledge capital as a result.

Training and development

Organizations need people to have the skills for the job. As jobs change, skill requirements alter. Although training and development are usually amongst the first areas to be cut back in hard economic times, organizations which maintain their investment in training and development, especially in skills and topics that should protect future revenues (such as leadership, innovation, teamworking and new business processes), are likely to reap the benefits of employee commitment and upskilling.

Example 10.5   B&Q

B&Q is one company that has maintained (or increased) its spending on training in recent years. It has also made a multi-million-pound capital investment in a learning management system. This initiative is seen by managers as a means of achieving the business strategy, with better bottom-line impact. B&Q's decision stemmed from a need to deliver better value to its customers, not least in terms of improving levels of service. The DIY industry has a relatively poor record on customer service, and the B&Q Board recognized the clear links between employees, service levels and profitability, since the Director of HR, Mike Cutt, was able to point to a direct correlation between customer satisfaction and sales.

The chosen option was e-learning, since 25 000 of its staff are located at 300 stores throughout the UK. While investment in training has increased by 100 per cent, the volume of training carried out has increased five-fold. B&Q has also directly tied compensation for staff to their ability to put their training into action. It has replaced an appraisal-based merit system with a series of inflation-linked 'spot' rates. Employees are now offered small incremental increases to their hourly pay rate, based on how quickly they progress through the learning and development programme. The system is not based on course completion but on applied knowledge. An existing scheme offering team-based bonuses – based on factors such as how well a store fares in sales, service and shrinkage – continues to run alongside the new compensation scheme.

B&Q has also implemented six-month 'fast-track' management training programmes, designed to promote employees through the ranks of team leader, store manager, general manager and regional manager (Rodgers, 2003).

There is an obvious organizational benefit not only in providing core skills training but also in providing 'fine-tuning' for key individuals at different stages of their career. Employees are keen to develop their employability. They want to learn leading edge methodologies, and have the opportunity to use enhanced skills and knowledge. There is a wider range of training and learning methodologies available, including online learning groups, e-learning in general, self-managed and action learning groups, conferences, workshops, mentoring and executive coaching, to name but a few. There is increasing emphasis on evaluation to ensure that training activities result in value added.

The link between training and retention

Training is more important than financial incentives in retaining telecoms staff, according to Watson Wyatt, who conducted a survey of fourteen telecoms companies in 2001 and found that training rated higher than increasing basic pay, bonus payments and career progression in addressing retention problems. Indeed, other studies have found that increasing pay may not make much difference in retaining staff when other problems remain unresolved. Money lets people know the value of their work to the organization and is closely related to recognition and status, but does not actually help to sustain motivation for most people in the long term. However, whilst people may be motivated more by other factors than by money, they may leave if they feel that they are not paid their worth.

Training must be relevant, and employees should have the opportunity to use the new skills acquired back at work. At IBM, training is considered a key part of career development. Since IBM is trying to attract highly skilled individuals, the employment contract has to be tailored to individual needs.

Coaching, mentoring, buddying

The most popular methods for dealing with retention are centred on new recruits, especially by providing training and development. A good induction process ensures that successful candidates are integrated within the organization in the shortest possible time. Affinity groups and buddy systems can be very effective in helping new recruits to settle in.

The 2003 CIPD survey suggests that the biggest increase in methods for improving retention is in offering coaching/mentoring/buddying systems to help new recruits to adjust as quickly as possible. Increasing pay to improve retention is not as popular as in previous years. The current most popular methods are assisting recruits to develop through improved training and development, and improved induction processes.

Blended learning

It is perhaps due to the increased use of technology that knowledge management appears to be moving up the management agenda. The main drivers of this are usually to improve internal efficiency and minimize wastage through sharing. However, knowledge management practices are still perhaps not generally well established in the workplace, and there appear to be few incentives for people to share or co-create knowledge. Typically, few organizations offer specific rewards for knowledge management activity. Similarly, e-learning is only slowly becoming more firmly established in the business world, with applications now extending beyond technical knowledge/skill acquisition to management development and leadership training.

'Blended' learning, combining e-learning with classroom and other methods, appears to be more popular than e-learning alone. Computers add a sophisticated channel of communication, enabling learners to connect with fellow learners and have access to interactive materials. Many learners still prefer a face-to-face situation. According to Kaye Thorne (2003), blended learning is:

> the most logical and natural evolution of our learning agenda. It suggests an elegant solution to the challenges of tailoring learning and development to the needs of individuals. It represents an opportunity to integrate the innovative and technological advantages offered by online learning with the interaction and participation offered in the best traditional learning.

The role of HR in building a high performance workplace climate

As discussed earlier in this chapter, various research projects suggest that in many organizations the workplace climate actually works against employees being willing to release so-called 'discretionary effort'. In Roffey Park's *Management Agenda* survey, for instance, people report that they are not empowered to do their jobs. HR can help build a positive work climate through helping managers to design challenging jobs that offer people responsibility, provide the resources to do the job and hold people accountable.

Managers may need help in standard setting, providing clarity of goals and targets and managing team dynamics. They may need coaching regarding their own leadership style and help in developing their ability to develop team members. HR can support the aim of developing competent employees through enabling job rotation, developmental assignments and relevant training. HR can also work with line management to design effective performance management systems that are relationship-based rather than a system-led process. They can build effective reward and recognition systems which differentiate and reinforce good performance, and offer a degree of individual choice in how performance is rewarded.

Conclusion

High performance is often the result of right people, right place, right time. Achieving high performance on a more consistent basis puts a strong emphasis on recruiting, motivating and developing talented people. Employees appear to give of their best when they have a clear customer-focused purpose and when they are empowered to do their jobs. This means giving them the tools to do the task – including clarity of objectives, high quality information, training and other resources – and removing some of the barriers to high performance, such as unprofessional practice, poor standards and political behaviour.

Managers have a disproportionate impact on high performance climates. As is often said, 'people don't leave organizations, they leave their manager'.

Managers need to be able to deploy a versatile management style, providing support and encouragement as much as direction and monitoring when necessary. Management needs to coexist with leadership behaviours which should be enabled at all levels. When employees are empowered and have the skills and authority they need to do their job, they are more likely than not to be responsible and accountable. In such cases, employees need have only the parameters of their role within which they can exercise self-management. In such conditions, discretionary effort is likely to flow.

Checklist: Meshing HR strategy and planning needs with operational requirements

- Design jobs that take into account employees' motivation (the 'want to do' factor), their knowledge of what is required (the 'know what to do' factor) and their ability to do what is required (the 'can do' factor).
- Provide training that enables employees to acquire critical new skills and approaches.
- Individuals and groups must be equipped with relevant facilities, skills and equipment.
- People must know what they are expected to do – the organizational area of activity must be defined, the intended direction communicated, and priorities and goals established.
- Ensure that work is structured to include the whole task – which produces greater flexibility and broader experience resulting in wider career paths.
- Reduce the administrative hierarchy and push decisions further down the organization, thus enhancing autonomy and responsibility.
- Ensure that 'high flyer' development emphasizes good people management practice.
- Build reward processes that are fair and reflect organizational needs and individual and team performance.
- Motivate individuals and teams to invest time and energy in improvement activities. Incentive systems designed round compensation for extra time and effort, and rewards for valuable suggestions, are required.

11

Performance management

In today's culture of partnership, pure performance appraisal is giving way to more 'holistic' performance management. It is argued that this is the best way of getting the best out of employees, teams and the organization as a whole.

(Management Today, 2001)

Introduction

In an ideal world, employees work hard and effectively, are responsible, accountable and flexible; they are willing to learn new skills and to share their knowledge with other people. They willingly 'go the extra mile', feel empowered and are willing to use their initiative to improve service, rather than leaving the task to someone else. However, empowered performance does not happen in a vacuum. In an empowered organization, employee activity has a clear focus. There is a shared sense of purpose and direction which employees find motivating. Performance is managed in ways in ways that generate trust, rather than resentment. Job roles and employee performance are closely linked to the requirements of the business. Learning and innovation are happening at all levels.

Empowerment only tends to happen when the conditions are right. The conditions for empowerment include a degree of flexibility and resilience, at both individual and organizational levels. To be empowered may require people to change behaviours that have stood them in good stead in the past, such as referring all decisions up the chain because decision-making feels risky. It will certainly require managers to listen to staff concerns and aspirations and be able to coach and develop others. Similarly, if a change in business strategy is to be implemented successfully, performance management and reward strategies need to be aligned with the new aims of the business. This assumes that people understand and buy into the reasons for change, which presupposes that communications are two-way and effective.

Empowered organizations tend to attract highly motivated employees. Theories of motivation are many and complex, but some of their common elements include the following:

- Motivation is internal and cannot be imposed
- It is, in contrast, easy to demotivate others
- Motivated individuals tend to release discretionary effort and experience 'flow'
- Motivated individuals are likely to persevere longer with tasks
- Motivated individuals are more likely to achieve their goals.

In this chapter we will look at how performance can be managed in ways that unleash and make the most of employee talents and motivations, rather than constrain employee potential.

Human capital

While the opening statement of many company reports is 'Our people are our greatest asset', in practice there is rarely any measurement reporting of the people or human capital dimension. In labour economics, human capital is the composite of acquired personal characteristics of employees (skills, knowledge and experience) that have an economic value. Knowledge is displacing capital as the key to corporate success. Managers in all sectors are having to rethink their priorities to make the maximum use of available knowledge, thinking ability and brain power in order to be competitive and effective. People, instead of being a 'cost' item, have become the source of long-lasting business results. The cost of replacing skilled employees is significant, especially as the pace of business increases, and the time needed for new employees to go through a learning curve can significantly reduce an organization's competitive advantage.

Measuring human capital is difficult, but attempting to do so should enable organizations to put a value on their human capital, and to manage their return on investment. By measuring a significant number of key people behaviours that affect performance, soundly selected indicators should provide as accurate a profile of people effectiveness in any organization as financials do of an organization's trading position. Measuring human capital should provide answers to questions such as:

- How are our organization's people performing relative to our competitors'?
- How much talent do we have?
- How good is our leadership?
- How innovative are we, relative to our competitors?
- What people actions are required in the future to increase shareholder and stakeholder value?

Focusing on employee commitment, rather than satisfaction

Although the link between employee motivation and willingness to perform has long been recognized, attention has generally focused on improving employee satisfaction. Indeed, this focus underpins the logic of the employee–customer–investor value chain, which assumes that happy and satisfied employees provide better service, which then builds customer loyalty and strong business results.

The cost of poor employee attitudes is evident in customer retention figures. Most people have been on the receiving end of poor service as customers. While receiving a Basil Fawlty-type of service may be rare, many of us may have been in receipt of faulty goods or have found ourselves stuck on the phone to a supplier for hours, struggling to break through endless recorded messages to speak to a real customer representative. We may have come across indifferent or grumpy shop assistants, waiters and others who are paid to provide service, or arrogant professionals who patronize their clients. From a customer perspective, the effect is frustrating to say the least. Where customers have options they tend to take their custom elsewhere, and the costs to businesses can be considerable. When individuals under-perform, achieving great business results becomes more difficult.

There are many reasons why such situations occur. For example, frequent changes in project can undermine employees' willingness to perform. However, managing for high performance is not just about giving employees what they want all the time, according to Hayday (2003). She argues that employee satisfaction does not automatically lead to higher performance, since it is only one part of a bigger picture. Achieving high satisfaction in itself can actually be passive in its effect, rather than energizing, since it may lead to complacency.

Instead, Hayday argues that commitment is a more active component of employee performance. Referring to her research in a major retailer, Hayday found that employee commitment had a higher correlation to customer satisfaction than employee satisfaction.

However, given the damage caused to the old psychological contract by the past years of organizational change, and the prospect of ongoing uncertainty of business prospects, much of the basis of employee commitment (i.e. trust) has been eroded. The shift towards self-managed careers and the growing confidence of many employees in their own employability means that employers cannot expect employees to be committed to the organization simply because they have a job.

Hayday suggests that employee commitment is a two-way street, and requires a proactive approach on the part of the employer to developing and valuing employees. The drivers of employee commitment include compatibility of values, pride in the organization, loyalty, job satisfaction and feeling fairly rewarded. Above all, commitment is the result of good, sustained people management.

The role of line managers in managing performance

Achieving high performance involves a delicate partnership between individuals and their organization. Most people want to do a good job. They want the chance to do it well and to be valued for what they produce. They want their performance to be assessed fairly. They want to feel valued for what they do.

As the organizational component of this performance partnership, line managers can and do have a direct and significant influence on individual performance. Managers have to tread the line between providing the clarity and support needed to help employees do a good job, and overly controlling what individuals do – especially if those employees are experienced and capable knowledge workers.

Managers can unlock an individual's ability and willingness to perform at high levels in many ways – for instance, by translating long-term goals into step-by-step plans, clearly stating expectations and holding people accountable. They bring the organization's vision to life by relating it directly to people's activities. Contact with the manager is known to be a motivating factor for many employees. Managers can inspire others by persuading them to move in a desired direction, expressing confidence in employees' ability to do the job, and recognizing and rewarding achievement. Empowering managers communicate well with all their stakeholders. They are aware of their own behaviour and of the need to be consistent in 'walking the talk'. They practise continuous improvement, and challenge themselves and others to become more efficient and effective. They identify and seek to remove the barriers to people's performance.

All of these behaviours can help to stimulate high performance in others. Interestingly, it is thought that by helping to find solutions to problems at work, managers can increase individual performance significantly (by 23.7 per cent), whereas recognizing and rewarding achievement increases performance by only 4.4 per cent (source: Corporate Leadership Council 2002 Performance Management Survey).

However, sometimes managers do not see the 'people' aspects of their role as significant, and neglect to manage performance. Sometimes, too, performance management becomes so systems-led and sophisticated that managers are reluctant to use the systems to their full potential, usually because they lack the skills to do so. Alternately, managers may prefer to use the system as a proxy for more relationship-based performance management, leaving employees feeling undervalued and cheated. There can be a lack of objective, measurable results for most jobs, requiring the use of performance ratings. There can be faulty performance appraisal systems, with poor cooperation from managers and often a leniency bias in appraisals. There can also be union resistance to such systems and to change in general. There can be a poor perceived connection between performance and pay, or the level of performance-based pay is too low relative to base pay, since the cost of more motivating programmes is usually prohibitive.

Performance management systems

An effective performance management system (PMS) can be helpful in breaking out of this spiral of underachievement. Since the late 1970s, performance management systems have been seen as participative, problem-solving processes concentrating on both task performance and development.

Performance management systems can be used both to reinforce the *status quo* and as part of planned culture change, since targets and rewards reinforce people's behaviour in specific (desired) directions. In designing a performance management system, the cycle begins with the business needs. Performance excellence should be defined in the context of the company's overall strategy, beginning with the mission and business plan, and the chief executive's own goals (Figure 11.1). A competency framework with behavioural indicators can help employees and managers translate strategic intent into how tasks need to be implemented – for example, with a greater emphasis on the customer, through demonstrating greater collaboration and knowledge-sharing. A programme of development for jobholders may be required. The appraisal of performance and discussion of broader development needs increasingly occurs as separate, but related processes. The reward strategy should then be redesigned through consultation and communication. Coaches should be assigned to senior people to help them manage their own behaviour change and role-model this to others.

Assessing performance only via an annual performance appraisal is no longer enough. Rather, effective performance management should be ongoing. Problems linked with not achieving a specified level of performance should also be swiftly addressed. Coaching and development should form a key part of the performance management process, along with appropriate reward and

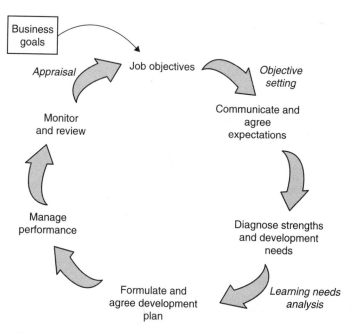

Figure 11.1 Performance management cycle.

recognition. In order to be effective, recognition and reward should be directly and speedily linked to performance and quality improvements.

The underpinning principles on which effective performance management systems are based are as follows:

- Effective performance results from a partnership between the jobholder and the organization
- The employee has adequate skills for the job
- The employee knows his or her role in the process
- The employee's responsibilities match her or his accountabilities
- The employee has access to the information needed, at the right time.

As a management tool, a good PMS should also enhance employee job satisfaction. To achieve these twin organizational and employee objectives, effective performance management should primarily be relationship-based, rather than system-led. A performance management system is neither just a reward system nor is it purely an appraisal system. It should be designed to enhance overall performance and be about the development of potential, not control. It should be company-wide, flow from the business plan, with senior managers having a clear idea of their own goals and modelling the process.

Appropriate levels of accountability

A common problem area that can affect employee performance and willingness to 'go the extra mile' occurs when individuals are genuinely unclear about where their job overlaps with that of other people, leading to gaps in delivery or duplication of effort. Roles should be designed to ensure appropriate levels of autonomy and accountability. Care must be taken from the outset to match appropriate jobs and targets to employee abilities and readiness. As we discussed in an earlier chapter, jobs should be designed so that they have an element of 'stretch' so that employees feel challenged and are able to grow through the jobs they do. Employees should also be helped to see the bigger picture and identify the interdependencies in doing their jobs. Service level agreements may need to be negotiated to manage accountability and service performance. Roles and responsibilities should be discussed and agreed with employees, together with any development required, so that they can become effective in new roles as quickly as possible.

To establish appropriate levels of accountability, people need to have the right type of information to enable them to understand what is required at least. Information systems should be refined to ensure that decision-making can be made at the lowest levels possible in the organization with the minimum of risk.

In order to build accountability:

- Agree (stretch) goals
- Clarify responsibilities
- Provide required development

- Provide necessary resources
- Manage performance
- Use progress reviews
- Take remedial action if needed
- Develop simple and motivational appraisal processes
- Impose sanctions if necessary
- Recognize and reward good performance.

Delegation

One of the common causes of under-performance is when managers are unwilling or unable to delegate tasks appropriately. This is often due to managers having little faith that teams can carry out new targets, perhaps because they have failed to develop individuals and teams with the relevant skills. Typically, managers continue to control not only what needs to be done but also how tasks are carried out. They thus limit the potential output from the team to that which the manager can directly influence. The manager in consequence becomes overloaded and less effective. Just as damaging is when teams lack the necessary skills and the manager delegates inappropriately, for example starting to operate a 'clear desk' policy for him- or herself without having developed employees' ability to deal with the delegated tasks. Then delegation is seen as 'dumping', which can overload and demoralize subordinates.

Goal-setting

In managing for high performance, it is important to relate desired outcomes both to organizational values and to the means to achieve them. Managers should attempt to ensure that the goals and targets set reflect the needs of both the organization and the employee. When senior managers are clear about their own goals, they are able to cascade the process of goal-setting via their teams. Goals and targets should be set on a team and an individual basis.

Typical elements of goal-setting include:

- The key results areas (KRAs) and key performance indicators (KPIs)
- The key objectives
- An action plan to achieve the objectives
- The other people involved/affected
- Perceived difficulty of the circumstances in achieving the goal
- Success and rating criteria.

According to Jones (1981), the following are essential if fine-sounding visions and missions are to be translated into meaningful goals:

- Provision of training in goal- and objective-setting for all concerned
- Leaders who model the process

- Reinforcing organizational values during goal setting
- Assessment of the clarity of goals in all work-oriented meetings
- Testing of commitment to organizational goals.

With goals flowing top-down, individuals should then have clear objectives and targets to reach and accountability for things that contribute to the business plan. On the other hand, the more an individual's work is focused on longer-term strategic needs, the less the approach to performance management lends itself to a top-down controlling and normalizing process. Managers may need training in goal-setting/agreeing key result areas. They may need help with developing the skills of giving feedback, coaching and appraising.

Lack of clarity with regard to goals can lead to disorganization, inefficiency and lack of commitment. During a time of major change, there will typically be so much activity that it will be easy for people to lose sight of priorities. Ironically, this is perhaps the very time when goals should be made more stretching. The rationale is that when people have big and meaningful tasks to accomplish they have to think outside the box, gain the collaboration of others and raise performance levels. This has the benefit of keeping people focused on how they are contributing to organizational success rather than worrying about the effects of change. At the same time, it helps people to develop themselves and teams.

Employees need to be involved in setting and agreeing objectives if they are to be committed to achieving their outcomes. Real participation leads to a sense of involvement, which in turn makes people feel ownership of the goals and a desire to achieve them. They need to be clear what unique contribution their job makes to their organization. Employees need to define areas of performance within their spheres of responsibility (typically, there will be about five to eight performance areas). Individual goals should be integrated with SMART business goals (Specific, Measurable, Achievable, Realistic and Time-bound).

Employees also need to be really clear about what the performance standards are and how they will be rated. Performance is often assessed according to conventional success criteria:

- Financial – for example, how much income is generated per month
- Time-bound – such as the number of items to be dealt with within a set number of days
- Quantity – the number of items to be dealt with overall
- Quality – measured by, for example, a lack of mistakes
- Customer feedback – which distinguishes between proactive and reactive customer handling.

If employees do not receive the performance ratings they deserve, or feel they do, they call into question the fairness of the standards or the way in which ratings have been applied, and performance usually dips. There must also be procedures for dealing with complaints and grievances.

Measurement

Measuring individual performance acts as an active element of performance enhancement by focusing employees' attention on what the organization considers important, especially as business needs change. At an organizational level, key performance indicators (KPIs) highlight business areas requiring management attention.

Given the symbolic and practical importance of measures, the challenge is to choose appropriate targets and measurement systems. The old dictum 'if you can't measure it, you can't manage it' should be balanced by the more recent rejoinder, 'if you only manage the things you measure you miss a trick'. If measures, goals and effort are mis-targeted, people will put effort into things that do not matter much at the expense of things that will make a positive difference.

Example 11.1   Loop Customer Management
Loop Customer Management is part of the Kelda Group. It manages customer services to Kelda subsidiaries and external clients, although it was originally formed to provide managed customer services to Yorkshire Water. The type of performance measures Loop used to use worked well in a utility environment, with performance measured on elements such as length of service and attendance at courses. When Loop moved to outsourced customer services, many performance management practices needed to change. Now performance in the round involves looking at a person's total performance – the outputs delivered, the skills that person has to do the job effectively, plus the behaviours demonstrated. It is the combination of these things that creates a measure of performance.

Loop created its 'Values in Action' framework', which forms the basis of performance management and development. First, Loop identified behaviours that drove 'great customer experiences' and developed behavioural statements that brought the brand values – performance, partnership, people, innovation and best value – to life. Employees were involved in identifying these behaviours and the performance standards and measures that derived from them. In turn, these elements form the basis of reward at Loop. Six new pay zones were created, in which similar jobs were grouped together, rather than paying people who worked in silos on different pay scales. Developing people is made easier since there are clear competencies at each ability level within the pay zones.

The framework was cascaded by every line manager and was issued electronically and in a detailed booklet so that people were clear what was involved and what was expected of them. They could see where moves could be sideways or promotional, whereas previously this was not clear. A bonus scheme is also being developed to reward innovation, good ideas and innovation beyond what is expected (Wilson, 2004).

The balanced scorecard

Traditionally organizations have paid most attention to their financial performance – if not, they would soon go out of business – and performance measures
have tended to focus exclusively on financial and productivity-related outputs.
However, financial results are usually the consequence of other actions that
have taken place to achieve business aims, and therefore represent the past.
These actions have been carried out by people, the company's employees.
Employee performance, then, provides the 'input' side of the performance
equation, which converts into business 'output' in terms of bottom-line results.
Therefore, focusing exclusively on financial results is akin to driving along,
looking at where you are going through the rear-view mirror rather than the
windscreen.

More recently, there has been growing awareness that sustainable business
results only tend to occur when attention is paid to what happens on the 'input'
side of the equation. If the 'inputs' are managed, the 'outputs' usually take care
of themselves. Various measurement/evaluation tools such as the EFQM framework and the balanced business scorecard, devised by Kaplan and Norton
(1996), have contributed to this growing awareness. These frameworks can be
useful in ensuring that goals and measures focus on the things that will make a
positive difference to the organization's strategic and cultural ambitions.

In the balanced scorecard framework, the focus on the past (financials)
needs to be balanced by a focus on the future (people). The focus on what goes
on to deliver the product or service (inside) needs to be balanced by the needs
of customers or other stakeholders (outside). Goals need to be set in each of
these perspectives to ensure that the organization is delivering its current service well and developing what its customers will require in the future. For
example, activity on the people dimension may take the form, perhaps, of
training, development and reward to ensure that the people capability is moving in the right direction to ensure future business results.

The interconnection therefore should be the business vision, mission and
strategy, or at least the organization's core purpose. These should guide
choices about which aspects of the people dimension to set goals in and how
they should be measured, such as through retention. On the horizontal axis, the
focus on customers (the outside) needs to be balanced by the focus on
processes (the inside). These too must flow from the vision and strategy.
Financial and non-financial metrics can then be used to create personal objectives for each person in the organization, translating the strategy into operational terms, making strategic initiatives everyone's job and making strategy a
continuing process. Performance management and reward systems can be connected to the strategy through this means. Scorecards can be created at whole
organization/strategic business unit, divisional and team levels to ensure consistency. Individual scorecards can be created to align every job with what the
organization is trying to achieve.

An indication of how far thinking has shifted towards a more holistic view
of what leads to business success is that, throughout the early 1990s, Michael

Hammer argued that business process was most important. While Hammer (2001) still considers business process as critical to business success, he now argues that effective management of human capital lies at the heart of real success. As he states, 'What I've learned is that re-engineering alone is not sufficient'. The people issues that he considers it is important to get right include training, education, communications and change management. He advises that companies are right to overestimate, rather than underestimate, their true costs. Measures therefore should be set around the creation of capabilities and systems. Penna (Finn, 2004) suggest a five-stage process for setting human capital measures:

1. Identify the key human capital programmes, such as a talent management programme, or other business critical people factors
2. Identify measures that indicate progress or monitor the current state against a benchmark
3. Select results of programmes that add value to the organization
4. Collect the data, report on trends and agree which, if any, will be reported externally; the data should set the agenda for further people priorities
5. Identify any correlations between people measures and fluctuations in key business objectives. Sears (*Harvard Business Review*, 1998), for example, was able to identify movements in staff satisfaction that were predictive of a profit increase or decrease.

Benefits of scorecard approaches

The benefit of using a scorecard approach is that everyone in the organization should have a more complete understanding of what the organization is trying to accomplish as it becomes a vehicle for helping people understand what the new strategy is. Robert Kaplan (Kaplan and Norton, 1996) describes how the measurement systems can be used to implement strategy:

> *Innovating companies today are using their Balanced Scorecards to (1) gain consensus and clarity about their strategic objectives, (2) communicate strategic objectives to business units, departments, teams and individuals, (3) align strategic planning, resource allocation and budgeting processes and (4) obtain feedback and learn about the effectiveness of the strategic plan and its implementation.*

The balanced scorecard provides a fundamental strategic control mechanism, and is at the centre of an organization's business planning process. It involves getting feedback to improve learning about how to proceed and then translating the organization's vision for each employee. The element of feedback on the strategy is critical because, as Kaplan and Norton point out, strategies should be treated as hypotheses, rather than as commandments written permanently in stone. Only by uncovering flaws and correcting them, using the shared intelligence of employees, does the strategy stand a chance of succeeding.

Example 11.2   Using the balanced scorecard

In one financial services company, financial performance in the late 1990s was poor and the outlook was no better. Management developed a vision to be a high performer in the sector, and set stretch financial goals to try and improve the situation. However, staff were demotivated; they had not received active training or development opportunities for a number of years and were therefore under-skilled to perform in the way the stretch goals demanded. Furthermore, they were working in the wrong culture to achieve the goals. If employees, who already worked long hours, were to be expected to 'go the extra mile' yet again, they needed encouragement and recognition from managers. Instead managers, who were themselves overworked, did not offer praise when people did outstanding work but were quick to criticize when things went wrong. In some cases, managers lacked the calibre required for their roles.

Not surprisingly, staff lost interest in providing customer service. Customer feedback became generally negative, and customers started defecting in large numbers to the competition. Internally, there were few processes to help people do their jobs well. Benchmarked against other organizations' processes, this company scored low. Customer enquiries were time-monitored, which meant that customers with complex enquiries were hurried through their calls. There was little follow-through on change initiatives and few handovers between departments, leading to duplication and slow, costly transactions.

The chief executive realized that, until customers came back to the company in large numbers, things could only go from bad to worse. He recognized that a turnaround would have to be achieved through employees being prepared to work differently – in other words, that people capability issues in the here and now are telltale signs of performance and financial problems still to come. Yet it was not until the company's figures really dipped and layoffs were imminent that staff became motivated by the vision and goals. Until then, these were seen as merely another pressure.

Ironically, the company's predicament started to drive a sharing of the vision. The chief executive introduced the balanced business scorecard as a means of focusing managers' effort. The HR team became involved in a task force set up to try to address the organizational challenges. They made a start on the people capability issues by collecting relevant people/culture-related data from within the organization, and relevant benchmark data from outside on capability and HR-related process areas. They fed the disturbing data back into the organization.

The key barriers to high performance were identified through this process. Goals were set and strategies developed in each of the four domains in order to achieve the goals. From this were developed the key measures and targets that provided a focus for improvement.

Selecting measures

In using the balanced scorecard framework, organizations choose the domains most relevant to them. Whereas conventional measures have included operational and historical data such as headcount changes, hires and terminations and total compensation, more strategic measures relate to employee motivation, leadership team capability and employee competency.

For example, one pharmaceutical company developed measures in the financial, customer, internal business and innovation perspectives as follows:

Financial perspective – 'How do we look to our shareholders?'

- Revenue growth
- Operating profit growth
- Debtor reduction.

Customer perspective – 'How do our clients see us?'

- Client satisfaction index
- Key accounts performance
- Client retention.

Internal perspective – 'What must we excel at?'

- Employee satisfaction index
- Service delivery quality
- Productivity ratios.

Innovation perspective – 'How can we continue to improve and create value?'

- New service development
- New market development
- New ways of working.

In setting measures, it is important to focus not only on the indicators that will tell you if you have actually achieved the task ('lag' indicators) but also on some of the activities which will help you achieve them ('lead' indicators). To identify these different kinds of measure:

- Take one of the goals and articulate three to four things that will be happening when the goal is achieved (outcomes). These become the critical success factors.
- Identify at least one critical success factor per goal that can form a lag indicator.
- Then define three to four broad ways in which the goal can be achieved. These become the strategies.
- Examine the broad strategies and select a minimum of two per goal that can form lead indicators. Ensure that each of the four domains contains a balance of lead and lag indicators with respective targets.

In the financial services organization described in Example 11.2, lead indicators with quarterly targets were established in all domains. In the People Capability domain they included the percentage of people taking part in critical strategic programmes and the percentage of people reporting that they had 'rich and meaningful' Personal Development Plans (PDPs) – the definition of what people meant by 'rich and meaningful' was left to individuals to decide, but the very description drew people's attention to the potential value of such discussions. They also included the percentage of performance management interviews checked against Best Practice and the mean psychometric ability scores of new hires. They set lag indicators with biannual targets. These were the mean multi-rater feedback degree scores against key competencies, the key cultural/climate indices, the percentage of people turnover and Team/Self/ Organization ratings.

Measures focused people's attention on what needed to be done. In the people domain, HR took responsibility for developing new PDP processes. HR also rapidly trained managers to play their part in these conversations and to act as leaders. As employees started to notice the effect of being valued by their managers, their morale improved and they became more open to trying new ways of working to improve the customer's experience of the firm. Teams started to feel empowered to address some of the key challenges for the business, and were supported with effective facilitation and skills development by their managers. Under-performing employees who were a drain on their colleagues were helped to leave, and as the business results started to improve, new, more capable recruits took their place. As success started to be evident, employees were delighted to receive a share of the financial turnaround through an employee share offer. (I am indebted to Nigel Springett for his insights into this process.)

Example 11.3   Tesco

Tesco is one of many retail companies applying balanced scorecard approaches. For in-store personnel managers, the goal is to drive the development of people and create effective, enjoyable and accessible training so that teams can perform to the best of their ability. Personnel managers are not divorced from the business, but take on duty manager responsibilities for 20 per cent of their time. In Tesco there is a belief that an intrinsic link exists between employees' perceptions of how their company values their contribution, their development, reward and morale, and the ability of the firm to sustain its reputation as a provider of high standards of service to customers.

Tesco aims to maintain these high standards of customer care by focusing on staff retention, which is key to competitive advantage in the retail sector. For personnel managers, their contribution to business success is by focusing on the 'people' domain of the scorecard.

People management priorities include ensuring that employee appraisals are carried out, training section managers, resourcing, and succession planning. Training for senior managers focuses on task analysis, drive, motivation, the development of people and technical skills. These senior managers are the guardians of productivity, since they coach and support other managers to achieve their targets. Section managers are delegated routine personnel tasks such as pay enquiries.

Coaching and feedback for higher performance

Coaching is a highly individualized form of development. When employees start a new job or are required to do work which calls on them to use new skills, they may require training. More likely, they will also require on-the-job development through coaching to equip them for their role. Line managers are in an ideal position to act as coach and developer of others, assuming that they have the skills to do this. However, many managers do not see coaching as part of their role, or feel unable to make the time to develop team members. Frequently they are poor at delegation. Training in coaching skills can be helpful or even essential. While managers do not need to be highly emotionally intelligent, they do at least need to be able to listen if they are to become effective coaches.

Coaching is not only useful in helping individuals to develop. In a Roffey Park study of coaching (Kenton and Moody, 2002), a fifth of respondents reported that coaching was being used as a culture change vehicle in their organizations. In the same study, managers reported that coaching was a highly effective tool to aid development, increasing not only the skill levels of the 'coachee' but also the leadership and management skills of the coach. It was felt that coaching was a cost-effective way of sharing good practice and speeding up the transfer of skills within the organization. People reported that coaching led to increased levels of motivation, since individuals felt that the organization actually cared about them and was committed to their development.

When managers provide coaching, they are adding value to the organization by helping people develop and grow. It's about creating the right conditions so that people can perform to the best of their ability. It's also about preparing people for tasks that they cannot already do. The starting point is often something that the learner wants to achieve. In addition to setting goals for the actual work to be done, the coach adds learning goals. The coach coaches the learner and gives him or her the necessary skills, knowledge and confidence to do the task. In coaching, learners receive immediate feedback about their performance, which helps reinforce successes and allows mistakes to be quickly corrected.

From the learner's perspective, coaching involves:

- Being clear what they want to achieve and expressing this assertively
- Asking the coach for help, taking the initiative
- Being open and honest about the reasons why coaching is needed
- Asking for feedback and suggestions
- Taking responsibility for their own learning.

From the coach's perspective, coaching involves:

- Understanding what the employee needs to achieve his or her goals
- Assessing the employee's level of skill and will (motivation) to achieve these goals
- Asking good questions, listening well
- Giving and receiving feedback
- Getting the learner to think through how he or she might approach the issue

- Helping the learner to explore a number of options/solutions
- Making suggestions/giving guidance only as appropriate
- Clarifying the action plan and follow-through.

Managers must want to coach if they are to be successful. They must be prepared to share their own successes and failures, give performance expectations and feedback, and ask for feedback on their own coaching. They need skills of observation and analysis as well as key interpersonal and communication skills. The quality of the relationship between coach and learner is crucial to the success of coaching, and there has to be mutual respect. Being able to build and maintain rapport during coaching is important. If people are visibly supported, helped and encouraged by their manager in the learning process, they are more likely to view change (and learning) in a positive light.

Assessing performance

While employees are usually clear what the targets are, they may be less clear how the performance management system works and therefore how their performance will be assessed. If the perceived credibility of the system is low, employees may not consider the latest targets as worthy of extra effort.

A performance management system should be based on the principles of fairness and transparency. Since the days have largely gone when people were promoted on seniority rather than on merit, and when senior people were usually given high performance ratings regardless of how they had actually performed, perceived fairness is a critical factor in making a performance management system work. Since the most productive employee can sometimes outperform others by two to three times the level of productivity, it is important in a performance culture that they are rewarded equitably rather than equally.

Progress review

Effective performance management systems typically have a number of formal reviews which take place each year, but the more frequent the interactions the better. In some companies, the formal review process involves separate stages for goal-setting, reviewing progress, appraisal and development discussions.

Progress reviews provide regular and specific feedback to employees and ensure follow-up so that the data can be used to inform better decision-making about who is performing well, and who should be promoted, trained and paid more. A first progress review should take place after three to four months, another after a similar interval, and individual appraisal at the end of the year following target-setting. Between progress reviews, jobholders may require coaching or other on-the-job development with respect to some aspect of their work. They may require behavioural skills- or knowledge-based training. A performance issue may require a system-based solution. Promotion decisions based on performance should usually follow the progress review and appraisal discussions.

Dealing with poor performance

One way of raising the levels of performance of a whole team is to recognize and reward people who are out-performing the norm. Perhaps an even more effective way to lift a team's performance as a whole is to deal with chronic poor performance. In many organizations employees feel aggrieved that colleagues who under-perform are allowed to get away with it, putting more of a burden on those who perform well. In times of change, when workloads typically increase, tolerating poor performance can add to the strain on employees.

Many managers have difficulty in addressing issues of under-performance. Rather than taking corrective action, they resist giving honest feedback to the jobholder, especially if he or she is assertive and likely to contest the feedback. A more common tactic is to avoid the issue, give average performance ratings at appraisal time and seek to transfer the individual to another part of the organization so that the employee becomes another manager's problem. Managers may hope to solve under-performance issues by making the position redundant, but sometimes this is not a feasible option.

While understandable, such behaviour is unjustifiable. Other employees usually feel aggrieved if they perceive themselves to be carrying a heavier workload as a result. Typically, employees then start to adopt a 'more than my job's worth' mentality, which means that, far from raising levels of performance, minimum standards are simply complied with. To break this loop, the causes of poor performance should be identified and appropriate actions taken to remedy them.

A more effective way of addressing the issue is to prevent the problem occurring in the first place by ensuring that there is a climate of development and responsibility, characterized by frequent feedback and coaching. Jones (1981) suggests the following:

- Experiment with consultative and consensus methods of decision-making
- Work to improve the unit's climate
- Provide training for managers in conducting performance reviews
- Look for informal ways to reward individuals.

Why do people under-perform?

According to Adrian Furnham (2003), many managers find difficulty in diagnosing why some employees under-perform. In some cases individuals may be lazy and believe that they can play the system, but in today's more demanding workplaces such behaviour is less likely to be tolerated than in the past. In general, there are five common causes why problems arise:

1. *Capability* – an individual may lack the ability to do what is required or may have been over-promoted, the job may have changed, or they cannot learn fast enough to keep pace with developments. The 'cure' may be to manage them out; send them to HR(!); or find them a lower-level job which they are capable of doing.

2. *Ignorance* – the individual may not have been taught what is required, or his/her skills may not have been upgraded. It is important to be clear what is required – is the lack a 'head' or 'heart' issue? The 'cure' may be found in training.

3. *Distraction* – the individual may have something happening in his or her private life which causes them to take their eye off the ball. If this is an otherwise high performing employee, the organization should offer support.

4. *Alienation* – these are the people who 'quit but stay'. The cures may be to set stretching targets so that the individual can ratchet his or her performance up, or offer the option to 'climb on board' or go. Sometimes sending people on an assessment course run by externals can help them to gain a more realistic view of their own performance. Voluntary severance should be seen as an option.

5. *Fit* – sometimes there is a mismatch between a person's temperament and the job he or she is in. Extraverts need stimulation to be at their best, while introverts prefer to close down stimulation in order to reach their peak performance. The match between the environment, the work to be carried out and individual work-style preferences is a delicate one. An open-plan setting may not be conducive to certain types of work, while remote working may not suit certain individuals. The 'cure' is to try and diagnose with the individual the kind of work to which he or she is best suited and, if possible, play to the individual's strengths.

Confront inadequate performance in a problem-solving way

Poor performance is often the result of systems limitations, such as being starved of relevant information, or having too heavy a workload, rather than a skill or motivation issue. In such cases the performance solution may not be coaching but, for example, reducing an employee's workload. Managers should ensure that they are clear about the basis of their judgements with regard to performance, especially as performance management is often a more emotionally coloured than objective process. Some organizations use behavioural competencies, with both positive and negative indicators to help managers develop an objective view about what good performance looks like and to understand what leads to effective performance.

While effective performance management processes should prevent underperformance from occurring in the first place, sometimes there is no avoiding confronting an individual about his or her performance. In such circumstances, a conversation structure such as the DELACT framework can be helpful:

Describe the performance discrepancy
Explain the implications of the discrepancy (for the success of the task, the team, the individual)
Listen to the views of the employee
Alternative courses of action to solve the problem should be developed, so that if one fails, others can be used

Contract/agree the way forward, together with planned actions, responsibilities, support, review points etc.

Thank the individual for his or her desire to put in good performance.

The action plan should involve specific improvement targets that can be monitored so that progress/improvement can be reviewed at agreed points. The manager should give the employee space to act but should keep close to the situation so that coaching or other support can be made available if the employee is under-performing due to lack of skill or knowledge.

Appraisal

Appraisal is a key part of the PMS, providing the basis for promotion based on merit, and recognition and rewards based on past performance. It is used as a formal review process at the end of a probationary period, and can be used as a warning about unacceptable performance, leading to lay-off or termination. It can lead to career development or training needs assessment on an individual basis, to demotion or reduction in grade, and to lateral reassignment.

Appraisal improves staff utilization by fostering improvements in work performance and ensuring that work is assigned more efficiently. It should assist employees to set career goals as well as keeping employees advised of what is expected of them. It can help meet employees' needs for growth, help them to recognize what is needed for development to managerial positions, and identify training needs. It can validate selection procedures and be used for evaluating training courses. It can be helpful in fostering better relationships between managers and their direct reports, and between work units.

Feedback is a vital part of the process, allowing individuals to modify their performance and managers to assess performance. Increasingly, multi-rater instruments, such as 360-degree feedback processes, are being used to evaluate performance as well as for development purposes. There is strong argument for doing this when there is a desire to spot potential. A US study carried out in the early 1990s at an American training base for would-be officers found that peer groups were most effective at spotting potential officer material. In the average workplace, it is subordinates who usually show most consistency in how they rate their manager.

However, problems can occur over the rating of performance. For instance, using multi-rater instruments can cause problems of distortion in feedback, depending on the purpose for which the data are collected. Various research projects suggest that raters will tend to exaggerate their rating positively or negatively according to what is riding on the outcome and whether the resulting data are being used for pay, promotion or development.

Appraisal should be motivational and reinforce high standards. Emphasizing the positive can have a major positive impact on employee performance, as can being specific on the outcomes of the formal performance review, such as promotion, and emphasizing employees' long-term potential within the organization. Rather than being just about a once-a-year discussion, the management of performance through observation, providing feedback and coaching, and taking corrective action if needed, should be an ongoing process.

In performance discussions, managers should be honest with employees as well as concerned about their wants and needs. As is often said, in an appraisal there should be no surprises. Managers usually need training in how to assess performance to agreed standards, and also how to give feedback, coach and develop others. It can be helpful, for instance, if managers are trained to be assessors at development and assessment centres so that they can develop their ability to observe and make relatively objective judgements.

One pharmaceutical company trains managers via a series of mandatory workshops focusing on recruitment and selection methods, performance appraisal, coaching for performance and managing unacceptable performance. The training incorporates systems and process training, and skills development using realistic case studies, role-plays and actors. The approach helps managers to develop both the skills and the confidence to give feedback. Employees too should be trained in how to structure a performance appraisal or other performance-related discussion so that they can take a responsible part in the discussion. The same pharmaceutical company has also started rating the performance of every employee on both what they did as well as how they did it, using a competency framework that also emphasizes the responsibility of managers to manage performance.

Reward

Conventionally, organizations have relied on the extrinsic motivation of reward schemes, often linked with incentivized performance-related elements, to encourage employees to apply their skills in particular directions. Reward systems play an important role in communicating the organization's values, performance standards and expectations. Rewards have two organizational objectives: to equitably recognize past performance, and to stimulate and motivate people to perform competently or differently in the future.

Rewards are an integral part of Vroom's expectancy theory. According to this theory, people expect that their effort will result in performance; they also believe that their performance will be rewarded; if the reward is to be considered appropriate to the performance, it has be of perceived value to the recipient. If people do not feel appropriately rewarded, they will tend to lower their inputs (reduce effort) or raise their outcomes (by getting a pay increase, stealing time by absenteeism etc.).

People need to feel that the reward they are receiving is fair. Equitable pay is a basis of trust, since people do not want to feel that they are being exploited or deliberately underpaid. Justice can be seen to be done by carrying out job analysis, wage surveys, objective work measurement or performance rating, and generally by high pay and benefits.

Focusing reward strategies exclusively around pay is problematic since theories about the motivational effect of money are contradictory. Kohn (1993), for instance, argues that when people are intrinsically motivated to do a good job, direct, specific monetary rewards actually reduce motivation to creative work. Conversely, Eisenberger (1989) suggests that money is amongst the most powerful of extrinsic motivations and that it shapes all behaviour. In moving towards a high performing, flexible organization, getting reward strategies right becomes extremely important.

What should be rewarded?

The legacy of the 1990s has seen reward strategies undergo transformation. According to some commentators, the function of all modern compensation systems is to promote greater awareness on the part of the employee of his/her contribution to the company and of the importance of business needs and the bottom line. When rewards recognize and encourage superior performance regardless of level, boundaries become more permeable and the hierarchy becomes healthier. If innovation is required of employees, rewards should be balanced to ensure that people's ability inputs (e.g. skills, qualifications, behaviour) are taken into account with their work outputs and results.

Rather than paying for jobs, so that people will be motivated to get the next job up, boundaryless organizations pay people for expanding their capabilities so as to make the maximum contribution to the organization. Organizations need to be able to tailor pay rises for talented individuals, people who perform the best or take on the largest workloads, or those whose skills are in demand in the labour market.

Typically, rewarding people for their individual contribution is usually based on their achievement of objectives, targets, profit, cost, volume etc., and involves assessing their outputs on a scale ranging from 'does not meet requirements' through 'meets some requirements' and 'meets requirements' to 'more than meets requirements'. In competence-based pay systems, outputs should also be weighed against the competency requirements of the role, from 'below required competence' through 'developing competence' and 'competent' to 'above required competence'.

In the move towards more flexible options, old-style grade structures have decayed and rewards for service and experience have been replaced by rewards for performance. During the 'War for Talent', employers introduced broad banding, job families, diversity/equality proofing, flexible benefits, competency-related pay, profit share, share schemes, gain sharing and recruitment bonuses. In competence-based reward systems, for example, organizational roles are defined and competence is profiled by team leaders, then challenged and agreed by line managers and reward specialists. Individuals moving from one organizational level to another would not get 'promotion' increases unless their reward package was lower than the minimum for that level. Normally, people moving to a role demanding greater competences would already be rewarded above the minimum for the higher level. Progression within each level (and movement between role families) would be based on an individual's contribution.

How do employees want to be rewarded?

While increased pay would be welcomed by many employees, incentives for higher performance remain a contentious subject for many employees. Performance-related (or merit) pay (PRP) is now the main form of reward practice in the UK, though these schemes generally receive a poor press. More sophisticated approaches, such as skill-based pay and flexible benefits, are increasingly being used alongside PRP to compensate for its limitations. In the 2003 and 2004 *Management Agendas* there were many comments from employees sceptical about the value of performance-related pay.

When organizations believe in the power of the financial 'carrot', bonuses have to be substantial in return for outstanding performance. While this can occasionally be effective, there are serious drawbacks: individuals can experience massive fluctuations in their income from year to year, often due to factors beyond their control, and the fundamental fairness of targets is a key issue (Crouch, 2003). When bonuses are small, or are withheld because of market conditions, employees can feel duped and develop a sense of grievance. For most people, the issue is one of fairness.

In the UK, as general pay levels have risen only slowly due to low inflation, the widening differentials with executive pay have put financial reward back into the spotlight, with many unfavourable press comments in 2003 about 'fat cat' pay deals. Despite this, many *Management Agenda* respondents felt that their pay was at least competitive, and that they had good benefits. Just over a third of the sample reported that their organization had introduced flexible reward packages. Of these, a staggering 96 per cent welcomed the change.

Most respondents commented that performance rewards should be a mixture of team and individual rewards, with more emphasis given to team success. Many people in the Roffey Park surveys appeared to prefer a move away from bonus payments to pay increases, and would rather have potential ownership, through share options, than small bonuses. All-employee share ownership plans and the enterprise management scheme are designed for organizations of all sizes, and aim to extend employee share ownership beyond large public organizations. For many respondents, tax-saving ideas, long service awards and reinstatement of final salary pension schemes were more desirable than individual performance bonuses.

One fast food retailer, wishing to stem the tide of high turnover, carried out an 'Employer of Choice' survey. They found that the staff who did stay went unnoticed – their pay remained just above the minimum wage, and they were given no special recognition. The company put this right by introducing various length-of-service benefits, such as an extra day's leave in a 'milestone' year, such as five years' service. Together with small ceremonies and parties, these rewards made longer-serving staff feel special and valued.

At Prêt a Manger, staff incentive schemes such as Save as You Earn (SAYE) enable employees to save regular amounts from their salary for an agreed period, before being offered the chance to buy company shares at an agreed price. This type of share plan has become popular and can help retain staff for longer periods. In its research, The Human Capital Index (European Survey Report 2000), Watson Wyatt estimates that stock ownership and incentives drive even more value. Supermarket chain Tesco operates a share-based profit scheme and SAYE for staff. Both schemes were set up in the early 1980s, and by 2001 staff turnover had fallen from 75 per cent to 25 per cent. These types of scheme act as an effective retention tool. In sectors where there is a high turnover of staff, or skills are in demand, it is common for companies to offer retention bonuses in addition to long service and other incentives.

'Total' rewards

What people in Roffey Park and other surveys appear to consider more meaningful than financial reward alone are holistic 'total' rewards. Non-financial rewards such as being recognized, praised, valued, given challenging projects, the opportunity for time off and also to work from home are important to many employees. Just being thanked by a manager can be rewarding in itself. For many employees, having the opportunity to be promoted is reward in itself, whether or not they receive a huge pay increase. Many people want professional development, more time for themselves, more involvement in formulating strategies and in business meetings to shape their company's future, and more authority. Some people want more social activities, and would value tokens of esteem, such as theatre/concert vouchers. Mutual trust and respect lie at the heart of non-financial rewards.

An enlightened approach to flexible working can be a major motivator, as can a genuine concern to help employees achieve a work–life balance. Many employees would like these but their organization does not offer enough flexible options, or people have to sacrifice their career ambitions if they opt for working flexibly. Interestingly, the 50 Best Companies to Work For survey highlights some interesting practice in this area – 78 per cent offer benefits for domestic partners, 82 per cent provide paid paternity leave, and 64 per cent provide private health insurance for their employees. There are bonuses for returning mothers, hardship funds for those in need, community work sabbaticals and free one-week holiday cottages. Career breaks and recognition awards that acknowledge outstanding 'one-off' contributions can be very motivating and aid retention.

Recognition

Recognition, apart from the financial tokens of appreciation, has the potential to have a dramatic impact on employee motivation and commitment. It is also an area where employers can be most creative and focus reward practices towards areas where they can be most effective. For many employees, having the value of their work recognized by their line manager and peers is a powerful motivator. At Timpson, the UK shoe repair and key cutting business, the company believes in praising ten times more than criticizing, and area managers issue so many prizes that many carry a permanent stock in the boot of their cars.

In many organizations, formal recognition schemes sit alongside the day-to-day recognition practices that are implicit in good people management. Companies in the US and the UK are increasingly revising their recognition schemes to make them more imaginative and reinforce behaviours which support the company direction. Dolland and Aitchison, the high street optician, has developed an 'Incredible Colleague Award'. Staff are encouraged to nominate their colleagues, and the winner is able to live out one of their 'incredible dreams', courtesy of the company. One US company has introduced a recognition scheme that acknowledges the contribution that employees make outside the day job, such as work towards charities, good causes and projects which will benefit the community.

Example 11.4   DCM

Recognition is a key element of building a high performance workplace at DCM. As the logistics arm of Unipart, DCM provides services for a number of other Unipart Group companies in the automotive, rail, defence and leisure sectors. Its operating objective is to benefit clients by adding value at every stage of the supply chain, whilst ensuring high levels of product availability and significantly reducing costs and capital expenditure. With this focus, the company has achieved a 30 per cent improvement in sales in the past five years, an increase of £800 million to £1.4 billion.

Much of this success is due to Unipart's development of best practice tools and techniques for continuous improvement, grouped together under one umbrella called the 'Unipart Way'. This activity operates within the framework of the British Quality Foundation's Business Excellence Model. Added to this, at the time of the company's buy-out from Rover in 1987 employees were offered shares in the company, and the 55 per cent equity currently held by management and employees has created an important sense of shared destiny and become a strong competitive differentiator.

The company also helps employees reach their full potential through Our Contribution Counts (OCC) quality circles. Circle members attend a recognition ceremony where success stories of continuous improvement are shared and certificates given. The OCC programme achieved cost savings for the company of £2 million in 2002.

An in-house university, the Unipart 'U', helps reinforce the company's core beliefs in employee development. The learning environment is an integral part of the workplace, providing the opportunity for every single employee to acquire new knowledge and skills and share that learning.

'Although many companies strive to become true "learning organizations", Unipart has been focused on this objective for longer than most', says Keith Jones, managing director. 'Sourcing knowledge and best practice internally and externally and feeding it back on a group and local level are quite simply integral to the way we work'.

(Source: British Quality Foundation)

Conclusion

When a performance management system is working well, it should enhance the overall performance of groups, individuals and the organization. It should help individual employees see how their own role contributes to the organization's goals and success. It should enable innovation at both individual and team levels. It should provide employees with clarity of focus, a developmental relationship with their manager and ongoing feedback which allows them to fine-tune their performance. Employees believe that they are adding more value and that their work is benefiting the customer.

For high performance working to occur, the conditions have to be right. These include having a clear link between organizational strategy and individual jobs, the right people in the right jobs with the right level of resources, manageable workloads and good performance management practices (Figure 11.2). People cooperate across organizational boundaries, and learning, problem-solving and innovation occur at all levels. Work can be its own reward if the work itself is of significance, if people are able to use a variety of skills and are clear about what they are aiming to achieve and why. Individual roles should be designed to stimulate personal motivations so that people release discretionary effort that can transform ordinary performance into the extraordinary.

People need to have the support necessary to do the work, as well as the autonomy and authority to carry out what is required. They need feedback on how well they are doing and how they can be even more effective. They need to know the actual results of the work they do. Empowerment is about employees retaining ownership of the work they do, having the trust of managers and using their initiative appropriately. When this cocktail of performance ingredients comes together, people tend to experience work as more meaningful and take greater responsibility for its outcomes. For individuals, engaged performance

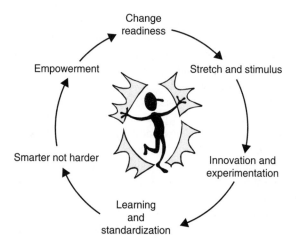

Figure 11.2 A virtuous circle.

results in personal growth, high intrinsic work motivation and job satisfaction. They grow in confidence and commitment. For organizations, the benefits are high quality work performance, low absenteeism and low turnover.

In enabling high performance, managers have a key role to play. The 'soft stuff' of management, i.e. people management, is in fact potentially the most potent way of building an organization's competitive advantage. The most effective combination of good people practices, such as job design, the development of skills through training, effective performance management, innovative reward methods (including rewarding group performance), and enabling teams of workers to use their skills and initiative, require management skill to implement effectively. The right blend of people practices should be tailored to each organization and its employees.

However, even good people-management practices are unlikely to improve organizational performance for long if the underlying psychological contract is weak. In later chapters, we shall explore how elements of the emerging psychological contract, or 'New Deal', can be brought to life and turn a workplace into a great place to work.

Checklist: Building customer-focused performance

How can HR and line managers help employees develop the skill and the will to be customer focused? These tips are about placing customers and employees centre-stage in performance:

- Use employee attitude surveys to take the temperature of the organization and to focus HR delivery on things that make a difference.
- Ensure that people are clear what their job is and how it relates to the customer. Role descriptions should help people see the whole process and how their job fits in with others in the value chain. Facilitate cross-boundary teams set up to address customer projects.
- Develop reward and recognition schemes, including 'spot' bonuses at managers' and team members' discretion, which reinforce great customer-focused performance. Design suggestion schemes that encourage innovative solutions to customer needs.
- Create performance management processes which provide people with meaningful feedback on how they are doing. Ensure that responsibilities are clear and that metrics reinforce the highest standards. Train managers to manage performance, including how to deal with poor performance.
- 'Command and control' management styles tend to produce 'more than my job's worth' employee styles. Train managers to coach and delegate more effectively, so that people become empowered to use their initiative and be accountable.
- Remind employees what it feels like to be on the customer end of bad and good service. Marks and Spencer used actors in training

roadshows to make staff aware of how small things can make a difference to how customers feel.

- Develop leaders at every level of the organization. Focus them on building an open, problem-solving climate.
- Train front-line staff in customer service. Train professionals in 'internal consultancy' and 'relationship management' skills. Train everyone in teamworking, problem-solving and interpersonal communication skills.
- Find ways of helping people work smarter, not harder. HR can work with line managers to develop effective knowledge management practices so that the wheel does not have to be reinvented each time, and to ensure that work processes are employee- and customer-friendly. Develop a range of flexible working options so that employees can achieve a work–life balance.
- HR should act as an excellent role model for customer service. Seek out customer feedback and aim to address customer needs proactively before they become problems.

12

The role of HR in building culture

Introduction

In this chapter we shall examine the role that Human Resources (HR) professionals can play in building a high performance culture. If high performance is generated by people, the people-specialist function should be uniquely well placed to act as change agent and culture builder.

In looking at HR's role in building high performance organizations, I shall draw on a range of Roffey Park research projects, including surveys and focus groups of HR Directors, CEOs and line managers (1999–2003). We shall look at some of the dilemmas facing HR as change agents, at how HR can add value in the short-term, and where HR can focus strategies to build sustainable high performance in the longer-term.

A function in transition

HR is itself a profession in transition, challenged to prove that, as a staff function, it adds value to business. The nature of what might be required of people in HR roles is likely to be contingent on a number of factors, including the nature of change experienced within the organization, the expectations of internal clients (line managers), and the state of readiness of HR professionals for more strategic roles. HR has a major role to play in improving the *status quo* – ensuring that employees have the skills and working conditions to give of their best and to be appropriately rewarded. HR should also have a significant part to play in developing the organization, by carrying out strategic recruitment and selection, building organizational capability, managing elements of the change process, and helping to shape the emerging culture through the development of effective people policies and practices.

The three 'traditional' main areas of HR responsibility are:

1. *Transactional HR* (administration, employment law, pay and benefits, special advice, recruitment and selection etc.)
2. Issues relating to *capability development and talent management* (management development, leadership development, training, performance management, retention initiatives, strategic planning)

3. Issues relating to *organization development and effectiveness* (cultural change, cost-reduction initiatives, knowledge management, innovation, performance climate, re-engineering initiatives, industrial relations/consultation, communications).

In carrying out these roles, HR professionals may be required to wear different 'hats' – as coach to line managers, architect of policies, designer of structures and facilitator of change processes, in addition to being expert in HR processes.

Working as business partner to line managers

In today's changing organizations, HR professionals need to work in partnership with line managers, who have direct responsibility for managing people. The challenge is to define how HR will work with line managers. In some cases it will be appropriate to provide the service/solution directly; in other cases it will be more appropriate to broker a solution, provide tools and train managers in how to deal with the issue by themselves in the future.

Typical organizational challenges faced by managers

The following issues are typical of the kinds of challenges managers face. Any of these issues, and many others besides, can be dealt with at a number of levels. They can form part of a team-level change project which can affect the success of a department or business unit, or can form part of a wider, system-wide change which effectively changes the culture of the organization as a whole.

1. Developing teamworking

Most organizations see the need at some stage to develop new ways of working and to change old patterns of behaviour. Developing teamworking, for instance, was seen as very important by 91 per cent of *Management Agenda* respondents. If the people who should be contributing to common tasks do not wish to work together, or face too many obstacles when they do, the organization will suffer.

2. Managing differences

Because people see things differently, conflicts are almost bound to arise between individuals and teams. Finding ways to use these differences constructively to generate new ideas and solutions can turn problems into opportunities. For change agents, the challenge is to build community by bringing people together; initiating meetings, not just facilitating them. They should push for humane treatment, dignity and fairness.

3. Creating conditions for high performance

Most organizations want their customers to have faith in their products, and they want their employees to take pride in what they are helping to produce or deliver. Finding work processes that facilitate high quality and consistent high performance is the Holy Grail. The changing business requirements should drive the culture agenda. To what extent is the current leadership able to create an adaptable, change-oriented organization in which accountabilities are clear, employees are highly motivated and committed, and where the culture is supportive of learning and innovation?

4. Encouraging innovation

The ability to innovate, think up new products and find ways of producing things in the most efficient ways possible underpins sustainable success. Typically, in a 'blame culture' environment (where people get punished if they make a mistake as they try new things) or where people are so busy they have little time to think, let alone experiment, innovation remains on the wish list. HR professionals should ideally be catalysts for change, working alongside line management to define the desired culture and find ways of changing attitudes and behaviours, especially those of people in leadership positions. In a Roffey Park survey of HR professionals, 83 per cent of respondents perceived that being a change agent was a critical part of the HR role. However, only 41 per cent of respondents claimed to be skilled in this area.

5. Working across boundaries

As companies increasingly operate in partnership with customers, suppliers and competitors, developing the skills needed to enable 'safe' collaboration, and importing skills and knowledge back into the parent organization are growing issues where HR can make a difference. Similarly, organizational success is increasingly dependent on employees at all levels being able to look beyond their organization's boundaries and import new ideas. Warner Burke (1997) suggests emphasizing the interrelationships of cultures, and recommends consulting in the domain of 'in-between-ness'.

6. Leadership

In the *Management Agenda* survey, inappropriate leadership and management styles were considered by many respondents to be hampering the success of their current organizations. However, relatively few HR professionals saw the development of their top team as a key priority for the future. It could be argued that HR has a critical role to play in building the leadership of the organization to create shareholder and other stakeholder value. This means not only developing succession for the medium term, but also critically evaluating the quality of current leadership.

For example, do leaders develop and manage effective relationships with internal and external stakeholders? Are they able to scan the environment for new opportunities for their organization? If not, what can and should be done to ensure that the organization has the leaders it needs? When employees do not trust their leaders, the challenge for HR as change agents is to provide coaching and feedback for executives to help them match the 'walk' to the 'talk' on values.

7. Employee motivation

Employee motivation issues are known to have a direct effect on retention, a topic that is high on the management priority list in many organizations. While individuals are motivated by different things, there are certain common factors that predictably have a negative affect on employee motivation, performance and retention. These include a lack of career progression, uncertainty, lack of balance, and inappropriate leadership and reward, including lack of recognition. Whilst it is one thing to be aware of the changing workplace and employee expectations, it is quite another to develop and implement innovative career practices.

While many HR practitioners in the Roffey Park surveys consider employee motivation issues important, only 52 per cent of respondents talk of employee morale and 49 per cent talk of career management as areas of future focus. Warner Burke (1997) suggests that change agents should foster career development by helping people to understand what they (a) are good at; (b) want in their work; and (c) desire concerning balance of work and other aspects of life.

Some of the issues that can have big effects on employee motivation suffer perhaps from falling into the less fashionable, 'soft' area of personnel practice in this, the era of strategic HR. Areas selected least frequently by survey respondents as areas for future focus included welfare issues (29 per cent) and ethics (20 per cent). Yet implementing employee-friendly policies on issues such as work–life balance, fairness at work and anti-bullying practices can have a positive effect on the image of organizations seeking to attract the best recruits.

8. Clarifying roles

Lack of role clarity can lead to job tension, dissatisfaction, political behaviour, duplication or gaps in delivery. It can also cause problems with regard to work–life balance. Warner Burke (1997) suggests that OD practitioners should model the way, seeking clarity regarding task expectations and goals/objectives; helping to provide feedback for employees; promoting reward systems based on merit and, perhaps, pay for performance.

9. Improving communications

Communications in most surveys are described as 'poor' – with too much data, not enough meaningful information, or a general lack of communication. Given that effective communications underpin employee commitment, the creation of new structures and processes that facilitate communication is a foundation for high performance. While formal communications are often managed by externally facing PR or Marketing functions, there is a good argument for saying that HR should have a lead role in coordinating and shaping internal communications, especially with regard to change.

10. Redesigning work

When employees find their work boring, lacking in challenge or repetitive, the additional workloads typically caused by the widespread use of technology can add to pressure rather than enabling employees to work 'smarter, not harder'. As more and more employees want to work flexibly, they often find the organization limited in its range of flexible working options. Conversely, as more and more organizations require people to work remotely, many employees feel cut off from the social processes of work through which they gained a sense of being part of a community or team.

HR operating as internal consultant

One way in which HR can work as business partner is by acting as internal consultant. Internal consultancy involves working with line managers on their people/business agenda. This can sometimes be very short-term and specific. It involves acting at local level to address problems managers face and helping to find systemic solutions so that problems do not recur.

Potentially this represents something of a vicious circle: without being responsive to line management, HR is unlikely to gain buy-in for people-related investments. On the other hand, the piecemeal nature of HR activity when working in a reactive manner reduces HR's credibility with line managers, who typically then stall on critical people-related decisions because they do not trust the function to deliver the 'big stuff'.

Breaking out of the vicious circle requires that HR is fully embraced by business units and is able to exercise influence around a leadership agenda. After all, there is no shortage of business problems that need people-related solutions. A lack of new products, failure to achieve market penetration or an unsuccessful merger may be linked to underlying cultural issues, such as the way innovation is encouraged or discouraged and the way managers integrate and manage teams. Broader people-related challenges, such as attracting and retaining high-calibre employees, talent management and the development of intellectual capital, all have a potential bearing on future business success. The HR task is to translate the organizational/people agenda into language which makes sense to business leaders and can clearly produce both short- and longer-term benefits to the business.

Examples of how internal consultants view the purpose of their roles (from Kenton and Moody, 2003) include:

Strategic alignment:
- To improve the alignment of people management practice to business goals
- To help managers understand their people in the context of organizational change.

Service:
- To provide an accessible point of contact for clients
- To improve overall service levels
- To provide bespoke, not generic, solutions.

Financial:
- To provide improved HR services at no extra cost
- To control burgeoning costs on external consultants.

Roles consultants play

In carrying out an internal consultancy role, it is common for both internal clients and sponsors (usually line managers) and the consultant to make assumptions about the nature of the role and relationship. Some clients, for instance, cast the consultant into the 'pair of hands' role characteristic of a contracting relationship. This is typical of the kind of 'purchase/sale' relationship often seen in tendering exercises, for example. This assumes that the consultant has some recognizable service to offer; that the client diagnoses both the problem to be solved and the solution; and that the consultant's job is to deliver the client's proposed solution. The client's role is to choose the right consultant to implement the results.

Such a relationship can be efficient when the client is accurate in their diagnosis of the problem. However, for the consultant who recognizes that the problem may be different – and indeed that the client might be part of the problem – the relative power dynamics of the relationship may prevent the best solution being applied. In such a situation, both client and consultant may suffer! This is a common issue for many internal consultants, who struggle to meet the challenge of 'being presented with the solution which someone thinks is right to implement rather than being allowed to research the issue/problem properly and complete a full consultancy process' (Kenton and Moody, 2003). While the client may continue to use the services of the consultant if he or she is satisfied, the transfer of learning between client and consultant may be low.

A further complication arises when the 'client' is in fact an HR business partner, commissioning a solution on behalf of an internal client. For people working on the delivery end of the transaction, in shared services for example, the right to carry out a diagnosis of their own with the client is often a major stumbling block and source for hard negotiation.

Another consultancy role that can be seductive but also contains dangers is the doctor–patient model. This works on the assumption that the consultant is the expert. The client invites the consultant in to deal with a 'problem' issue within the client system. The consultant accepts the 'problem' at face value and has access to the client group. The consultant identifies options for change and gets agreement from the client to implement a solution. The client monitors performance. Unless the consultant is able to diagnose the 'problem' accurately, there is a danger that a solution can be found to the wrong problem. The client then rejects the consultant's advice.

Perhaps a more appropriate internal consultancy approach for real business partnership is the process model. The client invites the consultant into the client system. At the start there is less clarity about specific issues and concerns, and attention is paid to the client/consultant relationship. In the process model, both parties share the task of diagnosing the situation. They act collaboratively to explore, identify, come to terms with and then act upon issues. They accept joint responsibility and ownership, and agree joint action. The client takes a prominent role in implementing solutions, and there is transfer of skills between the consultant and client. This deliberate focus on increasing the client's ability to address similar issues effectively is part of the organization development required as part of learning organization approaches.

These models do not represent either/or choices for the consultant. Rather, a contingency approach would be more appropriate, with relevant aspects of each model applied to specific situations. The choice of approach should always depend on the situation and the issue. The ability to switch roles and value different ways of working is a key skill required of any consultant.

The internal consultancy process

This is the process of engaging with the client to identify issues, generate options and implement solutions. Essentially, it involves the deployment of a set of skills while managing specific relationships to achieve client outcomes. The process typically follows a number of stages, with 'content' and 'process' issues at each stage (Figure 12.1).

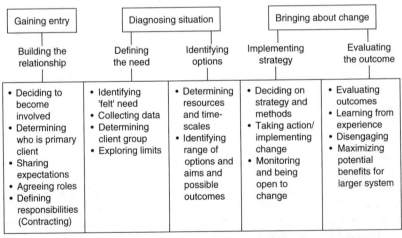

Figure 12.1 Internal consultancy cycle.

Gaining entry

In the early stages of the relationship between consultant and client, there is likely to be a wide variety of issues beneath the surface. Some of these are likely to be about consultant credibility and confidence, and client trust. According to Peter Block (1981), these may be dealt with indirectly (e.g. through the consultant acting in a trustworthy way) or directly (e.g. 'It sounds like you don't trust me'). If these issues remain unresolved, the consultancy is likely to be unproductive for all those concerned. If resolved (e.g. both parties are accessible, willing and able to work together), then client and consultant are likely to have a good basis for a working relationship.

According to Kenton and Moody (2003), ease of gaining entry depends on a number of factors, such as how visible (and therefore known) the individual consultant and function are; how well understood the consultancy role is within the business; and the individual's credibility and track record. Another factor is how ready the client is to work in this way. Beckhard and Harris (1987) suggest that the consultant should examine the client's attitudes, assessing the willingness of the client to work in this way, and to find out more about their motives and aims. It is also important for the consultant to assess how capable he or she really is to work in this way by taking stock of their sources of power, influence and authority, together with the skills and information required.

Contracting

This involves clarifying mutual expectations and responsibilities, and renegotiating the terms of the work if necessary. It is important at a 'process' level for consultants to be aware and willing to acknowledge their own limitations as a consultant. Contracting is a key skill that involves identifying and agreeing outcomes from the outset, as well as contracting on process and content issues. It is also important to clarify mutual expectations of the role – whether the client sees the consultant–client relationship as doctor–patient, supplier–purchaser or process facilitator.

Diagnosing the situation

This stage involves collecting data and making sense of it. It also involves generating options, making decisions and planning. At skill level, data collection involves choosing appropriate methods of data collection, asking pertinent questions and encouraging client ownership of data. The success of change is driven both by the accuracy of diagnosis and by the client's acceptance of the analysis. Most internal consultancy work is related to first-order, transactional change, where elements of the organization are changed but the organization as a whole remains fundamentally unaltered.

Diagnosis involves having a range of frameworks and models for understanding individuals, groups and organizations; maintaining a critical approach to models; being able to construct own models; and encouraging joint diagnosis with clients. For more information about diagnostic tools, see Chapter 4.

- *Generating options* involves techniques such as brainstorming and attribute analysis
- *Evaluating options* can involve techniques such as cost–benefit analyses, weighting and ranking
- *Design* involves being creative and purposeful in designing interventions; not relying on packaged, favourite interventions; being willing to redesign on the spot; and designing at the level of content and process simultaneously (Shaw and Phillips, 1998).

Bringing about change

This stage involves implementing the plan and taking action. The consultant may or may not be involved in implementation. The likely process issues at this stage are responsibility, risk-taking, commitment and willingness to learn. Again, these issues can be dealt with either directly or indirectly. If things are going well, then they are more likely to be dealt with implicitly. If, however, things are going badly, there will be the need to become explicit – e.g. 'You do not seem to have the power to implement this'.

Disengaging

A key aim of process consultancy is to help clients to help themselves in the future. Therefore, mutual dependency can defeat the object of the exercise. The consultant is often seen, at a process level, as an expert in a particular field (e.g. learning and process skills or HR practices). Indeed, this may be appropriate in some cases (such as giving advice on employment law or current training policy). However, the client may come to depend on the consultant's expertise, may and therefore feel less confident about ensuring that things get done. This may defeat the purpose of the exercise – i.e. to develop shared responsibility for learning and managing change. It is therefore important to help the client to take on his or her share of the work and consider how handovers can be made to those who will be involved in implementation. The consultant can prompt the client to take responsibility at a process level by asking questions that help the client find a solution that works (e.g. 'How can you do this differently?').

If successful, the client will take responsibility and ownership for the work and the consultant will be in a position to 'let go'.

Disengaging well from assignments involves reviewing learning from each project with clients. Sometimes disengaging can be difficult, especially if the process has been enjoyable and successful and both parties want to continue to work together. If the consultancy has not been straightforward, reviewing learning can be challenging. The consultant may have internal process issues to deal with – e.g. feelings, confidence, expectations and self-image. These issues can act as either constraints or opportunities, depending on how the consultant handles them.

HR as change agents

Within HR's strategic toolkit is a number of ways in which culture-building can be achieved. Short-term consultancy projects should always be carried out with an eye to the longer-term development of the organization. However, consultancy projects tend to be located in a specific team or business unit, or relate to a particular senior manager's agenda. Management Development is a key lever for change, and can undoubtedly influence the effectiveness of individuals, teams and, ultimately, the organization.

Some of the areas of focus for HR professionals as culture-builders and change agents include:

- Finding better and more cost-effective ways of getting the core administrative roles of HR done (e.g. through use of HR information systems, employee help desks, employee self-service, service centres, outsourcing, insourcing etc.), thereby making everyone's job easier and allowing HR to focus on higher value activities.
- Dealing with short-term local needs driven by business units (through internal consultancy assignments, facilitating team working, conflict management, coaching of managers, acting as broker to external consultants etc.).
- Building the organization's longer-term source of competitive advantage (by acting as adviser to top management; developing HR strategies focused on high quality learning processes; talent management; knowledge management strategies; work–life balance policies; change management, organization design; high performance work practices; leadership development; succession planning; and graduate recruitment).
- Managing change projects focused on business needs (e.g. restructuring, downsizing, relocation, continuous improvement etc.). They may, for instance, be required to carry out re-engineering and integration projects. According to Warner Burke (1997), this involves focusing on specific change targets that are critical to the success of the re-engineering effort (e.g. roles and responsibilities, the larger systemic picture etc.). Warner Burke advises HR to confront managers on the reasons for the decision, and test for constraining, cloning or learning forces. Connor (1988), suggests that HR's is an advocacy role:

> The difference between succeeding and failing to implement change is attributable to the advocate's ability to identify the right sponsor for a given change and to use the right kind of information to build that sponsor's commitment to the change.

Managing change is not something that HR generally excels at and therefore tends to shy away from the change agent role. In the *Management Agenda* 2004 survey, HR was described as 'reactive' by the majority of respondents (62 per cent) and proactive in only 25 per cent of organizations surveyed. Helping an organization to manage culture change was seen as important by

89 per cent of HR practitioners, yet only 63 per cent of respondents saw this as something they would be engaged in.

Whether this is because practitioners feel they lack the skills or the confidence to create culture change is not clear, although interestingly this was the main area of HR competence in which respondents felt they were personally least effective. Is this because HR professionals tend to favour strategies that play to their strengths, whether or not they meet business needs, and avoid working on things when they lack confidence in their ability to deliver, however important the issue?

Change agent skills

To be effective as an agent of change, the following skills are helpful (Shaw and Phillips, 1998):

- *Tolerance of ambiguity* – the ability to live with uncertainty and complexity without undue stress; searching for meaning without grasping at over-simplistic interpretations or rushing in with premature actions; tolerating incompleteness
- *Maintaining a long-term perspective* – helping clients to identify and articulate desired futures; setting short- and medium-term goals in the light of a longer-term sense of purpose
- *Maintaining a wide perspective* – attending to the wider context of one's work; not drawing boundaries too tightly; dealing with each subsystem's interaction with the overall system; keeping abreast of trends and developments in organizational, business and world affairs
- *Understanding the nature of change* – developing an intellectual and experiential understanding of change process (how and why people change; how and why they avoid change; how larger systems change or avoid changing)
- *Facilitating change* – encouraging widespread participation in the design and implementation of change; supporting others through the stress of transition; being aware of self as a catalyst and seeing possibilities of intervention in all aspects of own work and interaction with clients.

Organizational development

Building culture and organizational capability requires an organization-wide approach. Organizational development (OD) involves working with the organization as a system to bring about change. It is as much a perspective as a role, and is often defined through its activities, such as team facilitation, conflict resolution etc.

An OD perspective means diagnosing the health and performance of the organization (or team), and its ability to change. OD focuses on organizational culture, leadership and strategies. It takes an open system perspective, i.e. the interaction between the organization and its environment. It is concerned with the linkage between all the organization's parts, with any movement in one part affecting the other parts (systemic alignment). OD requires practitioners to be able to blend an understanding of organizational culture and group behaviour with more traditional management practices such as performance measurement, structure and process. Effective OD interventions are carefully planned to focus on the processes that deliver value to the stakeholders.

Warner Burke (1997), a pioneer of OD, suggests that issues on which HR are consulted can be translated into organization development initiatives by practical actions. He argues that, for every organizational consulting issue, there is an OD practitioner's agenda:

Organizational consulting issue	OD practitioner's agenda
Re-engineering	Focus on specific change targets that are critical to the success of the re-engineering effort, e.g. roles and responsibilities
Downsizing	Confront reasons for decision and push for humane treatment
Community	Bring people together; initiate meetings, don't just facilitate them
Employer–employee social contract	Seek clarity regarding task expectations and social contract goals/objectives; help provide feedback for employees; promote reward system based on merit
Employability	Foster career development by helping people understand (a) what they are good at, (b) their desires concerning work–life balance (c) what they want in their work
Trust	Espouse and live the value of openness; provide coaching and feedback for executives on the congruence of their words and actions

Dilemmas

When HR professionals act as OD practitioners they may encounter a number of dilemmas at a values level. They can experience tension in promoting the humanistic values of OD, such as growing the potential of individuals because development is a good thing in itself, versus the demands of the business agenda, such as maximizing productivity and focusing development only on areas that will make a direct difference to the bottom line. OD practitioners who successfully bring about change typically gain access to the 'inner sanctum' of power in their organization. They can then experience the tension of being driven by ego gratification, personal success and financial rewards versus continuing to champion the traditional humanistic values in the consulting process which underpinned their achievement.

For external consultants in particular it is difficult to avoid projecting their own values and beliefs onto client organizations rather than being only a facilitator for serving management's interests. There can also be tension between being marginally committed and on the fringe of the organization versus total immersion and involvement in large-scale change.

There can also be potential dilemmas in terms of practice. Church *et al.* (1992) highlight the challenge of being focused on large-scale systemic change using only a limited set of OD technologies, such as team-building. The way a culture change initiative is handled should reflect what is desired in the new culture. Yet it is easy unwittingly to reinforce aspects of the existing culture while ostensibly setting out to change it. Similarly, internal consultants in particular may feel under pressure to deliver a planned programme of culture change, which can easily be assessed in terms of 'success' or 'failure'. Yet culture is a living process, and it can be self-defeating to over pre-design development activity in this area. There is a natural design horizon which moves forward during the course of an assignment. Appropriate next steps emerge from the previous ones, and are agreed in close consultation with clients.

Understanding the nature of change required

Cheung-Judge (2003) describes OD programmes as long- and medium-term planned and sustained change efforts. They typically involve the following steps: sensing, diagnosing, planning and taking actions, evaluating, making adjustments, and repeating the sequence. It is an iterative process. Skilled activity is required at each stage.

In most organizations, change agents will be required to support both transactional and transformational change. Cheung-Judge advocates understanding organizational dynamics through the use of organizational models such as McKinsey's 7S or the Burke–Litwin model (Figure 12.2), which highlights

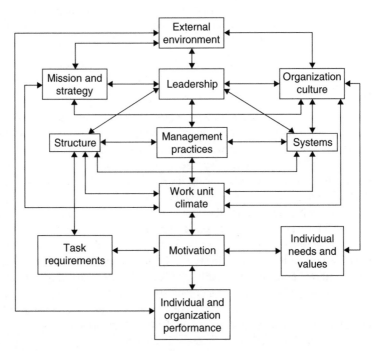

Figure 12.2 The Burke–Litwin organizational performance model.
Source: Burke (2002). Reproduced with kind permission from Professor Warner Burke.

the parts of the organizational system where transformational and transactional change can occur. Transformational change is more likely to arise from the external environment, changes in organizational mission and strategy, requirements to change the organization's culture and leadership. These often present as major strategic moves, crises or opportunities, driving the need for second-order change through which the organization is changed significantly.

Transactional change is more likely to arise from changes in other parts of the system. Structure should assure the effective implementation of the organization mission and strategy. Bringing about change in the climate of a work unit, for instance, requires an understanding of how other parts of the system are impacting on the unit, as much as of what is required by the system from the unit. For example, understanding the impact of management practices on the effective working of a unit involves looking at the specific behaviours of the manager; the way in which the manager makes and implement decisions; what the manager does and doesn't focus on; and how the manager treats people. Climate is the collective current impressions; the expectations and feeling of the members of local work units. These in turn affect members' relations with supervisors, each other and other units.

Developing an agenda for change

HR delivery, even short-term change projects, should be driven by the longer-term organization capability development agenda. Some issues, such as recruitment and retention for instance, present themselves as problems in the short term but may reflect longer-term systemic problems. To avoid treating only the symptoms of the problem, HR also needs to address some of the root causes of employee turnover while providing a short-term 'fix' in the here-and-now.

It is therefore essential that HR teams develop a clear and coherent picture of what will need to be strengthened or changed if sustainable high performance is to be achieved.

Developing an agenda for change involves taking stock of the organizational development issues that may progressively cause problems if they are not addressed, or may enable the organization to be more successful if they are strengthened. Some of these may be problems or opportunities now. Others may potentially have a major impact on the organization in the future.

For example, if a change in the business will affect the nature of skills required in the workforce, a strategic HR agenda will involve active workforce planning, targeted recruitment and development to build the skill base. In the short term, a relocation which may save money on leases but lead to a loss of key employees will signal the need perhaps to challenge the decision, and certainly to develop a strategy for smoothing the transition to the new location and building practical retention measures. The focus should be on maximizing the organization's capabilities to ensure both current and future success.

Developing a vision of a high performing organization

Any really strategic HR director will have a clear and shared vision about how the organization can be built over time to achieve sustainable high performance. The director will drive through the vision with energy and passion. A typical vision of a high performing organization is one that attracts and retains the best people, is a great place to work, and has high commitment work practices and strong corporate values to which people are attuned. Such an organization has excellent leadership and a culture supportive of innovation, flexibility, and knowledge creation and sharing, where people are able to work well across and beyond organizational boundaries.

This vision defines what needs to be reinforced, as well as changed, to create an organizational culture that enables people to fulfil business needs. It will underpin the choice of the key areas of longer-term focus, making some of the immediate priorities steps towards the vision in the short term. In selecting and devising the most appropriate strategies to achieve these objectives, a 'both/and' mentality is helpful. So how can short-term activities solve immediate problems and build to the future?

In a merger scenario, for instance, the short-term decisions about people and cultural integration can help create or undermine the basis of future profitability. Who gets what job, whether the processes are seen to be fair and whether people receive the support they need to move into new roles are all likely to predispose people to want to commit to the organization – or not. Harsh or inept handling of the people issues during a merger sends strong signals about the emerging culture, and people tend not to warm to cultural initiatives launched months after they feel they were badly handled during a change process. The culture becomes a reflection of what happens.

Thus all the members of the HR team, regardless of their roles and responsibilities, need to see how what they are doing contributes to the whole. Together, the vision and short-term needs will drive decisions about how HR should be structured, about the calibre and experience needed in the team, and the implications for line managers of any shift in HR roles.

Facilitating culture change

HR has a key role to play in facilitating culture change. Acting as change agents will involve working in an integrated way with line managers, teams, other internal and external change agents, using a range of change techniques and tools. It seems that with HR initiatives a planned approach is more likely to succeed, although if real culture change is to occur HR must 'plan for emergence' so that people within the organization can take ownership of the new practices and use them to generate improved performance.

Key levers of culture change

HR professionals have at their disposal some of the key levers of culture change. Kilmann and Associates (1985) suggests that for culture change to be embedded, change has to occur in each of five 'tracks' as follows:

1. *The culture track* – enhances trust, communication, information sharing and willingness to change among the members – the conditions that must exist before any other improvement method can succeed
2. *The management skills track* – provides all managers with new ways of working, coping with complex problems and hidden assumptions
3. *The team-building track* – infuses new culture and management skills into each work area, and encourages organization-wide cooperation
4. *The strategy–structure track* – alignment of structure, resources etc. with the new strategic direction
5. *The reward system track* – establishes a performance-based reward system that sustains all improvements by officially sanctioning the new culture, the use of updated management skills and cooperative team efforts within and among all work groups.

HR can also bring about (and embed) culture change by using a number of the following approaches to modify the different aspects of culture to more closely serve the organization's needs:

Structural approaches

Typical examples include altering existing structures; creating new structures; managing relocations; integrating personnel from different organizations; and changing role descriptions, work content and role relationships. Other examples include working with line managers to enrich or enlarge jobs; facilitating entrepreneurial groups; various forms of team-working; carrying out team-building with newly formed 'virtual' teams; setting up new HR processes for joint venture and other strategic alliance forms; setting up 'skunkworks' and other creative groups; establishing call centres; and developing career tracks.

Knowledge management can be facilitated by the deliberate development of operating networks, both as practitioners within the HR community and as facilitators elsewhere in the organization.

Other structural activities include:

- Organizational review and re-design
- Defining new work processes and practices relating to workflow
- Building flexible working arrangements
- Project management of relocation projects
- Feasibility studies on structural change
- Working in integrated teams to develop effective knowledge management processes
- Facilitating merger integration teams
- Facilitating cross-functional and remote team-building

- Development and facilitation of team interventions, including team-building, handling conflict within teams etc.
- Developing knowledge retention processes
- Review of HR to align skills with the new organization structure.

Personnel approaches

A variety of change tools fall into this category, ranging from changes to work scheduling, job-sharing, various forms of flexible working arrangement (including telecommuting), acting as a broker for external consultancy assignments, networking, changing the reward scheme, and developing effective diversity and work–life balance policies. Job rotation, open job posting and competency clarification fall into this category.

Similarly, HR excellence requires that transactional HR processes be carried out to high quality criteria and low cost. These processes are increasingly partly outsourced, or managers and employees are provided with IT-based solutions, such as help desks and relevant HR self-service software. Managers typically need training if they are to be able to use these processes effectively.

Other activities include:

- Developing competency frameworks
- Improving recruitment processes
- Mainstreaming diversity
- Facilitating teams to produce performance measures
- Designing and implementing performance management frameworks
- Redesigning reward systems to meet business needs
- Developing career tracks.

Employee development

Job-related training, coaching, counselling, information sharing sessions, IT, customer service, health and safety and quality improvement training are all means of not only equipping people for their roles but also communicating organizational values and new directions. In addition, career self-development workshops and job-specific training fit here.

Other activities include:

- Development of a range of learning and development services
- Designing a Training and Development intranet site
- Designing and delivering management training linked with performance measures (e.g. balanced business scorecard)
- Designing and implementating management development programmes
- Running personal development workshops
- Commissioning e-learning and blended learning solutions
- Brokering and quality assuring external training provision
- Evaluating training and development.

Technical approaches

These include providing HR-related expertise in learning and other systems, as well as specific tools such as brainstorming, and creative and problem-solving techniques generally. Collaboration with IT specialists to create effective knowledge management processes fits into this category. Ergonomics and lean production, total quality management processes, are growing areas within which HR teams are providing specialist expertise.

Leadership approaches

Given the impact of leadership on organizational performance, developing leaders is perhaps the key organizational development challenge for HR as OD practitioners. For Chan Kim and Mauborgne (2003), HR is better placed than anyone else to select and nurture leaders who can help an organization reach a 'tipping point' into positive change. HR should identify people who are natural leaders, who are well respected and persuasive, or who have the ability to unlock or block access to key resources.

Management and leadership development processes aimed at improving the quality of leadership include multi-rater feedback, training managers to coach others, performance management, business school executive development programmes, etc. Succession planning, graduate recruitment and high-flyer development also fall into this category.

Other activities include:

- Developing a management and leadership development strategy
- Designing and implementing succession planning processes
- Executive coaching
- Designing and delivering assessment and development centres
- Providing feedback on psychometric tests
- Mentoring managers to help them develop the skills needed to manage change
- Selecting people for a talent development programme
- Managing graduate and 'fast track' programmes
- Observation and feedback on group processes for leadership teams
- Arranging seconduents and sabbaticals
- Organizing business exchanges for business leaders.

Building a leadership 'brand'

When organizations start to become stale or complacent, the *status quo* does not need simply to be refreshed and improved but also to be transformed. Leadership plays a key role in making transformation happen. So important is this, according to Ulrich *et al.* (2000), that organizations should build a leadership 'brand' which represents what the firm aspires to be known for by customers. They give examples such as General Electric, which wants to be known for its capacity in e-business – so its leaders must become adept in their capacity to deliver e-business results.

Unlike many theories of leadership, which focus largely on the attributes of leaders, 'leadership brand' links attributes with results or outcomes which leaders must produce, given an organization's evolving strategy and market position. Results are clustered into four areas: employee, organization, customer and investor. Ulrich *et al.* (2000) argue that the nature of leadership focus will be very specific to the strategic aspiration of the organization, rather than being a generalized set of behaviours:

> *It communicates to employees how they should experience the transformation of leaders throughout the firm; it instils the transformation from one set of executives (for example, a top management team who conceived the transformation) to a distributed leadership cadre through a firm; it assures continuity in the transformation so that if any one leader moves, the transformation persists.*

They outline five steps for embedding a leadership brand. The first is achieving strategic clarity. This involves succinctly articulating, consistently communicating, and rigorously racking a new strategic proposition. Management systems such as resource allocation, compensation and training should then be brought into line to reinforce the new strategic proposition. The next step is developing the firm brand, which is its identity or reputation in the mind of its best customers in the future. When this external identity is brought to life for employees through policies, practices and management behaviour, the firm brand becomes the culture. The gap between the desired and current identity can be assessed, and actions taken to close the gap.

The third step involves defining the leadership attributes – i.e. the knowledge, skills and abilities of leaders required to bring about the firm brand. These attributes should derive from the strategic proposition and should focus on the future. They should be translated into specific behaviours, not just ideals, and form the basis of competencies which help leaders to determine how leaders should behave in a given situation. Having attributes alone is not enough for transformation. The authors stress the importance of linking them with results that flow from the strategy and mindset, and which must be measurable. The final step involves training and developing leaders at all levels so that the leadership brand becomes real.

An OD change process

When working on major organization development projects, HR professionals can find themselves playing a range of roles, from facilitator to expert, including:

- Objective observer/reflector
- Process counsellor
- Fact-finder
- Alternative-finder
- Joint problem-solver
- Trainer/educator

- Informational expert
- Advocate.

They can find themselves using a range of facilitation techniques, from the non-directive to the directive, such as:

- Questions to encourage reflection
- Observing problem-solving process and giving feedback
- Gathering data and stimulating thinking
- Identifying alternatives for the client and helping assess consequences
- Proposing alternatives and participating in decisions
- Training the client
- Determining policy or practice decisions
- Representing the client, arguing the case on the client's behalf.

The following process is intended to provide a possible roadmap through what can be a complex set of activities and elements.

1. Initiating the change programme

This involves defining the nature of the change to be made, and gaining involvement of key stakeholders. It may involve exploring different interpretations of the problem, and clarifying language. It may also involve challenging the thinking of key stakeholders and encouraging 'reframing'.

Facilitating involvement:
- Identifying the main stakeholders
- Clarifying expectations of project scope
- Facilitating strategic workshops
- Working towards participation of all
- Facilitating discussion among divergent groups
- Using knowledge of power/influence structures
- Selling corporate OD processes by influencing senior managers
- Buzz group facilitation.

Encouraging reframing:
- Managing and facilitating culture change workshops
- Creating opportunities for new attitudes and values to emerge
- Challenging beliefs, assumptions, values.

2. Diagnosis

Change may be needed in any (or all) of the 'five tracks' described earlier in this chapter. Using any tool is a change intervention in itself, since interpretation will be coloured by the instrument and method chosen to gather data. Similarly, the people who have interacted with the change agent during data-gathering will have experienced some reaction to what they have been asked to do. Typically, analytical processes focus people's minds on the problems they experience in their environment. In contrast, an approach such as Appreciative Inquiry (described in Chapter 5) focuses people on what is constructive and positive in their culture. The impact of using such a tool is usually to release energy for change.

Of course, any structured diagnostic tool can be too prescriptive or may need tailoring to the context. Ideally, OD practitioners develop their own diagnostic tools which can help them understand and make sense of their organizational context and issues. For Mee-Yan Cheung-Judge (2001), there is no finer tool than the 'self, as instrument'.

Many change agents have a relatively mechanical view of themselves and their role. They look for the 'tool kit'. However, Richard Seel (2000) points out that in a complex self-organizing entity the organization should be worked with, rather than worked on. Consulting from a complexity perspective involves working formally and informally, helping people to have conversations they might not otherwise have had. Consultants operating in this way work towards the organization becoming ready for its own transformation. They help to remove barriers and open up channels so that the system can self-organize to a critical configuration where change becomes possible.

Cheung-Judge suggests offering the client preliminary feedback of the diagnosis – the initial interpretation – and then having a general feedback session with all involved, to clarify the results, arrive at a final agreed diagnosis and generate alternative steps for responding appropriately to issues. Larger communication of results and action plans follows.

Through the process of diagnosis and any subsequent intervention, a good internal consultant can draw on a range of perspectives, recommend appropriate interventions and achieve long-term change. The total organization change programme may involve organization design (see Chapter 5), using large-scale interventions, future search conferences, introducing total quality management, appreciative inquiry summits, system survey feedback, and real-time strategic change. Profoundly democratic in their process, such interventions can produce a culture shift in their own right, since employees gain a greater sense of ownership of what they create.

3. Producing change

HR, working as part of an integrated team with line managers and other functional specialists such as IT and Finance, can create a coherent architecture for change, with short-term plans providing detail and milestones that can guide implementation for the next two to three years, during which time the initial change effort is built on and the fruits of the change effort start to be felt. Creating a meaningful plan involves distinguishing between those activities that need to be started or completed now and those which are better factored in to the medium term, such as relocations etc. Producing change typically involves:

- Critical path analysis
- Budgets, budgetary controls

- Performance measures and indicators
- Monitoring progress
- Ongoing communications, especially about progress
- Counselling managers affected by change.

HR may also have responsibility for developing a communication plan using the following inputs:

- The change programme itself
- The impact analysis
- An organization analysis
- Current communication effectiveness assessment
- Communication audience analysis
- Communication objectives/vision
- High-level messages for communication
- The communication strategy.

The plan outlines the communication events to be conducted throughout the change programme:

- Detailed communication schedule, by audience group, with proposed messages, messengers, vehicles and timing
- A communication record, outlining the details of each communication event.

4. Maintaining momentum for change

Once the initial change effort has subsided, other change agents usually revert to their day jobs and employees assume that the change is complete. HR can help maintain momentum for change by:

- Actively seeking opportunities to embed new behaviours
- Encouraging managers to act on options
- Action learning set facilitation
- Post-project reviews
- Evaluating the results
- Communicating new cultural symbols/values based on what has emerged
- Celebrating success.

Beyond specific culture change initiatives, HR must ensure that the organization is building the organization's capability for the future by attracting and retaining the best available talent, and ensuring that management practices are conducive to getting the best out of people. It is HR professionals, with line management, who need to work out what the key elements of the employer brand should be, and then how to make this real to current employees. In the context of a fractured psychological contract this can be a challenging task, but HR is central to developing appropriate strategies, policies and practices which are congruent with being a great employer.

Core skills for the HR practitioner

1. Credibility

In order to be effective at building culture, HR professionals need to have high levels of credibility. Credibility can be gained through personal actions, learning and reputation. Being externally connected, in touch with current thinking and able to impart best practice from elsewhere can all lead to increased credibility. None of these alone is sufficient, however, without practical application of insights gained. Benchmarking, for instance, may well build an individual's understanding of what needs to be done, but it is what you do with the knowledge gained, such as sharing research and experience with colleagues, that builds credibility.

2. Ability to influence senior decision-makers and other stakeholders

As a support function, HR is rarely able to impose its will, other than by designing processes and 'policing' them. Far more effective is the ability to bring about change through influencing others. Bringing about change requires being prepared to challenge the *status quo*. HR practitioners need to develop the confidence and judgement to challenge senior managers on the 'people' implications of their decisions – what Dave Ulrich (in MacLachlan, 1998) refers to as 'HR with attitude'. Supporting the job performance of an executive is a key responsibility for HR as strategic partner. This means being prepared to take well-calculated risks for the benefit of the business and, without being naive, treating senior managers as potential allies rather than adversaries.

HR professionals who are effective influencers tend to adopt similar strategies, as follows.

They develop champions and allies

Getting management teams to listen is about building and maintaining good relationships with the right people. Winning support for what HR wants to do often requires addressing a key priority for one of these influential individuals. They then become champions of HR, or 'cheerleaders', as Rosabeth Moss Kanter (1983) once described them.

Effective influencers work out who they need to influence and how to influence them. Influencing senior management is usually a highly political business, and trying to win everyone over is likely to be a futile exercise. Instead, effective influencers create a map of the influential players in their organization and pick out the key decision-makers and the people who influence them. These may not be the people who shout the loudest – they may not even be on the management team. The aim is to build productive working relationships with these individuals.

Influencers find out how the informal structures work, and assess who might resist cooperation and why. They work out how to address potential challenges. They map out how decisions get made, and what approaches have been successfully used with others. They develop respect from key influencers by delivering effectively. These champions then act as powerful third-party referees who can influence their peers without the need for HR to exert direct pressure – which may backfire.

Some HR professionals act as 'trusted adviser' or 'critical friend' to the CEO. They develop a workable and unambiguous set of mutual expectations. They are prepared to question these individuals to test their assumptions and confront real differences which may be making the relationship less effective. They are assertive and prepared to stand up for their own rights and those of others.

They think and act as a business-person – with specific value-added expertise

Effective influencers use 'business' language when talking about people issues. This avoids the need for senior managers to translate HR jargon into ideas that they see as relevant and important. They work out the likely implications of business aims for HR strategy and are prepared to challenge senior management about their key priorities if they foresee real problems. They are dependable and honest so that the management team can rely on them for an accurate reading of the 'people' issues for the organization and they are able to build trust.

They are also able to use formal influencing situations effectively. A polished, formal presentation that addresses both substantive and political concerns may be necessary to win further support. Senior managers are typically concerned about the potential rewards, the degree of risk involved and what their constituents will think. Effective influencers are prepared to argue their case using cost–benefit or other forms of analysis. Data, convincingly and concisely presented, can be a more powerful means of persuasion than simply appealing to hearts and minds. Influencers think and speak like a business-person first and a specialist second.

They discover the real objectives of key decision-makers

Having identified the influential individuals in their organization, effective influencers try to see them alone and on their territory. This gives both parties the chance to feel heard and in turn to hear what is being said. HR needs to have the confidence to ask members of the management team about their objectives, concerns and hopes for the business – and listen hard not just to the words but also for the meaning and the value the individual places on what is being said.

Finding out about people's real agendas requires 'emotional intelligence'. The more effective influencers do not fall into the trap of assuming that the strength of the business argument will win the day when they are looking for support. They become skilled at understanding people's likely motivations and how best to respond to them. They pay attention to clues in their colleagues' behaviour on an ongoing basis, so that they can recognize new priorities as things change. They are clear about the outcomes they want to achieve, but are flexible about achieving them. They regard winning the war as more important than winning the battle.

Developing the ability to see what needs to be changed may simply be a matter of making time to think – not easy in the daily grind of meetings and tasks. It requires focus, working collaboratively with business partners, using understanding and intuition to make good decisions and being able to bring others on board. One way to do this is to ask the business leaders what they think they need from the HR function. The various needs should be prioritized so that an achievable number of goals – maybe three or four – is identified and agreed. A service level agreement can then be reached so that line managers understand and know what they are getting. HR then has to ensure that these goals are achieved, even though this will mean dropping low value-add activities.

Having won support, they deliver brilliantly

As delivery starts to produce results, trust is earned. As the goals of the business are advanced, HR is perceived to add value. High quality innovative solutions, delivered ahead of schedule and at minimum cost, are popular with most management teams! Good diagnostic, negotiation, team-building, IT, planning and project management skills are the building blocks of effective implementation.

HR can sharpen up its act by being more selective about what it takes on, by focusing on the things which really do make a difference to the business and by making sure that appropriate resources and priorities are agreed. Effective influencers manage their time carefully. They establish clear goals and measures, prioritize plans and monitor progress, learn to anticipate and maintain enough flexibility so that they can exploit relevant opportunities.

Keeping senior managers informed of progress is easily overlooked, but is vital to the maintenance of credibility, especially if things begin to go awry. Developing a track record of positive contributions to the business is likely to ensure that HR is at least consulted before future key decisions are made.

Conclusion

Building culture is never easy, and may require HR to move beyond 'partner', 'consultant' and 'service delivery' modes into real business leadership. It may require challenging vested interests and being willing to take well-informed risks in the absence of hard and fast data about future needs. Effectively building future capability may always be a matter of intuition and informed guesswork, linked with determination and some luck.

HR leadership involves building for the future while attending to current business needs. Credibility will depend on high-calibre delivery in the here-and-now, and having the confidence to lead thinking and practice on strategic people issues. At the end of the day, it will require HR to role model high performance work practices and use all available HR tools in order symbolically and practically to lead the way to sustainable longer-term success.

HR can and does influence behaviours through its existing tools and levers, such as managing recruitment and designing the performance management and reward systems. HR can contribute significantly by rising to the challenge of developing organizational capability. By designing change processes that maximize engagement, and processes that embed behavioural change, HR can be a key enabling function of high performance.

In particular, HR can help build the organization's ability to attract and retain the best talent by strategically and practically building the employer brand. As the evidence starts to accumulate, it is becoming clear that organizations which are proactive in the development of a new basis for a psychological contract with employees become employers of choice. They attract and retain the best available talent. They are able to move swiftly and skilfully in the marketplace. They are the organizations that are most likely to enjoy sustainable success as businesses and employers. We shall explore what is involved in creating a 'great place to work' in the next chapter.

Checklist: Organizational capability

- What will the future capability need be?
- What is our current capability?
- What needs to change?
- Where is the 'talent pipeline' in this organization?
- What are the key roles within the business in which the key people are needed?
- Who are the key people?
- How are they developed to reach those positions?
- How is succession built for key positions?
- What aspects of culture do we wish to continue?
- What level of understanding is there about links between the business agenda and the capabilities of the people?
- What are the business requirements of the human resources strategy to ensure success?
- What are the human resource vision and goals?
- What initiatives are in place to support the business strategy?
- When customers think of the business, what image do we want them to have?

Part Two: Building Positive Psychological Contracts

13

Becoming a great place to work

The companies that make it on to our list have fared better than most during a bumpy year on the stock market. Whereas the FTSE All-Share index fell 15.6 per cent in the year to January 31, 2002, the listed companies among our top 100 fell a more modest 5.9 per cent. A study of performance over a five-year period is even more instructive. Share and dividend returns for these companies have shown 25.4 per cent growth year on year over this period, compared with 6.3 per cent for the rest of the All-Share index. Being a great place to work clearly pays in the long run.

(The Sunday Times *survey of the 100 Best Companies to Work For, 2002)*

Introduction

In previous chapters we have looked at some of the organizational practices that help to create a culture supportive of adaptability, innovation, knowledge-sharing and 'boundaryless' behaviour. These elements underpin dynamic stability – the mainspring of sustainable success. For 'practices', 'culture' and 'behaviour', read 'people'. Unless an organization is able to attract and retain talented individuals, on whose performance competitive advantage depends, strategic intentions cannot be translated into practice and sustainable success will remain a pipe dream. In this chapter we shall look at how organizations can make themselves employers of choice and better able to attract and retain the key talent needed for business success. In the following two chapters we will look in more detail at careers, work–life balance and the development needs of the 'new employee'.

Competition for talent

The challenges of attracting and retaining key employees are recognized as central to the quest for greater productivity. There is usually fierce competition to attract the best people. This is where the notion of employer 'brand' has been borrowed from marketing to apply to what the organization offers existing or potential employees in terms of its employment 'deal'. It recognizes that where talent is in short supply and employees have choice, the organization has to make its offer and substance attractive to potential recruits. Similarly, use of the term 'talent management' emphasizes the importance of people as the key business resource, and the need to activate policies and practices to make the promised employment 'deal' real and mutually beneficial.

The value of the 'employer brand'

Having an employer brand that attracts and retains the best employees puts a company ahead of the competition. When companies win the reputation of being a good employer, they have their pick of available talent. People therefore should be at the heart of the executive agenda. Jack Welch Jr, former CEO of GE, described as 'possibly the most admired business leader in the world and probably the most successful', was ranked among the top 40 power players in HR by *Personnel Today* because he places people issues at the top of his, and GE's, priorities. GE is believed to have the best executive talent in the US because of Welch's development programme. 'Graduates flock to apply to the company, despite unattractive interests, such as power generation. There are few better companies to benchmark against' (Beagrie, 1999).

Being a good employer pays off in business terms. The famous Sears case study (Rucci *et al.*, 1998) showed how the US retailer was able successfully to turn round its flagging business results by focusing on the things that mattered to its employees. Sears found that when their employees felt valued they gave better service to customers, who in turn became more loyal, spent more and made investors happy into the bargain. In Sears' case, even a small shift in this employee–customer value chain had a direct effect on business results. Effective leadership and HR practices were what made the difference.

Similarly, a well-trained and motivated workforce is likely to respond to change more favourably than one that feels it is a victim of change, since talented individuals choose to stay – they usually have other options available to them. And people tend to stay if they are being developed. Of course, when there is a strong employer brand, and organizations promote the idea that they are a great organization to work for, there is the danger that employees' expectations may be raised. There is also the danger that if the implied promise of the employer brand is not fulfilled, people will become disillusioned and leave. On the other hand, if organizations make little attempt to understand and appeal to the potential recruits they wish to attract, they will become uncompetitive in the labour market. The issue of trust and honouring promises is once again pivotal to being able to attract and retain the employees an organization needs.

Becoming a great place to work

With the new employment relationship in the process of being forged, Roffey Park has been exploring what employees consider 'a great place to work', based on what respondents to the *Management Agenda* have told us since the survey began in 1996.

What do talented people want?

According to this definition, a great place to work is one where people:

- Feel involved
- Feel equipped to do their job
- Are appropriately rewarded
- Can progress their career
- Can balance home and work life
- Are able to work flexibly to suit their lifestyles
- Can learn and develop.

Ingredients of 'a great place to work' reflect the new 'deal', and include having interesting work, the chance to grow and career development, yet still allow work–life balance. In the UK, the DTI is encouraging organizations that aspire to high performance actively to help employees improve the balance between work and home life. In return, employees are expected to show greater commitment, dedication and support to the business; be more willing to offer ideas; support the competitive strategy; and provide energy to sustain it and thus increase productivity.

In the 2002–2004 surveys, three additional 'wishes' have been added to the list of elements of what employees want from work. People want to be:

- Ethically led
- Supported and coached through periods of change
- Able to find 'meaning' in their working lives.

These represent different aspects of the emerging psychological contract. In previous chapters we have looked at the need to involve employees, design jobs to get the best from employees and reward employees appropriately. In the final chapters we will look at how organizations can become the values-based enterprises to which employees want to commit and give of their best.

Talent management

In the debate about how best to tackle to the issue of raising productivity there are underlying differences of emphasis. Economists argue that skills shortages must be addressed through recruitment – by attracting a wider pool of skilled candidates, using improved recruitment methods, and tailoring training and development to the needs of the business. Looking outside the organization can ensure that an organization brings in ready-made skills when it needs them. On the other hand, HRM places a greater emphasis on retention of key talent, arguing that the fragmentation of needs and the erosion of organizational loyalty of recent years mean that training and development, and other elements of the emerging psychological contract, must be largely tailored to the needs of the individual. The cost of losing an employee is usually estimated as being twice his or her annual salary, not only because of lost productivity but because others leave too.

Talent management should be a key leadership priority, with a strong focus on finding, developing and managing the people needed to help the organization succeed now and in the future. If these aspects of talent management work well, retention should follow. In thinking about its people, organizations should consider how they ensure that they are operating at the top end of the talent curve for all types of work. Reflecting on the following questions will help:

- How well does the organization know what it is really looking for?
- How well are roles and people attributes specified?
- How far ahead does the organization look?
- Where does the organization look for its talent?
- How are people assessed?
- What will the organization do with the talent it recruits?
- What processes will enable talent to be reviewed?

Before we examine what organizations can do to attract and retain the best employees, we shall first explore the backdrop to talent management – how expectations are changing with regard to the world of work, and how these impact on recruitment and retention.

The changing psychological contract

Much has been written in recent years about the changing nature of the psychological contract between employers and employees. First coined in the 1960s by writers such as Chris Argyris and Edgar Schein, the phrase 'psychological contract' describes a set of mutual expectations of the employment relationship. According to this psychological contract, employees looked to employers to provide job security and some means of career progression, while employers looked to employees for hard work and loyalty. These mutual expectations imply a promise, with mutual obligations.

Deal and Kennedy (2000) suggest that the turbulence of the 1990s, with widespread corporate mergers and downsizings and resultant waves of redundancies, undermined this implicit longstanding belief in the mutuality of interest between employer and employee.

Contract violation

When employees believe that the organization has failed to live up to its obligations and promises, or has abused their trust, the psychological contract can appear to be breached or even violated. A key area of perceived contract violation involves the undermining of job security. This has been deeply disturbing for many employees, especially those whose employment prospects elsewhere appear slim because of age or other reasons. For many employees work is a means of self-expression, and they value identification with their company.

Careers are another area of key concern for employees. Whilst it can be argued that the psychological contract described above has always applied only to a section of the workforce – professional and managerial workers – the 'myth' of career has long held sway. The implied promise of progression, together with higher financial rewards, has long been reflected in pay policies which offer low salaries in the early stages of career and higher levels of pay shortly before retirement. Pate *et al.* (2000) found that flattening organizational structures, which led to changes in traditional career structures, was viewed as a violation of the traditional contract and led employees to view their attachment to work in more calculative terms than before. We shall look at how 'new' careers are developing in Chapter 14.

The volatile nature of the evolving psychological contract is evident in the public comment about apparently inequitable compensation policies for senior executives. In recent times there has been an outburst of union comment on the 'fat cat' director pay arrangements that appear to survive poor business results because directors' pay is closely linked with the interests of shareholders. There appears to be a growing challenge to the idea that employees should pay the price of directors' mistakes with job loss. Pressure for change is coming from other stakeholders too. The rejection by shareholders (including employees) of the proposed pay deal for Jean-Paul Garnier, Chief Executive of Glaxo SmithKline in May 2003, which guaranteed a payout of $22 million irrespective of how the company performed after two years, suggests that shareholders too are beginning to feel that they are missing out on what should be theirs.

This reflects what Deal and Kennedy (1982) describe as an ever-widening fissure between the pay of those at the top and that of rank-and-file employees, fracturing the potential for a shared agenda or common purpose between management and the workforce. In consequence, employees put their own interests ahead of those of the organization.

For Andersson (1996), contract violation is evident in the nature of the workplace climate and business climate – for example, when harsh redundancy policies and practice are the norm, and when organizations fail to practice corporate social responsibility. Contract violation occurs when there is poor communication, a limited voice for workers, discourteous treatment, managerial incompetence and the frequent introduction of managerial fads that show little respect for employees' intellect or feelings. In a political climate, people do not trust each other. As Deal and Kennedy suggest, 'Now the premium is on keeping your mouth shut, your rear covered and your nose clean. It took years to break down the level of trust built up in strong culture companies. It will take many more years to get back to the former level'.

The nature of jobs and roles is another area of apparent contract violation. This includes the degree of role conflict, ambiguity and work overload. In addition to job losses, the redistribution of skilled work due to technological advances has also destabilized the employment relationship. Aronowitz and DiFazio (1999) argue that there is increasing proletarianization of work at every level below top management, except for in a few scientific and technical occupations. They suggest that Western societies may have reached a large historical watershed in which the link between 'work' as the Western cultural ideal and 'self' is in crisis, since both qualified and mass labour is increasingly considered redundant.

Leadership is another area where many employees appear to feel let down. In Roffey Park surveys, managers are widely reported to not be 'walking the talk' on values and the 'right' kind of leadership is in short supply. There appears to be a lack of strategic vision on the part of senior managers. Indeed, inappropriate leadership styles reported in many companies surveyed are perceived actually to be getting in the way of employees' ability to work well, and contributing to poor organizational performance.

Consequences of contract violation

Survey after survey suggests that old-style loyalty to employers appears to have waned, since people appear to have lost any expectation that their organization will safeguard their personal interests. Instead, people look after their own interests and become more affiliated to professional bodies or network groups than to employers. As one person in the *Management Agenda* survey put it, 'I turn to myself for security'. Similarly, the more transactional nature of employer–employee relationships is reflected in the comment 'loyalty lasts only until the next pay cheque', and almost half of the people who completed the survey were considering a job move in the near future. New entrants to the labour market are under no illusions about whether or not organizations are to be depended on for future security.

In addition, associated problems include loss of commitment and motivation amongst experienced staff; difficulty in attracting and retaining skilled employees, especially 'knowledge workers'; continuity problems in certain areas; loss of intellectual property; and failure to capitalize on the benefits of investments in training. Deal and Kennedy (2000) suggest that undermining the contract triggers a crisis of confidence that makes it difficult, if not impossible, to sustain people's loyalty, commitment and best efforts. They point out that it is not just the people who lose their jobs who suffer the consequences of job loss. Employees who survive the axe fear that they will be next. In place of the old promise of security, fear rules.

Perhaps one of the main negative consequences for employers of not taking psychological contract issues seriously relates to strategic flexibility. The fact that the erosion of the contract since the early 1990s has appeared one-sided has led to reduced levels of trust and increased employee cynicism. For Pate *et al.* (2000), job insecurity is a major influence on the quality of trust relations. These researchers found that with increased employee cynicism comes greater difficulty in achieving strategic change.

The 'new deal'

It is therefore increasingly in the interests of employers to develop and clarify a new relational contract (or 'deal') with employees. While the major organizational changes of recent years have challenged the idea of employees being assets, a reassessment of the value of an individual's worth to the organization is taking place and a new employment relationship is crystallizing. The 'new' workforce of better-educated employees can offer employers more. They also expect more from employers. When employees are valued as assets, empowerment and development are prerequisites of a highly skilled, flexible, coordinated, motivated, committed and productive workforce.

Deal and Kennedy (2000) argue that such a relational contract is fundamental to preserving a positive work culture. Relational contracts are often described as open-ended, characterized by a developmental and social relationship as well as financial exchange. High-trust relations are thought to be at the heart of such relational contracts (Bigley and Pearce, 1998).

One of the best-known texts about the emerging psychological contract (or 'social' contract), by Peter Herriot and Carole Pemberton (1995), describes elements of the 'New Deal' as follows:

- In place of promotion and job security, employees should focus on employability and job portability
- In place of loyalty, employers should focus on enabling high performance and developing high-commitment work practices.

They contend that the new deal is also mitigated by workloads, equal opportunities (including perceptions of fairness and bullying in the workplace), pay and performance, and working conditions. They argue that the new deal is violated from an employee perspective mainly in these areas rather than careers.

Guest and Conway (1999) argue that, from an employee standpoint, the value of the new psychological contract will be assessed according to:

- The extent to which the organization has kept its promises/commitments about job security, careers and the demands of the job and workloads
- Trust in management to keep its promises and look after employee's best interests
- Fairness of treatment in general, and specifically with regard to reward allocation.

Positive contracts embracing fairness and trust between employers and employees result in high levels of commitment and job satisfaction. Guest suggests that what predicts or explains variations in the psychological contract most strongly are HR practices such as appraisals, interesting and challenging work, care when selecting, opportunities for development, guarantees of no compulsory redundancies etc. Direct participation in decision-making with regard to such issues is also a strong factor.

Organizational benefits of good HR practices

Guest (2000, in Scarborough, 2003) suggests that HR practices have a significant effect on the growth of human capital and the working of the 'new deal'. He identifies HR practices influencing performance through:

- Their impact on employee behaviour
- Increasing employee skills and abilities
- Promoting positive attitudes that result in a committed workforce
- Providing expanded responsibilities that make full use of employees' skills and abilities.

Good people management practices are required if trust is to be built and cooperative employee relations maintained. Various studies on the evolving psychological contract suggest that trust is most likely to return when there are certain safeguards in place. For some people this will mean job security, for others it will mean clarity of career path, while for others it will mean being made more employable. Guest's research, and Roffey Park *Management Agenda* findings, suggest that employees working for large organizations are likely to experience a poorer psychological contract than those working in small and medium-size organizations.

Higher productivity is not the only benefit to organizations. A study by Watson Wyatt in 1999 found that good people practices overall increase a company's value. It found that high scores in 30 key areas of human capital management related to about a 30 per cent gain in terms of market value or return to shareholders (Scarborough, 2003). If employees feel more committed and motivated to give of their best, the organization is likely to see reduced staff turnover and absenteeism, a higher rate of innovation, successful introduction of new forms of work organization, and a better ability to react rapidly to threats and opportunities, leading to improved competitiveness.

The link between people practices and business results is evident in the market research company AC Nielson. Following the company's separation from Dun and Bradstreet in 1996, it was suffering from low morale and millions of dollars in losses. AC Nielson adopted a service-profit chain model in 1996, which included using a business effectiveness survey made up of 50 questions on 12 core competencies, such as leadership, performance management and career development. The survey findings helped scope a strategy. Changes were made to managers' compensation, linking bonus pay to the performance of their business units as an incentive to commit to the business model. Since the model's introduction, the company has quadrupled its operating income, reduced staff turnover by 34 per cent and increased employee satisfaction by 33 per cent.

However, the current deal in many organizations appears to be a long way from what employees want. Many people, for instance, would like to see improvements in the availability of flexible working, career development and balance. Given that it is in the organization's interest to do so, managing talent effectively involves having a twin focus on recruitment and retention, and achieving a happy balance of both individual and organizational needs.

Recruitment

Around 30 million people change jobs in Europe each year. In the UK, recruitment is likely to become a key challenge, with many employers suffering the consequences of a tight labour market and skill shortages. Recruitment problems are getting worse, according to the annual recruitment and retention survey conducted by CIPD. Of organizations attempting to fill their vacancies, 93 per cent are experiencing recruitment difficulties, as against 77 per cent in 2002. Most organizations expect their difficulties to continue (IRS, 2003), and the wider trends regarding unemployment and skill levels confirm their expectations.

Generation Y

The struggle to attract the best and brightest school leavers and graduates is fierce once again. Given the competition for the best recruits, organizations are having to adapt their styles of recruitment and employment packages to the needs of recruits, rather than placing organizational needs at the forefront of the process. The recruits most highly sought after are those of the so-called Generation Y (people in their early to late twenties). This generation is stereotypically described as being very different from Generation X (late twenties to mid-thirties) in a number of ways. Whereas Generation X was often characterized as having strong value-sets and wanting to find more meaning in life than through work, Generation Y is characterized by 'warp-speed processing of information and the need to speed through their careers' (Philipson, 2002). Generation Y-ers started seeking their first jobs at the end of the 1990s.

This media-savvy generation appears more highly motivated and conventionally ambitious in the workplace than its forebears. They have more economic power than their parents, and demand open, two-way communication from their employers. Ilene Philipson, who has studied Generation Y in their workplaces in the US, believes that their apparent strong identification with the workplace poses some risks. She says a new condition, called 'chronic workplace anger' now affects one in four young people at work. In the UK, a related phenomenon, 'competitive stress syndrome', has also been identified, which causes young people to compare their heroically gained, stress-related complaints and seek ever more expensive, high-status palliatives for them. These driven young people are hungry to succeed at whatever cost, and want to gain the material badges of success.

Aspirations

The aspirations of young people entering the workforce reflect broader social changes and new developments in information technology and exchange. 'Generation Y' employees tend to have a strong sense that their employer is not to be trusted to provide for their long-term future employment. Theorists are predicting that, increasingly, progressive, entrepreneurial and talented people will be unwilling to commit their working lives in a typical pattern to one employer. Rather than security lying with the organization, security comes from within. Rather than a career being largely within one organization, careers will be developed in many organizations. People will prefer to work as independent entrepreneurs, and employees will increasingly work from home. People in knowledge-based functions will act as consultants. Attracting, motivating and retaining key employees will become major challenges.

Demos and other research suggests that young people are attracted to join 'winner' organizations in which they can look good in the eyes of their peers. These are organizations that are future-oriented and developing and using new technologies. They are places of work where people apply their minds to adding value, such as consultancies, and where employees are involved in exciting projects. 'Loser' organizations are those where people's intelligence and individual contribution are perceived to be of only limited value, such as primary manufacturing. Given that many young people defer their entry into the job market, graduate recruitment may need to be seen as an ongoing activity rather than one linked purely with the 'milk round'. This may mean that graduate development schemes may need to be designed along flexible lines to accommodate people with different levels of experience.

Recruitment methods

Recruitment methods are evolving fast. Gone are the days when potential candidates just searched newspapers for employment opportunities. An estimated 5.4 million people in the UK use the Internet to look for work, and recruitment has been one of the largest growth areas online. As a sector, it has created hundreds of new businesses offering online recruitment services and career portals. Advocates of online recruitment typically speak of four key benefits:

1. Speed – the complete campaign happens faster
2. Cost
3. Effectiveness – eliminates elements of human error inherent in manual processing
4. Exposure – the Internet's ability to reach audiences who might not otherwise be captured via traditional recruitment methods.

To address the recruitment challenge, Sinclair (2003) suggests the following strategies:

1. *Increase the pool of potential applicants.*
   - Use a variety of advertising media; look beyond traditional recruitment pools; offer apprenticeships or work placements; look within the organization by offering development opportunities such as secondments or offering more opportunities to temporary workers.
   - Use the Internet to reach 'passive job seekers' (i.e. those not actively seeking work who have an interest in the company's activities). According to the CIPD survey (2003), the use of corporate websites for attracting applicants has increased, while the use of commercial job board websites has decreased in recent years.
   - Use different methods concurrently to maximize their effectiveness.
2. *Understand the labour market.*
   - Targeting recruitment efforts strategically avoids wasting time and money hunting down elusive talent. Organizations will need to re-examine job criteria (e.g. qualifications, hours to be worked) that exclude large sections of the available labour force.
3. *Be accessible.*
   - Organizations need to make themselves accessible to potential applicants, using all available technology (answering machines, corporate websites, e-mail etc.), while taking care not to exclude potential candidates who do not have ready access to technology.
   - Offer candidates extra ways of applying, providing recruitment documents in different formats (e.g. large print, disc etc.) and be more flexible in offering dates, times and locations of interviews; these can all help in encouraging applications.
4. *Make the job more attractive.*
   - Numerous studies suggest that there are many different factors that make jobs appealing to different individuals and groups. There does appear to be consensus that pay and opportunities for advancement are key attractors (Williamson *et al.*, 2002). A third of organizations in the CIPD survey have improved starting salaries or benefits packages for recruits as well as improving the promotion of flexible hours of work and work–life balance opportunities.
   - Offer good and appropriate training opportunities; this can both appeal to potential candidates and tackle skills shortages and retention issues, once the candidate is in the organization.
   - Work–life balance is increasingly important as more employees are no longer prepared to put work ahead of everything else that is important in their lives (McCartney and Holbeche, 2003).
   - Employees want the chance to do something worthwhile, and 75 per cent of UK professionals take social or ethical considerations into account when changing employer (Article 13, 2003).
   - At the same time employers must avoid overselling, as this can result in later problems if recruits feel they were misguided at recruitment. Simpson

(2003) reports that one in four new employees in the UK quits within a month of starting a new job. A simple and honest message about what it is like to work there is most effective for recruiting and retaining employees.

5. *Sell the brand.*
   - As well as selling the job, the organization also needs to sell the brand to potential applicants. This can only work if the organization is seen as an attractive place to work by its current employees. External benchmarking to evaluate management systems, reward practices and working conditions against the competition can help organizations to know what they offer compared to competitors.

6. *Effective selection procedures.*
   - The effectiveness of interviews is very dependent on the skills of the interviewer, who needs professional recruitment and selection techniques and high-level skills in interviewing, questioning and listening. According to Simpson (2003), two out of three interviewers have no training in interviewing techniques, even though some form of face-to-face interview is used by most organizations. Some training is key to ensure that interviewers use appropriate practices, guard against biases and adhere to legal issues, including Equal Opportunities. Interview panels should be balanced in terms of gender and ethnicity to guard against the 'cloning' that can inhibit creativity or productivity.
   - Structured interviews (i.e. with pre-prepared questions and benchmark answers or scales to rate responses) offer superior results over unstructured interviews (IRS, 2003). Interviews should be interactive, two-way processes. Behavioural assessment centres and interviews with psychologists are increasingly used.
   - Sound procedures should be applied, such as clear job descriptions and person specifications based on job analysis techniques, the use of objective and transparent selection criteria, and the use of application forms rather than CVs alone.
   - Using tests and employing more than one selection method should minimize the risk of unsuitable candidates being selected, and make the process fairer. Psychometrics and practical tests are increasingly focused on identifying emotional intelligence and creativity.
   - Group activities, work sampling or 'trial days' can be useful to assess the 'fit' of candidates. The Psychological Testing Centre has been established by the British Psychological Centre to give information to candidates and employers about using tests (www.psychtesting.org.uk).

7. *Speed.*
   - IRS (2003) found that one in four organizations believe it is losing good candidates because of the length of time recruitment takes. Speed up the recruitment process by using the Internet to accelerate the receipt of applications and delivery of responses, offer online applications incorporating 'self selection' tests which can help screen out unsuitable applicants, and devolve responsibility for recruitment to line managers. Ford Europe has revolutionized its recruitment process by using online

application processes, and has cut the application/interview/job offer process from six months to as many weeks.

Recruiting from within

As well as widening the external net, many companies are hoping to develop an appealing employer brand for existing employees and grow the talent they need. Tesco is one such company. It has a policy of grooming shop floor workers who show management potential – several of its main board members have worked their way up the company. Every manager is trained to be a talent spotter, and staff can put themselves forward without waiting for someone else to spot their potential.

On the other hand, few organizations appear really to know what their internal talent pool consists of. Data must be gathered from various sources if best use is to be made of existing talent. Typical processes that can aid recruitment from within include:

- Clarifying role assessment measures
- Performance management information
- Assessment centres
- Succession planning
- Internal job vacancies – open posting
- Talent review panels.

Some firms set up executive resource boards to ensure that talent belongs to the organization, not the line manager. These should involve the CEO or board members. Their role is to oversee the development of high-potential people and remove barriers to their progress. Comet, for example, has a management organizational development review process, which is a formal opportunity to review talent coming up through the ranks. Another company uses Talent Bank Boards, with senior managers from different parts of the business looking on a quarterly basis at action plans for high flyers and retention plans for key employees.

Conventional succession planning, with named successors for every key role, is still with us, but increasingly organizations are aiming to develop a cadre of people who can take on senior roles, rather than just a few high flyers. In most succession planning processes, potential successors are identified as 'planned' for a specific role, or 'emergency' replacement, or 'potential' successor. In selecting successors, managers should question the assumptions they are making about the role and why specific individuals have been identified as successors, to ensure that good talent elsewhere in the organization is not being overlooked. While fast-track schemes appear to satisfy the desire for conventional career development for a few, any organization that 'puts all its eggs in one basket' is potentially leaving itself exposed in the longer term. Employee loyalty can no longer be taken for granted, and Roffey Park research suggests that promotion does not guarantee a desire to remain with an employer.

The future of fast tracking?

Of course every organization has a responsibility to attempt to secure its future, and many now recognize that developing people who will supply present and future success is key. The degree to which fast-tracking should be seen as the main means of achieving this remains open to question. After all, conventional succession planning generally works best when an organization's environment, market conditions and structures are relatively stable and predictable.

Understandably, in times of change the basic parameters of planning, such as knowing where the organization is going, the skills needed for the future and the resources the organization currently has, are difficult to establish. Planning around roles seems short-sighted in such circumstances. Perhaps a more useful model is based on identifying the skills and experiences that the broad business direction suggests will be required in the future, and planning around developing people.

An important question to answer when taking stock of current employees is, who is key now and in the short- to medium-term future? The answer to that question may be different now from what it might have been several years ago. Similarly, organizations need to think through what they mean by potential, and how to assess it. Some organizations insist that potential can only exist out-side, and hence rely heavily on external recruitment to source key management positions. Often the tendency to rely on external recruitment is due to a com-bination of factors, including a widespread ignorance of the current skills of the existing workforce. However, such policies seem to have a largely negative effect on the morale of existing employees.

A more useful approach might be to widen access to such schemes to include internal people who might have missed the fast track first time round, if they appear to have the skills and attitudes which the organization needs as it moves forward. W.S. Atkins uses assessment centres to identify talent and create devel-opment plans. Individuals can apply to go to such a centre, and since the scheme was introduced the turnover of people who have been through the process has dropped to 3 per cent against an average of 20 per cent for those who have not.

This is not a purely philanthropic approach. Taking into account both the cost of external recruitment, especially if the new recruit does not 'fit' and soon leaves, and the value of the often irreplaceable knowledge of existing employ-ees which only becomes apparent when they become disillusioned and leave, it appears that fast-tracking should be a continuous, wide-based process rather than a scheme.

Retention

While a certain level of turnover is desirable to ensure a flow of fresh ideas and approaches, employers need to ensure that they do not invest so much time and energy looking for new talent that they neglect their current workforce. Keeping the right people is vital to an organization's competitive advantage. Skills, knowledge and know-how are not easily or quickly replaced. Organizations therefore need to take a proactive and strategic approach to developing and retaining existing talent.

According to a CIPD survey (2003), alongside difficulties with recruitment, retention problems in the UK have also increased dramatically, with 72 per cent of respondent organizations reporting difficulties in this area compared with 50 per cent the previous year. Over a quarter of these organizations lose people particularly both at under six months' service and at about two years' service. Often this is due to a lack of induction or mentoring to help the person 'bed into' the organization. Usually, though, people leave quickly because the company in reality does not match its brand image as an employer. In many cases, managers are unaware how much talent their organization loses in a year; nor do they know why people leave, because there is rarely an established process through which this information can be gathered.

Reasons for leaving

The key question is, does an organization really know why people leave? Even when exit interviews are used at the time people leave, the practice is often inconsistently applied and the reasons given often suggest that people are leaving for more pay. However, this is often a socially acceptable proxy for the real reasons, and may give misleading signals about why the organization (or parts of it) are losing key staff.

A growing practice is to outsource exit interviewing to a third-party supplier, with whom the former employee can feel completely open. This type of service tends to work best when the interviews take place some three to six months after the person has left. In the case of 'star' employees, such a process can also help to get the person back into the organization. One personnel director in the construction industry makes a practice of ringing former employees after a few weeks to offer them their job back. In many cases, former employees are delighted to have the approach, especially when they have become aware that the grass in the new organization is not in fact greener than in the job they left.

Some of the commonest reasons for staff turnover relate to aggressive workplace cultures and lack of challenge, accomplishment and recognition. However, the main reasons usually relate to management styles, and it would seem that there is some truth in the old dictum that people leave their managers, not the organization. Another common reason for leaving is having few opportunities for development and progression. (We shall look at development in Chapter 15.) Increasingly, too, as more and more employees feel sufficiently confident of their employment prospects that they no longer feel obliged to comply with the organization's demands for long hours and overseas assignments, the main reason for leaving is lack of flexibility. This can be exacerbated if the employer brand implies that employees are valued and can exercise choice.

Retention factors

If employees are feeling less dependent on organizations and have developed their employability, what do organizations have to get right in order to encourage employees to commit? The best retention strategies are tailor-made to fit each organization's unique circumstances, with talent management initiatives closely aligned to the organization and its changing goals.

Some of the commonest reasons why people stay fall into a number of categories. First, they are cultural: typically, people tend to stay in organizations where there are high levels of trust, open and honest communication, where they are enjoying their work, there is cooperation with colleagues, and where people are encouraged to challenge the way things are done. Then there is the nature of the job: challenging roles, supportive management and autonomy to go ahead and deliver results are all important factors. Next there is the nature of the employment 'promise', such as whether or not people feel that they receive appropriate reward and recognition, that they have challenging roles through which they are growing, and that they can work flexibly. These and other factors influence employees' decisions to stay with or leave their organizations.

Roffey Park's research suggests that people are more likely to stay with their organization if there is genuine support for home-working, career progression for those who achieve work–life balance, and a range of career tracks at all levels. In one company, for instance, employees working in call centres are offered the ultimate flexibility – they can work any time and for as long as employment law allows them to. Since introducing this flexibility, the company has halved staff turnover, which has had a positive bottom-line impact.

HR practices

Purcell *et al.* (1987) found that multinational organizations tend to perform better than their domestic counterparts in their ability to attract and retain high-potential employees. They found that some of the key differences lie not so much in the policies and practices they use but rather in how they implement those practices. The link between business requirements and employee needs in such companies appears strong.

For instance, referring to Purcell *et al.*'s study, Hiltrop (2002) points out that companies that are pursuing a strategy of high product innovation are likely to have career guidance programmes, specialized career paths, and some type of personality assessment of job candidates. This intense focus on getting the right deal for the right employees is a strategic priority in such companies. In contrast, according to their study the companies that were competing on the basis of cost were more likely to use formal planning to determine future staff requirements, and to recruit using *ad hoc* rather than formal procedures. Service companies were more likely than manufacturing firms to share information among employees, link pay to performance and delegate authority to the lowest possible level. In contrast, manufacturing firms were more likely to offer job security, flexible working arrangements, and financial support to employees who wished to take external training courses.

A wider range of HRM practices was used when top managers saw their workforce primarily as 'a source of talent that must be developed' rather than 'a cost factor that must be reduced'. Managers who saw employees as a source of talent were also more likely to delegate responsibility to the lowest possible level, offer flexible working arrangements, openly share information about goals and results of the company, and use quality circles to seek out the ideas of co-workers. None of these practices occurred when employees were viewed primarily as a cost factor.

Hiltrop lists a number of factors that represent the types of policies and practices employed by international companies to attract and retain a group of qualified and motivated people. They include:

1. The extent to which the company is able to offer employment security
2. Opportunities for training and skill development
3. Internal recruitment and promotion from within
4. Career development and guidance
5. Opportunities for teamwork and participation
6. Equal benefits and access to perquisites for all employees
7. Extra rewards and recognition for superior performance
8. Openness of information about corporate goals, outcomes and intentions
9. Proactive HR planning and strategic HRM.

Hiltrop points out that there is no one combination of practices that represents the ideal in all circumstances, but that the best combination is specific to the situation. For example, large food corporations in the study (such as Nestlé) scored above the sample mean for recognizing employees' contributions, openly sharing information, helping employees to develop their personal growth and capabilities, and offering employment security. 'Knowledge-intensive' organizations (such as consulting firms) score below the mean on employment security but above the mean for recognizing and rewarding high performance.

Job security

To commit to an organization and give of their best, people need assurances of security. In order for a company to rebuild a constructive culture, it must remove the fear of arbitrary job loss. The DTI's consultation paper on High Performance Workplaces recognizes this as an issue, and talks about the best organizations 'reaching agreement concerning employment security in exchange for flexibility on the part of individuals as to how they will be deployed'.

Organizational commitment means that the organization shows that it genuinely wants the relationship to last – that people are not going to be the first casualty of any business downturn. Hurley *et al.* (1997) suggest that human resources practices should be changed to reward tenure. That way, individuals with potential to reach the top can develop the core skills, flexibility and breadth of experience relevant to the organization.

If further cost-cutting is foreseen, companies should design and publish fair criteria for deciding which jobs or people are to go or be retained. Rover, for example, has an explicit psychological contract of no compulsory redundancies in return for personal mobility and the willingness to learn new skills and apply them where needed. At the car group, some former headquarters middle managers work in or with the 'extended enterprise' – dealers or suppliers. A few work in the community. While Rover does not claim to give unconditional employment guarantees, this learning contract is at the heart of developing success.

Pension arrangements

Similarly, the widespread changes looming in the pensions industry are adding to employee insecurity and feelings of betrayal. The Pickering Report on the condition of pensions contends that employers require more flexibility and that the pensions industry requires simplification. If the Pickering recommendations are adopted, employers will be able to compel staff to enter their pension plan as a condition of employment, and index-linked pensions will be abolished. While generous final salary schemes have made matters easier for people who have worked for the same employer for 30 or 40 years, people who have a more flexible career will need to set aside large percentages of their income from the moment they enter the labour market. Under money purchase schemes, the investment risk is transferred to the employee. Already, many employers (such as BT and ICI) have closed final salary pension schemes to new entrants.

Pensions are likely to become a key differentiator in the labour market, with those employers still offering final salary schemes being seen as better employment options.

Workplace culture and retention

A compelling picture of the future

Employees want to believe in, and have confidence in their company's future, so organizations should market their image and direction to customers and other stakeholders. Increasingly, employees want to feel that they work for an ethical organization (see Chapter 14). Staff turnover at Prêt a Manger, the food retailer, fell by 30 per cent in a year following the development of a culture of innovation. Managers focused on making the company culture friendly, open and cooperative for its 2300 staff. Each recruit attends a culture workshop within a month of joining the company. Each potential new member of staff spends a day at one of the chain's outlets before their final interview. The decline in staff turnover has also been helped by the company paying better than the competition.

Listening to employee needs

At Microsoft, the culture is geared to listening to employee needs, with a knock-on positive effect on employee commitment. People policies are so strong that if an employee attempts to leave, it's their families that force them to rethink. This is because Microsoft's policies reflect an understanding of the needs of employees' families. They include childcare provision and annual children's parties. There is free private healthcare (including 'life partners' and family) and a four-month (unpaid) sabbatical after four years. Microsoft also uses its commercial strength to benefit the wider community. The company gave away just under 10 per cent of its UK pre-tax profits in 2002.

Asda, too, takes family needs into account. It has developed flexible working schemes that allow people with families to play a valid role in the workplace. One initiative, called 'shift swap', allows employees to change shifts around at short notice if, for instance, a child falls ill.

Motivating climate

Richer Sounds continues to embody the entrepreneurial approach of its founder, Julian Richer. His views on staff motivation and running a successful business are described in his book *The Richer Way* (Richer, 1995). Promotion from within is the norm, and the majority of head office staff have worked on the shop floor. Staff rate Richer Sounds highly for its support of good causes, which staff consider to be sincerely meant rather than just for publicity. They also believe that they are fairly paid relative to others in the company. Communication at the firm is excellent, with all staff given ample opportunity to give feedback at seminars, suggestion meetings and branch dinners. Salaries are high for the retail industry, and the perks are impressive. The company offers employees the loan of holiday homes in locations such as St Tropez and Venice, trips in the company jet, and free massages. There is even a 'take your pet to work' scheme.

Sense of community

At Flight Centre, a global travel business, the sense of community is strong. The company is divided into 'tribes', 'villages' and 'families'– the teams of workers on the shop floor – and the focus is on developing and rewarding individuals. Store managers, known as 'team leaders', take 10 per cent of profits and can buy 20 per cent of their business.

Using activities external to the workplace to utilize talent

Shell allows young executives up to three months to work for a charitable organization. Both parties appear to benefit, with Shell's employee development needs and social motives being matched by charities' having access to business talent.

Showing people they are valued

Fun

Many companies provide generous social budgets, which help build team spirit. Fun and creativity seem inextricably linked. At the computer games company Electronic Arts, the UK headquarters building, designed by Sir Norman Foster, has meeting rooms with names like 'the Black Hole'. There is also a bar (with free drinks on Friday from 5 pm to 6 pm), a gym and a recording studio. Prêt a

Manger spends £250 000 on staff parties twice a year, with subsidized Friday night drinks at trendy bars. At SAS UK, a subsidiary of SAS Institute, staff who do not want to be disturbed can wear a silly hat. There is a basketball net in the Glasgow office that they can take a shot at as a reward for good work.

Using reward schemes imaginatively

Prêt a Manger runs a career development scheme, and offers up to £1000 for business ideas from employees. In addition, £250 is presented to individuals who are promoted, which they must distribute to those staff who have helped them. In addition to its long service awards, the company has a number of customer service incentive schemes tailored to motivating its younger staff (38 per cent of Prêt employees are under 25). The Mystery Shopper System enables employees to share a team bonus every week. Weekly mystery shopper visits can potentially earn each team member an extra 75p for every hour they work that week, and outstanding performance can gain them an additional £50 cash bonus (Damon, 2002).

Benefits bonus

Another company gives long-serving staff an extra day off after three years, where they can do anything they want at the company's expense. Some companies allow employees to trade in flexi-time for share options, and sell/buy-out a week's holiday. UBS Warburg piloted a concierge service which can organize anything from social events to domestic help. This is in a bid to help employees balance work and home lives and so enable the firm to recruit and retain the best talent. At Ulster Carpets, the carpet weavers, hard work is rewarded. Employees of the month are offered a free trip to South Africa to visit the company's Durban factory, with five days' of sightseeing thrown in.

Similarly, the Alliance and Leicester Group, which has grown out of the Leicester Permanent Building Society, wanted to improve productivity, retention and customer service, and improve management and reward of staff. The company launched and communicated a new corporate brand called 'living life better'. A new recruitment website was introduced, and staff were given more flexible holiday arrangements, 24-hour rest areas were introduced and the company invested £4 m in the 'Valuing Individual People' scheme. The company found that leadership improved, employee turnover dropped by 11 per cent in the first year, and more than 17 per cent of vacancies are filled via staff recommendation.

Improving the quality of management and leadership

Many surveys suggest that relationships with managers, including levels of appreciation and recognition, make the biggest difference to retention because of their impact on morale and motivation of teams. Managers who are unable to delegate, contribute to a poor work climate and set unrealistic targets can actually depress performance. Organizations must improve the skills levels of poor managers, or replace them with those who can communicate more effectively.

Relevant skills

To meet business needs and to enable employees to develop skills that increase their employability, there needs to be a strong connection between the business goals companies are trying to achieve and the sort of skills being developed in their management teams. Usually, the connection between what the business is trying to do and how it invests in management development is weak, and development is focused on individual needs. According to Philpott (2002): 'Sustained improvement in organizational performance is more likely when the education and development expectations of individuals and organizations are aligned around strategic objectives'.

Middle managers often find themselves in the least satisfying situation, with pressures from above and below them in the hierarchy. They are usually the people who have to deliver tough news to others. Sun Microsystems in the UK had to make 9 per cent of staff redundant in 2002. Managers were given workshops to help them deal with difficult changes.

Senior management assessment and development

Shell has addressed this issue through a detailed senior management assessment. Annual strategy planning divides the business into 50 units. Personnel matters are part of this, although previously the main focus was on the skills required for new businesses. The annual talent review is being integrated with business planning so that management capability is reviewed every time business improvement is discussed. Each individual is assessed to gauge the job level she or he could ultimately achieve with Shell (Eglin, 2000).

Dixons Group addresses both individual and organizational needs through its executive development programme. It uses assessment centres to pick out 20 people to join the programme each year. Any middle manger can opt into the company's management development programme, but those with high potential can be considered, with their director's support, for the executive development programme. The company is considering removing the need for a director to support a nomination, in order to widen the catchment pool (Upton, 2003).

Safeguarding employee health

West Bromwich Building Society is one of the UK's oldest building societies. It employs 750 staff and has 49 branches, making it the ninth largest building society, with assets of around £4bn. In 2003 the Society won a Personnel Today award for managing health at work. The company had been concerned about levels of sickness absence, averaging six days per employee per year. It wanted to address the issue by raising health awareness among staff and reducing absence levels at the same time.

Consequently, a health awareness programme to improve provision was introduced, along with new health benefits through local providers, reducing costs and building links with the local community. Various health benefits were introduced, such as gym membership, flu vaccinations, alternative therapists, health assessments and an employee assistance programme. The project was developed in-house for the first two years, saving on consultant costs, and software was developed for surveys to track how employees were responding. The results of these initiatives was very positive, with sickness absence down to less than four days per year per employee, along with improvements in employee satisfaction and morale.

Similarly, Standard Life Healthcare introduced a range of initiatives to improve staff engagement. They implemented an online health assessment and, in response to the results, developed health fairs, nutrition seminars and subsidized massage. The impact on the business was demonstrated by a rise in new business of 26 per cent; customer retention rose by 2.2 per cent and staff turnover fell by more than 60 per cent. At Volkswagen Group's UK operation, the Milton Keynes site has a medical suite offering therapies such as reflexology and stress counselling.

Well-being

Microsoft too takes employee health seriously. At the company's UK Reading offices, a well-being clinic offers everything from a mechanical massage chair to well-man clinics (including classes on how to detect testicular cancer). There is a 'bump' club to help pregnant mothers before their eighteen weeks' fully paid leave, there are onsite nurses and a doctor, and even a facility to donate bone marrow. Not surprisingly perhaps, the sports company Adidas offers a holistic well-being programme, which has resulted in improvements to not only employees' physical health, but also their mental attitudes to work and to the stresses of everyday life.

Developing a meaningful employer brand

Employer branding is a way of standing out in the labour market. An employer brand has to meet the needs of both the business and its employees if it is to be effective. It should have a key value. Managers need to understand the concept of employer branding if the implied promise is to become reality. To be truthful, an employer brand should reflect what the organization is trying to do as a business; if the message is geared only to the aspirations of potential recruits, the demands of the business will always create a gap between the employer brand promise and reality.

In one company, the HR Director followed the following process to achieve understanding and buy-in of managers to the idea of employer branding:

- In a first meeting with senior managers the HR Director outlined the philosophy of branding, encouraged them to think through the business benefits of taking such an approach, and gave several other organizational examples of employer branding
- The group then examined the company mission statement, exploring in particular how the company was performing with regard to the behaviours required to fulfil the mission
- They then looked at the obstacles to implementing a good (business) and (employer) brand
- They thought through how these might be overcome
- They decided how to move forward
- The employer brand was backed up with extensive training for managers at all levels, and a few key initiatives driven by employee choice as well as deriving from the mission statement.

In another company, developing a meaningful employer brand was achieved via the values route. The process was as follows:

- Work with a diagonal slice of the organization
- Confirm, in working sessions, that everyone knows what the organization is trying to achieve
- Explore what the organization values should be to help achieve this
- Work through the practicalities of living the values, e.g. developing specific recognition schemes
- Develop indicators that will let us know if we are living the values
- Make part of Directors' bonuses dependent on how well they live the values.

In another case, the top team defined the five words that the organization was meant to live by. Employees were consulted about what these words meant to them. Staff were actively engaged in the debate about the 'what' and the 'how', resulting in widespread ownership of the ideas and their translation into practice.

Conclusion

Employer branding should take into account the ways in which employee needs are changing. While individuals are motivated by different things and there are dangers in relying on stereotypes, there are clearly some trends which suggest that, for the foreseeable future, current and potential employees are likely to want to work for ethical, successful and well-managed organizations. They are going to want a degree of flexibility and choice alongside a platform of relative security. They are going to want challenging, interesting and worthwhile work and the chance to grow. In the next two chapters we shall explore what careers and work–life balance mean in today's organizations, and what the development needs of 'new employees' are likely to be.

Checklist: Becoming a great place to work

- What are your long-term resource planning requirements?
- What type of talent do you need to bring in?
- What will be the source of candidates with the right capabilities?
- What do individuals want?
- What does the market demand?
- What are your internal and external selection markets?
- How effective are your selection methods?
- How satisfied are employee with the level/type of recognition and reward they receive?
- How creatively can/do you use your reward systems?
- What systems are in place to support the well-being and development of all employees?
- What career paths are in place?
- What are the matching processes?

14

Careers and work–life balance

Introduction

As the 'baby boomer' generations near retirement, approaches to work and careers that they represented are passing with them. Given the waves of downsizings and major changes to organizational structures of recent years, few employees now expect to have a career for life in one organization. Few trust their employer to safeguard their interests. On the other hand, many employees still aspire to a career that goes 'onwards and upwards', even if this is not in one organization.

Indeed, few management issues are as cliché-bound as that of careers. According to many pundits, 'careers are dead'. 'Onwards and upwards' is supposed to have been replaced by lateral growth. Employment relationships are supposed to be more transactional and short term, and careers more mobile. Organizations need flexible structures and processes, and employees are expected to be adaptable and open to continuous learning.

The new career is 'protean' rather than corporate. Employability, rather than job security, is the watchword.

Despite the rhetoric, careers continue to be a prime focus and concern for many employees. So important are career and development issues that seven out of ten German employees, despite their involvement in the running of their enterprises, would change jobs for better prospects, more flexible hours or better pay, according to a survey carried out by Gemini Consulting. Similar findings were reported from thirteen other developed nations. Insecurity is a major factor behind the findings, with two-thirds of those polled having been directly affected by downsizing or restructuring (Whiteley, 1999).

In this chapter we will focus more specifically on careers and work–life balance as elements of what makes an organization an employer of choice for key employees.

The shifting power balance with regard to careers

Until relatively recently, much management literature has focused on the negative sides of the 'new deal' for employees, with messages about 'manage your own career' being interpreted as corporate abdication of responsibility towards employees. This has been compounded by actual practice, with many employers appearing to interpret the 'new' contract to mean that that the employer has no responsibility at all with regard to career development. Herriot (1998) also argues that not all employees have accepted the new *status quo* voluntarily, and some have been reluctantly bullied into a new psychological contract by employers who demand compliance in return for a job.

However, employers are starting to see some negative consequences of putting the full burden of responsibility for career management onto employees. As more employees start to exercise greater control over their careers, employers are faced with the potential threat of increasing turnover, especially amongst more marketable/employable staff. They are also having to face hard bargaining from potential recruits they are trying to secure. Denise Rousseau (1996) argues that this is a reflection of the fact that employment contracts have moved in recent years from a longer-term relational basis to a shorter-term transactional one. Research by Douglas Hall in the USA found that if, in a given year, the contract was not met for either party, the employee was likely to leave the organization in the following year (Hall and Moss, 1998).

Hall suggests that some employees now demand that the career transaction should be more explicit, in contrast to the old implicit contract. Interestingly, Guest and Conway (1997) propose that people working on fixed-term contracts experience a better psychological contract than permanent employees for precisely that reason. The more transactional nature of the employment relationship is apparent in such cases, and people are more likely to negotiate hard to achieve the elements of the contract that are important to them rather than to rely passively on paternalistic benevolence on the part of the organization. Guest also suggests that organizations do not like to be clear with employees about career prospects for precisely that reason, while employees want clarity.

The end of career?

Various writers have predicted the end of the career and of job security. Alvin Toffler (1981) predicted two decades ago that many employees would end up working from home in their 'electronic cottages'. Handy predicted that portfolio working would become a common career model. William Bridges (1995) argues that in the USA at least, some of these trends are already under way. These shifts are usually introduced to meet changing business needs, rather than employee preferences. Bridges suggests that technological and economic shifts are making the notion of a fixed 'job' obsolete; fixed jobs are becoming flexible roles. Even the notions of part-time and full-time work are becoming anachronisms. If Bridges is correct in suggesting that jobs as we know them will disappear, the notion of 'career' takes on a different significance in terms of its meaning to individuals, the definitions of career success and the means to have a satisfying career.

New career patterns reflect changing business demands within cyclical economic patterns. Business demands for flexibility and the consequent new career patterns may favour women, who have traditionally followed more cyclical than linear career patterns. Women are apparently better than men at networking, for instance. According to Judy Rosener (1996), the key career trends suggest that:

- Money will become less important than equality in the workplace, in particular people being judged on their own merits
- 'Shifting down' will become an acceptable choice, rather than always striving for the top job
- Integrating work–life will replace the traditional work focus
- Multiple careers, once the domain of women, will become acceptable for men
- Many people will change their careers radically
- Flexibility and moving in and out of careers will become more acceptable.

How strongly are these predictions being borne out in practice? In the UK at least, the trend towards individuals opting for portfolio careers appears under way but is less well established than in the USA. However, the increasingly flexible nature of the workplace may mean that more people move into self-employment and various forms of contractual work in years to come. There is a perceptible rise, for instance, in the numbers of successful executives in their thirties and forties opting for a variety of employment types, blending part-time, voluntary and creative occupations.

In many organizations, people work according to the demands of projects rather than to any pre-assigned schedule, and under arrangements too fluid to be called 'jobs'. Work is increasingly outsourced to former employee groups and supplier/partners who have an ongoing relationship with a company but no guarantee of business continuity. In the software industry in particular, people often work in project teams in which they are not directly accountable to management but to other members of the project team. In such a context, individual performance is very visible and 'career' prospects are dependent on the individual's ability to establish his or her credibility in every project. Traditional marks of status count for little. In such project teams a leader's authority lasts only for that project, and today's manager may be tomorrow's team member.

However, the dominant form of employment contract still appears to be full time, with research (Hay Management) suggesting that average job tenure is seven years. Even in the USA, research suggests that employees may be staying around longer than organizations think (Crenshaw, 1994). The Roffey Park survey population have been with their current employers on average eight years! Although many people continue to enjoy continuity of employment, the spectre of forced redundancy or some other destabilizing effect of change continues to haunt employees. The idea of a more fragmented and mobile approach to career development appeared to have little appeal for *Management Agenda* survey respondents, the majority of whom still appear to prefer a work situation characterized by job security rather than by ongoing uncertainty. Similarly, my research into the career aspirations of high flyers in 1998 suggested that the majority were looking for career progression (vertical) in the same firm (preferably) or industry (Holbeche, 1998).

It would seem that a key element of retention is whether or not people feel they can progress their career within an organization.

The 'new' career

Of course, careers can be looked at from both an individual and an organizational perspective, and the interests served may be different. As Peter Herriot (1998) has pointed out, there are many types of individual career. It is therefore surprising how much consensus exists about some key features of the 'new career'. One area of general agreement is on the subject of employability. For years now people have been told that organizations cannot manage careers and that people should develop their skills if they wish to remain employable. For 'employable', people have been encouraged to read 'able to get a job elsewhere'.

On the other hand, Hall and Moss (1998) describe the new deal from the employee perspective as being a shift from the organizational career to the 'protean career'. This is a process which the person, not the organization, is managing. Rather than with the organization, the new contract is with the self and one's work. Growth and job satisfaction are therefore key elements of the protean career contract. Other features are that:

- The career is a lifelong series of experiences, skills, learning, transitions, and identity changes; 'career age' counts, not chronological age
- Development is continuous learning, self-directed, relational and found in work challenges
- Development is not (necessarily) formal training, retraining or upward mobility
- The ingredients for success change from know-how to learn-how, from job security to employability, from organizational careers to protean careers, from 'work self' to 'whole self'
- The organization provides challenging assignments, developmental relationships, information and other developmental resources
- The goal is psychological success.

Kanter and other commentators suggest that careers are inherently becoming more mobile and, from an organizational perspective, less stable. The 'new', more mobile careers envisaged by Kanter are 'entrepreneurial', based on the growth of organizational and personal value. In 'boundaryless careers', individuals' careers take them across organizational boundaries. Career assets are enhanced through cumulative learning experiences in different contexts (Arthur and Rousseau, 1996). Career progress comes not from intra-company vertical promotion, but from inter-company self-development.

Career partnership

My ongoing research into the current state of careers suggests that, from the organizational perspective at least, careers have dropped off the corporate radar screen. Yet career issues remain high on employees' agendas, with 85 per cent of the 2004 *Management Agenda* sample considering them to be important. Indeed, along with frustration over various aspects of organizational culture and long hours/heavy workloads, a lack of career opportunities is the commonest reason why people want to leave their current organizations. Conversely, the opportunity for learning and growth is a common reason why people want to stay or would be attracted to new organizations. More than two-thirds (70 per cent) of respondents asserted that the environment of constant change has resulted in them thinking more short term in relation to their current position. This presents a possible risk area for organizations, which potentially could lose capable managers.

The need for workforce flexibility is being mirrored by the notion that careers will from now on become ever more mobile, and that individuals will need to be able to adapt to constantly changing environments. However, when the career partnership can be made to work, both employees and organizations benefit:

> *In those organizations where it has worked best, the new career contract does not represent a discontinuous corporate trauma. Rather it is simply an intelligent response to a turbulent and unforgiving economic climate. In this environment, 'success' comes disguised as an ongoing and difficult struggle, but one with a clear sense of values and vision, an appreciation of the crucial role of employees in achieving that vision, and a lifelong process of continuous learning.*

> *(Hall and Moss, 1998)*

The emphasis in much writing about careers in the past few years has been on what individuals can do for themselves to survive and thrive in turbulent times. The new 'post-corporate' career may involve periods of employment, self-employment, voluntary work and studying. Only those who have the capacity for continuous learning and for coping with ambiguity are likely to survive and thrive. To these self-empowered individuals, success often means working as part of a highly effective team and developing broader skills, rather than simply achieving conventional status. They are most likely to adapt to horizontal and/or more mobile careers and accept responsibility for managing their own career. They thrive on change and constantly look for new ways to improve their practices and challenge the *status quo*. Such new-style employees actively negotiate development opportunities as part of their recruitment package, and take responsibility for their own learning. They have a clear sense of what is important to them, and indeed are likely to be identified by their employers as key contributors.

However, employees are not the only parties involved in shaping the new career scene. Employers, governments, trades unions, leaders of industry and financial institutions all have a role to play. Ironically, some of the greatest brakes on changing career patterns are to be found at this level, rather than in the willingness of employees to adjust. The problem is that by the time institutions have woken up to the need for change, individuals have lost heart and reverted to expectations and practices more suited to the past.

My research, mirroring work carried out by McGovern in 1995, indicates that it is the organizational side of the partnership that is most lagging behind. Despite employees' willingness to adapt to new career models, few viable career alternatives seem to have appeared. The support that people might expect to help them embrace the realities of the new career appears thin on the ground. This therefore adds to the confusion about what the 'new' career looks like, and produces a few ironic effects:

- While employees appear to be adjusting to the notion of employability, few people seem to be actively contemplating portfolio careers. The average job tenure of Roffey Park respondents is eight years, suggesting that most people would rather develop their careers within their current organization.
- Organizations are interested in graduates and high flyers again. They are typically bringing back fast-track schemes which maintain or reintroduce conventional forms of career management. However, these may also do more harm than good, since they reinforce stereotypical expectations about rapid advancement for members of an elite group. Although people still aspire to onwards and upwards, they are frequently not prepared to make the longer-term commitment to the organization that such schemes often require. Where fast-track schemes exist, they are often subject to a high 'churn' rate.

This research suggests that people are becoming more willing to contemplate lateral career development as a viable alternative to vertical promotion. However, because lateral development seems to be as difficult to obtain as vertical promotion, and organizations still attach more symbolic and financial value to vertical promotion, people are discouraged from taking lateral development seriously.

This fairly basic mismatch between what employees are asking for and what organizations are offering is perhaps to be expected, since it is thought that employee attitudes adjust some seven years earlier on average than organizations' capacity to deliver. Yet, since many of the major drivers of the changing career will continue unabated, organizations need to develop their side of the partnership if they want to get and keep the best. This is in everybody's interest, because most employees still want to grow their career in the same organization. If those people have both the skills and knowledge the organization needs, maintaining an active career partnership makes sense. Some employees may be willing to shift away from aspirations for 'onwards and upwards' if the organization can supply the right degree of support for a different kind of career.

Employability – a double-edged sword

One of the most striking findings in *Management Agenda* surveys is the extent of confidence people express about their employability. A resounding 98 per cent of our respondents believe that they have now developed their employability to the extent that, should the worst happen, they believe they could get a job elsewhere, particularly in sectors where there is a buoyant job market.

For most of our respondents, 'employability' appears to mean the ability to be employed outside their current organization, rather than within it, and a quarter of respondents are currently looking to develop their careers in other organizations. This is hardly surprising since, as Charles Woodruffe (1999) points out, organizations which send messages that employees should develop their employability may come to regret it. 'Manage your own career' and 'develop your employability' may be understood by employees as a lack of commitment by the organization to the individual in the longer term. Without this commitment from the organization, many employees believe that their best interests are served by moving elsewhere.

What employability means may vary in different industries and types of role. However, if this really is the Information Age, or era of the knowledge worker, the kinds of employment opportunities and the skills required, regardless of sector, may be different from in the past. A key element of employability seems to be the market value and demand for an individual's skills. People report that becoming an expert makes them more employable, as long as that expertise is tempered by commercial acumen, effective interpersonal skills and pragmatism. Not all went as far as one person, who described himself as 'a key expert with rare skills – I can command my price'.

For many Roffey Park respondents, employability seems to be about a mix of experience, track record and key skills. These include flexibility, people-management skills, creativity, change-management skills, teamworking skills and openness to continuous learning. Most have built their employability through training, networking and challenging work assignments, and a few have been helped by a mentor. Many people pointed out the transferable nature of their asset, and while such mobility may be good news for individuals, the cost to organizations of losing key employees may be high.

This highlights possible tensions over individual and organizational interests in career development, as Iles (1997) points out:

> *Issues of intellectual property rights, the visibility and mobility of high-potential employees, the transparency of their contribution to added value and organizational performance, the relative bargaining power of high-potential individuals and organizations, and the embeddedness of capabilities in organizational routines and processes rather than in individuals will all need to be addressed.*

Of course, organizational careers are not independent of the broader technical, social and economic shifts affecting organizations themselves. Nor are careers merely matters to be negotiated between employers and employees. There are other interested stakeholders. Ironically, tax laws and pension arrangements in the UK may undercut the very job mobility and career self-management that the new career deal is supposed to deliver.

Woodruffe suggests that the rhetoric of the new career will appeal more to people who see themselves as passing through the organization than to those who stay. He argues that they are less worried by a half-hearted message of commitment to them, and are more likely to have a transactional relationship with the current employer and to expect development opportunities. Ironically, perhaps, the best development deals of all are enjoyed by people on various forms of short-term contract who negotiate what they expect from the contract up-front. It is the people who still cling to the hope that their organization will manage their career who are likely to miss out on growth opportunities if they maintain a low profile or are not seen as a high flyer.

Thus organizations may be caught on the horns of a dilemma of their own making. They may not be able to attract truly employable people without offering a development package, yet retaining such people may be difficult since they will owe little allegiance to the employer – especially if the transaction (i.e. opportunities to build skills and experience) breaks down. Applying the 'manage your own career' message to talented individuals whom the organization wants to retain may be unwise, especially if they are open to staying and building a relationship. Training and development geared to building internal employability may be the best option.

The organizational side of the new deal

In a high performing organization, with its focus on nurturing human capital, maintaining a productive psychological contract becomes a key investment in an organization's continuing success. Herriot and Pemberton (1995) suggest that, while responsibility for career development now lies primarily with individuals, the new psychological contract still represents a form of partnership of mutual interests, with different requirements of both 'partners'.

It is therefore increasingly in the interests of employers to clarify their role in the career partnership. The organization should support employees in developing their employability, while employees should commit to ongoing learning and development, along with increased flexibility and versatility.

Key players

Who is meant to supply the organization's side of the bargain? Various 'players' have different contributions to make. Clearly top management has a role to play in supporting development by granting resources, taking an active interest and creating a strategic framework within which development can take place. Senior managers in particular need to take an active lead in developing new career processes. They should look for talented people of whatever age wherever they are based in their organization. They should have a vested interest in doing this; after all, these people may be their future successors. Keeping people moving around the organization should create both vertical and horizontal openings. Horizontal moves will keep employees learning and interested even when there are no openings for them at higher levels.

Line managers

However, the key players in this partnership are likely to be line managers at all levels and others who are responsible for helping employees to develop. For the past decade in organizations of all types, including the British Civil Service, line managers have been encouraged to embrace the role of coach and developer. Being in the front line of gaining employee commitment, they are meant to empower, delegate to and involve employees. Managers are the gate-keepers of organizational policies. The reality of work–life balance policies, for instance, reflects line managers' attitudes with respect to flexible working.

In addition, line managers' roles are becoming more complex. Typically, however, line managers continue to have responsibility for doing the 'day job' in addition to their responsibilities to their teams. Often spans of control have expanded, and the creation of sophisticated appraisal and development planning processes has in some cases only added to the pressure line managers are under.

Human resources management

Other key suppliers of the organizational piece of the partnership are HR professionals, since many aspects of the new psychological contract are likely to form part of HRM policy. HR generally provides the strategies for development and designs the structures within which people work. Managing career management interventions may mean doing a few things well, rather than dispersing effort in a myriad of initiatives. A key challenge will be to create exciting and innovative career tracks that keep knowledge workers motivated. Line managers need to be trained up to play their part in the career partnership. This is largely about coaching and being prepared to engage with employees' career concerns. There needs to be a focus on helping people to achieve their self-determined career aspirations, not simply the organization's interests. Line managers may need incentives and practical support – such as smaller spans of control – to enable them to help people with their development as well as performance.

It might be argued that the objectives behind much HRM policy and activity are geared to safeguarding the organization's interests, which might not be the same as those of individual employees. Enabling career mobility, for instance could create problems of labour turnover and loss of talent. However, for employees, mobility may be a key means of ensuring career 'success'. Boxall (1992) points out that HR practices such as reward systems, communication systems and training programmes are often designed to retain employees and limit flexibility. Similarly, many career development programmes and hierarchical career paths are designed to build company-relevant expertise and encourage loyalty and career dependency of the employee on the organization. This kind of thinking sees employees as resources of the organization.

According to Parker and Inkson (1999), much of the 'new deal' thinking reverses this argument, seeing organizations as resources for individuals. Employability depends more on flexibility and versatility, and less on experience gained in a single organization. More mobile employees are less likely to be attracted to organizations that encourage career dependency. Parker and Inkson suggest that creating a stable organizational 'core' in such a fluid situation is difficult.

What does the organizational side of the new career deal look like?

While employees in our survey generally acknowledge that they are responsible for their own career development, to what degree are organizations playing their part in the career partnership? For Hall and Moss (1998) the organizational side of the deal is about brokering opportunities for enhanced employability, if not providing development directly.

Roffey Park research suggests that the organizational side of the partnership is lagging behind employee willingness to change tack. According to Hall and Moss this is only to be expected, since it appears to take approximately seven years for an organization and its members to reach an understanding of the new relationship. In the Roffey Park *Management Agenda* we found a number of ways in which organizations seem to be violating the emerging psychological contract:

- There is a big contrast between people aspiring to work flexibly, and actual numbers engaged in it or managing flexible workers (83 per cent : 33 per cent). There are limited options regarding types of flexible working, especially for professional staff; managers do not know how to manage staff who work flexibly or remotely
- Work–life balance is still growing in importance, especially among young high flyers – it is seen as an increasingly desirable element in career choice, but not easy to achieve without having to sacrifice career progress.

Some of the biggest frustrations were expressed by respondents in specialist roles. This is rather ironic, since these are likely to represent the much heralded 'knowledge workers' whom organizations are said to be keen to attract and retain. On the whole, scope for conventional career development through technical or professional roles appears limited. If people stay in specialist roles they are often squeezed out of promotion opportunities by generalists because the only promotion route available is through management. In many organizations career paths are currently confused, making serious career choices difficult. One person suggested that what was required in his organization was 'clarity about what is required in managers – specialists or generalists'.

On the whole, our respondents were slightly less optimistic about career opportunities within their current organization (60 per cent) than about those within the sector as a whole (67 per cent). The main reasons given for this were lack of opportunities for lateral growth, lack of clear career paths, 'dead men's shoes', unimaginative career practices and lack of management support.

One of the ironies in our findings is that though people seem to be adjusting to the idea that career development means sideways as well as up, with 59 per cent believing that their career will follow a lateral path, opportunities for lateral development are noticeably rare. So keen are people to take on lateral moves that 81 per cent stated that they would accept such as move even without a salary increase. This suggests that people are not only willing to take some risks, but also want to break out of potential career bottlenecks. However, because lateral development seems to be as difficult to obtain as vertical promotion, and organizations still attach more symbolic and financial value to vertical promotion, people are discouraged from taking lateral development seriously. Clearly, although it would be in many organizations' interests to support such internal career mobility, not enough is being done in practical terms to make this possible.

These findings suggest that employee willingness to embrace the new career deal is moving ahead of organizations' ability or desire to keep their side of the bargain. Employees are focusing on building up relevant competencies which will equip them to succeed in today's increasingly boundaryless world. If employees are as confident of their employability as they suggest through our survey, they are unlikely to want to remain in organizations that do not provide what they regard as meaningful opportunities for career development.

Career initiatives

However, change does appear to be under way. Organizations that recognize the value of these specialist knowledge workers are now attempting to retain and motivate them by offering a range of ways in which people can develop their careers. Nationwide, for instance, the UK's ninth largest bank, saving and lending organization, and the world's biggest building society, was keen to help the company's workforce take advantage of career opportunities while increasing staff commitment and improving customer service. Managers set up a project team to develop better career guidance and provided career advice through an intranet site. They enabled staff to select a database of job types and register interest in vacancies, and provided exercises to help career planning. As a result, all staff have access to career advice, and the intranet tools help staff to achieve stretch goals.

Similarly, Getronics, an information and communication technology company with 1500 UK staff, has overhauled its career development framework, and built business objectives into career progression. The initiative involved profiling all roles and responsibilities and defining career paths and promotion criteria. Spirit Group, the pub company, prepared for flotation by developing a transparent career path for staff, available in all 1000 outlets. Retention of retail managers has improved by 9 per cent in one year and internal manager appointments have risen by 11 per cent. Asda, which is part of the Wal-Mart group, offers career breaks after three years' service. Job-sharing is open to all, including managers.

Example 14.1   Scientific knowledge workers
In a public sector employer of scientific knowledge workers, an innovative approach to career development was created to satisfy the needs of highly qualified employees who tended to leave the organization because of poor career options. The nature of the work is highly skilled. Employees have until recently had two broad career options open to them; either to follow

a project management route to more general management, or to progress up a technical ladder. People have had to choose early on, and since the management route appears to offer more promotion possibilities, many younger employees have moved away from scientific roles, with some regret. Given restraints on public sector pay, they are then more likely to be attracted to private sector work, which pays better, once they have acquired more experience and are at their most valuable to their current employer.

In response to these challenges, a team working within the organization has in recent years produced various helping mechanisms to enable people to develop their careers more actively, such as clear technical and managerial competencies and open job posting. The team developed a framework for defining the kinds of roles people can engage in to match the levels of their own development. This was intended to offer people a clear insight into a wider range of choices and the kinds of development needed to support those choices. Now there is a real opportunity for people to develop their scientific career with a commercial mindset, or to take a general management route or a hybrid combination of the two.

It is in the interests of both employers and employees to make the new deal work. In today's confusing career scene, the way ahead may not always be clear. Given half a chance, many people in Roffey Park surveys would prefer to pursue their career in the same organization, and few contemplate a portfolio career. The individual side of the career partnership has to include an intelligent assessment of respective needs, goals and opportunities, and a willingness continuously to learn.

Sadly, the organizational side of the career partnership only seems to get addressed when some crisis point has been reached. If organizations are to keep pace with employee expectations, they cannot afford to wait until the way ahead looks clear. As Iles (1997) points out:

> *Firms may enjoy 'human capital advantage' through recruiting, retaining and developing talent through training and career development; they may also enjoy 'human process advantage' through encouraging learning, co-operation and innovation. Innovative high potential career management strategies may, if durable and hard to imitate, contribute to sustained competitive advantage by retraining and developing high potential staff who do not leave or de-rail, and who do not under-perform because of the firm's reneging on their side of the new employment contract or because of a lack of trust or commitment.*

Career systems

Career systems are where these potentially conflicting interests can be reconciled or driven further apart. Career systems are both the formal and deliberate career management practices within organizations, and the informal methods – the way in which career development happens in practice. Many organizations have abandoned conscious attempts to manage careers in recent years. However, it is argued that some kind of career system, detectable by the patterns of recruitment and advancement, will be in operation. Some kinds of career system will be easier to adjust to the 'new deal' than others. Gunz *et al.* (1998) define three recognizable types of career system; command-centred, constructional and evolutionary. The first two systems assume that the organization grows according to a particular pattern.

Command-centred career logic, typical of retail chains and banks, consists of moving between a series of similar managerial jobs that differ in the size of their responsibilities and status. Usually the most prestigious city unit is referred to as the 'flagship', and is the highest point in the career ladder to which managers can aspire. As managers move from position to position, they are generally doing the same kind of job within the same broad function. Development involves becoming aware of the subtle differences in roles, and learning to perform the job on a larger and more prestigious scale with each move. In this kind of system, managers are often being prepared for a particular kind of job.

Constructional career logic is used in organizations where career development is dependent on the accumulation of different kinds of experience. People acquire this experience by working in as many parts of the organization as possible, often demonstrating innovative job moves. Typical of matrix organizations, this kind of career system relies on managers being able to understand, and work well within, the organization's complexity. In such a system, people worry about getting stuck in one specialism and therefore avoid becoming expert at anything. People measure their progress by how fast they are moving, how many roles they have had and the size of the role. Managers have to assume that the experiences they have acquired will be relevant to what they find at the top of the firm when they reach there.

Evolutionary career logic is evident when managers get involved in something new to the organization and make it their own venture. The organization evolves alongside the managers. The job expands, responsibilities are added and the role grows. Managers generally stay with their project unless it runs out of steam, and managers' moves are driven mainly by the lifecycle of the project rather than the development needs of the individuals.

In theory, the career system in place should reflect the organization's strategy, which may change as competitive pressures mount. When organizations attempt to redefine their career logic in order to achieve greater flexibility or achieve strategic advantage, the result can be confusion for employees who are used to the current system. Moving from a command-centred logic to a constructional one, for instance, typically produces retention problems, since the clear means of progression becomes fuzzy. However, as career ladders shorten, and the importance of knowledge becomes more apparent, career systems that favour generalism may be out of step with business and employee needs. Lateral development may not seem a viable career path to knowledge workers who want to develop their expertise as part of their own career competitive advantage. Just changing the career-management system may not be enough. The organizational structure and 'success models' may also need to be modified, and people helped to bridge skill gaps.

Repositioning lateral moves

West *et al.* (1990) found that people who took a lateral move often explained this by referring to 'personal reasons', indicating that stigma may be attached to any move other than vertical promotion. The implications of such findings for organizations include the need:

- To have transparent selection and promotion processes
- To provide appraisal and development processes that encourage open, honest and realistic feedback
- Deliberately to reposition lateral moves as being career opportunities
- To find alternative forms of status to replace lost symbols of progression
- To remove all forms of status and 'democratize' the workplace
- To provide employees with challenging development opportunities
- To provide flexible reward strategies
- To help employees to gain a sense of involvement in decisions that fundamentally affect them.

If lateral development is going to be the main means of career development for many, such moves will have to be seen in a more positive light and seized for the opportunities they contain.

Career plateaux

Within any career system, most employees sooner or later reach a structural plateau beyond which they are unlikely to be promoted. If promotion is a key element of employee expectations/aspirations under the 'old' psychological contract, flatter organization structures in particular lead to more employees reaching a career plateau at an earlier age. With wider gaps between layers, it is likely that employees will stay in the same roles for longer. This in turn carries with it the danger of stagnation and bottlenecks in key areas where 'information is power'. The 'survivor syndrome' may prove to be more difficult to deal with than decisions to change the organization's structure.

Leaner organizations, with fewer opportunities for promotion, can affect groups and individuals in different ways. Research (Bray and Howard, 1980) suggests that some managers whose career has hit a plateau can adjust to reduced opportunities for career mobility, and in some cases with relief. There would appear to be a tendency amongst people whose career has plateaued to change their view of the fairness or otherwise of promotion and reward systems. Evans and Gilbert (1984) and McEnrue (1989) discovered that people who reach a career plateau are more likely to think that promotion systems are based on things out of their control, such as luck, fate, age etc. On the other hand, people whose careers have not yet become 'stuck' are more likely to ascribe career success to factors over which they feel in control, such as their skill, performance and ability generally. If the more mobile employees identify more opportunities ahead, they are likely to perceive the system as fair.

Graduates and careers

A study carried out for the Careers Research Forum, known as the 'First Ten Years' study (1999), examined the reactions of graduates to company policy and practice, their attitudes towards careers, and whether these were shaped by the recruitment and selection process in their first ten years of employment. The study found that graduates retain unrealistically high career ambitions when the traditional career paths apply to relatively few graduates. On the whole, graduates aspired to move 'onwards and upwards', possibly within the same organization, as long as the organization could deliver such progression. Loyalty appeared conditional on the organization doing the 'right things' by individuals.

To some extent, the First Ten Years' study, focusing as it does on graduates working in large organizations with conventional graduate recruitment schemes, calls into question the nature and reality of the new psychological contract. Graduates in this study still appear to expect a conventional career. Having a sense of progression and help with career management appear strongly linked with organizational commitment and intention to quit. Hierarchy still matters and is perceived to be there despite the rhetoric of 'flat' structures.

What is different is the general acceptance that with the amount of change going on, life is less stable. There is a recognition that, with the pace of change being driven largely by technology and markets, keeping abreast of what is new is important and learning processes are therefore essential. There is also acceptance of the more complex nature of organizations, and a recognition that a key skill for managers may be the ability to manage subcontractors on whose skills the success of an organization may depend.

Work–life balance as a key ingredient of the 'new deal'

The First Ten Years study found that career ambitions tend to adjust down over time to be supplemented with aspirations for work–life balance. The extent to which people believe that they can achieve work–life balance in their job appears to be an important emerging element of the new psychological contract. It seems that as people move up the hierarchy they have to work longer hours, leaving many people unhappy with the impact of working hours on other parts of their life.

However, various researchers suggest that balance is moving up the business agenda rather than being seen as simply an organizational issue. This is due to increasing difficulties in attracting recruits to organizations, especially high-technology companies where many employers are competing to attract the 'best' recruits available. 'Soft' issues such as this are beginning to affect return on investment and other business measures when failure to attract and retain key employees becomes apparent in organizational performance. The UK government too, concerned about the increase of 'stress-related' absence from work, has encouraged and funded a variety of workplace initiatives relating to work–life balance.

According to US management writer Bruce Tulgan (1998), members of 'Generation X' – or people under the age of 35 – are less likely than their predecessors to put up indefinitely with a lack of work–life balance. Research carried out by Demos in the UK examined how lifestyle aspirations affect the attitudes of these young people to life and careers (Cannon, 1997). One of the characteristics of people in this age group is their high educational attainment.

The numbers of young people entering further or higher education have increased dramatically in recent years. More than 340 000 students entered university in 1998, which was more than double the numbers entering in 1990. During the 1970s only 5 per cent of 18-years-old had the opportunity to gain a university degree, whereas today more than 30 per cent of young people are pursuing further or higher education, and the UK government aspires to up to 50 per cent of young people in higher education by 2010. This brings young people in the UK more in line with their counterparts in other European countries, especially Germany, where higher qualifications have traditionally been valued.

There are some important differences, however. In Germany there has been a tradition of making good use of skills and higher education when the individual enters the job market (and indeed many qualifications are vocationally oriented). In the UK, by way of contrast, many of the jobs on offer to graduates have not changed from those that might formerly have been offered to school leavers. Employers who might once have recruited A-level students for management trainee positions are now becoming graduate recruiters. Job literature produced for university 'milk rounds' continues to imply early opportunities and the rapid promotion of yesteryear. In practice, graduate recruitment is followed by quiet streaming as genuine high flyers are selected from the rest.

Unrealized expectations about exciting careers can lead to disillusionment and cynicism amongst young employees. Indeed, various newspaper reports have documented the phenomena of the 'TIREDs' (or thirty-something-educated-radical-dropouts) and the TATTs (tired-all-the-times). Employers in the knowledge economy are already recognizing the need to attract skilled employees by having a well-articulated set of values that really work in practice. Highly employable people seem now to be looking for roles that appeal to their personal values, and money may not be the main consideration. More cross-sectoral job moves may be likely, including moves in and out of the voluntary sector. People may increasingly choose to take career breaks or work flexibly in order to have more of what they consider important.

The Demos research suggests that people within this age group have been exposed to a range of experiences to which previous generations did not have access. These experiences may have shaped their expectations and values in ways that can be hard to grasp from other vantage points. Whilst there are dangers in generalizing about generations, various research projects indicate that members of Generation X have been exposed to more information than their predecessors through TV and other media, and are used to receiving information in simplistic form at a fast rate. They are heavy users of technology, including the Internet, and are able to see some of the potential applications of transformational technology. This generation appears to learn and absorb information quickly, particularly about areas of interest to them, such as consumer products and services. They expect things to happen quickly.

Many Generation X-ers value their freedom and appear to look for control over their work life so as to be able to enjoy other aspects of their lives. They are also accustomed to travel and are considered the first truly 'global' generation, even if the links are only through a common currency of consumer products. The Demos research suggests that young people want money, greater control of their time, and the chance to use some of their intellectual potential.

These experiences have potentially shaped their attitudes in a number of ways. They expect honesty from employers, especially with regard to career opportunities, and dislike feeling manipulated. There is a perceived lack of trust, particularly in employers, since they do not provide secure employment, and a wariness about committing to anything long term. Loyalty to an employer is therefore not an appropriate concept. Organizations that promise career growth through international assignments, for instance, and then fail to deliver may produce cynical employees who leave when they are at their most valuable to their current employer.

Managing work–life balance

The issue of work–life balance has become extremely topical in recent times. The turbulent 1990s highlighted the need for organizational flexibility. At the start of the 1990s, flexibility meant employers being able to dispose of employees who were surplus to requirements or whose skills were linked to 'non-core' parts of a business. There was little talk of employee work–life balance at that time, as job insecurity was a much more topical feature of the employment landscape.

Work–life balance first became a high-profile issue in the mid-1990s, when it was seen as part of the Equal Opportunities agenda, mainly focused on the needs of women to work flexibly in order to care for their families. Balance also grew in importance because of the long hours culture and the growth of the stress industry. Managers faced increasing workloads and heavy pressure as organizations became leaner. They not only had to cope with increased workloads of their own, but at the same time were faced with the need to motivate their teams and concentrate on the people side of managing.

In fact, it would seem that managers in particular are usually the worst 'victims' of a lack of balance. In some of the organizations studied by Roffey Park (Glynn et al., 2002) managers do ensure that other staff are able to have balance, but it is managers themselves who tend to work extra hours if the job demands it. In that sense, managers tend to be the least 'protected' of employees. Even top managers can seem unable to address the issue for themselves – unlike

Henry Steward, founder and Chief Executive of Happy Computers: 'You have to recognize what's important to you. I once felt that I couldn't spare the time to go to my children's school, but talking about it afterwards I realized that their school experience is one of the most important things in my life. After that, finding a morning a week wasn't a big deal' (in Rice, 2001).

What can organizations do to enable work–life balance for employees while at the same time protecting business interests? Respondents to Roffey Park's *Management Agenda* make some interesting suggestions. One suggestion regards strategic clarity. If people understand what needs to be done and why, they can be more proactive about prioritizing their own workloads. Better and more realistic planning and involving employees can be helpful. Other enablers of work–life balance include the elimination of duplicated work, and an increase in human resources – building some slack into the system.

What do people mean by work–life balance?

Of course defining what is meant by work–life balance is tricky, since people's motivations and life situations differ. Most people perceive their work and life to be in balance if they feel they can exercise some control over their time and their workload. While a 'workaholic' might feel stressed if forced to down tools at five o'clock, other people may become stressed if they are regularly pressurized to work beyond five o'clock. Developing a blanket policy on balance can therefore be difficult. However, flexible working is a common factor to many work–life balance initiatives.

Lack of work–life balance remains a key issue for employees, and balance is now seen both as a reward when it is achievable, and as a form of harassment when it is not.

A pivotal issue

Over the years since Roffey Park Institute began researching the issue of work–life balance, public recognition of the importance of the issue has grown exponentially. Indeed, the shift in emphasis is reflected in the increasingly common reference to 'life–work' balance. It has been interesting to note how, emerging from the Equal Opportunities and Diversity agendas, work–life balance has become a central element in the UK productivity debate. Technology has been a key driver, with the removal of time and location boundaries resulting in increased volumes of business activity around the clock. Far from enabling employees to enjoy more leisure time, as was predicted in the 1980s, technology has instead ensured that the boundaries between work and non-work have virtually disappeared.

From being seen as a mere fringe issue relating to part-time working, the damaging effects of the long hours culture on public health and well-being, skills shortages, and the need for business flexibility have led to direct government involvement and a variety of major initiatives to 'fix' the problem of work–life balance. The UK 2003 'right to request' legislation (the Employment Act), enabling parents or carers of young children to apply to work flexibly, has been a small but significant step in acknowledging that work–life balance is not exclusively a gender issue but one that affects society as a whole. Employers vary widely in their response to the initiative, with some organizations (such as Marks and Spencer) proactively embracing the spirit of the legislation, extending the right to request to all employees with carer responsibilities. Other employers grumble that even complying with minimum requirements will increase their costs and may make them uncompetitive in the global marketplace.

Changing attitudes to work–life balance

The issue of work–life balance is becoming a pivotal focal point with regard to the changing psychological contract. It also highlights the current transition between different economies, where the key production factor is shifting from capital to knowledge. Employer attitudes are also in transition, with 'old economy' management practices sitting uncomfortably alongside the needs of the new economic order. The shift is also evident in employee attitudes, where the work ethic of the 'baby boomer' generations is being replaced by expectations that employees are entitled to expect to have both a career and a life. As discussed earlier, the stereotypical 'Generation Y', even more than their predecessors 'Generation X', recognize that no organization can be relied on for job security and that they must move on from organizations where they are not being developed or where they lack the right balance for their personal needs.

It is perhaps because the 'tipping point' in attitudes has not yet fully been reached that take-up of work–life balance initiatives remains small, despite the proliferation of schemes and forms of flexible working. Roffey Park research suggests that many employers still fear that working flexibly or remotely will cost them career progression, where 'out of sight means out of mind'. After all, there are still relatively few senior women managers who are able to demonstrate a flexible career path to the top, and even fewer men. Moreover, in today's organizations, company politics mean that you have to be seen in order to influence and safeguard or advance your position.

Similarly, the link between successful work–life balance policies and productivity remains frustratingly vague. While there is much anecdotal evidence of improved employee morale, better retention rates and customer satisfaction as a result of policies, lack of 'hard' evidence tends to undermine the business case for work–life balance, leaving the sceptics unconvinced. Another key factor is that many managers find managing a flexible workforce difficult, at one extreme neglecting employees who do not conform to the full-time employment model and at the other extreme tending to 'meddle' because of lack of trust.

Business drivers for work–life balance

Work–life balance is one issue in which individual, organizational and national needs will increasingly coincide. On the plus side, the multiple levels of attention and activity with regard to work–life balance suggest that, while it may be in fits and starts, progress is being made. Whereas a few years ago flexible working options were very limited, now the range is wider and is driven by business need. In a context of growing skills shortages, employers are having to look beyond the traditional labour catchment pools to recruit the people they need. As more women and members of various minority groups look to gain access to parts of the labour market from which they have long been excluded, work–life balance has become part of the diversity agenda.

In certain sectors, such as fast-food retailing, high turnover rates and the expansion of the sector means a constant search for employees who can keep outlets operating over the many hours of opening. In the supermarket sector, the shift to 24/7 working and the increased numbers of supermarkets has meant that just to keep a store staffed means having to develop new ways of thinking about working patterns. Not only are people working in shifts, on various forms of flexible working, but staff are also being drawn from previously disadvantaged minority groups.

The Health and Safety Executive has identified work-related stress, depression and anxiety as the second most common group of self-reported work-related illnesses. This is forcing employers to recognize that the psychological well-being of their staff is as important as their physical health. In an effort to mitigate some of the effects of work-related stress, many organizations have introduced employee assistance programmes. It is thought that around 65 per cent of employees in the USA are supported by an EAP (Sanders, 2000).

Stress, and its negative impact on health, is also driving employers to develop flexible working options. The Ideal City Workplace survey found that nearly half of city workers worldwide think a better work–life balance, with better policies and more opportunities to telework, would reduce stress in the office. More than a third of respondents want to work from home (*Personnel Today*, 18 April, 2001), yet 33 per cent of respondents in a CMI survey (2003) confirm that their employer has made no provision for this.

Balance is becoming central to organizational aspirations to become a great employer and so attract and retain employees. Staff retention was a primary reason for implementing work–life programmes in many US organizations, according to research carried out by Mercer (2000). According to Dana Friedman, co-author of the William M. Mercer (2000) report:

> *Leading companies recognise that work–life initiatives can contribute to their cutting-edge competitiveness in a tight labour market. Not only do they offer the most generous and innovative initiatives, they focus on creating a supportive working environment as a way to become the employer of choice in their respective industries.*

Flexible working

Flexible working is thought to be one of the key solutions to meeting both organizational and individual needs. The number of permanent employees is expected to fall within three years, according to a CMI workplace survey

(2003). Of managers in the CMI survey, 82 per cent agree that companies will increasingly seek to reduce their property and office costs, thus boosting the number of individuals and organizations working remotely. Organizations also want a flexible talent pool. With round-the-clock working patterns and the development of new technologies, many companies are already experiencing skills shortages that are hard to fill.

Many employees also want to work flexibly, to help them deal with the impact of change and heavy workloads. After all, technology now means that there are few logistical reasons why employees should be co-located, or be 'at work' during the same time periods. Flexible working is therefore increasingly being seen as the answer to a number of problems and needs – the needs of parents, the need to save money on office space, the need to extend opening hours of business etc. It is a key plank in developing a more diverse and representative workforce.

While the 2003 Employment Act acknowledges the fact that parents of young children in particular need to have the option to work flexibly (and research suggests that women still shoulder the greater share of responsibility within the home, and are twelve times more likely than men to do most of the childcare), the coming into force of the 'right to request' flexible working has put employers under pressure to extend the right to all employees, regardless of carer responsibilities. Of respondents, 88 per cent suggest that there is a growing demand for a more flexible working pattern in their organization, and 68 per cent of the sample state that they would like to work flexibly. However, in most organizations the range of flexible working options is inadequate, with only 44 per cent of respondents reporting an increase in the range of options available.

Even when flexible working options exist, many employees fear that working flexibly will undermine their career prospects. Some organizations are working hard to develop career tracks, and changing meetings and other organizational arrangements to enable flexible working. The number of role models working flexibly and still reaching top positions is tiny, but is steadily growing.

Currently, around 29 per cent of UK employees work part-time or in some other form of flexible working pattern. In most of the organizations in the Roffey Park *Management Agenda* surveys, flexible working accounts for up to 25 per cent of the workforce. Part-time and shift working is of course well established in the retail and leisure industries. The number of part-time jobs is increasing faster than the number of full-time jobs. By 2006, the number of individuals working part time is expected to increase to 31 per cent as a result of both organizational and individual needs (DfEE, 1997–8).

Implementation of balance policies

The William Mercer survey found that work–life balance policies in the USA are leading the way in terms of implementation. Employers who were considering the adoption of popular work–life balance policies two years before, went on to implement the programmes. The most prevalent work–life benefits offered are casual dress and reimbursement of tuition fees, offered by 90 per cent of employers. Nearly one in five of the employers surveyed sponsors a childcare centre. Back-up care is also growing in popularity as a solution for employees in need of childcare in an emergency or on a holiday basis.

In the UK, the picture is less positive. The long hours culture was recognized by the UK government as problematic. Stress-related absence and additional burdens on the NHS cost the country millions of pounds each year. The 'Challenge Fund', set up by the DTI, was given the remit to fund workplace initiatives regarding work–life balance. The Working Time Directive should have curbed the excessive hours culture, but early indications suggest that there is little change. The work–life balance agenda is now seen as an issue that is not gender-specific since the Employment Act 2003 gave parents of either sex with children under the age of six the right to apply to work flexibly.

Despite these initiatives, take-up of the various options appears patchy. Implementation is proving the biggest challenge, given that many employers still restrict career development to people who are prepared to show their commitment by working long hours. In many companies the problem is lack of availability of flexible working options. Research by the Joseph Rowntree Foundation (2003), which explored the needs of the growing population of informal carers as the workforce gets older, found that an additional problem was that staff did not know what flexible arrangements were available. Moreover, staff were worried that they would be labelled 'needy' if they applied for carers' leave or counselling services.

Two groups of people have key role to play in making work–life balance possible for others; HR and line managers.

HR's role in enabling work–life balance

Human Resources personnel can help by demonstrating commitment to innovative work–life balance policies which really work. If HR professionals are looking to find ways to make a difference to their organization's success, they should focus on flexible working as an enabler of work–life balance and organizational flexibility.

Developing a wide and readily accessed range of flexible working options is a key contribution HR can make to enabling employees to achieve balance, though developing such options can take time and involve a different way of thinking about the workforce and recruitment practices. Managers may need training in how to manage people on job shares, or who work remotely, for example.

Flexible working is 'culture-sensitive', and has to be customized to fit the individuality of the company. HR policies can also address some of the cultural barriers to work–life balance identified by *Management Agenda* respondents. These include long hours, unmanageable workloads, lack of time, lack of organizational commitment to work–life balance, lack of control over workload, frequent travel, and lack of recognition of people who are able to achieve balance and still do a good job.

Policies can incorporate some of the respondents' many suggestions about how work pressures could be alleviated. These range from 'organizations should recognize the pressure' and 'provide an environment where it is OK to say you have problems' to 'train managers to let go/stop dabbling' and 'plan better/embed skills and knowledge'; also 'recognizing and rewarding people who do the job and manage their own balance'. Career management strategies should reinforce this.

Policies need to address real employee needs. The BBC, for instance, has approached the issue through innovative flexible benefits schemes. A number of packages have been introduced in recent years. Full-time staff have full use of the BBC Club Lifestyles fitness centre, a range of insurance through BupaCare, and the extension of sick pay to full salary while staff are ill.

The role of the manager in enabling balance

While policies are useful, the other key players in enabling work–life balance are line managers. Managers should review team workloads regularly to ensure that they are manageable, and that unnecessary work is replaced by more important activities. Some companies are now training managers in how to manage a more flexible workforce, including people working remotely. This requires strong communication skills, the ability to coach at a distance, and the ability to manage outputs rather than inputs. *Management Agenda* respondents also suggest that better performance management, including tackling poor performance and preventing extra work from falling onto the shoulders of 'the willing' employees who always deliver.

Managers are central to developing open lines of communication with staff and understanding the specific issues faced by individual employees. Roffey Park's extensive in-depth study of work–life balance issues found that managers who are able to role-model good work–life balance practice are usually not only successful at achieving business results but also thought to be good leaders by their teams. They tend to demonstrate genuine concern and empathy for others (Glynn *et al.*, 2002). At Napp Pharmaceuticals, for instance, managers are expected to know the names of every production floor worker, their partners' names and their personal situations. This enables the manager to grasp when there is a genuine need and address problems as they arise.

At Penna Consulting, where managers have considerable autonomy in how they manage the work–life balance of their teams, at the time of the research there were no formal work–life balance policies in place. When asked if they would like to see such policies developed, managers expressed a need for general guidelines only – they were wary about policies being too prescriptive and limiting their freedom to make situation-specific decisions regarding individual situations. Above all, they demonstrated trust in employees and empowered them to be self-managing. Rather than finding their trust abused, managers have generally found that team members tend to 'go the extra mile'.

Mutual trust lies at the heart of the issue. Employees too must reciprocate by being loyal and trustworthy and by attempting to self-manage. Managers must learn to manage people who work remotely or on various forms of flexible working pattern, in supportive rather than controlling ways. At Allied-Domecq, the manager's role, supported by the organizational culture, is one of facilitation rather than enabling balance directly. Managers have to ensure that the conditions are in place for work–life balance, but after that it is up to individuals to manage their own work–life balance.

Flexible working options

In the Roffey Park surveys, the most common form of flexible working on offer is part-time work, followed by fixed-term contracts. Job shares are also on the increase, but are still relatively rare in professional roles. Less common are term-time only working, 'key-time' working, voluntary reduced hours, associate schemes etc. What is less clear from our survey is whether the flexible working patterns have been developed to suit employers' needs, or whether employees have been able to opt for them. For example, a number of people described how they had been forced into roles that are short-term contract based in contrast to their previous full-time employment, making firm planning for the future difficult.

Teleworking is on the increase. In the UK in 2003 there are estimated to be 700 000 people working from home. Work that does not need to be carried out in an office, such as sales, insurance etc., has long been carried out from a variety of bases, including employees' homes. The idea appears to be gaining ground that a much wider range of jobs can be based away from an office environment, thanks to technology. Companies such as BT, who supply the electronic infrastructure and are introducing other technologies such as Solstra to enable people to work from home, have seen this side of their business grow significantly in recent years. BT currently employs 6000 home-based workers.

Caroline Waters (2003), HR Director of BT, suggests that the capability of technology to enable work to be done at home is opening up employment opportunities to people who might otherwise have been excluded from the workplace because of difficulties caused by their physical disability. Waters argues that as long as the organization and employee are clear what outputs are expected, employees can create their own working pattern. When employees love what they do, work when they choose and are effective in their outputs, the definition of what is 'work' and what is 'leisure' changes.

Asda has an impressive range of flexible working options. It has 259 stores across the UK, employs 122 000 people, and has one of the highest part-time workforce contingents of the Sunday Times top 100 companies. The supermarket operates an in-store shift-swapping scheme, and allows students to switch to their home store during holidays. There is 'school starter' leave (an unpaid half-day for parents or grandparents) and a 'big break' (an extra-long holiday for a special occasion such as a family wedding). Asda also offers job-sharing to all, including managers, and there is religious festival leave.

Many supermarkets are seeking to meet their flexible working needs by retaining or recruiting reliable older workers. They are providing a wide range of services, such as transport to and from work so that staff can work unsocial hours, which allow employees to meet family commitments and enable the store to extend its opening hours. Asda wanted to increase the number of staff aged over 50 from 15.4 per cent to 20 per cent by the end of 2003, and produced a new recruitment toolkit. The company introduced the Asda 'Goldies' store campaign to promote benefits to older staff, including grandparent leave (allowing older workers to take time off for the birth of a grandchild). Among the more unusual benefits is a three-month unpaid 'Benidorm Break' from January to March. Asda increased older staff by 3.5 per cent to 18.9 per cent, and reduced staff turnover and absence.

In other sectors, the value of older workers is increasingly recognized. Arup, for example, appears to have embraced 'age-friendly' policies, and has more than 10 per cent of its employees in the over-55 age category. Old Arupians are invited to an annual get-together hosted by senior staff, so even when staff retire they remain part of the 'family'.

King's Healthcare NHS Trust in Lewisham suffered a serious shortfall of nursing professionals. In the year before an imaginative work–life balance scheme was launched, 18.9 per cent of midwifery and nursing posts remained unfilled. A group of managers, clinicians, HR and staff-side representatives came up with a ten-point package of flexible working practices, known as 'Kingsflex':

1. Part-time working
2. Job-sharing
3. Temporary reductions in hours for specific periods to help employees deal with special circumstances
4. Staggered working hours – staff can determine their working patterns on a planned, weekly basis
5. Annual hours – work can be spread unevenly over the year, giving employees scope for reducing their hours during school holidays, for example
6. A phased return to work – staff can build up their number of weekly hours over a period after an absence such as sickness or maternity leave
7. Special and parental leave – staff can take time off for specific needs (fostering, for example)
8. Working from home – this is an occasional option as long as normal work is fulfilled
9. Career breaks – employees can take unpaid leave for up to two years in order to travel, pursue further education or fulfil carer responsibilities
10. 'Personalized' annual leave – individuals can buy or sell days of annual leave, adjusting their entitlement by up to ten days and increasing or decreasing their salaries accordingly.

In the year following the scheme's introduction, nursing and midwife vacancies fell to 13.5 per cent (Mahoney, 2000).

Employee well-being

Increasingly, companies are likely to have a wellness plan running alongside their business plan. HSA has built its business around health insurance, so it is perhaps no surprise that the company takes staff well-being seriously. There are more than 50 patterns of working, including flexible hours and a compressed working week, and three-quarters of HSA employees say that they can find the right work–life balance. Newly renovated offices are bright and colourful, with relaxation rooms on every floor and workstations that are designed with the help of an ergonomics specialist. Life insurance is eight times salary, and everybody can join the free family health plan.

As more and more companies encourage employees to work remotely, there is often the assumption that the work–life balance dilemma has been solved. In practice this is often far from the case, especially for parents of young children. It can be very difficult for people to separate personal and work space at home and, typically, there are no safeguards in place to prevent them from developing workaholic tendencies. The problem can be solved to some extent by helping staff to establish a community with other home-workers in their neighbourhoods and, if possible, giving them the chance to 'hot-desk' at regional offices. BT brings home-workers together so that they can learn from each other.

Similarly, some companies are selecting people who have the right sort of approach (relatively independent and self-managing) for home-working. BT recommends that employers must take account of the adjustments that have to be made by employees working away from the office and realize that if people are going through this change to flexible working, the employers who do not help are storing up problems for themselves. Employers also need to set up a training agenda which equips home-workers with the skills they need to cope efficiently on their own – for instance, time management, IT and marketing skills.

Above all, perhaps, organizations can address the problem at its root by increasing the number of employees and 'building in some slack'. By good planning, communicating with teams and understanding workloads, balance can be achieved without sacrificing productivity. In fact, managers recognize that happy, well-rested employees are more productive, loyal and motivated. Perhaps the most effective way of enabling work–life balance is by building a climate of mutual trust where people feel it is OK to achieve the form of balance that is right for them.

Conclusion

In a high performing organization, with its focus on nurturing human capital, building a productive psychological contract should be seen as a key investment in an organization's continuing success. The changing workplace has radically altered the nature of the psychological contract on offer. Many elements of the old contract, such as job security and promotion, are still aspired to, even by people entering the job market for the first time. Yet 'old' styles of career development are not necessarily the solution to retaining the most talented employees. It is as if some of the accompanying elements of the old deal, such as unquestioning loyalty, patience and a willingness to carry out unpopular assignments as a means to make progress, are no longer prices employees are willing to pay.

Employers who want to attract and retain young talent will have to adapt to the values of the generation that is rejecting the norms of their elders, such as working all hours and being grateful to have a job, and is looking for a work– life balance. Issues such as the environment are also important. Many want to work for an employer that is a responsible world citizen, not one that is solely interested in shareholder value no matter the cost. Employers will therefore have to strengthen their brand recognition if they want to attract these graduates – and the employer brand image will need to be reflected in reality, if employers wish to retain them. This will mean providing interesting work, plenty of opportunities for growth, and good career development.

In the next chapter we will look at the skills likely to be needed by the high performing organization and its employees.

Key points

- Organizational change and uncertainty have eroded the old psychological contract; the notions of loyalty to the employer in return for security of employment and career advancement have been replaced by more transactional relationships
- Given that people are the potential main source of competitive advantage, organizations are having to take the new 'deal' or 'social contract' seriously if they want to attract and retain key employees
- High performance depends on people having the skills, the will and the commitment to innovate, work hard and produce innovative, high quality customer solutions
- Employees are looking for career and skills development and expect their employer to partner with them in achieving these; interesting work, work–life balance are key elements of the new deal
- Employees increasingly choose to work for organizations with a strong developmental and ethical track record.

15

Key skills to survive and thrive in changing organizations

Introduction

In this chapter we look in more detail at some of the skills that appear to make employees effective and employable in today's changing organizations, and at how organizations can retain people by developing them.

The importance of development

Perhaps the key factor in keeping people motivated and retaining their talents is offering them opportunities for individual and career development. Development is crucial in that it ensures that talent is refreshed and renewed. Without development, talented people leave. Speaking in 1998, Richard Brown, CEO of Cable and Wireless, suggested that, even in down times, organizations should 'train and develop your critical people, managerial and technical. Nothing is more important than growing your "A" players, which is conducive to better retention, and promptly dealing with "C" players. This is an opportunity for exercising leadership'.

The need for workforce flexibility is being mirrored by the notion that careers will from now on become more mobile, and that individuals will need to be able to adapt to constantly changing environments. The emphasis in much writing about careers in the past few years has been on what individuals can do for themselves in order to survive and thrive in turbulent times. Many organizations have been reluctant to spend money on training people who may well leave, yet research suggests that where training and development are geared towards increasing internal employability, people enhance their skills and stay longer with their current employer. With specialist knowledge work being in short supply, this has to be a good thing.

This more adult–adult relationship between employers and employees is based on the increasing power of the knowledge worker to redress the balance of power, which until recently had swung heavily in favour of organizations.

This is particularly marked in some of the oil companies, where overseas assignments as part of a broad career route for high-calibre employees are becoming increasingly difficult to fill. This is explained partly by the rise in the number of dual-career families, but also by the increasing unwillingness of employees to make sacrifices if they are not guaranteed promotion on return from the assignment. There is already a good deal of anecdotal evidence that employees with transferable skills and experience are more confident of being employable and less tolerant of the frustrations of poor management, inappropriate reward and few growth opportunities. Ironically, the very skills which many employers crave – such as the ability to get things done, be innovative, customer oriented etc. – are precisely the skills that will help people to get jobs elsewhere.

An organization is only as high performing as its members. Successful organizations need people who are skilled, committed and willing to go the extra mile as the goalposts are raised still higher. Companies such as Federal Express, which recognize the importance of retaining and developing employees even during downturns, are able to reap the rewards of employee commitment and rising stock prices in the here and now.

Development should be geared to both increasing people's effectiveness in their current roles and helping to prepare them for future roles.

How are managers' roles changing?

In the knowledge-based economy, it is no longer sufficient for managers to be the 'best of the rest'. In any case, managing teams of knowledge workers in particular may mean that the manager has less technical skill than team members. Some pundits argue that there will be little need for managers, since knowledge workers, given enough relevant information about the organization's needs, are supposed to be inherently self-managing. Others suggest the converse is true, and that 'people management' is needed now more than ever. Managing such workers usually involves having a light touch, understanding how to create a motivating climate, and providing protection for employees from the organization's bureaucratic pressures.

What is more generally agreed is that managing large and complex projects calls for specific forms of management and coordination, combining both strategic and implementation processes. Often managers are managing teams comprising a diverse range of employees and contractors. They are sometimes working across organizational boundaries in various kinds of alliance. Managers are expected to provide the 'glue' to keep the task together, and their role becomes that of a facilitator/coordinator. They are the 'close by' leaders, who are also frequently responsible for relationship management with clients.

Since people management is very clearly a key part of their role, managers need good interpersonal, team leadership and motivational skills, and to be supported by integrated management and communication systems. The increasing emphasis on corporate social responsibility, supported by employment legislation, means that employee relations need to be exercised in an open, fair and partnership manner. Managers need to be able to manage constructively the interests of different groups of employees, such as ensuring that part-time and temporary employees, as well as contractors, are fully integrated. Many managers struggle with the multiple and often contradictory foci and how to help staff deal with these.

Many theorists predict that the manager's conventional role will diminish, with employees increasingly required to learn and self-manage. The manager's role will be about strategizing and problem-solving, managing information flows, hiring and retaining, monitoring performance and intellectual property, and keeping up with technological advances. Many managers report being aware that their organization expects them to find new ways of doing things and to encourage innovation in others. Typically, line managers continue to have responsibility for doing the 'day job' in addition to their responsibilities to their teams. Often spans of control have expanded, and the creation of sophisticated appraisal and development planning processes has in some cases only added to the pressure on line managers.

Not surprisingly, many managers find the multiple demands of their role may be mutually contradictory. Middle managers in particular may feel under-empowered for their role, often due to lack of training or because they are not involved in the strategy formulation process. If communications are poor, managers may be as ignorant of the organization's direction as other employees and therefore unable to provide much needed clarity, especially with regard to career options. Little wonder then that line managers have difficulty providing their contribution to the 'new deal'. Many experience the personal challenge of staying focused and motivated in their 'darkest hour'.

The complexity of managers' roles is evident in findings from the *Management Agenda* survey. The majority of respondents (83 per cent) reported that change has affected their role, bringing a greater emphasis on the people side of management. For 64 per cent of managers, this increased responsibility for people management is in addition to maintaining their normal workload. However, a longer-term shift appears to have taken place, with even traditionalists now recognizing the need to motivate knowledge workers, manage performance and engage in team-building.

Of managers, 58 per cent indicated that they now have to work in different types of teams, including cross-boundary project teams. The majority of managers indicated that they are expected to create highly productive workgroups, and 92 per cent of managers reported that they are finding themselves having to manage their teams through change. This includes the need to keep their teams motivated and committed through change. This involves engaging the hearts and minds of their team as well as coaching and developing others. Typical challenges include:

- How to recognize key strengths in their teams and get the best out of people
- How to get the 'extra bit' out of staff
- How to manage mediocre performance.

Managers are in the front line of career matters, and typically receive little practical help to enable them to make a good job of this. It is likely that wide spans of control will shrink to enable managers to really carry out the performance management and development sides of their role.

Leadership, too, is becoming a key issue across all sectors – much craved by employees and generally perceived to be lacking in UK organizations. Leaders will be expected to demonstrate high levels of emotional intelligence, especially self-awareness. The multi-rater feedback and executive coaching industry looks set to burgeon. Some of the issues that a focus group of senior managers were grappling with included:

- How to manage the tension between 'top-down' and 'bottom-up' demands
- Which approaches to change are appropriate at different stages of an organization's life cycle
- How to show that you care as a senior manager in a large organization
- What skills are most helpful in managing change?

Many senior managers struggle to adjust their leadership styles to suit a political climate, developing effective working relationships with boards, governing bodies and other stakeholder groups. Many 'distant' leaders new to a top job wonder how to effect change from, and how they can have an impact on, the quality of what goes on 'at the coalface' when they may be at several levels removed from front-line staff and team leaders. The loneliness of the top job is often remarked upon, and increasingly executives are turning to external coaches or taking on non-executive roles so that they can 'learn the job without having to ask people in the organization'. One new Managing Director, for instance, was somewhat daunted by the challenge of replacing a well-respected and experienced male MD when she was younger, female and unknown within the organization. This new MD was not alone in wondering if she as top leader should take on the organization's values if they are different from her own, or whether she should not take on the job at all.

Employability and skills

In such complex management roles, certain skills seem key. When we asked *Management Agenda* respondents what they believe to be the skills needed for success in changing times, they highlighted:

- Networking skills
- Flexibility
- Political skills
- Project management
- Change management
- Communication
- Coaching and mentoring
- Team-working

- Performance management skills
- Extreme competitiveness
- Ability to forge useful alliances
- Cultural awareness
- Strategic leadership.

A number of respondents also emphasized the need for technical competencies, including:

- E-commerce skills
- Video-conferencing skills
- Internet and web-related skills
- IT skills, especially the ability to manage large flows of IT-processed data.

Employability is likely to be enhanced by a set of core skills such as these, underpinned by good interpersonal, leadership and communication skills. The ability to take a strategic view, and to think and act as a business person, whether from a generalist or specialist perspective, will be key to most roles.

If it seems that people are generally attuned to the idea that career security may lie in learning new skills, what are the skills that seem to be required in changing organizations? Of course, what constitutes employability may vary in different industries and types of role. However, Allred *et al.* (1998) suggest that the following five key types of skill, knowledge or aptitude are likely to be critical to future career success, whatever the sector:

1. *A knowledge-based technical specialism*, including computer literacy, since being able to make information of practical use will create competitive advantage. People management will not automatically become the means to career advancement. Indeed, people managers may well work remotely from the people they are managing, maintaining contact via e-mail, the Internet, fax and telephone. Being knowledgeable may not be enough; becoming expert in highly marketable knowledge/skill areas is better. Continuous learning will be essential to ensure that skills are leading edge.
2. *Cross-functional and international experience*. Managers will need good project management skills. They will need to be culturally aware and able to adapt to changing and unfamiliar situations. Managers will increasingly be required to get the best out of multicultural and virtual teams, as well as managing people who work on different forms of contract, such as contractors, and also employees working flexibly.
3. *Collaborative leadership*. Since projects will be both temporary and ongoing, people's ability to integrate quickly into new or existing teams will be critical to success.
4. *Self-managing skills*. Since there is likely to be less hierarchical management of knowledge workers, people will need to exercise self-governance, including the willingness to act ethically. Continuous learning will be essential, as will the ability to manage for themselves an acceptable work–life balance.
5. *Flexibility*, including the ability to lead on one project and be a team member on another.

Successful employees are likely to be customer-oriented, able to contribute to the continuous improvement of processes, products and services, and, at the same time, committed to personal development and flexible. As the new career evolves, development will not be linked to a long-term future within one organization. There will be a greater emphasis on the skills and competencies required for 'employability'.

Some pundits suggest that the key skills for the future include visioning and planning; information handling; influencing and negotiating; creativity and learning; change management; teamworking and leadership. Others point to strong collaborative, partnership and relationship skills. Kiechell (1994) highlights self-reliance, including risk-taking, initiative and self-motivation. To develop these skills requires people to have intellectual curiosity, be able to balance work with non-work, be physically active and be able to seek support when they need it. I would add to this list *personal credibility*, built on being good at delivery, confident, well-networked, and able to develop knowledge with others and grow knowledge assets.

Skills for handling continuous change

Perhaps the most essential skills of all are those that help individuals to deal with continuous change. First there are the relationship skills – sound interpersonal skills, networking ability, and being able to build influence and respect. Positive political skills are part of understanding how organizations really work, but only part. People need to become knowledgeable about the issues affecting their business, sector and industry, and use the language of business. They need good thinking skills and mental flexibility. They need good project management skills and the ability to lead or be part of integrated teams. They will benefit from the learning implicit in being part of cross-boundary teams. They need to be able to manage their own networks and visibility.

Some people are naturally inclined to embrace change, and relish the opportunities change provides. A key requirement for employees in changing times is to keep their skills up to date with changing needs. Individuals will need good coping strategies, including managing the work–life balance that is right for them at that point in time. Change can also throw up many uncomfortable challenges. Even survival can be a success, as change situations can throw up challenges from all sides. The most important thing is to be true to yourself in such circumstances. According to Broussine (1983), there are three levels of choice when confronted by difficult situations – for example, if you disagree with what is being done. The first choice is to argue the case for the decision to be different, working hard to change the proposals but accepting that you may be unsuccessful. The second is to accept the changes as given, and then put your effort into making them work with as much energy as if they were your idea in the first place. The third option is to find an outlet for your talent elsewhere.

In particular, people who thrive on change are clear in their own minds about the proactive and reactive elements of their role. Employees need skills in (and an attitude of) independence, being willing to take responsibility for managing themselves and developing the capacity to be enterprising and innovative. Organizations want people who can make things happen. Organizations need employees who can deal with uncertainty, since this is likely to be an ongoing characteristic of the workplace. This means not being a perfectionist, and being able to handle anxiety and to take risks. It means having a sense of self-belief, which comes with a sense of self-acceptance. It means having a sense of purpose and emotional commitment while not being over-attached to particular outcomes. Above all, it means developing emotional resilience – i.e. the ability to bounce back after setbacks or criticism.

Career self-management

The so-called 'post-corporate career' is really starting to happen, and will become a more clear-cut trend as people's confidence increases. The evolving career form may involve periods of employment, self-employment, voluntary work and studying. Only those who have the capacity for continuous learning and coping with ambiguity are likely to survive and thrive.

Career resilience is likely to be the key determinant of successful career self-management, linked with the ongoing quest for learning and new skills. Individuals need to accept responsibility for managing their own career. For this they need solid self-confidence and well-developed interpersonal skills. There is greater emphasis on managing their own image within the organization and learning to pay attention to, and deal with, organizational politics. People need to be able to market themselves and use their visibility to good effect. They also need to be able to handle many different personal/organizational changes, seeing learning and change as a way of life rather than an exception. They will therefore need to thrive on organizational complexity and ambiguity.

A number of characteristics of people who manage to make career headway, even in ambiguous and changing circumstances, have been identified. The most important characteristics are the ability to work with a wide variety of people and to take early overall responsibility for important tasks. A need to achieve results and leadership experience early in a person's career are indicators of later career success. Similarly, having wide experience in many functions before the age of 35, an ability to negotiate and do deals and a willingness to take judicious risks are all important.

Being an original thinker, having more ideas than other colleagues, make a person's contribution richer. Being stretched by the boss helps to provide development challenge, stimulates learning and builds confidence. Being able to change managerial style to suit the occasion, a desire to seek new opportunities and becoming visible to top management by the age of 30 are also important. Having family support, sound technical training and a manager early in your career who acted as role model can help set your career course. Overseas experience, experience of leadership in the armed forces and special 'off the job' management training are all useful in preparing for effective career self-management.

Characteristics of the successful 'new' employee

The textbook employees most likely to succeed are those who successfully adapt to horizontal careers and accept responsibility for managing their own career. They have a positive and cheerful attitude. They are nice people to have around. They are enthusiastic about what they do, and believe they can make a difference with their clients. They see their clients as potential allies rather than adversaries. They thrive on change and constantly look for new ways to improve their practices and challenge the *status quo*. To these self-empowered individuals, success will involve working as a team and developing broader skills rather than simply achieving conventional status. They work hard to form good relationships with a large number of people, and have a wide network of contacts throughout their organization, their industry and field of expertise.

Such new-style employees actively negotiate development opportunities as part of their recruitment package and take responsibility for their own learning. They have a clear sense of what is important to them, and indeed are likely to be identified by their employers as key contributors. They are clear about the outcomes they want to achieve, and are flexible about achieving their outcomes – they regard 'winning the war' as more important than 'winning the battle'. They have a track record of achievement, and get things done consistently, on time and within budget. They meet or exceed others' expectations of them. They have a good reputation in their firm or industry, and are known and talked about positively by people beyond their immediate circle of contacts. They take responsibility for their behaviours and their actions and do not blame others for their failure to influence.

They are assertive, standing up for their own rights and the rights of others. They are perceptive and able to 'read' people from their body language and subliminal behaviours. They are authentic, behaving in a way that is true to their own needs, beliefs and feelings, and are honest with themselves and others. They are emotionally intelligent.

Emotional intelligence

Change occurs in a context of human social interactions. It generates strong feelings. Work has also been described as 'emotional labour'. According to McBain (2000), the management of culture is the management of emotions: 'Leaders must first be able personally to identify these norms and values, and then use their emotions and those of their followers to help build and maintain a collective and meaningful identity for the organization'.

Managers have traditionally ignored or misunderstood the importance of feelings in the workplace, and business people are unused to sharing much of their private feelings and reflections with colleagues (Zohar, 1997). Being able to recognize and harness people's emotional commitment is perhaps the key to developing a high performance culture. As Mindell (1992) points out, it is imperative for successful leaders to work with the natural energy of their followers that arises from changing moods, tensions, emotions, roles and time spirits. The narrow path that the leader must follow is a path that the followers themselves create and can accept, and leaders need to realize that the energy of their followers cannot be completely controlled or predicted.

There is growing recognition that 'emotional intelligence' underpins leadership ability. Popularized by writers such as Daniel Goleman, the key ideas relating to 'emotional intelligence' (EI or EQ) revolve around self-awareness and self-control. These are very different from the application of analytical thinking skills which characterized many of the leadership development frameworks of the 1980s. Goleman (1995) suggests that emotional intelligence is nearly six times as important as IQ and technical skills in distinguishing between effective and ineffective leaders. He described leaders with lower emotional intelligence as dissonant leaders, emotionally off-key with those around them and having no sense of the pulse of their groups.

Leaders' awareness of their own emotional states, and their ability to control those emotions, can help to discount those emotions which are not relevant to a decision. They can become more aware of the moods of their followers and more accurately gauge how employees are feeling. They can repair negative states and rebuild confidence if they are able to tap into the emotional undercurrent in the workplace. Leaders need to learn more about themselves and others, and improve how they use their knowledge of themselves and their organizations.

Increasingly used as the basis of leadership development, emotional intelligence breaks down into four categories:

1. *Social awareness* – empathy, organizational awareness, service orientation
2. *Social skills* – influence, leadership, developing others, communication, change catalyst, conflict management, building bonds, teamwork and collaboration
3. *Self-management* – self-control, trustworthiness, adaptability, achievement orientation, initiative
4. *Self-awareness* – emotional self-awareness, accurate self-assessment, self-confidence.

The essence, for leaders, is being aware of their emotions as they are occurring, being emotionally literate, able to identify and discuss emotions, and able to communicate directly and clearly. It is also the ability to empathize with others and make intelligent decisions based on a healthy balance of emotion and reason. Emotionally intelligent leaders have greater self-awareness and greater empathy with others. This is key, according to Goleman, to developing trust within groups, and is a clear advantage in accomplishing the leadership task of building commitment.

Self-awareness can be raised through many development routes. Typical processes include formal or informal training, mentoring, work-shadowing, performance reviews, networking with peers from other industries, task forces, and the use of multi-rater feedback tools. Feedback processes are an effective way of helping leaders to 'walk the talk' on values. Increasingly, executives also appear to be turning to one-to-one coaching so that they confidentially explore their own development and think through their organizational strategy.

Political influencing skills

In today's organizations, just doing a good job is no longer any guarantee of success or even survival in an organizational context. A key ingredient of success is building political acumen, or developing micro-political savvy. Hard-core rationalists and idealists may wonder why they have to play political games to get what they believe in accepted. Sadly, perhaps, in an uncertain environment where clear-cut ways of getting things done are hard to find, having the ability to use political skills to get things done is a necessity.

Ask almost anyone about their experiences of organizational politics and they will have colourful stories to tell of having been the innocent victim of some malicious plot by an unscrupulous colleague or boss. 'Back-stabbing' and 'scape-goating' are typical of the phrases used to describe what happened. These incidents, even if they occurred years ago, remain vivid and often painful memories for those recounting them. To make matters worse, the link between politics and career progression in many organizations – 'climbing the greasy pole' – makes politics a dirty word to hard-core rationalists who believe in fair play, and others who feel that doing a good job should be enough to ensure career success.

Yet individuals are not the only victims of political behaviour. Roffey Park's *Management Agenda* survey findings suggest that office politics are not only rife but are also having a damaging effect on organizational performance. People report that the negative effects of politics – the lack of trust and game-playing tendencies – trigger risk-averse, compliant behaviour, and prevent employees from giving of their best. Worse still, most respondents believe that little can be done about this state of affairs since politics is part of the human condition and an integral part of organizational life, with 63 per cent of respondents acknowledging that political behaviour is needed at work just to get things done. If that is the case, does political behaviour always have to be damaging? If not, how can politics be used more constructively?

A Roffey Park research project, *Politics in Organizations* (Holbeche, 2003), looked into these issues. One area that everyone agreed on was that politics lies beyond the realm of the rational and involves the use of a range of sophisticated influencing strategies and tactics. Another area of general agreement was that politics involves self-interest. This does not mean that individual purposes must be achieved at other people's expense. What distinguished 'politics' from 'influencing' (or 'good' politics) to people in our study is the perceived motive behind the behaviour. Influencing involves achieving a win–win outcome for the individual and for the organization, while 'bad' politics usually serves only individual interests, often at the expense of other people. Thus most people in our study see themselves as influencers and other people as politicians.

Another aspect of politics is the link with power and control. In a sense, organizational politics is the stuff of power in action, beyond what happens in the formal organizational processes and structures. If conflict theorists are to be believed, organizations are made up of shifting coalitions which occasionally contend with each other for resources such as money, status and influence. As the Roffey Park study suggests, political behaviour tends to be more obvious in times of change. When the *status quo* is disturbed, some people take the opportunity to enhance their own position, often at the expense of others, while other people appear to use political behaviour to defend their 'patch'. In relatively stable times, office politics seems to be more about balance of power, resource and status issues.

In any role, but especially a functional role such as HR (which usually involves getting things done through influence rather than direct authority), 'good' politics is an essential part of making things happen, especially when the people whose support is needed have more power or status in the pecking-order. Winning support for ideas, mobilizing effort and dealing with tough issues can be very difficult for an individual whose views are easily discounted or who has few power levers to pull. HR professionals have to be willing and able to deploy a wide range of micro-political strategies and tactics that are in line with their own morality and organizational ethics if they are wish to win friends and influence people. More to the point, if they actually want to make change, HR is inevitably going to have to deal with potential opposition – so actively developing a constructive political repertoire should be seen as part of the job.

So how do you build political skills? In our study, some of the commonest tactics used by people described as effective political actors included networking, building up a support system or power base for themselves, getting others to buy into their vision, and seeding ideas at different levels in the organization simultaneously. In short, the most effective politicians developed and used their *nous* about people, the way things get done and who needs to be influenced.

The way people use micro-political strategies produced a slight, but interesting, gender skew. Men were a little more willing than women to admit to enjoying playing politics at work, yet women reported using micro-political strategies more frequently than men. Men reported more frequently than women grasping every opportunity to increase their visibility. The difference seemed to be that men were more selective about how, when and for what purpose they deployed those strategies than were women in our survey. Women were more likely to build wide networks and reported themselves as sharing information more freely than men. Men were more specific and purposeful in how they used their networks to locate sources of information, and then used that information selectively.

Amongst the commonest strategies reported by women to win influence was presenting strong arguments, ahead of adapting their behaviour to the situation/role/person involved. Men reported using these strategies in the reverse order. Women reported themselves as putting organizational interests ahead of personal goals and directing others' personal goals towards corporate goals, while men did not. Given that women tend to outnumber men in junior and middle management HR roles, these tactical differences may be significant for progression to more senior HR roles.

There are faint echoes in our study of the political behaviour differences of men and women described by Louise Barton, a city analyst who unsuccessfully brought a case of sexual discrimination against her employers on the basis that she did not earn as much as her male colleagues even though her earnings for the firm were at least as good as theirs. According to the *Evening Standard's* report of the case (2 October 2002), 'Crowing is as much part of City success as being clever, well-informed and having a great contacts book. It's something she {Barton} tells young City women to do – although there were very few in the company she worked for – especially as she thinks she's paid the priced for underselling herself'.

It would seem that for people in the research study, political behaviour can straddle the boundary between the ethical and the unethical. For our respondents this was a line most were not prepared to cross. For instance, only a few admitted using tactics such as releasing information selectively, being selectively supportive of others and manipulating people. For most of our respondents, the end would not justify the means if it meant being unscrupulous, even if they themselves could benefit by such behaviour.

Despite these reservations, most respondents recognized that political behaviour can be deployed positively to the benefit of organizations as well as individuals. One of the reasons this does not always happen is that developing the skills of positive politics is rarely taught in formal management development. People tend to learn more from observing others (usually negative role models), through bitter experience or by instinct. One person described learning positive politics by observing her own CEO:

> *She is a fantastically gifted CEO. I trust her entirely. If she happens to use these tactics to get us to the right place, well fine. She has two Board Directors who have a joint responsibility to deliver something but they had a disagreement. She could have stood there and banged the drum and said, 'You must do this' but she didn't. She set up a series of meetings and events and bits of information and you could just see it happening. The two Directors had no awareness of what was going on. She was playing them, putting two people together at the right time with the right information.*

Positive politics depends in part on having a clear agenda – a vision for change and a strategy for achieving that vision. That means individuals being clear about what they want and do not want – what they are prepared to trade off against something more desirable in the long term. The best agendas take other people's agendas into account, particularly those who are vital to success. Politics works within the informal system, and there are no route maps to what is a changing and potentially hazardous landscape. It is important to map the terrain before attempting to enter it by working out what channels of communication are the most effective ways to both hear and be heard, and then to work out the principle agents of political influence and what motivates them. What support for your ideas can you muster? How can you maximize your chances of success of your ideas being supported by blending others' needs with yours?

Networks are a vital resource, but effective micro-politicians are purposeful in figuring out whose help they might need and developing relationships with those people. Being prepared to horse-trade and co-align different interests is a way of mobilizing support. Building up your own power base and reputation – through membership of professional groups, relationships with credible people, being

Table 15.1 Reported tactics of constructive political actors

Tactics	Percentage of respondents mentioning
Establishes effective relationships	85
Understands individual agendas	85
Builds strong support for proposals	70
Creates win–win situations	66
Acts in a principled way	63
Uses face-to-face communication	60
Is well connected externally and internally	59
Builds a strong reputation	51
Treats everyone fairly	48
Exposes negative political behaviours	25

Source: Politics for the Greater Good Survey (Holbeche, 2004).

plugged in to what is happening, and being prepared to use your 'expert' status from time to time – and most of all being able to build up so-called 'referent' power where other people recommend you as a result of your excellent work, are all means of surviving and thriving in a political landscape.

In addition to networking, other constructive political strategies are presented in a table detailing the results of my survey of managers concerning perceptions of the personal characteristics of effective political actors (see Table 15.1).

These results are consistent with Bucher's emphasis on articulateness and previously described characteristics of being skilled at diagnosing situations and being willing to use that knowledge. At the same time, the reader should be cautioned that these are perceptions of characteristics, and may reflect widely held stereotypes and myths as much as any empirical reality.

Simon Baddeley and Kim James (1987) have developed a descriptive stereotypical model of political behaviour. This four-part model works on two dimensions – awareness of the political dimension in organizational life, and eagerness to play the skills required. They characterize the resulting quadrants with animal stereotypes. In the 'clever' category is the psychological games-playing, highly aware creature which reads the organization – the 'fox'. In human terms, fox-like behaviour is demonstrated through being interested in power and in associating with the locus of power. Individuals may seem unprincipled, inner-goal oriented and not ethical, and they may not display feelings spontaneously. They get support, are good at ingratiating themselves and are aware of other people's viewpoints. They can recognize and exploit key weaknesses in allies and opponents.

The caricature of game-playing tendencies married with lack of awareness is the 'donkey', or the 'inept'. In human terms, such people are not skilled inter-personally and are emotionally illiterate. They are usually unprincipled and unethical, hate to be ignored and like to associate with authority. They make judgements based on feelings rather than on knowledge of the organization's procedures or bureaucracy. In contrast, the 'sheep', representing innocence (given that they act with integrity but are politically unaware) stick to ethical, organizational and professional rules. They believe in expert and position power, and have a strong sense of loyalty. They tend to rely on authority, and do not network or know how to get support.

Finally the 'wise' owl, representing political awareness combined with acting with integrity, is interested in direction in association with power and purpose. 'Owls' can cope with being disliked, and are non-defensive. They use coalitions, and know how the formal processes work. They have a sense of loyalty, know how to make procedures work for them, and are open, sharing information. In human terms, such individuals are excellent listeners and are aware of others' viewpoints. They take account of other people personally, and recognize who knows, who cares and who can.

Writers on organizational politics agree that if managers want to get things done in their organizations, the following micro-political skills and strategies can be helpful.

1. Agenda-setting

Politically, agendas combine a vision for change with a strategy for achieving that vision. Creating and exploiting ambitious but relevant opportunities requires high degrees of self-discipline. This involves developing an understanding of how organizational structures work, having good time-management skills, nurturing flexibility, exploiting information networks, and researching and preparing moves. According to Jeffrey Pfeffer: 'Many people think of politicians as arm twisters, and that is, in part, true. But in order to be a successful arm-twister, one needs to know which arm to twist and how' (Pfeffer, 1992, in Bolman and Deal, 1997).

Writers consistently agree that effective leaders develop this agenda from a clear sense of what they want. Being clear about what you want and do not want, and what you are prepared to trade off against something more desirable in the longer term, is essential. In setting an agenda, effective micro-politicians are able to give recognition to the concerns of the major stakeholders, and often make use of 'pull' influence styles in gathering information about others' views.

2. Mapping the political terrain

Politics work within the informal system, and there are no route maps to what is a changing and potentially hazardous landscape. Pichault (1993, in Bolman and Deal, 1997) believes it is important to take four steps in establishing the political landscape before attempting to enter it:

1. Determine the channels of communication that are the most effective way to both hear and be heard. Building an information network is critical. This can occur through membership of committees, associations and key projects, and contact with key people.
2. Identify the principle agents of political influence. These may not be the most senior people, but people who are influential with them.

3. Analyse the possibilities for both internal and external mobilization. What support for your ideas can you muster? How could your idea be implemented, and what resources can help you to achieve success?
4. Anticipate the strategies others are likely to employ. Your political allies and opponents are not neutral. How can you maximize the chances of your ideas being supported by blending others' needs with yours?

3. Networking and coalition-building

A memo to your boss is sometimes an effective political strategy, but it is more often a sign of powerlessness and lack of political skill and sophistication. The political frame emphasizes that no strategy will work without a power base. Managers always face a 'power gap'; managerial jobs never come with enough power to get the work done (Kotter, 1985). Managerial work can only be done with the cooperation of other people – often large numbers of people. Moving up the ladder brings more authority, but it also brings more dependence because the manager's success depends on the effort of large and diverse groups of people, sometimes numbering in the hundreds or thousands (Kotter, 1985, 1988). Rarely will those people provide their best efforts and fullest cooperation merely because they have been told to. If you want their assistance, it helps a great deal if they know you, like you, and see you as being credible and competent.

The first task in building networks and coalitions is to figure out whose help you need. The second is to develop relationships with those people. You want them to be there when you need them. Kotter (1985) suggests four basic steps for dealing with the political dimensions in managerial work:

1. Identify the relevant relationships (work out who needs to be led)
2. Assess who might resist cooperation, why, and how strongly (working out where the leadership challenges will be)
3. Develop, wherever possible, relationships with those people to facilitate the communication, education or negotiation processes needed to deal with resistance
4. If step (3) fails, carefully select and implement more subtle or more forceful methods.

4. Build a power base

Having power is about determining events. Being powerful enables a person or organization to exert some degree of control over events and situations. The root of power is having the right 'currency' to lever that control. Leverage comes from having a form of power that the other party values. There are many sources of power. French and Raven (1959) identified the following as being of particular significance in the workplace:

- Reward power – how much you can control the behaviour of others by reward or, conversely, have to 'jump to someone else's tune'.

- Coercive power – how much you can exercise power over others by force, directly or indirectly; conversely, how much your ability to exercise force on others is withheld by, for example, a bullying boss.
- Referent power – how much your reputation speaks for you and helps you. How much are others attracted to you and identify with you? Good working relationships with peers, subordinates, subordinates of subordinates, bosses, customers and suppliers are all helpful.
- Legitimate power – how much does your role and position in the hierarchy entitle you to exercise power, or be subject to power?
- Expert power – your knowledge base. How much is your expert status a source of power because people have to come to you to gain access to that expertise? Conversely, do you lack expertise and have to go to others who may withhold their expertise, perhaps without your being aware?
- Information power – how much are you plugged in to what is happening? How good are your networks and information sources, enabling you to get ahead of the game when opportunities or threats beckon?

Other sources of power include:

- Control of resources – how much you can grant or deny people access to scarce resource, including technology.
- Connection power – how well connected you are to significant persons inside or outside the organization. A well-connected leader tends to induce compliance because others aim to gain favour or avoid the disfavour of the powerful connection.
- Physical power – how much you can exert your will by physical force
- Personal power – how much you are willing to take responsibility for your actions in any situation; knowing when to stand your ground and when to give precedence to others' needs; personal skill; an intelligent agenda for action; and a good track record.
- Political power – how plugged you are to the strategic relationships available which may cut across formal lines of authority and be a means of tapping into someone else's positional power.
- Professional power – how connected you are to a professional group which spans organizations; resource networks.

According to John Kotter (1977), managers who are successful at acquiring and using power are sensitive to what others consider legitimate behaviour in acquiring and using it. They have a good intuitive understanding of various types of power and methods of influence.

5. Become more visible

- Develop a positive image
- Be present and contribute at key meetings
- Publicize achievements.

6. Bargaining and negotiation

'Horse-trading' and co-aligning different interests present the challenge to many managers of 'how do I do this in an ethical way?' Fisher and Ury (1991) developed an approach to negotiation based around a principled search for an agreement beneficial to all parties. Their 'principled negotiation' model reflects four rules:

1. Separate the people from the problem
2. Focus on interests, not positions
3. Search together for creative options
4. Establish objective criteria for the solutions.

7. Idea-selling

Kanter (1983) found that middle managers seeking to promote change or innovation in a corporation typically began by getting preliminary agreement for an initiative from their boss. They then moved into a phase of 'pre-selling' or 'making cheerleaders':

> *Peers, managers of related functions, stakeholders in the issue, potential collaborators, and sometimes even customers would be approached individually, in one-on-one meetings that gave people a chance to influence the project and the innovator the maximum opportunity to sell it. Seeing them alone and on their territory was important: the rule was to act as if each person were the most important one for the project's success.*

Once you have cheerleaders, you can move on to 'horse trading' – that is, promising rewards in exchange for resources and support. This builds the resource base that lets you go to the next step of 'securing blessings' – getting the necessary approvals and mandates from higher management (Kanter, 1983). Kanter found that the usual route to success at that stage was to identify the senior managers who had the most to say about the issue at hand, and develop a polished, formal presentation to get their support. The best presentations responded to both substantive and political concerns, because senior managers typically cared about two questions:

1. Is it a good idea?
2. How will my constituents react to it?

Once innovators got the blessing of higher management, they could go back to their boss to formalize the coalition and make specific plans for pursuing the project (Kanter, 1983).

The basic point is simple: as a manager, you need friends and allies to get things done. If you are trying to build relationships and get support from those friends and allies, you need to cultivate them. Like it or not, however, political dynamics are inevitable under conditions of ambiguity, diversity and scarcity (Bolman and Deal, 1997).

Opportunities for growth

Of course, while someone with high levels of such skills is likely to be valued by their current employer, the skills themselves are all highly transferable and make an employee very employable, potentially elsewhere. This begs the question of how much organizations should do to enable people to develop these skills. Organizations may be caught on the horns of a dilemma of their own making. They may not be able to attract truly employable people without offering a development package, yet retaining such people may be difficult since they will owe little allegiance to the employer – especially if the transaction (i.e. opportunities to build skills and experience) breaks down. Applying the 'manage your own career' message to talented individuals the organization wants to retain may be unwise, especially if they are open to staying and building a relationship.

Training for internal employability

Training and development deliberately geared to enhancing internal employability may be a better option.

My proposition is that employees are more likely to stay with an organization where they feel appreciated and where development is taken seriously than in one where development is purely the responsibility of the employee. It would seem that many organizations are directly benefiting from sponsoring people to acquire qualifications, for instance. Not only do employees tend to stay with their employer for at least the time needed to complete the qualification, but the increasingly vocational nature of many qualification programmes, with project work based on the employing organization, should also bring immediate returns on the investment made.

Providing training in the new skills needed, such as training managers to become better coaches and developers of others, should be a vital part of an organizational development strategy. It would seem that organizations that have achieved Investors in People (IIP) status often do better than other organizations on this front. To motivate and retain key employees, organizations must show them that they can realize their ambitions inside, as well as outside, the company.

How can organizations develop talent?

Hall and Moss (1998) argue that the organizational side of the career partnership should take the form of brokering, creating learning opportunities, facilitating lateral moves and enabling employees to build interesting jobs. Here are some of the ways in which a focus group of managers described the ways they attempt to develop others:

1. *By providing stretch/challenge.* This may take the form of continuous management development, challenging jobs, variety, objectives that seem just

about feasible rather than impossible, and not having quite enough resources to do the job but being called upon to use initiative, with senior management being aware of the outcomes.

2. *By giving responsibility.* This may include identifying opportunities for each team member to grow on the job, having a specific area of responsibility that causes the person to look beyond the boundaries of his or her job, and empowering people to make decisions and use their own judgement.

3. *Through job moves.* Typical mechanisms include job shadowing; sabbaticals; conferences; expanded opportunities; new assignments.

4. *Through cross-functional working.* This may include encouraging people to take part in cross-functional project working, providing briefings for other teams about the work of their own team, having a greater variety of support/technical/specialist roles for people to choose from, and being 'less status-oriented'.

5. *By taking people out of their comfort zone.* This may be through wider networking, speaking at conferences on the company's behalf, representing the company at a trade delegations etc., and giving managers training in how to have 'tough conversations'.

6. *By providing mentors.* Frequent conversations where people can talk in depth about their career, aspirations and work are key elements of helping people to grow their talents. The City of Westminster Council, for example, provides managers and new recruits with mentors from outside their own function.

7. *Through having a good manager.* Good performance management with regular feedback, together with coaching and longer-term developmental mentoring, is critical. A Personal Development Planning process can help. Encouragement to study and support from colleagues can stop people from losing interest in their role.

8. *Through having greater flexibility.* Many employees want greater flexibility; most want the chance of a better work–life balance and more reasonable workloads. More flexible pay structures can enable individual choice. Positive organizational factors reported by *Management Agenda* respondents who believe that flexibility exists in their organization include the variety of roles available, sufficiently generic roles meaning that leadership can be achieved no matter what role you are employed in, a wide range of roles being available at the same level, and less hierarchy.

9. *Transparent processes.* Employees still want to have a sense of future directions, in terms of both organizational strategy and career paths, so that they can better develop their career to their satisfaction. Though Hall says that career planning does not really fit the new career paradigm but job planning does, in practice our research suggests that people do want to know what routes are available to them so that they can start to navigate their way through the career jungle (Hall and Moss, 1998).

Various kinds of feedback process, including 360 degree, are now widely used for development purposes and to ensure that managers know what is expected of them. These are most effective when used in combination with development coaching. Other processes include open appointment systems, encouragement to staff and managers to have a personal development plan and move across functions, and recognition of the worth of lateral moves.

In many ways, participants in the focus groups conform to the 'self-starter' image, and have developed as a result of a wide range of experiences. However, the importance of having support and recognition from an effective line manager, mentor or management in general comes through. This seems to be all the more important in the cases where people feel that aspects of the organization's culture, such as rivalry among peers or micro-politics, prevent people from advancing in the way they would like.

Developing high flyers

In a study exploring high flyers and the changing nature of succession planning (Holbeche, 1998), I looked at what appear to be helpful or hindering factors in high-flyer development. The sample consisted of 400 people from different sectors who were described as high flyers in their organizations. On the whole, the younger group (aged 25–29 years) in the study saw fewer obstacles to their development. This might be explained by the fact that most people in this group are on fast-track development programmes, claim to have supportive managers and may not as yet have had to overcome many setbacks.

However, nearly half of the entire group (49 per cent) said that something or someone had got in the way of their development, more so amongst people aged between 35 and 39 years. This was particularly the case in the public sector group. Women were proportionately slightly more likely than men to say that someone or something had hindered their development.

Blocks to development

Some of the main factors considered to be unhelpful to development relate to people. The biggest obstacle to development and the greatest source of frustration, especially for women respondents, appears to be unhelpful management. Twenty per cent of the group, especially those in the 40–44 age group, said that specific individuals had hindered their development. This reflects findings from research carried out by Lewis (1994), which suggests that women encounter more difficulties with their superiors than do men. A key issue here is the role played by organizational politics – 17 per cent of women and 6 per cent of men claimed that politics had worked against them.

The other factors relate to luck and circumstances. A small number of respondents talked about being held back by their own shortcomings, by ageism, the cost-cutting economic climate and by business tensions. Fourteen per cent said that they had not had the opportunity to develop. This was particularly the case with men, especially those working in the manufacturing sector, which generally underwent widespread downsizing over the last decade. Fourteen per cent also blamed 'culture', which included discrimination on the grounds of gender, and 23 per cent of women and 9 per cent of men considered their organization's culture to have had a negative effect on their development. This was particularly the case in the public sector organizations in the survey.

Eleven per cent also stated that physical constraints of time, resources and location had been inhibitors. Typically, being unwilling to relocate, work weekends or undertake extensive overseas assignments seem still to be considered proof of a lack of commitment, even though organizational value statements suggest that individuals are valued and encouraged to have a good work–home life balance.

Helpful factors in high flyer development

Respondents were asked if anyone or anything had helped them to develop within their current organization. Most (77 per cent) acknowledged this to be the case, though people over 50 years old were noticeably more likely to say that they had received no help from others and that their success was 'self-made'. These made up most of the 7 per cent who claimed that the biggest help to their development was 'myself'.

Of the 'helpful' factors, most appear to be about people. The biggest factor appears to be supportive management, especially 25–29-year-olds. This appears to be linked to the attention paid to groups of people on high-flyer development programmes, through which participants are generally exposed to a wider group of senior management, and where any project work undertaken by programme participants is taken seriously.

Almost a third (30 per cent) said that supportive colleagues had helped them. This was particularly the case with people in the 40–44 age band, especially those in the public services/government sector. We found numerous instances of well-established networks of individuals who developed collegial relationships, despite individual differences and rivalries, in the face of common organizational challenges. One example was a group of senior civil servants who were now required to have a more 'hands on' people management role in addition to policy work. They developed self-help networks following training in leadership and continue to support each other in developing skills in their new areas of responsibility.

Over a quarter of the group acknowledged help from a mentor, especially people in the 35–39 age band. Twenty per cent said that recognition by their line manager had been helpful to their development. This was especially the case with those aged 25–29, who appreciated the value of coaching and feedback in accelerating their ability to perform effectively. Women were slightly more likely than men to talk of having a helpful line manager.

Interestingly, the main ways in which our respondents felt they had been most helped to develop related to contact with people who were really interested in the high flyer's development. By contrast, many of the conventional ways in which people are thought to develop, such as through having a clear career structure, carrying out an international assignment, managing a special project or managing a team, appear to be considered less important.

How do high flyers learn best?

Respondents were asked what their greatest learning experience had been. This produced a wide-ranging response. For the majority of high flyers in our survey, the main sources of development appear to be being given a major challenge and the opportunity to study, particularly to do an MBA. Interestingly, learning from other people such as mentors or supportive bosses hardly featured in this section.

'In at the deep end'

The biggest factor (14 per cent), especially in manufacturing type organizations and the financial services, appears to be 'being thrown in at the deep end', although in the public sector group the main response was 'achieving against all the difficulties'. This is hardly surprising, given that high-flying individuals are thought to have a strong need to achieve. Seven per cent said 'achieving against all difficulties', and 9 per cent said special projects. This also applied to unexpected promotions.

This 'macho' drive to take on major challenges appears strongest in the 25–29 age group, when people are attempting to prove their worth, and in our sample the group considering 'achieving against all difficulties' as their biggest learning experience appear to be aged 35–39. However, a key issue is whether the individual's efforts are noticed. Lack of recognition of a major achievement is disheartening for anyone, but appears to be particularly damaging to a high flyer.

Studying/training

The broadening effect of studying, especially doing an MBA, comes next, with 12 per cent suggesting that they believed that they were operating at a higher (intellectual) level on completing their course. Several people commented that doing an Open University degree or a PhD had been major learning experiences. Training (7 per cent) as a whole is seen as less significant, except in the public sector, where it appears to be valued rather more. Specific forms of training do, however, appear to be formative:

- 'training as a paratrooper with the TA'
- 'learning to fly aeroplanes'
- 'being in the Royal Navy'
- 'studying stress management'.

We asked respondents who had obtained further qualifications (58 per cent of the total) if their company had supported them to do this. A significant majority (92 per cent) said that they did receive support. This was primarily (86 per cent) in the form of financial sponsorship, and two-thirds also obtained time off for study. Few people reported receiving support or encouragement from their boss or an internal mentor. Other support included job placements and the provision of an external mentor. Only 8 per cent believed that they did not receive any form of support, whether in terms of finance, time off to study or simply encouragement. For all the people who took qualifications, the biggest obstacles appear to be lack of time to study and a sense that the learning was not valued by their employer since it was usually not directly used in the business. What therefore appears to be particularly valued is the combination of time to study, financial support, moral support from the boss, recognition of achievement and the chance to apply the learning.

Qualifications are increasingly required or valued in many walks of life, but it seems that the main motivation for doing an MBA is to be more effective in the current role, rather than to obtain promotion elsewhere as is commonly assumed. Organizations can benefit from sponsoring people to do a qualification in a number of ways. Not only are they likely to retain the person while he or she is studying, but the programme studies should also ideally be relevant to the workplace. However, one of the commonest complaints made by the high flyers who had taken their MBA was that their organization did not specifically use the enhanced skills and knowledge arising from the studies. The challenge for organizations is to provide the level of support required, typically through the provision of an interested and credible mentor, and to ensure that the benefits of work-based assignments are reaped.

Learning to deal with politics

Dealing with organizational life is also seen as a learning experience by many. Ten per cent of respondents said that dealing with organizational politics had taught them a great deal (12 per cent of women and 9 per cent of men). It seems that it is thought important to become effective politically from the earliest part of a career, since 17 per cent of people aged between 25 and 29 in our survey saw this as their biggest learning experience. Comments included:

- 'learning to protect my back'
- 'learning to temper my enthusiasm'
- 'shouting doesn't get things done'
- 'learning to stand alone and who to trust'
- 'finding out that not everybody is as committed as me'.

Dealing with people

Dealing with people is an important learning experience. For a few of the older people in our survey, acting as a mentor was a major learning experience for them, as much as for the 'mentees'. Ten per cent found most learning from managing a team, less so in government departments. This appears proportionately a bigger learning experience for men (13 per cent) than women (4 per cent), and for 18 per cent of people aged between 35–39. Comments included:

- 'managing a big and then a small team'
- 'problem-solving'
- 'learning about the fragility of motivation'

- 'meeting members and dealing with their questions'
- 'working with different people as a consultant'.

Doing the job

Just getting on with the job and gaining practical experience was seen as developmental by many respondents. To a lesser extent, people derive learning from dealing with structural change and the challenges of their current job. Comments included:

- 'changing into a commercial organization'
- 'working in a multicultural environment'
- 'managing corporate change'
- 'becoming independent due to a change in funding'.

Learning about yourself

Some learning experiences appear to relate to simply 'growing up' in organizational terms, coming to terms with reality and acquiring greater self-knowledge. Women appear more likely than men to consider these as learning experiences, and the younger age group (25–29) in particular appears to have taken the 'career self-management' messages to heart:

- 'realizing that the individual is responsible for one's own growth'
- 'I recognize that it is my responsibility to learn new skills'
- 'I have learned about myself ... and I like who I am'
- 'I have learned to be myself, not to pretend to be something else'
- 'learning to rely on my own decisions'
- 'becoming confident in my own ability'
- 'learning to adapt to the world'
- 'learning to be patient'.

Risk-taking

Other comments regarding learning experiences involved the invigorating effect of changing personal direction and risk-taking:

- 'changing jobs after ten years with the company'
- 'starting a company which I don't own'
- 'starting up a business'
- 'starting a completely new job'
- 'voluntary work'
- 'moving into a project environment'
- 'taking a completely new job'
- 'going from a specialist to a generalist role'
- 'going from university to the workplace'
- 'being in the police force before the law'
- 'having a career as a competitive swimmer'.

Learning from hardships

Learning from adversity is important:

- 'taking the wrong job and getting through it'
- 'job rejections'
- 'learning how difficult it is to teach others'
- 'watching the rise and fall of others'
- 'learning from mistakes'
- 'redundancy'
- 'dealing with the City'
- 'getting my fingers burnt'
- 'six months in prison in the Yemen'.

International experience

Eleven per cent of respondents said that life experience or travel had broadened their minds, proportionately more from manufacturing type organizations, with 7 per cent having learned a great deal from an international assignment:

- 'moving to the UK from the USA'
- 'doing my MBA in the USA'
- 'travelling through West Asia for six months'
- 'travel after university'.

Family/life experiences

Family and personal reasons and just day-to-day living are considered growth experiences, especially by people in their 30s. Women are proportionately more likely to consider these as learning experiences than men. Verbatim comments included:

- 'being part of a family'
- 'having children'
- 'motherhood'
- 'marriage'
- 'sister dying from cancer'
- 'my father'
- 'coping with extreme stress and its effects'
- 'learning to cope with change'
- 'having flexibility between work and parenthood'.

Above all, having the opportunity to achieve and the chance to prove something to oneself and others stands out as critical to high-flyer development. Development processes that provide people with increased challenge, personal growth and the opportunity to really achieve do seem to motivate people and increase their commitment to the organization, for a time at least.

Fast-tracking

Organizations are interested in graduates and high flyers again. They are typically bringing back fast-track schemes which maintain or reintroduce conventional forms of career management. However, these may also do more harm than good, since they reinforce stereotypical expectations about rapid advancement for members of an elite group. Although people still aspire to onwards and upwards, they are frequently not prepared to make the longer-term commitment to the organization that such schemes often require. Where fast-track schemes exist they are often subject to a high 'churn' rate.

Increasingly, organizations are recognizing that potential for top jobs may exist among current, mature employees, who may not have been classified as high flyers when they first joined their organizations.

Senior managers in particular need to take an active lead in developing new career processes, looking for talented people of whatever age, wherever they are based in their organization. They should have a vested interest in doing this; after all, these people may be their future successors. Keeping people moving around the organization should create both vertical and horizontal openings. That way, individuals with potential to reach the top can develop the core skills, flexibility and breadth of experience relevant to the organization. Horizontal moves will keep employees learning and interested even when there are no openings for them at higher levels.

Building the 'pool'

Fast-tracking, then, should become almost a state of mind as well as a development route. The 'fast' element should include opportunities to acquire the skills and experience needed by the organization in the short and medium term. One UK financial services organization has introduced a three-year structured development programme for a large group of existing and new employees of different levels and ages. The short-term payback to the organization is high morale amongst programme participants, and widely applied learning. An international bank is introducing fast-tracking to accelerate the development of an international management cadre. HR staff are aware of the danger of setting up an elite, and work is underway to develop career tracks for employees at all levels.

All fast-track processes need managing, and individuals on such tracks need ongoing monitoring and support to ensure that they are delivering what was intended and are able to make the progress implied. Some organizations make extensive use of mentors for this purpose. Fast tracks can happily coexist alongside other development routes, but any organization that ignores the need for some form of development for the bulk of its workforce may be doing itself a disservice.

The HR role in development

HR should aim to move in the direction of building internal talent, and deploying it well, rather than relying on contingency approaches. Rather than fighting against a rising tide of employee mobility, HR can help by developing relationships and joint ventures with various parties involved in development. These include employable workers themselves, their managers, suppliers of training solutions, consultants and employment agencies. A key challenge for HRM will be to seize the opportunity to transfer the valuable skills and learning of incoming employees so that they become part of the organization's culture and strategy. In particular, HR can work with line managers to help them identify development solutions, prepare practical and relevant development processes that managers can use with their teams, and train managers as coaches. They can assist in ensuring that the value of 'off-the-job' training and development is transferred to the workplace by helping line managers to follow through and evaluate improved effectiveness.

HR policies, especially with regard to work–life balance, can make a positive difference. HR professionals can train managers in how to support employee work–life balance, and in how to recognize and reward people who perform effectively and manage to achieve balance. While few organizations can guarantee job security, HR professionals can provide training and development geared to internal employability. They can encourage the adoption of 'new' career practices, such as continuous management development, sabbaticals, wider networking and open appointment systems. They can facilitate cross-organizational career moves and reward people who make lateral job moves. They can design more flexible pay structures and a greater variety of roles through which people can gain leadership experience and the chance for learning and growth.

HR can also design a wide range of flexible working options to suit employee and organizational needs, helping line managers to communicate effectively and get the best out of a more flexible workforce. Employers are likely to have to develop 'revolving door' policies for departing employees whose skills are in demand. They will have to be prepared to negotiate appropriate deals to attract talent back into the organization, which may be more expensive than having good development possibilities in place to start with.

Conclusion

When the psychological contract is weak, the cost to the organization is felt when it becomes difficult to recruit and retain key people. This is forcing organizations to develop new and more meaningful relationships with such employees if they are to reap the benefit of their talent. Becoming a great place to work is about developing a new 'employee deal' which responds to employee needs for work–life balance, development and career growth. In conjunction with a good workplace climate, this deal is likely to go some way towards repairing damaged trust and forming the basis of employee commitment and retention.

The relative advantages of the new deal are still unclear, but, for the time being, employers appear to be benefiting from employees' willingness to adapt to new ways of working. The message about employability seems to be firmly established, and some groups appear better placed to survive and thrive in today's more flexible workplace. While the more employable people may be those who have the eminently transferable skills, it would seem that active organizational partnership, in the form of training and other development opportunities, is a real retention factor for the most highly skilled employees. Investing in development therefore makes sense for an organization wishing to build an active partnership with its employees.

16

Becoming a values-based organization

How can an enterprise build capabilities, forge empowered teams, develop a deep understanding of customers, and – most importantly – create a sense of community and common purpose unless it has a relationship with its employees based on mutual trust and caring?

(Robert Waterman, 1995)

Introduction

Why do highly talented people choose to come to work and give of their best? For many, the reasons go far beyond financial necessity. It is through work and their experience of the workplace that many employees attempt to meet their 'psychological', emotional, social, creative and personal achievement needs. Some would go further, arguing that work fulfils a greater role, connecting people through affiliation and purpose to sources of meaning that might be described as 'spiritual'.

In earlier chapters we have seen that people's expectations about the extent to which they can rely on others, especially their employer, to protect their interests, have been reduced. So, for example, there is now widespread recognition that people will need to continue to learn and develop throughout their lives and that they are responsible for managing their own careers. We have looked at what organizations can do to enable employees to meet some of their psychosocial, creative and personal achievement needs in the workplace. Employers are recognizing that employees have a life outside work and they take the balance issue seriously – even though the successful examples of good practice may be few and far between. They are providing training and development in areas where both employees and employers can benefit.

We have looked at some of the other ways in which organizations are attempting to build a new psychological contract with employees, based on mutual commitment and enrichment. For example, in some businesses leaders are helping their organizations to become change-able by getting better at encouraging innovation and knowledge-sharing. They are handling change in ways that involve employees, and helping them to regain a sense of control over their own destiny. The basis of trust is the honouring of promises, both explicit and implicit. By matching organizational and individual needs, they are attempting to rebuild trust and commitment.

However, there are still other aspects of the 'deal' which we have not yet explored, which seem to be at the heart of the new psychological contract and can lead to a new basis for trust between employers and employees. Increasingly, employees are stating that they want to work for a values-based organization, one whose core purpose and products are at least not harmful and at best fundamentally worthwhile. They are also saying that they want their experience of work to be meaningful.

In this chapter we shall look at how organizations can operate effectively from a values base, and at what can make employees' experience of work meaningful, such that talented individuals willingly choose to give of their best. We will explore how employees pursue their quest for meaning through work, and look at whether organizations have a responsibility to respond to even deeper individual and community needs. We shall consider if and how the quest for meaning forms part of the 'psychological contract' – the unwritten set of mutual expectations between employers and employees. In other words, is it appropriate for employers to attempt to satisfy employee needs for greater meaning, and if so, how might they go about doing this?

Why values matter

Work represents the dynamic intersection between social, business and an individual's personal needs and values. Most people have personal values, even if they never consciously think about them. They only become aware of their values when they feel discomfort or, worse, when they are placed in a position of contravening their own values. All organizations have values, or beliefs which they hold dear, whether or not these values are socially acceptable or evident in written statements. A typical smattering of value statements would include the words 'teamwork', 'integrity', 'customers', 'community', 'passion', and 'innovation'.

Employees understand what is real about these values, not so much from what is written but from what is put into practice. For example, if an organization claims to value its customers but in practice condones poor customer service, employees are more likely to believe what they experience rather than the words. Of course, no gap between espoused and actual values is the ideal, though many organizations claim that their values are aspirational and intended to encourage preferred behaviour. However, if the gaps between the 'walk' and the 'talk' are large, employees are unlikely to trust their organization to look after their interests, or be willing to commit to it emotionally.

Ideally, of course, employees are 'attuned' to their organization's values. For organizational values to truly have a deep impact on behaviour, according to Collins and Porras (1994), they must reflect the inner needs, beliefs and aspirations of employees. However, if individuals' values are very different from those of their organization, they are unlikely to stay long. If the match between individuals' values and those of their organization changes over time, especially if the organization changes direction, employees can feel betrayed and become cynical about change.

Rhetoric versus reality

Typically, a mismatch of values with actual practice can take place at a number of levels:

- Strategy and corporate values – companies continue to deal with 'rogue states' or pressurize suppliers despite the rhetoric of values
- Policy and practice – diversity, flexible working and corporate social responsibility typically are implemented only to a level that is expedient
- Brand image – often at odds with workplace practice and customer experience
- Personal values – do not chime with organizational values
- Role – top managers do not act as leaders
- Behavioural – managers at all levels do not practise values
- Procedural – people can still be rewarded with promotion despite not practising values.

In the 2003 *Management Agenda*, 80 per cent of organizations are reported as have a published set of values. According to Collins and Porras (1994), for values truly to have impact they must reflect the inner needs, beliefs and aspirations of employees. However, in the Roffey Park survey 49 per cent of respondents felt that these values did not reflect the actual values of management, and wanted managers to 'walk the talk'. Similarly, in the 2004 survey 88 per cent of organizations were reported to have value statements, yet 52 per cent of respondents were sceptical about them. They reported:

- Failure to follow though on policies such as diversity, work–life balance etc.
- Concern about practices that appear unfair
- High levels of political activity
- Barriers to progression into senior management – women (39 per cent), ethnic minorities (34 per cent)
- Corporate Social Responsibility (CSR) statements as 'window dressing'.

As one participant put it, 'Values are seen as the organization trying to be politically correct'. The values 'gap' was evident in the following comments, which are representative of many others:

- As a public sector organization we espouse values related to improving the quality of life. It may well be that the people who work for us do so because, even if not overtly, they share those values. As such, there is not an obvious search for greater meaning at work, indeed there are times when I would hope for greater 'buy-in' to the organization values. As a specific instance to refer to, there is a partnership with a local clergyman who acts as a notional industrial chaplain who visits once a month to be available to staff on a confidential 'listening' ear on matters secular as well as spiritual. So far he has very, very few customers!

- Performance management driven by political priorities has resulted in cynicism at the loss of integrity.
- The County Council has in the last year created an excellent, thought-provoking, list of 'values'. All make good sense. The staff are encouraged to practise those values but in reality they may be easily compromised when other pressures are exerted.
- ... being underfunded/decreasing support whilst world attention is drawn elsewhere.
- Adoption of new values has been enthusiastic by some {but there is} cynicism by others who claim to have their own values.

When respondents were asked what would need to change to remove discrepancies between espoused and practised values, the majority (68 per cent) suggested that all managers should model organizational values. They described the ideal as being when values were identified, relevant to stakeholders, known, talked about, shared, grounded, communicated, checked, debated, reviewed, 'held by cleaners', embraced, celebrated and implemented.

They felt that to make this happen managers would need strong encouragement to 'walk the talk'. First, this would involve setting the appetite; their behaviour should then be monitored; then they should be rewarded or 'addressed' by their peers if they failed to live the values. Culture change (58 per cent) was also considered important, along with making the organizational values realistic in the first place.

In practice, disenchantment with the workplace is evident in this research, especially since many people work long hours and feel under heavy workload pressure. Many people (39 per cent) experience tensions between the spiritual side of their own values and those of their organization. In our survey, women (44 per cent) were more likely to report that they experience these tensions than men (35 per cent). For many *Management Agenda* respondents, finding a values 'fit' is sufficiently important that they are considering leaving their current employer to find a better fit elsewhere.

Employee cynicism

In previous chapters we have explored how the search for success and the way change is managed can often end up, perversely, destroying the foundations of future success. This occurs when change undermines the psychological contract, leading to loss of trust and employee commitment. Many senior managers argue that this is a price worth paying, since business pressures require speedy and sometimes draconian actions in order to ensure business survival.

Typical components of employee cynicism include the following (Dean and Cassidy, 1990):

- *A belief that their organization lacks integrity.* We have seen how loss of public confidence in formerly respected institutions, and the economic uncertainties of the future, create a difficult backdrop for positive organizational change. For organizations in every sector, being ethical and trustworthy is becoming a cornerstone of sustainable business success.
- *Negative affective attitudes and emotions towards the organization.* This is evident in frustration, contempt for managers, hopelessness and disillusionment.
- *A tendency for employees, consistent with their beliefs and emotions, towards disparaging and critical behaviours of their organization.* The targets of such cynicism are usually senior managers, the organization in general, and corporate policies and programmes.

An arid platform for high performance

Most organizations have the bold statement 'our people are our greatest asset' somewhere in their company rhetoric. In practice, instead of valuing employees and building new, more constructive psychological contracts, many organizations are actually going in the opposite direction – whether they have been affected by economic downturn or not. Shutdowns, downsizing, cost-cutting, headcount reduction and slashed training programmes are the order of the day. In the search for organizational flexibility, people become dispensable, with job security becoming an issue again in many sectors. The greater emphasis on performance, pressures on employees to work long hours, the focus on outputs and inputs, lack of management vision and lack of consultation add up to quite a bleak picture.

This cocktail of ingredients conjures up an image of a working climate that is psychologically, if not physically, reminiscent of a Dickensian sweatshop in some organizations. Organizational politics and lack of trust simply add to the problem, causing people to focus on watching their backs rather than going the extra mile for the customer. People claim that they simply don't have time to be creative, to share knowledge and all the other things that organizations say they want, and that employees want too. The endless emphasis on doing more with less ends up becoming a zero sum game, particularly when employee cynicism rises.

The drive for ever-higher performance can also adversely affect employee retention and innovation. We have seen that an organization's future business success depends to a large extent on its ability to innovate and maximize its intellectual capital. This ability is essentially based on employees' willingness to deploy their creativity on behalf of the organization. In turn, this willingness depends on how employees feel about their organization, which is generally reflected in the health of the psychological contract and is measured by instruments gauging levels of employee 'engagement'.

The danger of employee cynicism

The more employees develop an attitude of cynicism and futility towards change, together with a negative attitude towards change agents, the less likely they are to show motivation, job satisfaction and commitment. As Reichers and Wanous (1997) observe, there is something of a self-fulfilling prophecy at work in this, and, importantly, employee cynicism affects most seriously an organization's ability to be flexible and change-able. As Pate *et al.* (2000) suggest: 'when organizations are trying to secure important organizational changes, low trust relations and high degrees of cynicism may combine to significantly limit the degree of change that can be achieved'. For these authors, this downward loop helps explain why the organizations that have the greatest incentive to change, particularly following threats of downsizing or closure, often lack the ability to do so.

How success can breed failure

Employees like to feel part of a successful organization. Many are proud to be associated with a famous or well-reputed brand name. This becomes a source of concern when the image of the organization becomes tainted by scandal or failure. The decline and fall of many proud and successful companies is often ascribed in part to the challenge of complacency at best, and arrogance and dishonesty at worst. Many studies, from Peters and Waterman's (1982) review of the 'Excellent' companies of the 1980s, showing how many had slipped from their pedestals, to more recent reviews of the sharp decline in fortunes of major corporations such as Worldcom, Marconi, Adelphi, the cable giant, and Enron have suggested that success can in due course become the source of failure.

It is often when companies are at their most successful that cultural values can be ignored or perverted. Similarly, when a leader becomes synonymous with the company, things can become unhealthy if that leader becomes so sure of his or her instincts that he or she fails to listen to the staff at the 'coalface'.

Simpson (2002) suggests that triumph can lead to hubris when large stock options and dubious diversifications fatally weaken a company's culture. If executives are given the kind of stock options where share prices are key, they will inevitably be driven by the short term, not the long term. Described by Simpson as 'Victory Disease', one of the symptoms is where executives become obsessed with perks and get isolated from the market, leading to poor decision-making.

The quest for meaning

Work takes place in a broader social context. Our turbulent world and our greater awareness of it has had the effect of challenging many people at a deeper personal level.

It would seem that many individuals are now actively looking for more meaning in their lives. Evidence for this can be found in Roffey Park's annual *Management Agenda* survey. In the 2003 survey, 47 per cent of all respondents reported that they were looking for more meaning in their lives, with 82 per cent of 20–30-year-olds in our sample apparently looking for more meaning in their lives. In 2004, 70 per cent of employees of all ages reported that they were looking for more meaning at work.

We were curious to know whether these individuals were responding to the *Zeitgeist* at the turn of the new millennium, or whether there was something more profound going on. We also wondered, if there was evidence of a shift in employee needs for meaning in the workplace, how organizations and their leaders could or should respond. We decided to investigate the issues further, using our existing research vehicle, the *Management Agenda*, and other methods. We called the study 'The Quest for Meaning at Work' (QMW).

Why the growing interest in meaning?

Various possible explanations for the growing interest in meaning are suggested:

- People generally spend longer at work than on other parts of their lives
- Change and the 'dog-eat-dog' ethic in many workplaces are making relationships more transactional and mistrustful, and consequently people are feeling less 'connected'
- Reported higher levels of employee cynicism over a range of issues, including 'hollow' ethical policies such as diversity and corporate social responsibility, 'fat cat' pay issues and accountancy scandals, cause people to doubt the purpose of their organization and the integrity of leaders
- Community as a whole has undergone a moral/values transformation in recent decades to a more commercial, secular society
- The plethora of 'alternative' therapies and self-help groups suggests that many people are experiencing a lack of community spirituality – they want to fill a 'God-shaped' hole
- Society in general and employees in particular are becoming increasingly distrustful of people in authority, especially leaders.

Konz and Ryan (1999) suggest that individuals are searching for meaning in their work – a meaning that transcends mere economic gain. Much of the available recent literature on the subject appears to come from the USA. It suggests that many people feel a lack of meaning in their work, and that this is prompting a quest to discover a higher sense of purpose in life. According to Cavanagh (1999), there are three major new causes for this:

1. The mid-life crises of the idealistic baby boomers
2. Downsizing and additional work hours
3. Landmark events such as the year 2000, birthdays etc.

The last decade has seen widespread socio-economic and political change on a global scale. As ideologically opposed power balances have shifted after the collapse of the Soviet Union, the role of capitalism has been put under the spotlight. Environmental issues have been a source of major international debate, largely sparked by a series of environmental disasters during the 1990s, such as the after-effects of Chernobyl, the chemical pollution at Bhopal, and oil spillages off the coasts of Canada and Europe, for which corporations refused to accept responsibility. Similarly, the proposed sinking of the Brent Spar oil platform by Shell, which was opposed by Greenpeace on the grounds that it could cause environmental damage, became a *cause célèbre* in stimulating debate about corporate social responsibility. The refusal of the US government to sign the Kyoto Accord seemed yet another sign of the rights of corporations and particular nations being placed ahead of the collective good.

Ethics, too, has become the focus of attention as a series of scandals have rocked the financial world. In a few cases, business leaders of major corporations have been found to have done deals with terrorist groups and despotic governments in return for business advantage, or, like Robert Maxwell, have used pension funds inappropriately and deprived former employees of their rightful income. Accountancy practices have been brought into disrepute in the Enron, Worldcom and other scandals, and the role of executives as ethical leaders has come to the fore.

Tischler (1999) uses Maslow's hierarchy of needs (1968) to explain the growing interest in spirituality as a theory of social consciousness and motivation. Maslow's theory suggests that there are five basic levels of need in this hierarchy: physical or survival needs, security needs, social needs, achievement needs and self-actualization needs. Tischler argues that over the past 200 years there has been an evolution from an agrarian society of little change for the majority of people through an industrial society that, through a machine orientation, has created:

- Comparatively enormous wealth for most people in developed countries
- A mass society with attendant changes in social structure and social consciousness
- An unimaginably faster and increasing pace of change.

We are now in a post-industrial society that focuses on individual achievement and self-actualization growth for as many people as possible in a socially, economically and environmentally sustainable and responsible manner. As knowledge has become an increasingly important competitive factor, companies have increasingly to offer their educated employees many new kinds of opportunities and benefits. As workers decreasingly look to outer situations, people and their structures to motivate their behaviour and impact their feeling and thinking, they look ever more inward for direction, esteem and the creation of their own happiness.

Similarly, in the Roffey Park study we found that the search for meaning, although a perennial issue, has been brought into high relief by wider economic and political instability. It has also been strengthened by disenchantment at work. People are working long hours, and the boundaries between work and non-work are blurred (anyone with a mobile phone becomes contactable at all times). As a result, people who might have become involved in their local community – by running a scout group, for example – now don't. Work becomes the focus around which the rest of life revolves. Within the workplace, relationships at work have become more transactional, characterized by mutual suspicion and lack of trust. People feel increasingly 'disconnected'. People are sensing a void, wanting some 'space' where they can 'be' rather than 'do' all the time.

Webster (2002) argues that work can be part of the problem that people look to spirituality to overcome. Work can be insecure and oppressive; it can seem purposeless and meaningless – or, worse, it can make us feel part of unjust, oppressive systems. Work can isolate us and leave us disconnected from our fellow human beings, or it can make us feel very connected to our colleagues but disconnected from others (e.g. our families and friends). Freeman and Gilbert (1988) speculate about how much more meaningful work and organizational life would be if people were able, in fact, to bring their whole selves to work; to engage in personal 'projects' in which they truly believed and that provided a source of shared purpose and identity.

Organizational benefits of developing a values-based culture

Why should organizations be concerned to address these deeper levels of meaning for employees? In practical terms, there are potentially many business benefits to be gained in developing a values-based culture. This is no 'soft' option. One argument is that developing a more meaningful work environment leads to greater organizational cohesion. On the other hand, organizational coherence can have its downsides, as Tourish and Pinnington (2002) point out. They argue that corporate cohesion is usually achieved at the expense of internal dissent, and that such dissent is a vital ingredient of effective decision-making.

Positive effects on performance

On the whole, though, theorists and researchers tend to point to the business benefits of taking such issues seriously. Neck and Milliman (1994) claim that spirituality positively affects organizational performance. Organizations that attempt to promote spiritual development of their members report increases in creativity, satisfaction, team performance and organizational commitment (Laabs, 1995; Mirvis, 1997). Similarly, empowerment is an integral aspect of spirit at work. Other aspects include enthusiasm and commitment, emotional expression (Bracey et al., 1993; Dehler and Welsh, 1994) and personal relationships (Miller, 1993).

When people experience greater meaning, they appear to be 'in flow', able to give of their best. Conversely, when work and the workplace lack meaning, morale suffers and people start to look for other jobs or consider self-employment. Konz and Ryan (1999) suggest that individuals are expecting organizations designed to promote their search for meaning and transcendence. For Csikszentmihalyi (1992), people tend to reach 'flow' or optimal experience in situations where there are clear goals, total immersion in the activity, transcendence of ego boundaries and merging with the environment, and high levels of motivation, self-confidence, competence, enjoyment and other intrinsic rewards.

In practical terms, there are many business benefits to be gained in developing a values-based culture. This is no 'soft' option. Neck and Milliman (1994) claim that spirituality positively affects organizational performance. Organizations that attempt to promote spiritual development of their members report increases in creativity, satisfaction, team performance and organizational commitment (McCormick, 1994; Brandt, 1996; Leigh, 1997; Mirvis, 1997).

Ability to manage change effectively

The notion of spirituality has been employed to explain and understand organizational change as well as numerous other organizational phenomena, including value systems, managing, leadership, executive development and empowerment. Emotion in general, and spirituality more specifically, represent core concepts within the organizational transformation framework. When employees feel a strong collective sense of purpose, they tend to be committed to what they are doing and view change as a potential opportunity for improvement, learning and personal growth. Our research suggests that such an organization retains its key people with ease and manages change effectively.

Ability to attract skilled employees

Highly employable people seem now to be looking for roles that appeal to their personal values, and money may not be the main consideration in job choice. More people in the UK are making cross-sectoral job moves, especially to the voluntary sector. Work–life balance in particular is becoming a major issue for many employees, and is a growing factor in people electing to leave organizations and look for alternatives, including self-employment. People are increasingly choosing to take career breaks or work flexibly in order to have more of what they consider important. Employers in the knowledge economy are already recognizing the need to attract skilled employees of generations X and Y by having a well-articulated set of values that really work in practice.

The study

We first explored what people meant by the term 'meaning' and found, not surprisingly, that the word signifies different things to different people. Meaning can be triggered by key events that provide moments of elevated experience, such as holding one's baby for the first time. For many people, it was about experiencing 'flow'. The underlying themes are feelings of belonging and connection; harmony and balance; everything being in order; having the freedom to be genuine and fully oneself; giving selflessly; release; and being at ease with oneself. It is in these states that people feel most able and eager to give of their best.

For some people, 'meaning' was about the search for spirituality, whether or not this was faith-based. According to Millman and Ferguson (1999), spirituality usually involves deeply held values and deals with 'who am I?', 'what is my purpose in life?' and 'what is it that I offer?' questions. According to Konz and Ryan (1999), spirituality is defined as the particular way the human person in all his or her richness, the relationship of the human person to the transcendent, the relationship between human persons, and the way to achieve personal growth are envisioned. Spiritual experiences, however they may be defined, take place at a much deeper level than do our 'normal' experiences.

To some extent, we lack the vocabulary in everyday life to express such ideas. This may be because, as Wilber (2001) suggests, we are less familiar with, and tend to ignore in Western studies, the subjective and inter-subjective elements; the interior individual 'I' in which consciousness, emotion, sensations, perceptions, ideas and spirituality are to be found and the interior 'we', where cultural identities are found. The current popularity of ideas around emotional intelligence in leadership development suggests how novel such concepts are to Western ears. It seems that they have to be labelled and reduced to a few manageable characteristics before managers can grasp or apply the ideas.

How people experience lack of meaning at work

Weick (1977) noted that people in organizations invest their settings with meaning and then come to understand them. Weick called this an enactment process, or a creation of reality. Similarly, Shaw (2001) suggests that 'our human capacity for narrative self-making means that we create our sense of continuity and change, stability and instability as a single movement of living experience'.

In order to understand how people interpreted 'meaning', we decided to use Ken Wilber's (2001) four dimensions of phenomena (Figure 16.1) to analyse our research data.

In the Roffey Park study we found that people who suggested that they were looking for more meaning tended to work for large organizations which had flattened their management layers and gone global. People ended up having large spans of control, many responsibilities and pressures. These people were generally looking for other jobs. Typically they were looking for roles with the same or less responsibility, and many were considering a self-employed situation.

Similarly, many people experience lack of meaning if their organizational climate is competitive and demanding. People have neither the time nor the

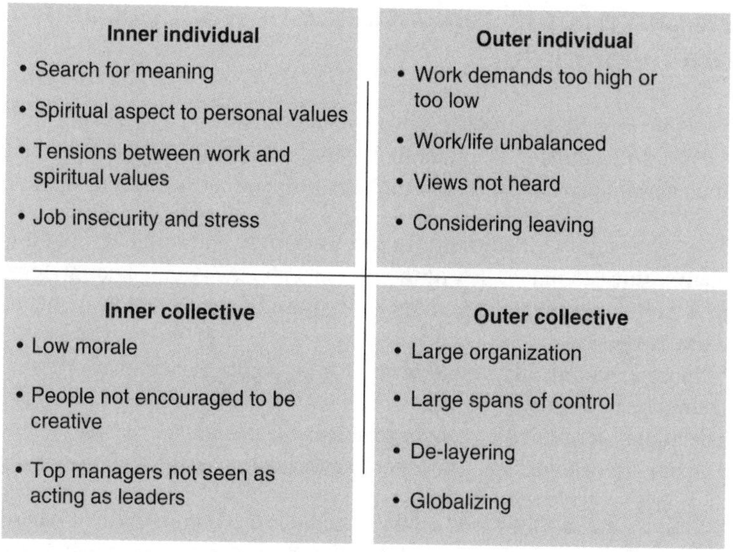

Inner individual	Outer individual
• Search for meaning	• Work demands too high or too low
• Spiritual aspect to personal values	
• Tensions between work and spiritual values	• Work/life unbalanced
	• Views not heard
• Job insecurity and stress	• Considering leaving

Inner collective	Outer collective
• Low morale	• Large organization
• People not encouraged to be creative	• Large spans of control
	• De-layering
• Top managers not seen as acting as leaders	• Globalizing

Figure 16.1 Search for meaning – a multidimensional perspective, adapted from Ken Wilber's model (2001).

encouragement to be creative, and they report having low morale. In the survey data, there was a clear correlation between top managers not being seen to act as leaders and employees experiencing lack of meaning. In our study, the search for purpose and the desire to do something worthwhile causes many employees to question the work which they do and to be sensitized to differences between their organization's espoused and actual values. As one QMW respondent put it: 'principles are more important than "talk"', while another typical comment was 'ethical practice is important to people'. These people typically wanted to work for a more ethical organization.

The search for meaning also correlated with work demands being too high or too low. There were strong links with people reporting a lack of work–life balance. In many cases they reported that their views were not heard, and that they little chance to make them known. These people typically wanted a more flexible working pattern.

We also found correlations between people looking for more meaning and experiencing tensions between their personal and spiritual values. Of the respondents, 66 per cent maintained that their personal values have a spiritual aspect to them. Over half the sample experienced tensions between the spiritual side of their values and their daily work, and 70 per cent were interested in learning to live the spiritual side of their values. These people typically experienced job insecurity and stress, especially if they felt they had to conform and play politics just to survive. Typically, they wanted to achieve a better match between their own values and those of the organization. They valued the opportunity of discussing spirituality in the workplace with colleagues.

How can people's experience of work become more meaningful?

The UK's Council for Excellence in Management and Leadership (CEML) research into leadership suggests that longer-term sustainable performance is built on certain principles that should underpin how organizations operate:

- The achievement of diversity in the workforce and at all levels, in all its many forms, to match that of their clients and customers and the locations in which they operate, and to make best use of the talents available across these categories
- Finding economically viable ways of moving to higher levels of environmental responsibility
- The adoption of good employer practices for all staff
- The pursuit of high standards of ethical behaviour and social responsibility.

Sustainability is here based on the so-called 'triple bottom line', where taking the needs of different stakeholder groups into account appears to be the key to good business results.

Applying these principles should lead to the development of a high performing and connected organization which can rightly play its part in the broader community. For many employees, such principles are closely aligned to their own values. Working in an organization that operates according to these principles is therefore likely to be meaningful to such employees.

Central interconnected aspects of a meaningful workplace involve a dramatic shift in both the fundamental hierarchical and the power relationships toward a more collaborative model. We need collaboration as much as competition to survive as the interconnectedness of the world grows more apparent. It is a symbiosis, mutuality – or, in organizational terms, collaboration and interdependence – on which success is built.

This perspective contradicts the dominant values of business-aggressive competition.

Acting as a community

Central interrelated aspects of workplace spirituality appear to be the organization acting as a community, and having a cause or important purpose. Developing community is an exercise of spirituality. It is part of what Wilber (2001) calls the 'left-hand' side, the internal expressive side of life, as opposed to the external, empirically measurable and observable aspects of the world. For Conger (1990), this includes developing more hospitable work spaces, rendering services to both organization and community, while strengthening organizational objectives and performance.

Community, where it can be found or created, can be a countervailing force to the stress, isolation and anomie that characterizes organizations that have cut out too much of what was community in their efforts to become competitive.

Community implies care, joint meanings and mutuality, and commonality of purpose, history, norms and values.

Arguably, community, caring, being with others who care, working toward or being in something bigger than us, becomes as important as having more of the goods that are pervasive in developed societies globally: 'By itself, shareholder wealth provides an incomplete sense of identity and uniqueness and does not motivate long-term creativity the same way community does' (Anderson, 1993).

Waddock (1999) suggests that work organizations are replacing other types of communities in many Americans' lives. Many people live in suburbs, not knowing their neighbours, working 50–60 hours a week in what is too frequently meaningless work; where 'face' time is as important as real contribution, and where pressure to do more substitutes for teamwork. Lay-offs, downsizings, re-engineering and restructurings of all sorts combine in the devaluing of local communities, not to mention community among employees. Too frequently jobs are structured to provide the most control for management and the least for those who actually perform the work. In addition, there are numerous virtual organizations where people interact less frequently than in traditional organizations.

These shifts arguably occur at some cost to community. It may well be an imperative that our institutions, market-based, public and civil, recognize and deal with this need for community and spirit if they hope to be successful in the future and tap the best of human energies. Miller (1993) suggests that people are searching for a way to connect their work lives with their spiritual lives, to work together in community, to be unified in a vision and purpose that go far beyond making money. Many people discover that, from a certain point, money is not going to make their lives better. Turned off by work that is at its roots meaningless and in some cases even unethical, many people opt out of their organizations psychically, turning their productive energy and attention to family or civic matters, or self-development.

Waddock argues that people need and want to belong to communities where they can make meaningful contributions that build a better world. For Waddock (1999), organizational prosperity and survival depend on building structures and relationships that permit people to make meaningful contributions and fulfil a fundamentally spiritual need for community. Empowered and autonomous individuals need to be held together by some sort of 'glue' if they are to be productive for the organization or a community.

Being interconnected with others

In Roffey Park's research into meaning, people felt that meaning in the workplace was linked with affiliation and the opportunity to be interconnected with others. Some people questioned whether the trends towards virtual working and self-employment would produce a backlash for individuals working in these ways, due to a sense of isolation and disconnection. Work can also enable people to transcend themselves.

However, participants highlighted the danger that work can also leave us connected to our colleagues but disconnected from other people, affecting our beliefs about ourselves and others. Similarly, valuing others and relationships to others were clearly important to many participants. For one person, meaning at work was essentially about 'the colleagues with whom I work above all else'. Typical comments included the following:

- Care and concern for people
- Relationship to others is significant
- The colleagues with whom I work, above all else, give meaning
- Treating all employees and team colleagues with dignity and respect, building trust; creating an environment at work where people feel their contribution is noticed and valued; empowering them to question and challenge in a constructive way to achieve business success, rather than collude with stale procedures which need challenging and improving.

Several people in management roles saw their responsibilities as being about creating greater connectivity – 'To build an environment that is based on much more than transactional relationships' – and involving care and concern for people. For one manager it involved 'Treating all employees and team colleagues with dignity and respect, building trust'. For another manager it was about 'Creating an environment at work where people feel their contribution is noticed and valued. Empowering them to question and challenge in a constructive way to achieve business success, rather than collude with stale procedures which need challenging and improving'.

Moynagh and Worsley (2001) suggest that a revolution in the workplace is under way because of a shift towards networks. They predict that three types of community are likely to become familiar. *Fragile communities* are formed when competitive and financial pressures force workers to adapt to organizations. Individualized contracts are widespread, and workers are paid by results. Organizations transfer as many risks as they can to the individual, but individuals still have the benefit of working within fairly stable networks. However, this is not a stable situation, since the need for innovation and new expertise can disrupt an existing network. *Stable communities* are driven by skills shortages. Organizations are forced to adapt to the needs of their workers – for example, by investing in measures to improve work–life balance. While this is the ideal for many employees, the authors question how viable it is, given the pressures from the global economy and public sector constraints.

Disposable communities occur when intense market competition requires workers to adapt to organizations by shouldering a heavy burden of risk. They are paid by results, even though these are not entirely under the individual's control. Labour is seen as a commodity. Knowledge is stored electronically. There is a global pool of skilled labour, and power lies with the employer. Pushed too far, organizations meet with resistance. Workers downshift or take early retirement, thus causing skills shortages and forcing employers to adopt more employee-friendly practices.

While organizations are likely to see evidence of all three of these different kinds of network at different stages of their evolution, the question remains of how to get the best out of people in a world where employers will be more concerned about skills shortages than unemployment, and where people will increasingly expect to be treated as individuals.

When the Body Shop reluctantly had to close its manufacturing arm in a small southern town in the UK, the company was true to its values. Concerned that the economy of the small town depended to a large extent on the incomes from workers at the factory, the Body Shop gave every support to departing employees to get them established in small businesses or find alternative employment, preferably locally. The Body Shop itself became one of the key clients for many of the small enterprises that were set up. The small town's economic stability was maintained.

Similarly, when BT's business focus changed in the 1990s it had no further need of a number of warehouses, where hundreds of semi-skilled workers were employed. BT took responsibility for retraining warehouse staff into other roles, granting the equivalent of £800 per employee for retraining of their choice. The way the change was managed produced positive benefits for BT (in terms of cost savings) and for employees, many of whom had the opportunity for new kinds of roles of which they might never have considered themselves capable in the past.

Something I can believe in

If people are to believe that the company means what it says with regard to values, there needs to be a conscious drive to ensure that their intention is matched by action. Some organizations are vigorous in ensuring that their values are practised on a daily basis, and use a variety of means to reinforce them. Virgin Holidays, for instance, brings values to life by having rooms set side for physical representation of the company values. These light-hearted room visual aids enable staff to picture what practising the values really means in behavioural terms. Such practices reinforce what the organization holds dear.

This search for purpose and the desire to do something worthwhile is causing many employees to question the work they do and to be sensitized to differences between their organization's espoused and actual values. According to John Seely Brown (in Dearlove and Coomber, 1999): 'When it comes to attracting, keeping and making teams out of talented people, money alone won't do it. Talented people want to be part of something they can believe in, something that confers meaning on their work and their lives'.

A higher sense of purpose

In a busy and business-like work environment, it is easy to forget that most work involves humans interacting as individuals within communities. While at various periods of history people as a whole can be 'bonded' together by a shared crisis or loss, such as the general outpouring of grief at the death of

Princess Diana in 1997, in workplaces such unifying dramas tend not to occur in ways which engage people's hearts and minds and catalyse them to greater efforts or higher endeavours. Many business plans and key performance indicators fail to excite.

The link between having a cause or important purpose and sustainable high performance is evident in much of the literature. Purpose is positively linked to employee health, well-being and motivation. Sandelands (1998) suggests that: 'Employees perform most energetically, creatively and enthusiastically when they believe they are contributing to a purpose that is bigger than themselves'. Purpose can excite and mobilize the members of an organization to work in greater alignment to each other – but not just any purpose; in commercial organizations, serving clients and customers may be tapping into similar motivations.

Living with passion in organizations requires bigger meanings and purposes, aimed at something beyond the 'goods' contained in dollars and products, and something of the common good that is engendered in relationships of care and community, commonality, among all stakeholders in an enterprise. Vision and values can create meaningful work within these autonomous units and serve as a source of 'glue'. Tom Chappell, CEO of Tom's of Maine agrees. He wrote in *The Soul of a Business* (1993) that 'common values, a shared purpose, can turn a company where daily work takes on a deeper meaning and satisfaction'.

Meaning provided by work itself

Meaning can be derived from work itself. Norman Bowie, a professor of Business Ethics at Minnesota University, considers that:

> *meaningful work is work that is freely entered into; that allows the worker to exercise their autonomy and independence; that enables the worker to develop their rational capacities; that provides a wage sufficient for physical welfare; that supports the moral development of employees and that is not paternalistic in the sense of interfering with the worker's conception of how they wish to obtain happiness.*

Adrian Furnham (2003) suggests that work provides a source of creativity and mastery – the feeling that one has achieved something worthwhile and useful.

Work provides a source of identity – it gives people a sense of their status in society and value. Work gives a sense of purpose – it makes people feel needed and stops alienation. This theme was evident in the Roffey Park research, with people suggesting that they were looking for jobs that they could relate to. This generally meant that people were looking for jobs that were inherently worthwhile, and they wanted to work for organizations they could respect.

Sandelands emphatically distinguishes between feelings *of* work (work effect, emotion and job feeling) and feelings *about* work (feelings about work are reflected in such concepts as job attitude and job satisfaction). Just as the wind itself cannot be seen, so spirit has been defined as an 'animating force, an energy that inspires one towards certain ends or purposes that go beyond self'. Freeman and Gilbert (1988) speculate about how much more meaningful work and organizational life would be if people were able, in fact, to bring their whole selves to work; to engage in personal 'projects' in which they truly believed and that provided a source of shared purpose and identity.

Making a difference to others

The desire to do things for other people is evident in much of the literature. For Waddock (1999), stakeholder value is replacing shareholder value as the primary business motivator for employees: 'The successful companies will be those able to rethink and adjust their business model to one that aims to contribute to the economic, social and environmental welfare of a wide set of stakeholders'.

In the Roffey Park study, many people reported that they are motivated by a desire to do something for the greater good/'put things back'. Working to provide shareholder value had little appeal, whereas making a difference to other people did. Employees whose organization was shareholder-focused tended to be looking for more meaning and suggested that their organization did not enable people to be creative. Employees working in organizations with a customer-focused purpose tended to trust their leaders more, believe that they were appropriately rewarded and recognized, have higher morale, experience less stress, and believe that their organization supported creativity.

This desire to do things for other people characterizes much of the literature. The challenge is to be able to harness employees' latent altruism and to stimulate the collaboration and interdependence on which success is built. Within organizations, these behaviours are precisely what organizations seek to encourage through knowledge management and team-building. Yet this perspective contradicts the dominant values of business-aggressive competition. In a 'dog-eat-dog' world, how easy is collaboration? Countless attempts at strategic partnerships founder on mutual suspicion, unwillingness to share information, and protection of individual interests.

Individual employees may be unwilling to share their knowledge and skills because they know that if they do their ideas will be plundered, and they will become dispensable. Trust is once again the key catalyst for collaboration. When trust exists, people are able to give more fully of themselves. Csikszentmihalyi (1992) suggests that it is entirely possible to live daily life in what he calls 'flow'. He describes Joe, an assembly line worker who created a meaningful work environment by learning everything about all the machines and becoming a tremendous resource for his co-workers. The critical question is, how can we transform our organizations so that more – all – of them permit this kind of individual self-expression, yet retain the context of the larger enterprise's meaning, purpose and goal achievement?

Gardner *et al.* (2001) suggest that:

people who do good work ... are clearly skilled in one or more professional realms ... they are thoughtful about their responsibilities and the implications of their work. At best, they are concerned to act in a responsible fashion with respect toward their personal goals; their family, friends, peers and colleagues; their mission and sense of calling; the institutions to which they are affiliated; and lastly, the wider world – people they do not know; those who will come afterwards, and in the grandest sense, to the planet or to God.

These authors suggest that thoughtful practitioners should consider three basic issues:

1. Mission – the defining features of the profession in which they are engaged
2. Standards – the established 'best practices' of a profession
3. Identity – their personal integrity and values.

A person's own background, traits and values ... add up to a holistic sense of identity: a person's deeply felt convictions about who she is, and what matters most to her existence as a worker, a citizen, and a human being. A sense of identity includes personality traits, motivation, intellectual strengths and weaknesses and personal likes and dislikes.

(Gardner et al., *2001)*

A central element of identity is moral – people must determine for themselves what lines they will not cross and why they will not cross them.

Corporate social responsibility (CSR)

As the interconnectedness of the world grows ever more apparent, employees increasingly feel part of something bigger than themselves when their organization has a deliberate focus on its social and environmental responsibilities. The notion that an organization is responsible to the wider community is reflected in the plethora of corporate social responsibility initiatives under way. Good corporate citizenship requires clear principles, engagement with stakeholders and good communications so that everyone understands a company's approach – its 'honest disclosure'. Organizations will soon have to report on their social policy, and need to be able to evaluate it systematically in order to do this.

David Ballard (2003), Director General of the British Safety Council, argues the case for organizations actively embracing their corporate social responsibilities:

All organizations should support education, skills training, community development and public health initiatives. But corporate responsibility goes beyond mere support and involvement. Fundamentally it is integral to the way everyone should do business each and every day. Issues of safety, environmental protection, accountability and ethics are central to every business decision

and process. A commitment to corporate responsibility is a basic require-
ment for attracting and retaining the best people, being the best partner and
achieving the best performance. All are essential to long-term success.

Employees, too, think this is completely right. In the Roffey Park study, for instance, 88 per cent of respondents believed that organizations should act exercise social and environmental responsibility towards wider society; 41 per cent of respondents' organizations have a CSR statement compared with only 21 per cent three years previously; 77 per cent believed that their organization is socially and environmentally responsible; and 83 per cent of respondents confirmed that this is important to them.

Yet the gap between organizational policies and actual practice remains wide, with many employees suspecting that their organization regards CSR as a PR activity and nothing more. While 55 per cent of respondents felt that their organization acted responsibly to some extent, many commented that such policies were no more than window dressing as defensive, risk-management initiatives, or to achieve some commercial advantage, or to redress negative images of previous corporate neglect of the environment. In many cases, the policies were scarcely being implemented.

Diversity, for example, is noticeably absent in many companies. While the policies exist, management and HR practices tend to perpetuate monocultural identities. Similarly, voluntary service in the community used to be the pre-serve of senior managers approaching retirement or of young high flyers. This was very much in line with successive governments' aims to push responsibility for public services towards the private and voluntary sectors. In practice, in economic downturns such practices have been cut back in many companies, leaving community groups 'high and dry'.

On the other hand, some organizations are going out of their way to ensure that what they do does not harm the environment or disadvantage employees, customers or other stakeholders, and that they are properly governed, with appropriate checks and balances in place. Shell already proactively produces an annual social and environmental responsibility report, and other organizations are beginning to follow suit. In the construction sector, HBG monitors its practices under the 'considerate constructor' scheme and puts actions in place to consolidate its good practice.

Volunteering, as a means of contributing to the local community, is once again starting to be seen by some companies as a means of providing career development for individuals while fulfilling some organizational aims around corporate social responsibility. IBM has a 'Days of Caring' programme; Boots has a 'Skills for Life' programme; BP operates a mutual mentoring scheme; Nokia has a 'Helping Hands' programme; and TXU operated an 'Energy for Action' programme, delivered in conjunction with Community Service Volunteers. At Ulster Carpets, employees are given paid time off for charity work, and the company matches staff donations.

However, British firms tend not to be as generous as their American counterparts in giving to charity, with few giving more than 1 per cent of pre-tax profits away. However, Microsoft is far ahead of the rest, giving away 9.58 per cent of pre-tax profits in 2002 in the UK. In one initiative, the company gave 10p to the NSPCC every time an employee went home before 5.30 pm. The firm also matches what staff raise by up to £7500 each per year. Richer Sounds is also socially responsible, giving away the highest proportion of pre-tax profit (5 per cent) of any UK company. It is not surprising that 86 per cent of staff say they are proud to work there. According to Jonathan Austin, managing director of Best Companies (2003): 'Employees within companies that are active in local and wider communities feel significantly better about themselves and their organization'.

Example 16.1   Southwest Airlines

One of the best-known cases in the literature of an organization that operates from a values-based model is that of Southwest Airlines: organizational spiritual values drive business and employee plans and goals. These in turn drive HRM practice to reinforce Plans/Values that drive outcomes such as organizational performance and employee attitudes and spirituality.

SWA employees feel they are part of a cause – their airline offers the lowest airfares, frequent flights, a personable service characterized by fun and humour. This cocktail of elements has made SWA a success story among airlines. Even in the aftermath of September 11 and the war in Iraq, when the travel industry generally and airlines in particular have suffered downturns due to people's unwillingness to travel outside their own country, SWA has fared better than its competitors.

SWA has a strong emphasis on community – teamwork, serving others and acting in the best interests of the company are central aspects of this value. Employees always come first, and their families are often invited to participate in company activities and celebrations. SWA employees are also actively involved in community-based service projects. SWA is careful about who it invites to become part of the employed community, and places great importance on the selection process. SWA also encourages employees to be individuals – really be themselves, rather than conforming to some corporate 'type' (Millman and Ferguson, 1999).

Diversity

Though the economic drivers are strong, the diversity of its workforce also reflects an organization's values. For instance, demographic changes and skills shortages mean that the workforce mix is changing. It is predicted that by 2010, 80 per cent of new entrants to the workplace will be women. Flexible working is seen as only one means of plugging skills gaps by enabling women and people with carer responsibilities to participate in the workplace.

Similarly, the global marketplace is also influencing the thinking of senior managers about the kind of workforce needed. After all, there is growing evidence that in today's multicultural world, workforces must represent the customer bases they serve. Addressing the skills shortages issue means that many employers are reaching out to a wider labour market than would perhaps have been the case in the past. As a senior manager in Astra Zeneca put it, 'Diversity is a business need'.

Anyone who works in the UK public sector will be aware of the Labour Government's drive to achieve greater diversity in the workforce. Diversity represents a key plank in the drive to close the UK's productivity gap with other developed economies because, aside from any egalitarian motives, diversity makes business sense. There are also research studies galore that suggest that it is through diversity, rather than sameness, that innovation arises.

The growing emphasis on diversity as a business imperative is reflected in the practices of some major private sector companies. For instance, Sir John Brown announced in June 2002 that he wished to change the culture of BP away from 'membership of a golf club' to more representative of society as a whole. Diversity policies aim to be inclusive of people who may have suffered discrimination on grounds of disability, race, gender, sexual orientation and religion. BP has changed its policies to extend the same benefits and pension rights as heterosexual couples to same-sex couples. The emphasis is on 'mainstreaming' diversity, rather than sidelining diversity practices to affected parties only.

However, it would seem that, in many organizations, diversity is light years away. While there is increasing evidence of diversity at more junior levels in organizations, the numbers of women and members of ethnic minorities achieving roles at senior levels in UK organizations remain disproportionately and disappointingly small. Even in the Sunday Times 100 Top Companies to Work for survey, only seventeen had women making up at least one-third of senior managers. In the *Management Agenda* survey (2003), 40 per cent of respondents overall believed that barriers exist to inhibit women's progress into senior management, and 33 per cent believed the same is true of ethnic minorities. As one senior manager of a construction company put it: 'it will probably take another couple of generations before society has moved on enough to make diversity an everyday reality'.

Why should this be? After all, equal opportunities, the philosophy that preceded diversity, has been reflected in employment legislation in the UK since the 1970s. These two related philosophies are subtly different. While the basic premise of equal opportunities is that people should be treated the same regardless of difference, diversity suggests that differences should be valued and harnessed for the good of the organization. Post-September 11, 2001, diversity as a business issue has gained urgency and credibility, since monocultural focus can blind people to what becomes obvious in retrospect.

Often linked to US-led globalization, diversity reflects a business-driven, rather than a 'social good' imperative. Critics of diversity suggest that by focusing on the business imperative, notions of equality of opportunity get hidden. Do organizations tend to embrace people-related issues fully only when they have to, because economic and other pressures force their hand? Mostly this seems to be the case. On the other hand, some go considerably further. BT has led the field in equipping disabled as well as able-bodied employees with the technology to work remotely, thus benefiting from a wider skill base while enabling a broad range of employees to contribute productively.

This mixed picture is reflected in *Management Agenda* survey findings. Compliance with what is expected of good employers is evident at one level. Whether they are in private, public or not-for-profit sectors, most organizations are reported as embracing diversity within the workforce, and roughly one-third of all organizations in our survey have had equality/diversity policies for over ten years, with the public sector marginally leading the field at 37 per cent. Interestingly, nearly ten per cent of private sector organizations surveyed have no formal diversity policy at all.

However, when asked for how long their organization had treated equality and diversity seriously as a business priority, respondents gave very different answers. Those reporting 'ten years or longer' were as follows: public sector (22 per cent), private sector (19 per cent), and not-for-profit (24 per cent). Respondents reporting that their organization does not treat diversity seriously included 9 per cent from the public sector, 22 per cent in the private sector and 17 per cent in not-for-profit organizations.

Ironically, although the public sector is expected to role-model good employment practice to other sectors, it would seem that policies alone are not enough to ensure more than compliance with the letter of the law. Embracing the spirit of the law is something else. For instance, when people were asked to say if they thought that barriers existed to inhibit women's progress into senior management in their organizations, 51 per cent of public sector respondents said 'yes', while 35 per cent of private sector and 27 per cent of not-for-profit respondents agreed. With regard to ethnic minorities, barriers to inhibit progress into senior management were perceived to be strong in 48 per cent of public sector organizations, compared with 40 per cent of not-for-profit and 24 per cent of private sector organizations.

The *Management Agenda*, and Roffey Park focus groups, suggest that many of the real barriers to equality and diversity are to be found in HR practices, such as recruitment, promotion and succession planning, where the tendency to 'clone' and perpetuate the existing cultural and gender mix at senior levels is commonplace. Similarly, 'unfriendly' cultures with fixed working arrangements, long hours and inflexibility, lack of cross-cultural awareness and vested interests tend to work against diversity. Often described as 'the permafrost layer', manager attitudes can effectively work against diversity.

Managing for diversity

Given that, despite the strong business case, progress towards creating a diverse workforce at all levels appears slow, diversity needs to be managed rather than left to chance. Executives and HR professionals need to make and communicate the business case for diversity. Leaders, especially those at the top of organizations, need to really understand and provide long-term commitment to the implementation of diversity policies. They need to set and sell goals and targets, hold managers accountable for these, and change the organizational culture to embrace diversity.

Ingham (2003) suggests that when developing a diversity policy it is important first to analyse your business environment, internally and externally, to see how diverse your employee base is and whether it reflects the customer base. Then it is important to define diversity and its possible organizational benefits, such as becoming an employer of choice through the development of its employee value proposition (EVP) and an improved external image. The diversity policy should be integrated into the corporate strategy and woven into the organization's values. Staff at all levels need to be involved in diversity, through initiatives such as setting up diversity councils and diversity action groups. The policy needs to be communicated internally and externally, with regular updates and through a variety of media.

Diversity should be embedded into core HR processes and systems. Some external help may be required to kick-start the process. Examples of approaches used by a variety of public and private sector organizations to achieve greater diversity include:

- Policy development
- Equalities monitoring, including turnover and the reasons why people leave
- Levelling up the workforce through positive action, active recruitment, development of relationships and investing in the under-represented groups within the current workforce
- Ensuring that diversity and Equal Opportunities are integrated across the whole range of activities, from business planning to induction and performance management
- Management development for the whole workforce and for disadvantaged groups
- Recruiting high flyers from under-represented groups
- Supporting people so that they do not feel isolated
- Diversity sessions which raise awareness of the interpersonal and organizational processes that may promote or undermine equality
- Printing business cards in large print and Braille
- Encouraging members of under-represented groups into senior positions, using mentors and shadowing
- Use of diversity 'champions'
- Bringing 'success stories' to the forefront
- Introducing remote working.

Leaders need to measure the impact of equality on business performance. Evaluation, including benchmarking progress at regular intervals, should enable progress to be measured and success stories circulated.

Conclusion

Trust is becoming more widely recognized as a cornerstone of high performance, since it affects an organization's ability to attract and retain key employees and to maintain high levels of motivation and commitment. Building an organization to which key employees want to commit means going beyond the rhetoric of values statements and corporate social responsibility policies. It is about managers and leaders 'walking the talk' and building a new basis for trust.

Roffey Park's research into the issue suggests that there is a real business case for taking questions of meaning seriously, because our findings suggest that lack of meaning goes hand in hand with employee cynicism. As various writers have suggested, employee cynicism makes people more, not less, resistant to change. Similarly, people tend to work less hard if they experience no sense of meaning. With more employees actively looking for more meaning, organizations are likely to see a haemorrhage of key talent unless they at least become aware of the issue and attempt to meet employees halfway.

On the other hand, there appears to be a clear link between employees experiencing meaning and:

- An organization's ability to manage change successfully
- The ability to retain key people
- Greater employee engagement and high performance.

For many people, meaning is about connection, being at peace and in balance; having a heightened understanding of what is really important, of what it is to be human. Meaningful moments appear to elevate people's focus and desire to give to others and fulfil themselves.

In the workplace, meaning appears to link to a sense of community, to having a higher sense of purpose, especially a customer-focused purpose. It also links to consistency of behaviour and congruence between personal and organizational values. People want to work for ethical organizations and to see greater transparency with respect to values. People want to feel involved and treated like adults, and able to balance work with other aspects of their lives. They want to have the opportunity to discuss spirituality in the workplace with colleagues. They want challenging jobs through which they can experience personal growth.

In high performing organizations, leaders have to ensure that the gap between policy intention and actual implementation is closed. For instance, they need to ensure that diversity is actively managed and becomes a reality. They must also insist that there is greater alignment of reward and recognition with constructive behaviour, so that practices consistent with ethical standards are reinforced. They need to challenge existing promotion and appointment practices to ensure that they are fair. Organizations most likely to be able to recruit and retain the best employees will be those that demonstrate open and honest practices, both towards wider society and towards employees themselves.

Checklist: Building a climate of trust

While many of these suggestions apply to leaders, they also apply more widely to line managers, HR professionals and employees themselves.

Clarify strategic direction:
- Provide an outline vision and strategy
- Engage employees at all levels in developing a higher-level purpose, not just shareholder value
- Involve employees in decision-making at appropriate levels
- Improve communications – both the quality and quantity and range of communication channels used, and by making communications two-way
- Demonstrate trust and respect for employees – use fewer but more effective controls, and consult and listen
- Provide parameters for experimentation.

Build a high performance climate:
- Develop leaders at all levels
- Promote leaders who act as role models for desired behaviours
- Ensure that organizational values are realistic and credible to stake-holders
- Set targets for closing the gap between espoused and practised values
- Deal assertively with organizational politics, unprofessional behaviour and harassment
- Set high standards, especially with regard to honesty, social and environmental responsibility and ethical practice generally
- Be consistent in reinforcing practice with regard to values
- Use multi-rater feedback and other mechanisms to encourage leaders to 'walk the talk'
- Manage diversity proactively, including monitoring how policies are working
- Clarify lines of accountability
- Use flexible rewards, with a degree of individual choice
- Remove some of the blockers to creativity and other aspects of high performance.

(For more details, see Holbeche, 2003b)

Build high performance skills:
- Use team-building when teams are formed and establish effective team processes
- Train managers to coach others, and provide honest feedback and recognition
- Train managers to establish stretching but achievable standards and targets
- Increase opportunities for employees to develop partnering skills
- Encourage people to use their initiative

- Review learning, rather than blame, if things don't work out first time
- Ensure that employees have time to be creative.

Dealing with stress:
- Ensure that workloads are well designed, scheduled and managed
- Review workloads on an ongoing basis, and be prepared to stop doing some things in order to make time for others; encourage people to use their initiative; review learning, rather than blame, if things don't work out first time
- Eliminate as much bureaucracy as possible
- Develop e-mail protocols (e.g. e-mail-free Fridays)
- Design and manage the physical environment so that it is healthy, congenial and 'fit for purpose'
- Train managers in delegation
- Monitor employee well-being
- Ensure that decisions are taken at the right level by clarifying roles and responsibilities, and providing the skills training required for those involved
- Develop management procedures for combating harassment and bullying
- Support managers in their often stressful roles
- Train managers in how to manage flexible workers
- Consult employees on how the organization can help them manage their well-being.

Stabilizing the employee deal:
- Build the range of flexible working options on offer, including genuine support for home-working
- Ensure that people who work flexibly can still achieve career progression
- Maintain employee benefits, especially pensions
- Provide job security where possible
- Maintain investment in employee training and development
- Create horizontal and vertical career tracks
- Ensure that individual roles offer employees the chance to achieve, enjoy their work and help others succeed
- Recognize that work represents a form of meaning beyond the pay-cheque; build a sense of community and belonging; ensure that work is worthwhile and makes a real contribution; build connections between different parts of the organization to increase a common sense of purpose
- Provide flexible retirement options
- Create a 'fun' working environment
- Celebrate success.

17

Leading for sustainable high performance

Introduction

To paraphrase Butts (1999), the notion of meaning at work is an idea of revolutionary potential. Applying the idea to work, especially in terms of personal satisfaction, peak performance and overall business success, can also enrich communities, cultures and the Earth itself.

In this respect I share thinking with various authors who suggest a potential causal relationship between a more holistic approach to management, one that takes account of emotions and people's deeper needs, and improved business performance. Deal and Kennedy's study (2000) of 'winning' organizations suggests that the one thing that sets the top-ranking companies apart is their robust cultures. A robust culture in a cohesive enterprise is committed to a deep and abiding purpose. Developing an organizational culture in which employees can experience a deeper sense of meaning is, therefore, central to high performance.

Building a culture of high performance places a special emphasis on the quality of leadership within an organization. While definitions of leadership abound, one of the core elements of most theories is, as Bennis and Nanus (1985) suggest, that the leader creates the 'social architecture' for an organization, which 'provides context (or meaning) and commitment to its members and stakeholders'.

Creating an organizational climate conducive to innovation, knowledge-sharing, collaboration and high performance is a major part of a leader's responsibility, wherever they sit in the hierarchy. Top leaders in particular have a symbolic role with regard to the nature of organization climate and culture that evolves. Whilst what may be required is context-specific, in practical terms this could involve, for example, taking action consciously to build trust, to suppress political activity, to create challenging and rewarding roles, and to address areas of imbalance on work–life. Bringing about the kinds of culture change called for may be less about 'leading from the front' and more about providing some clarity of direction while harnessing people's ideas and energies around the process of change.

In the light of recent corporate scandals, many writers are urging senior managers to redefine their corporate purpose. As we saw in the previous chapter, a values-based organization is one where there is a deliberate emphasis on practising what is preached with regard to company values. Two aspects of leadership in particular appear important in this regard: employees want their leaders to act ethically, and they also want leaders to support and coach them through periods of change. In this chapter we shall look at aspects of leadership that appear to be intimately linked with creating a meaningful context for work to take place.

A leadership vacuum

However, regardless of sector, employees suggest that they are not getting the kinds of leadership and management that they feel they and their organizations need. In many cases there is a wide discrepancy between what employees expect of managers and what they experience, creating a sense of leadership vacuum. In *Management Agenda* surveys, employees report:

- Managers failing to 'walk the talk'
- Failure to follow though on policies such as diversity, work–life balance etc.
- Corporate social responsibility statements as 'window dressing'
- Promotion of people who act unethically
- Managers who hold staff back
- Leaders who pursue personal rather than organizational agendas
- Macho, competitive styles
- Fiefdoms.

Managers at all levels are tending to 'act a level down', over-controlling people's work. Of the survey respondents, 92 per cent stated that being a leader is part of being a good manager yet only 49 per cent maintained that top managers in their organizations act as leaders, with senior managers in particular not embracing the leadership aspects of their roles. Particular criticisms included a lack of ability to listen, and discriminatory and prejudiced thinking patterns of senior managers whom respondents would like to see offering more strategic direction, championing good management practice such as performance management and 'meddling' less. Respondents typically want managers to utilize their skills in a more rewarding way, provide guidance on priorities and review working methods regularly. They also want senior managers to tackle underperformance of senior colleagues and train managers to 'let go'.

What undermines trust

Both managers and leaders have to work at building trust and an organizational culture conducive to meaning-making. In many organizations, values are more often espoused than practised. Employees want managers to 'walk the talk', demonstrating a visible personal commitment and an orientation towards deeds, not words. While 80 per cent of *Management Agenda* (2003) respondents reported that their organizations have a published set of values, 49 per cent of respondents felt that these values do not reflect the actual values of managers.

Trust is the key catalyst for collaboration. When trust exists, people are able to give more fully of themselves. As Roffey Park respondents tell us, the basic integrity of senior managers is the most important element of finding meaning at work. However, trust appears to be in short supply, with only 24 per cent of respondents trusting senior managers to a great extent. The most trusted group are subordinates (59 per cent), followed by peers (49 per cent).

Respondents were asked what they perceive to be the biggest issues that effect trust at work. Themes included:

- Unclear vision, leaving employees unable to buy-in to the direction, leading to confusion and mistrust
- Lack of communication and consultation, combined with lack of transparency and openness
- Bullying, which seems to be quite widespread, with the main perpetrators seen to be senior managers (56 per cent) and colleagues (33 per cent)
- Unprofessional behaviour, including malicious gossip and other political activity
- Lack of honesty, with double standards and economy with the truth, especially over future staffing levels
- Broken promises, especially with regard to policies on bullying and blame
- Political behaviour, with hidden agendas and internal competition
- Poor performance management, including inconsistent approaches to pay reviews, and favouritism
- Poor leadership, including conflict at the top of the organization.

Far from experiencing their organization as a community united by a shared purpose, people remarked on tensions at board level and a management focus on personal agendas. Above all, employees want to see a more open, democratic form of leadership, which treats employees as adults. A number of respondents (male and female) suggest that having more female leaders and adopting some of the styles of communication of the best 'virtual' managers would produce better leadership.

According to Deal and Kennedy (2000):

> These troubling patterns have arisen from assault and default. The assault has often come from outside the business environment and creates new demands. The default comes from executives and managers who have either forgotten or ignore what makes a well-run business tick. They fail to pay attention to the real cultural bonding people need to function effectively at work.

Cultural bonding is not something that leaders can just 'do' as an agenda item. Releasing energy and creativity from people goes deeper than that. Filling the leadership vacuum requires leaders to 'step up' to the challenge of being an instrument for change, not just an instigator of change initiatives.

The role of business leaders in creating meaning

For many authors (Kotter, 1988; Conger, 1989; Schein, 1993), a key function of leaders is to create meaning for their followers. As Bennis and Nanus (1985) also observed:

> Great leaders often inspire their followers to high levels of achievement by showing them their work contributes to worthwhile ends. It is an emotional

appeal to some of the most fundamental human needs – the need to be important, to make a difference, to feel useful, to be part of a successful and worthwhile enterprise.

However, other authors suggest that, in practice, this function is ignored in preference to bottom-line considerations. Indeed, Millman and Ferguson (1999) argue that many CEOs will not justify a practice unless it favourably impacts the bottom line. They suggest that research is needed if we are to create a paradigm shift in CEOs so that they incorporate spiritual principles into their organizations.

Springett (2004) argues that leaders should not only be judged by the worthiness of their intentions but also by the extent to which they deliver against those intentions: 'This adds an important discipline that encourages leaders to refrain from articulating overly lofty or idealistic purposes. It means that a leader is morally obliged to search for a corporate purpose that is not only meaningful and elevating for followers but also practically effective'.

A new management style?

That is not to say that leaders should start to think of themselves as corporate 'high priests' but that they should more fully embrace the moral, ethical, dimensions of their role. These include creating a community to which employees want to belong and give of their best; which operates to the highest ethical standards and where 'good work', as described by Gardner *et al.* (2001), is carried out; which serves a higher purpose and provides a valuable contribution to the broader community; and where employees can have healthy working lives. Leaders create symbols and rituals which can form the basis of meaning. Their behaviour, and what they pay attention to, assumes a disproportionate significance, since leaders benefit from the 'amplification effect'. They have various forms of power through which they can exercise their will. Leaders therefore have to carefully consider how they can use themselves as an instrument for unleashing high performance in the organization.

Such an approach may require a shift in emphasis for many people currently in leadership roles. The quest for sustainable success is a theme running through this book. Leaders need to focus on both short- and long-term success, and plant seeds for tomorrow's organization. It might be argued that the conventional command and control management paradigm was based on a belief that others are incomplete and not to be trusted and over whom power should be exercised. Counterbalancing power-coercive approaches are the more transformational approaches which focus on 'getting people and organizations to undertake willingly the challenges of transforming dreams into realities' (Kozmetsky, 1985). Here, the role of the leader is to create a symbolic environment that people can relate to and do not rely on information so much as on people's need to share meanings and have a commitment to those meanings.

'Stepping up' to leadership

From the research data which has underpinned the high performance organization model, the form of leadership that comes closest to what employees say they want is not 'charismatic', 'transformational' or any of the other established stereotypes of leadership, but is more like that practised by the 'Level 5' leaders described by Jim Collins (2001).

Collins distinguishes between merely 'good' leaders and 'great' leaders. He identifies that the difference between the (Level 5) leaders of 'great', as opposed to the Level 4 leaders of 'good', companies is that Level 5 leaders are incredibly ambitious not for themselves but for the institution. This ambition manifests itself in a paradoxical blend of personal humility and a professional, almost maniacal will. Unlike other leaders, Level 5 leaders tend to be less charismatic and ego-driven but more enabling. They give credit where it is due, but support people's learning by being prepared to take the blame if something goes wrong.

Whether or not organizational success and leadership style are in a cause-and-effect relationship may not be important. The fact that they are correlated is interesting. In fact, Collins suggests that charismatic leaders can sometimes do their organization more harm than good, since they are likely to make the organization dependent on them.

Zohar and Marshall (2000) believe that a person with high spiritual intelligence is likely to be a servant-leader, bringing higher vision and value to others with the ability to inspire, to understand that the whole can be greater than the sum of the parts. Such a leader is not afraid to ask questions or to say 'I don't know', and look for achievement through many facets, not solely in the bottom line. The leader is:

- Flexible – open to suggestion, surprise and change, and able to cope with ambiguity
- Self-aware – both reflective and self-confronting
- Led by his or her own vision, values and sense of purpose
- Able to learn from adversity and turn bad experience into wisdom
- Holistic – considers the whole purpose, whole system;
- Welcoming of diversity
- Independent and willing to take a stand on issues
- Questioning – especially 'why?' questions
- Able to reframe situations – give new perspectives, creative alternatives
- Spontaneous – alive to the moment, and not afraid to respond or initiate.

Emotional intelligent leaders

In the context of the key leadership tasks, 'emotional intelligence' is essential (see Chapter 15). As one *Management Agenda* respondent put it:

> *Our senior teams have to inspire and take account of employees' emotions. Logical decision-making and communicating is not enough as it fails to recognize human hopes and fears.*

Leaders need to learn more about themselves and others, and improve how they use their knowledge of themselves and their organizations. As Mindell (1992) points out, it is imperative for successful leaders to work with the natural energy of their followers that arises from changing moods, tensions, emotions, roles and time spirits. The narrow path that the leader must follow is a path that the followers themselves help to create and can accept. Leaders need to realize that the energy of their followers cannot be completely controlled or predicted.

For Dehler and Welsh (1994), emotions are essential to the new management style since this paradigm says that managing people is managing feelings. Work is an emotional experience, yet for the most part this point has been neglected by management theory. For Daniel Goleman (1995, 1998), emotional intelligence requires managers and workers to develop a higher level of self-discipline, interpersonal and ethical skills, to know and manage their emotions, to develop self-motivation, recognize emotion in others, and handle relationships.

Robert Cooper (1997), in his article 'Applying emotional intelligence in the workplace', says: 'How often have you thought: "Let's just keep emotions out of this and deal with things rationally"?'. He goes on to say that research shows that emotions, properly managed, can drive trust, loyalty and commitment – and many of the greatest productivity gains, innovations, and accomplishments of individuals, teams and organizations. He quotes a former leader of an executive team at Ford Motor Company, Nick Zeniuk, who said: 'Emotional intelligence is the hidden advantage'. Taking care of the 'soft stuff' means the 'hard stuff' will take care of itself.

Claudia Heimer (1998), co-author of *The Dancing Giant*, refers to the 'encouraging sign of a renaissance of emotion in the workplace'. This, she says, challenges the idea that a management role is purely a rational one. The demands on a manager tend to be to stick to the rational, the linear, the factual, the defined rather than the emotional 'fluffy stuff'. In contrast, research shows that innovation, increased profitability, good decision-making and effective performance are brought about by managed emotions.

Leaders as guides

Dehler and Welsh (1994) suggest that leaders should facilitate the spiritual development of their followers, making it possible for employees to experience a higher sense of meaning through their work. According to various writers, managers are now seen as guides who help create meaning and purpose for their subordinates. No transformation is easy, especially one as significant as the role shift from manager to spiritual guide. Being a spiritual guide is not part of any manager's training. Even if they felt such a role to be appropriate, the difficulty faced by managers is the diversity of spiritual traditions and experiences individuals bring to the workplace.

The spirituality of the organization's leaders maintains the spirituality of the organization through its influence on the socialization of new employees. Anita Roddick, co-founder and former CEO of The Body Shop, describes her personal growth in her book, *Business as Unusual* (Roddick, 2000). For her, the spiritual dimension of life underpins everything. She cites Matthew Fox

(2000), who claims in his book *The Reinvention of Work* that reinvention begins when a values system is attached to work and that spirituality is an active energizing principle running through every aspect of daily life.

Although spirituality is not automatically associated with religion, the link between spirituality and business is evident in leaders from many faiths. Farooq Kathwarai, CEO of Ethan Allen Interiors, says that the Koran influences business decisions. Ranwal Rekhi, CEO of Cyber Media, says that Sikhism affects his management style. Forbes (1998) quotes executives on how their religion and spirituality affects them and their business. Max DePree, ex-chairman and CEO of Herman Miller, spelled out his religiously based philosophy of management in 1989. James Autry, ex-CEO of Meredith Communications, did the same in 1991.

Delbecq (1999) interviewed executives as part of a leadership study of CEOs dealing with rapid change environments in the 1980s. He found that many leaders with a Christian perspective saw their role in the form of a 'calling' to service, not simply a job or career. Since all creation is deemed good, being involved in co-creation through industrial enterprise can be an act of love. These leaders saw their own role and the function of the business enterprise as a form of service, in this case the design and provision of goods and services that meet important societal needs. They saw a complete integration of their spirituality with their work, rather than a 'private life of the spirit' and a 'public life of work'.

For Delbecq's interviewees, leadership in the private sector is a role worthy of the highest form of servant-leader. He suggests that leaders need courage to stay on course and survive with dignity the special challenges of executive leadership, which daunt the brightest and the best. These leaders describe how they continually strive to lead through a vision that is bold and courageous, yet remain flexible in order to accommodate continual change. This calls for a detachment from what is comfortable and familiar. It requires excruciating public presence, with the constant need to interface with diverse stakeholders. Through personal reflection and meditation, leaders manage to balance the dangers of over-extension and burnout. They also consider the major cause of leadership failure to be hubris.

Future-oriented

Leaders need to monitor employee attitudes and morale, as well as how the organization is functioning. However, *Management Agenda* respondents are clear that they would like leaders to focus on the future, not just monitor the present. They want leaders who encourage and enable risk taking *and* risk management. They want top leaders who can make wise judgements on what is important, not senior managers who obsess about minor 'hobby horses'. They are looking for leaders to take a more collegiate, corporate approach, and to be open, honest and consultative. They expect the leadership group to act as a team, with a shared set of leadership values and skills. They feel that individuals in top management positions should be reviewed, echoing some of the recommendations of the Higgs report into Non-Executive Directors, but applying them to senior management (McNulty *et al.*, 2003).

Providing direction

Top leaders need to be able to create a shared sense of purpose and direction that engages people and captures their energy and imagination. Ellsworth (2002) published data indicating that companies which focus on delivering value to customers outperform their industries by an impressive 36 per cent. Springett (2004) explains this by suggesting that a customer-oriented purpose generates superior financial performance by enabling strategic focus, investment in people, and creative capability. Ellsworth argues that: 'A purpose grounded in the service of others, such as serving customers, and vigorously promoted by the company's leaders, can act to raise the moral level of the individual members of the organization'. Leaders at all levels need to communicate a clear imperative and vision for change, set clear objectives and identify the priorities for the year. In Roffey Park research, employees want leaders at all levels to provide clearer direction and steer, yet be prepared to listen. They want leaders to consult and involve people at all levels. At the same time, employees want leaders to be able and willing to take hard decisions, not procrastinating until a problem has become chronic.

Championing change

Leaders need to champion change, having a set of beliefs about what makes change successful. Leaders need higher degrees of adaptability than others. They must be resilient and able to cope with the stresses of their role. They need to demonstrate how to manage change effectively. They must be visible at all levels, using two-way communication, especially face-to-face, rather than relying on e-mail, videos and other remote methods. They need to show that they can listen. They need to lead by example and safeguard their credibility by acting in ways consistent with what they recommend for others. They need to respond effectively and sensitively to employees' personal concerns, in order to secure lasting commitment. They must overcome resistance and build commitment to the changes to be implemented by involving people meaningfully in the change, giving them a sense of control and managing their available capacity.

Influencing others

At the very heart of the leadership task is the ability to influence others to achieve what the organization needs to do. Leaders need to be willing and able to influence others and inspire others, showing commitment and enthusiasm. They must be optimistic and positive, yet be able to empathize with people who may feel differently. 'The leader's subtle use of language may also be a factor in determining his effectiveness, both in enhancing his credibility and in managing the influence process' (Pondy *et al.*, 1983). According to April

(1999), good leaders understand and are attentive to language, and they know the power of words.

Use of symbolism

Schein (1993) suggests that, in breaking down that which is taken for granted and gaining acceptance of the new, the use of symbolic devices such as myths and stories is important. When organizations make changes, they often discard or destroy old symbols and artefacts in favour of the new. Symbolic acts on the global stage include the toppling of the Berlin Wall and of the statues of Saddam Hussein. Leaders are also attentive to the use of ceremonies and aware of the communication value of these. Kouzes and Posner (1995) argue that 'in the performing art of leadership, symbols and artefacts are a leader's props. They are necessary tools for making the message memorable and sustainable over time'.

Practising ethical leadership

For employees, even this long list of leadership tasks is incomplete if a values-based organization is to become a reality. The missing link is ethical leadership, whereby top leaders become the organization's ethical custodians and standard-bearers, setting the strategic direction but imposing less control. Roffey Park survey respondents want to see a more open, democratic and ethical style of leadership, which treats employees as adults. Under such leadership employees develop a strong, shared sense of purpose to which they can readily subscribe. 'Walking the talk' on values is essential if people are to take them seriously.

A moral contract

Greenleaf (1998), along with Burns (1978), describes how leadership is more than skills and situational know-how, and is, instead and more fundamentally, a moral contract between leaders and followers to bring out the best in each other for the good of the whole:

> *Such leadership occurs when one or more persons engage with others in such a way that leaders and followers raise one another to higher levels of motivation and morality ... transforming leadership ultimately becomes moral in that it raises the level of human conduct and ethical aspiration of both leader and led, and thus it has a transforming effect on both.*
>
> *(Burns, 1978)*

In high performing organizations, leaders are proactive and persistent in implementing corporate social responsibility policies that really make a difference to the 'triple bottom line'. This can take courage, given the short-term focus and pressures from shareholders. Sir Adrian Cadbury (Pickard, 2003) defended his decisions to continue doing business in South Africa under apartheid on the basis that he felt that the company had a responsibility to stay in South Africa and play its part in bringing about change in the country. In the end, he said, Cadbury did not lose shareholder support to any great extent.

Similarly, leaders who practise ethical leadership ensure that diversity is actively managed and becomes a reality. They champion good management practice and 'nail their colours to the mast', so they deal assertively with unprofessional and political behaviour. They work to the equity principle, and they ensure that people receive 'true' performance appraisals, where management practice is based on fairness rather than expediency. They insist that there is greater alignment of reward and recognition with constructive behaviour, so that practices consistent with ethical practice are reinforced. They challenge existing promotion and appointment practices to ensure that they are fair.

Articulating a higher sense of purpose

Living with passion in organizations requires bigger meanings and purposes, aimed at something beyond the 'goods' contained in dollars and products, and something of the common good that is engendered in relationships of care and community, and commonality, among all stakeholders in an enterprise.

The key leadership role is to articulate core beliefs or a higher cause which creates meaning. Deal and Kennedy (2000) distinguish between fundamental beliefs and strategies. Strategies lay out steps to achieve competitive advantage. Strategies come and go as conditions shift in a company's market. Fundamental beliefs, in contrast, speak to sustaining, non-negotiable values that shape life inside the workplace. Fundamental beliefs cannot be altered easily without unravelling the cultural fabric – a company's enduring ethos. Fundamental beliefs persist, whereas strategies change. This is echoed in similar studies by Arie de Geus (1988) and Collins and Porras (1994).

According to Bennis and Nanus (1985):

> the spark of genius in leadership must lie in the transcending ability, a kind of magic, to assemble a clearly articulated vision of the future ... The absence or ineffectiveness of leadership implies the absence of leadership and the absence of vision, a dreamless society, and this will result, at best in the maintenance of the status quo, or, at worst, in the disintegration of our society because of lack of purpose and cohesion.

Tom Chappell, CEO of Tom's of Maine, agrees. He wrote in *The Soul of a Business* (1993) that 'common values, a shared purpose, can turn a company where daily work takes on a deeper meaning and satisfaction'. Zohar (1997) suggests that leaders should focus on building business that benefits others ('spiritual business') – that is, 'other'-centred rather than 'self'-centred. She points out that leaders and organizations have the option to be in harmony with other people, rather than in strict competition – what she calls 'competing altruism'. This also dramatically shifts both the fundamental hierarchical and power relationships toward a more collaborative model.

For Jim Collins (2001), developing a compelling vision involves what he calls the 'hedgehog' concept (because the hedgehog survives by knowing only one big thing). This is where leaders focus the corporate effort on what they feel passionately about, what they can be the best in the world at, and what drives their economic engine. The best visions derive from where these three factors intersect. Collins suggests that organizations aspiring to greatness should preserve the core values, but continually change goals, strategies, culture and operating policies as circumstances warrant.

For Dehler and Welsh (1994), internalization of the vision as an emotional response suggests that the organization's mission has intrinsic value to individuals – i.e. meaning in-and-of itself. Alignment occurs when the vision is used by management to infuse work with spirituality and meaning. Purpose can excite and mobilize the members of the organization to work in greater alignment with each other. For Waddock (1999), a higher cause is the 'glue' that holds empowered and autonomous individuals together, keeps their disparate efforts focused on a common purpose, and enables them to be productive for the organization or a community. Vision and values can create meaningful work within these autonomous units. For subcultures to work together, there must be informal rules or guidelines for how these independent entities are supposed to relate to one another or are linked to the corporate whole. These rules are derived from a historically anchored set of beliefs about what the corporation stands for.

'Walking the talk'

Organizations in every sector have published sets of values. For Dehler and Welsh (1994), leaders raise the consciousness of subordinates about the importance and value of organizational endeavours. The leader's values are the standards against which all organizational activities are measured (Conger, 1990; Chappell, 1993). Conversely, many authors point out that failure by leaders to 'walk the talk' on organizational values is a major impediment to organizational effectiveness, since it is likely to give rise to employee cynicism, which in turn is thought to make people more resistant to change.

Keep values explicit

The Body Shop reminds employees and other stakeholders of its values in very practical ways. Anita Roddick's famous remark 'If I see a man on a bike I think there's hope for the world' is echoed in a line painted across the company car parks. People who have done great things which reflect the company's values have their photos displayed on a 'wall of heroes'. Such practices reinforce what the organization holds dear.

For real impact, values must be modelled by leaders at all levels. 'Walking the talk' on values is essential if people are to take them seriously. Leaders need to be able to lead courageously, having a strong value base from which to draw. Bass (1985) describes transformational leadership as a process by which leaders raise followers to greater heights of awareness so that they are prepared to sacrifice their own self-interest for the good of the organization: 'This heightening of awareness requires a leader with vision, self-confidence, and inner strength to argue successfully for what he sees is right and good, not for what is popular or is acceptable according to the established wisdom of the time'. Employees want greater transparency; for managers to be more open, honest and consultative; to reduce political behaviour; to provide a clearer direction and steer; and to be decisive and willing to take risks.

A key challenge for leaders is closing the gap between espoused, surface values and real values. Various theorists suggest that leaders and managers should focus attention on values and keep them explicit wherever possible.

For John Jones (1981), leaders need to share their own values with their subordinates, make value considerations a valid part of the agenda at meetings and avoid win – lose arguments about values. Leaders should monitor the extent to which people espouse a common set of assumptions, philosophies and purposes. They should also monitor the way people exhibit value-oriented behaviour and assess the 'fit' between organizational values and those of employees. They should update the organization's organizational values and set goals that are consistent with them.

In high performing organizations, leaders make values real to stakeholders by practical actions.

Raising standards

Leaders need to have high expectations of colleagues, and to empower individuals. They need to be able to influence the organization's climate so that it becomes motivational, purposeful and constructive, as well as enjoyable. They need to allow delegated decision-making and give people freedom to act. They need to provide regular feedback to drive accountability, maintain momentum, increase confidence and stimulate learning. They need to focus on developing the culture – on championing practices that foster innovation, knowledge creation, teamworking and continuous improvement. They need to see employee development as a priority.

Managing conflict

In many organizations, conflict between groups and individuals is an everyday occurrence. This is often because people feel strongly about something but have few outlets to exercise influence other than 'digging their heels in'. Where there is contention, leaders should not see this as a threat but aim to harness the positive of power of conflict. They need to tackle cultural misalignments, which are reflected in the conflicts and inconsistencies in the culture and can create barriers to lasting change.

Leaders must develop clear protocols for dealing with conflict, asking tough questions and initiating the 'straight talk' needed to open up dialogue. If the energy and ownership implicit in conflict situations can be put to good use, the organization can benefit. Leaders should schedule team-building sessions for groups that are in conflict with each other, before staging an inter-group meeting to confront the differences and find a way forward. More broadly, leaders should foster a climate of team-working, collaboration and achievement.

Problem-solving

When attempting to improve the organizational climate, leaders should deliberately include people who are feeling disaffected, as well as those who are satisfied with the current climate, so that key issues are surfaced. Leaders should focus on problem identification and problem-solving in reporting relationships, communication patterns, decision-making procedures, the accountability system and the reward system, ironing out inconsistencies and dealing with the root cause of perennial problems. In problem-solving, they should question values as well as facts and procedures, looking for value differences ('should' and 'ought') underneath conflict situations. They should push for visible results.

Developing leaders

In today's rapidly changing environment, the analytical, rational approach to management needs to be complemented by the more intuitive and inspirational aspects of leadership. Conventional business education does not always provide for development of the three broad areas of skill that are increasingly recognized as part of the 'kit-bag' of effective leaders. These are emotional intelligence, spiritual intelligence and strategic leadership.

Spiritual intelligence

Alongside emotional intelligence (see Chapter 15), spiritual intelligence is coming to be seen as key to effective leadership. Eggebrecht (2003, in Holbeche 2004) describes spiritual intelligence as follows:

Western psychology rests on two processes – the primary (EQ) and secondary (IQ) – the latter seen by Freud as the more superior. Along with IQ and EQ, SQ (Spiritual Intelligence) has been identified as the third key area of human intelligence with a direct impact on human performance. The third Q, SQ or spiritual intelligence, has its origins from the collective evidence of psychology, neurology, anthropology and cognitive science. Some argue that the quest for meaning through our evolution is the thing that has brought us down from the trees. Danah Zohar and Ian Marshall argue that SQ is uniquely human and the most fundamental of IQ, EQ and SQ. They see computers as having IQ and animals possessing EQ and in a situation each can respond, but neither ask why.

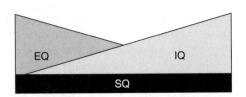

Figure 17.1 EQ, IQ and SQ.

IQ and EQ are associated, and in order to think effectively we need to feel; SQ is where we solve the problems of meaning and value we place on our actions and lives (see Figure 17.1). They support one another, and each has its own area of strength and can function separately. There is an argument that Gardner's multiple intelligences are variations of IQ, EQ and SQ linked to one of the three basic neural systems in the brain.

SQ operates out of the brain's centre and introduces a third, which unifies and integrates the two processes and acts as a dialogue between reason and emotion, mind and body providing a support for growth and meaning-giving centre. SQ gives us a moral sense – to temper rigid rules with understanding and compassion and to see where these two have limits. It helps us recognize existing values and discover new ones making religion possible though not dependent upon it. Being religious does not guarantee a high SQ. EQ (Goleman) allows me to judge what situation I am in and to behave appropriately whereas SQ allows me to ask if I want to be in the situation at all.

Our SQ gives us the security to question and to look at the familiar in an unfamiliar way, including ourselves. That security needs to be intrinsic as managers are expected to be ever more flexible and innovative which can in itself appear a paradox. Zohar and Marshall suggest paths to greater spiritual intelligence:

- *You must become aware of where you are now – self-awareness and reflection day to day*
- *Feel you want to change if you or some area of your life could be better*
- *A deeper level of reflection on your motivations and getting to know yourself*
- *Discover your obstacles and what is holding you back and how these can be removed*
- *Identify what paths you need to follow to move forward*
- *Commit yourself to a path and look for meaning*
- *Remain aware there are other paths and honour those who walk them.*

Spiritual intelligence is our 'compass' or guide, at the edge in the chaos theory, in the border between order and chaos or what we are about and being lost. We tend to throw ourselves into immediate pleasure and satisfaction and limit our horizons to the merely human, cutting ourselves off from wider meaning and broader perspective. Being human has laid in reason (our IQ) in logic, and science with origins in Aristotle's philosophy where thinkers defined man as a rational animal.

The East and West perspective on humanism has differed – with the former being based on a deep sense of interconnectedness of life and responsibility for the whole world, an awareness of self, meanings and values which could be described as spiritually intelligent. We have forgotten many of our meaning skills.

When insight and energy flow freely through the channel from inner to outer we become centred and whole, our SQ works to unite all the levels of being. Recollection, the vehicle of SQ means to re-collect, to pick up, and gather the fragmented pieces of ourselves. Recollection is SQ in action and SQ is never absent – only our sight of it and, therefore, our ability to use it, may be blocked.

Strategic leadership

The UK Chartered Management Institute's 2001 report, Leadership, the Challenge for All, suggests that the top three characteristics leaders in all sectors should possess are: inspiring (55 per cent), strategic thinker (41 per cent) and forward-looking (36 per cent). In a similar vein, J. Van Maurik (1996) describes the essential characteristics of strategic leadership as follows:

- *Wisdom* – able to create visions of the future, and pursue them; intuitive, yet wise in the way the vision is pursued; judges people and situations well; has thoughts and opinions on the future of business methods and the nature of work; inspiring when necessary; capable of being a mentor at all times; adept at influencing and persuading others; able to see the big picture and to recognize trends; capable of dealing with organizational politics – a communicator and networker
- *Integrity* – demonstrates to others that they are worthy of trust; does not operate on hidden agendas; is open and honest in dealing with others; does not shrink from candour when necessary; able to give bad news
- *Sensitive (in approach)* – can operate as a coach; good listener; able to empower and develop others; understands the power of teams and how to work with them; understands the constituents of good process and how to achieve it; capable of continuous learning; a facilitator of learning and of situations; looks for future opportunities in everything that happens; looks for opportunities to motivate others
- *Sensitive (in thinking)* – conforming in approach when necessary but capable of non-conformity; able to challenge the conventional wisdom of situations, to bust paradigms; able to handle diversity of approach and opinion; understands that different things motivate different people and applies this understanding; creative; can think outside the box; able to think strategically and to communicate the strategies; familiar with a number of strategic tools; a risk-taker when necessary – adventurous and courageous

- *Tenacity* – dynamic, energetic; hard-working yet able to balance home and work life; capable of handling own stress as well as that of other people; disciplined in approach; able to handle failure and setbacks; tenacious – doesn't give up; understands and copes with the pressures of power; able to handle uncertainty and to help others to do so; demonstrates optimism; handles change well; plans it and makes it happen.

HR's role in building values-based leadership

According to Simpson (2002), HR can play an important role in helping organizations to avoid the corporate scandals of recent times by placing high priority on the calibre of, and succession to, the board. Good strategic HR management should 'ensure that managers do not exploit shareholders' by ensuring that there is a reasonable diversity of opinion on the board, rather than the CEO's 'clique'.

HR must monitor perks and salaries, 'creating a mechanism which allows proper scrutiny and lets HR define what is culturally acceptable'. Appointing company 'ombudsmen' is one way in which organizations can avoid the danger that internal dissent and whistle-blowing of unethical/illegal practice is silenced. Since behaviour tends to follow reward, HR has a key lever for focusing executives' attention onto what matters. While executives may prefer the simplicity of stock options, HR must devise a broader set of criteria which balance short and long term, cash and shares, basic salary and bonuses, hard and soft goals. As Simpson suggests, why not reward managers for increasing staff retention as well as increasing profits?

Similarly, HR can help senior managers to understand the ways in which mergers and acquisitions might change a company's culture. It is HR's job to assess the implications of any acquisition and ensure that staff in the newly acquired subsidiary understand and buy into change.

Building succession

Given their key role in building a change-able culture, leaders should be nurtured at all levels in the organization. Investing in leadership development should therefore be seen as a critical activity. This contrasts sharply with company practice. Only 62 per cent of US chief executives interviewed in *Fortune* magazine said that they had a successor lined up (Connolly, 2003).

Yet high performing organizations, such as the 'visionary' companies described by Collins and Porras (1994), are all careful to institutionalize their ideologies in various ways. They tend to select people for their organization who share similar beliefs, and to grow their own and have well-developed succession planning. According to John Kotter (1995a), the transformational leader ensures that the next generation of top management embodies the new approach. Jack Welch, for example, former CEO of General Electric, was a long-term employee of GE. Even when the CEO is not a long-term employee of the company, the visionary organizations tend to manage the transition towards a new era by ensuring that the new CEO builds on the achievements of the previous CEO, rather than ignoring them. According to Collins (2001), great leaders 'set their successors up for spectacular success'.

HR also has a key responsibility to ensure that the organization is building successors for future leadership roles. They should have accurate and up-to-date data on, and personal knowledge of, potential leadership candidates. They must act as guides and consultants to their organizations as they head into a new era of succession planning. In the past, in relatively stable times, succession planning used to be simple replacement plans for key roles. Now succession planning needs to be an ongoing process of finding and developing a pool of leaders who can meet the organization's current and future needs. Given the need for flexibility, identifying rising talent becomes more difficult. Yet organizations need to beware the old tendency of recruiting in the CEO's image, since what was required for success in the past may not be the same in the future. Succession planning therefore needs to ensure leadership continuity, while maximizing and diversifying the pool of executive candidates and talent pools at every level.

Succession planning also involves identifying gaps in capabilities, future skills and management development processes. For Eastman (1995), succession planning that works always:

- Receives visible top-management support
- Is owned by line management and supported by staff
- Is simple and tailored to unique organizational needs
- Is flexible and linked with strategic business plans
- Evolves from a thorough human resources review process
- Is based upon well-developed competencies and objective assessment of candidates
- Incorporates employee input
- Is part of a broader management development effort
- Includes plans for developmental job assignments
- Is integrated with other human resources systems
- Emphasizes accountability and follow-up.

HR can work with top management to design the criteria for promotion to future leadership roles. They can review HR practices, identifying those (including compensation, recruitment and performance reviews) that could discourage effective succession planning. They can develop learning assignments that can give companies a reliable reading of future leaders' strengths and weaknesses. If a high performance culture as described in this book is to be achieved, it is essential that the people who do get promoted to top management demonstrate ethical leadership as well as business acumen. HR can play an active role in developing senior managers, enabling them to expand their horizons and awareness of other leadership approaches by arranging benchmarking visits to other company management teams, for instance.

Tesco and Unilever have both managed to gain sustainable, profitable growth over many years. Both have well-developed succession planning systems in place, and both seek to improve what they do by learning from the experience and insights of others. Many other companies believe it is important to know what experience and abilities are available within their employee base, and where further experience and training are required. Some companies classify managers according to the level of job they are judged to be ultimately capable of filling, and whether they will be ready in two to five years' time, or further ahead, or now. Other companies consider such classifications unnecessarily restrictive and periodically review their talent base, sometimes spotting an overlooked 'star' amongst experienced employees.

Given that the leadership skills required at one stage of an organization's life cycle may be different from the skills required at another stage, according to Hunt *et al.* (1988), it is essential that leadership skills be reviewed regularly.

Developing leadership teams

Management Agenda respondents expect their leadership groups to act as a team, taking a more collegiate, corporate approach. The UK Chartered Management Institute's leadership research found that, for long-term success, the company needs to depend on the whole leadership team, not just the CEO, because it has a broader reach into the company. It is therefore important that senior teams see their own development as a team as a strategic priority. Researchers found that the best teams focus on business performance issues first, and only after the event do they reflect on the manner in which they did it, so discovering how they function as a team. Team-building retreats and facilitated workshops tended to be seen as less helpful in creating an effective team. It can be helpful to use the services of a credible facilitator, who can help executive teams manage their decision-making process. Increasingly, executives appear to be turning to one-to-one coaching so that they confidentially explore their own development and think through their organizational strategy.

Example 17.1   Marriott Hotels

Marriott Hotels recognizes the importance of developing its senior managers. All are expected to complete 40 hours training off-site each year. For example, departmental managers are encouraged to attend a three-day service leadership programme, which is about how they manage their priorities as managers and in individuals. This is a holistic programme that encourages them to focus on their work, personal and spiritual lives. Marriott also involves senior managers in delivering its international leadership programme. There is considerable kudos in being part of the network of managers who are allowed to deliver this programme. First the senior manager attends the programme as a delegate. Such managers might then observe a programme and act as a third 'hand' before running their own sessions and finally becoming certified to run their own programme (Carrington, 2002).

Supporting development of self-insight

Executive coaching is now a common form of leadership development. There are many reasons why people ask for coaching, ranging from access to technical advice (for instance, concerning specific business challenges) to increasing personal effectiveness as a leader by developing deeper levels of self-insight. Often entered into at a time of personal transition for the coachee, one-to-one coaching can provide disproportionate benefits to the organization if it helps a senior manager to 'correct' unproductive behaviour.

Contemporary training is extending to include more holistic perspectives on leadership. For instance, Shell Directors receive lectures from Buddhist monks, aligning priorities beyond simply the work part of working life. Companies such as Unilever and Kellogg send employees off to question their work and spiritual attunement, cultivating intuition as one part of a more perceptive mind state. In its staff development, Cadbury Schweppes includes raising awareness on personal aspects, including those of a spiritual and emotional dimension. These companies acknowledge that these are the skills required in order to generate trust and good industrial relations.

Recruitment consultants specializing in the job market in the financial sector say that many of their clients want the qualities associated with EQ and SQ, although they may not use those terms. Some organizations are offering their staff the opportunity to have psychometric feedback from instruments such as the Myers Briggs Type Indicator and other instruments such as the Enneagram, which explores deeper levels of motivation and personal identity.

Conclusion

Roffey Park surveys suggest that many employees want to see a more open, democratic and ethical style of leadership. Under such leadership, employees are treated as adults and organizations have a strong sense of purpose to which employees can readily subscribe. In such contexts, employees are more likely to commit to the organization and want to give of their best. Conversely, failure to practise values and a leadership vacuum are more likely to increase employee cynicism and reduce commitment. While organizations in every sector have explicit sets of values, some are more vigorous than others in ensuring that these are practised.

Given the importance of leadership, HR can play a key role in ensuring that managers practise company values by using multi-rater feedback and reward processes as a means of drawing managers' attention to the importance of demonstrating leadership behaviours. Investing in leadership development at all levels should be seen as a priority. Building a new psychological contract with employees will be ever more key to attracting and retaining people in the future.

18

Conclusion

We stand at the edge of the deepest power-shift in human history. In years past, power equated to manpower and horsepower. Today, and more so in the future, knowledge and information are power.

(Toffler, 1991)

It would be easy to dismiss the argument that business success will follow good people management practice as a pipe dream, or aspirational at best. Yet the proof of the pudding is in the eating, as they say, and through research and consultancy practice I am seeing evidence that what is often regarded as the 'soft stuff' of management is in fact the 'hard stuff', which more successful organizations tend to get right.

Throughout this book I have suggested that today's volatile and competitive global economy demands new models of doing business, built around strategic flexibility and resilience. For Van de Vliet (1994), the emphasis should be on 'adaptability, intuition, paradox and entrepreneurial creativity in the face of an unpredictable, indeed inherently unknowable future'. As open systems, organizations have to respond to the changing requirements of their environment. This will required new and widely shared working practices. Great business results are increasingly likely to depend on an organization's ability to scan the environment, move quickly to develop customer-focused offerings, continuously improve and innovate while driving down costs, and use the talents of employees to the utmost.

The boundaryless and fluid nature of today's global economy may seem to suggest that organizations are mere passive pawns, compelled to keep pace with change as and when it occurs. However, I would suggest that this is a time of strategic opportunity and agree with Jennings (2004) that a new 'Darwinian' perspective is emerging according to which organizations which aim to survive and thrive need to proactively interact with, and shape their environment, or else atrophy and die:

Strategic adaptation is now a much more creative process, recognizing that reactive flexibility is a necessary, but not sufficient condition. Only those organizations with visionary leadership able to conceive and enact a strategic fit will be able to survive. Survival does not depend upon achieving optimal outcomes, merely on being in sufficiently mutually beneficial exchange relationships with external stakeholders in ways that other competitors cannot emulate.

Organizations therefore will have to change how they see themselves and their purpose. They will need to recognize and accept that they have a broader role to play within the wider community, whether this is at a local, national or global level. As Clive Morton (1998) suggests: 'Those companies that are inclusive in their relationships inside and with their communities stay the course, are more consistently more profitable and better able to make strategic choices for the future'.

Today's context calls for new approaches to leadership and management. Change must not be 'change for change's sake' but be carried out with clear longer-term purpose and benefit in mind. According to Edward De Bono (1992):

Managers are still in 'maintenance mode'. That is to say housekeeping, quality, cost control etc. That is because they are promoted that way. Most managers still think of creativity as a peripheral luxury. They do not realize that as competence, information and technology become commodities, the only thing that is going to matter is 'value creation', and that requires a different sort of thinking. Managers just want to survive, not succeed.

Looking ahead, success in the first quarter of the twenty-first century, will depend on an organization's ability to act like an entrepreneur, to continually generate and put resources behind new ideas, whatever their line of business. If they wish to stay ahead businesses must:

1. Act in the short-term with the long-term in mind.
2. Take advantage of global markets – collaborate as well as compete.
3. Develop a real proactive focus on the customer.
4. Develop new products – fast.
5. Create vision and leadership in your business.
6. Put people's needs first.

The role of culture in creating competitive advantage is coming of age.
For Zuboff (1988):

The 21st century company has to promote and nurture the capacity to improve and to innovate. That idea has radical implications. It means learning becomes the axial principle of organizations. It replaces control as the fundamental job of management.

Leaders have to rise to the challenge of their role as culture-builders if the learning potential of organizations is to be activated. Knowledge, especially access to knowledge, will increasingly play an important role with regard to power, which is inherent in all social organizations and systems.

Changes in the nature of demands on a workforce have important implications for human capital. People will have to maintain their learning power to maintain their earning power. Self-esteem will no longer be gained from money, power and control, but from ideas and innovation (Strange, 1993). Knowledge reduces uncertainty, and supports flexibility in attitude and behaviour. A well-educated workforce will anticipate, accept and eagerly support change. There will always be value and demand for such a workforce. The modern organization must flex to meet the needs of an increasingly self-aware and diverse workforce.

The trend towards greater use of mind-based skills and talents, rather than the application of physical power, will accelerate. In a world of knowledge-based work, the output is limited only by the mind (Morrison and Schmid, 1994). For organizations, garnering the talent of employees to generate future revenues will be key to success. With the sources of productivity and innovation therefore being essentially voluntary, organizations must increasingly engage with their workforces, taking employee needs into account. For example, *The World of Work* (Strange, 1993), an international report on jobs, concluded that jobs from now on must offer greater opportunities for entrepreneurship, social interaction, individual achievement and personal recognition. In the future, competitive success may depend critically on how countries balance paycheques with these psychic rewards.

Developing change-ability

Leaders therefore need to be able to transform their organizations regularly to create ongoing competitive advantage, in an environment where change is becoming more challenging and complex. Change is risky, since the very process of change can destroy elements of meaning for employees – connectedness, relationships, trust, continuity, clarity of purpose, balance, community and even a sense of identity.

Since the rapid pace of change is likely to continue, people will have to adjust their perspectives on what differentiates 'change' from 'steady-state'. Effectiveness cannot be postponed until 'normality' resumes. Therefore, leaders need to understand what can be stabilized while other things are transformed, using language and symbols to signpost the progress being made as the organization moves forward. Of course, true implementation goes beyond mere installation. Building an organizational culture that is change-able requires equipping a critical mass of people with the ability to see change as the norm which unleashes both organizational potential and individual opportunity, and *vice versa*. That way people become less daunted by, and more committed to, the change effort. They become more willing to change and sustain their new behaviour long enough for the benefits to be realized.

Change leaders need to think beyond the process of change to what the change is meant to achieve, and let outcomes dictate methods. Above all, effective change management requires taking into account the human, emotional aspects of change. If the change is to result in new ways of working, leaders need to find ways to engage people in the organization's vision and mission, actively involving them in developing the organization through dialogue and conversation. This is a key means of increasing commitment, since people tend to own what they help create.

Creating a change-able organization requires that organizations demonstrate that commitment is not a one-way street. Change programmes should not only focus on customer and shareholder needs but also on employee welfare and satisfaction. When an organization demonstrates its commitment to individuals, those people tend to show commitment in return.

The people dimension of organizations is therefore paramount in achieving sustainable high performance. At the end of the day, great business results are produced by great people who have the skills and the will to do their job to the maximum of their ability. In a change-able organization, building an open and positive culture in which people can give of their best is the key leadership challenge. Effective leadership is perhaps the key enabling component in the successful twenty-first century organization. According to Schein (1993):

> *culture and leadership ... are two sides of the same coin, and neither can really be understood by itself. In fact, there is a possibility ... that the only thing of real importance that leaders do is create and manage culture, and that the unique talent of leaders is their ability to work with culture.*

Developing a high performance culture is about providing the framework within which employees can realize their potential. A committed, diverse and talented group of employees needs only bounded freedom, rather than strict controls, if they are to deliver the desired outputs. Employees need a clear understanding of the desired direction, and to be empowered with the right degrees of information, autonomy, authority, resources and accountability for their roles. They need to be supported by managers and leaders who have the styles and are of the calibre appropriate to the task in hand.

I believe, in common with April (1999), that:

> *when an individual has less concern for the ego associations of leadership, and more for the mission to serve by liberating and redirecting individual resources and energy, potential expands. People do more than they had been doing because they feel freer to be more than previously they had felt possible to be. As a result of the greater energy available, through the more actualised individuals, there is more possibility for creative change in organizations.*

Building positive psychological contracts

At the very heart of the leadership task is the ability to influence others to achieve what the organization needs to do. It is becoming evident that where the psychological contract has become more transactional, or has become tainted by deep cynicism about the one-sided nature of the deal, organizations are likely to find change harder to manage, to experience difficulties attracting and retaining key employees, and to find that achieving higher levels of creativity and productivity will become more challenging and expensive. If companies genuinely want to develop innovative, customer-focused, values-based cultures that will be the foundation for future business success, they will need to focus on building a new relational psychological contract with the people on whose performance business success depends.

Gratton (1999) points out the dangers of not taking seriously the people issues of organization:

> *I believe passionately that the reality in organizations falls well short of the rhetoric that 'people are our greatest asset'. Until we face up to this gap, until we can stare reality in the face and until we can care as much about feelings as about finance, we are doomed to create organizations that break the soul and spirit of those who are members – and that reduce, rather than build, human potential.*

Given that the previous psychological contract broke down as employers appeared to renege on their side of the deal, it is in the interests of employers to be proactive in forging the elements of their employer brand into something that will inspire employees and encourage them to commit to the organization, rather than waiting for employment legislation to enforce good practice. If they want to safeguard the possibility of sustainable success, leaders have to stoke the engine of high performance by giving priority to the drivers of employee engagement and commitment.

Engagement

True engagement comes when people feel that they are valued for who they are and what they bring, as well as what they do. Leaders, aiming to create successful organizations that can cope with the demands of an ever-changing world, need to enable others (and themselves) to find meaning, balance and fulfilment. This is about allowing people the space, time and energy to explore their true feelings, beliefs and attitudes – both to themselves and others – which change and shape the way they experience each other. By enabling a shared meaning and purpose to emerge, leaders can help create a meaning-full community to which people want to belong.

Engagement involves helping to create a shared sense of destiny within the workplace. Our findings suggest that employees experience this when they:

- Are informed and involved
- Believe that the organization has a higher-level purpose
- Share the values that underpin this purpose
- Feel that their leaders 'walk the talk' and are worthy of respect
- Believe that their work is meaningful, in and of itself
- Have a means of doing something for others, especially customers
- Feel treated as adults and respected by others, especially leaders
- Feel they can be themselves in the workplace and are right to trust others because politics are kept to the minimum or absent
- Feel part of a community.

The organization's higher sense of purpose needs to reach people at an emotional level and raise people's aspirations to achieve something they perceive to be worthwhile. Serving customers, rather than shareholders, calls on an altruistic motive – the willingness to give of one's best and be useful. In the process, shareholders do benefit, but more obliquely than when shareholder motives come first.

People also like to feel connected, part of a community. Appropriate types of symbolism and ritual can help to reinforce the sense of belonging, without the need to kit employees out with uniforms! Employees also want to see their leaders acting congruently with values, whether this is at policy level – such as ensuring that corporate social responsibility, diversity and other ethical policies are implemented – or in management practices and behaviours. They seem to be looking for the 'Level 5' type of leadership described by Jim Collins, where the leader drives the organization forward with passion but is able to release people's potential – giving credit where it is due and taking the blame when things go wrong.

Commitment

Of course, employees can feel little commitment to an organization but still feel committed to doing a good job. However, what seems to distinguish 'contained' commitment from its more 'active' cousin is the greater energy and enrichment that occur when employees really want to do their best because they feel their effort is worthwhile. What are the practical drivers of employee commitment? The following factors all demonstrate how much organizations really care about, and value, their employees.

First, *safety and security* (physical and psychological) is critical. As a basic requirement, employers should ensure that the workplace is safe and that people are trained and equipped to do their jobs, whether they work from home or in the workplace. Employers should aim to ensure employee well-being. As far as possible, employers should aim to provide a reasonable degree of job security and to adopt continuous employment practices.

Trust is an enabling mechanism of greater innovation and responsibility. Trust is both an input and an output. It is essentially reciprocal. When trust is present, employees are respected and have autonomy to make choices. They are assumed to act with integrity and judgement. For trust to be present, employees need to feel fairly treated, that their managers are honest and that their organization has worthwhile purpose. In return, employees need to be prepared to learn new skills and develop the flexibility such an organizational commitment to them requires.

Secondly, *rewards* (remuneration, benefits and 'holistic' rewards) are important. Goals and incentives should be aligned. These should be equitable and reward contribution, not just short-term performance. People should also be rewarded for engaging with change and for behaving in new ways. Non-financial rewards should be imaginative, and tailored to the individual where possible. Benefits should offer a degree of choice. Final salary pension schemes should be maintained or generous alternatives offered, rather than transferring all the risk to the employee. Managers should be trained to recognize good performance when they see it. Building a stress-free environment, with manageable workloads and opportunities to develop personal projects alongside company projects, can be very motivating. Just giving people a little time and space to reflect can be mutually beneficial.

Thirdly, *affiliation* (the extent to which employees feel part of the team) is significant. Wanting to be part of something larger than self is part of human psychology. For home-workers, the social connection with co-workers can be noticeably lacking. Bringing teams together from time to time so that they can connect socially and share learning can be of advantage to both employers and employees. Creating opportunities for people to take part in cross-functional teamworking and other means of expanding their networks and understanding of the organization can help employees feel part of a whole. Managers should develop projects that help to generate team spirit and pride in achievement. Celebrating success and encouraging a climate where work is fun, rather than pure pressure, reminds people that the best work can be enjoyable.

Fourthly, *growth* (the opportunities for learning and gaining experience) is important. If individuals are to be motivated to ever-higher levels of performance they need jobs that are stretching and stimulating, providing opportunities for variety and initiative. Employees need the chance to learn the skills required for their jobs, and to be coached and developed in their roles. They need to be clear about how their role helps the organization achieve its strategic goals, and about their scope for experimentation. As they experiment with new approaches, they need to be encouraged and supported, rather than blamed if things go wrong.

Whatever their age, most people want to continue to learn and develop. Investing in training and development is a key way not only of demonstrating organizational commitment to the employee but also in growing the organization's human capital. Opportunities should be found to facilitate people's

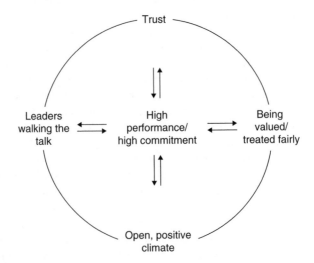

Figure 18.1 The reciprocal nature of high performance.

career growth within the company. There should be active support for employee self-development, and practical options available to employees, even in tough times. People should be enabled to apply their developed skills in ways that benefit them and their employer. The key to this is mutuality of interest. I agree with Kanter (1979) that 'the productive capacity of nations, like organizations, grows if the skill base is upgraded. People with the tools, information and support to make more informed decisions and to act more quickly can often accomplish more'. People also want the time to reflect and learn from other employees. Building some slack into the organization, and enshrining in the culture the notion that reflection is vital and not a waste of valuable activity time, will bring benefits to all.

As new 'good practice' emerges, generic learning should be 'captured' and disseminated so that others do not have to reinvent the wheel, but not so rigidly enshrined in process terms that it removes chance for further refinement and ownership by others. As new learning proliferates and people see the benefits of sharing knowledge, they are able to genuinely work 'smarter, not harder', thus freeing up time for both work–life balance and new opportunities for the business. In such a context, success breeds success and empowered individuals willingly share the rewards of their efforts with the organization and *vice versa*.

Finally, *work–life balance* is a touchstone of the health of the employment relationship between organizations and their employees. For many employees, being able to achieve the right work–life balance is increasingly important. Being in balance is about feeling fulfilled and 'at one' with the world. It is about managing personal commitments and having some flexibility alongside delivering high performance in work. One set of needs should not preclude the other. When organizations put effort into helping employees to strike the right balance, they show that they value the individual as a person, not just as a worker. Such attention, through flexible working arrangements, reviews of workloads and innovative policies, pays off. When employees can have both a career and a life, they tend to remain with an employer 'with a heart' who values them to this extent. Then the employer brand becomes a reality, and trust, the cornerstone of active commitment, is rekindled.

Essentially, organizations can only gain if they create a meaningful context in which employees – their source of competitive advantage – can flourish. I have argued that, for all concerned, high performance and its results should be reciprocal, with mutual risk and return. I have suggested that organizations which are able to rap into their employees' deeper motivations, amplifying potential from the individual to the organizational, have the greatest chance of achieving high performance. Better still, organizations which are able to harness the enduring human desire for learning and growth are likely to find that their ability to achieve high performance is self-renewing. When an organization becomes a locus of heightened experience in this way, sustainable high performance is the logical consequence.

References and further reading

Abrahamson, E. (2000). Change without pain. *Harvard Business Review*, July–August, 75–79.

Allen, R.W., Madison, D.L., Porter, L.W. *et al.* (1979). Organizational politics: tactics and characteristics of its actors. *California Management Review*, 22(1), 77–83.

Allred, B.B., Snow, C.C. and Miles, R.E. (1998). Characteristics of managerial careers in the 21st century. *Academy of Management Executive*, 10(4), 17–27.

Anderson, J.R. (1993). *Rules of the Mind*. Lawrence Erlbaum.

Andersson, L.M. (1996). Employee cynicism: an examination using a contract violation framework. *Human Relations*, 49, 1395–1418.

April, K.A. (1999). Leading through communication, conversation and dialogue. *Leadership and Development Journal,* 20(5), 231.

Arkin, A. (2000). Motional intelligence (Profile: Donald Sull). *People Management*, 6(21), 56–58.

Aronowitz, S. and Difazio, W. (1999). The new knowledge work. In: J. Ahier and G. Esland (eds), *Education, Training and the Future of Work 1*. Open University Press.

Arthur, M.B. and Rousseau, D.M. (1996). *The Boundaryless Career: a new employment principle for a new organizational era*. Oxford University Press.

Article 13 (2003): Corporate social responsibility – a source of competitive edge for SMEs. www.article13, June.

Ashkenas, R., Ulrich, D., Jich, T. and Herr, S. (1998). *The Boundaryless Organization*. Jossey-Bass.

Atkinson, G. (2000). Are you ready? *Training Journal*, March, pp. 14–17.

Baddeley, S. and James, K. (1987). Owl, fox, donkey or sheep? *Management Education and Development*, 18(1), 3–19.

Baldridge, V.J. (1971). *Power and Conflict in the University*, John Wiley.

Ballard, D. (2003). *British Safety Council publication*, http: www.britishsafetycouncil.co.uk

Barham, K. (1991). Developing the international manager. *Journal of European Industrial Training*, 15(1), 12–16.

Barham, K. (1993). International teams and leadership. *Transition*, September.

Bahrami, H. (1992). The emerging flexible organization: perspectives from Silicon Valley. *California Management Review*, 34(4), 33–52.

Baldridge, V.J. (1971). *Power and Conflict in the University*. John Wiley.

Ball, S.J. (1987). *The Micro-politics of the School*. Methuen.

Ballard, D. (2003). Ignoring social responsibility hits the bottom line. British Safety Council Press Release, March 10.

Barger, N.J. and Kirby, L.K. (1995). *The Challenge of Change in Organizations. Helping employees thrive in the new frontier*. Davis Black.

Barham, K. and Heimer, C. (1998). *ABB – The Dancing Giant: Creating the Globally Connected Corporation*, 1st edn. Financial Times/Prentice Hall.

Baron, A. and Walters, M. (1994). *The Culture Factor*. IPD.

Barratt, E. (1992). *The Strengths and Weaknesses of the Corporate Culture Analogy 'the glue that doesn't stick'*. Henley Management College.

Bass, B.M. (1985). *Leadership and Performance Beyond Expectations*. Free Press.

Bass, B.M. (1990). From transactional to transformational leadership: learning to share the vision. *Organizational Dynamics*, 18, 19–31.

Beagrie, S. (1999). Top 40 power players in personnel. *Personnel Today*, 15 April.

Beaudan, E. (2002). Leading in turbulent times. *Ivey Business Journal*, 66, i5.

Beckhard, R. and Harris, R.T. (1987). *Organizational Transitions: Managing Complex Change*, 2nd edn. Addison-Wesley, Cambridge Mass.

Beer, B.M., Eisenstat, R.A. and Spector, B. (1990a). Contrasting assumptions about change. *Harvard Business Review*, November–December.

Beer, B.M., Eisenstat, R.A. and Spector, B. (1990b). *The Challenge of Change in Organizations*. Davis Black.

Beer, B.M. and Eisenstat, R.A. (1996). Developing an organization capable of implementing strategy and learning. *Human Relations*, 49(5), 597–617.

Beer, B.M. and Nohria, N. (2000). Cracking the code of change. *Harvard Business Review*, May–June, 133–141.

Bennis, W.G. and Nanus, G. (1985). *Leaders*. Harper and Row.

Bennis, W.G. (1989). *Why Leaders Can't Lead*. Jossey-Bass.

Bergson, H. (1907/1983 edn). *Creative Evolution*. University Press of America.

Best Practice Forum (2003). *Driving Business Success*. University of Surrey.

Bigley, G.A. and Pearce, J. (1998). Straining for shared meaning in organizational science: problems of trust and distrust. *Academy of Management Review*, 23, 405–421.

Block, P. (1981). *Flawless Consultancy*. Jossey-Bass.

Block, P. In D.M. Hosking and I.E. Morley (eds), (1991). *A Social Psychology of Organising*. Harvester Wheatsheaf (available at http://www2.warwick.ac.uk/fac/sci/psych/people/academic/imorley/).

Boddy D. and Macbeth, D.K. (2000). Prescriptions for managing change: a survey of their effects in projects to implement collaborative working between organisations. *International Journal of Project Managements*, 18(5), 297–306.

Bolman, L. and Deal, T. (1997). *Reframing Organizations*. Jossey-Bass.

Boxall, P.F. (1992). Strategic Human Resource Management: beginnings of a new theoretical sophistication. *Human Resource Management Journal*, 2(3), 60–79.

Bracey, H. *et al.* (1993). Managing from the Heart, Dell Publishing, N.Y.

Bramley, P. (1996). *Evaluating Training*. Institute of Personnel and Development.

Bray, D.W. and Howard, A. (1980). Career success and life satisfactions of a middle-aged manager. In: L.A. Bond and J.C. Rosen (eds), *Competence and Coping during Adulthood*. N.H. University Press of New England.

Brewster, C., Hegewisch, A. and Lockhart, T. (1991). Researching Human Resource Management: methodology of the Price Waterhouse Cranfield Project on European Trends. *Personnel Review*, 20(6), 36–40.

Bridges, W. (1992). *The Character of Organizations: Using Jungian Type in Organizational Development*. Davies Black.

Bridges, W. (1995). *Jobshift*. Nicholas Brealey.

Brightman, B.K. and Moran, J.W. (2001). Managing organizational priorities. *Career Development International*, 6(5), 244–288.

Brightman, B.K. (2004). Why managers fail and how organizations can rewrite the script. *Journal of Business Strategy*, 25(2), 47–52.

Broussine, M. (1983). *Surviving as a Middle Manager*. Routledge Kegan Paul.

Brown, S.L. and Eisenhardt, K.M. (1997). The art of continuous change: linking complexity theory and time-paced evolution in relentlessly shifting organizations. *Administrative Science Quarterly*, 42(1), 1–34.

Buchanan, D. and Boddy, D. (1992). *The Expertise of the Change Agent: Public Performance and Backstage Activity*. Prentice-Hall.

Buckingham, M. and Clifton, D. (2001). *Now Discover Your Strengths*. Gallup Organisation.

Bunker, B.B. and Alban, B.T. (1997). *Large Group Interventions. Engaging the whole system for rapid change*. Jossey-Bass.

Burke, W.W. (1997). The new agenda for organization development, *Organizational Dynamics*, 26(1), 1.

Burke, W.W. (2002). *Organization Change: Theory and Practice*, Fig. 9.2, p. 199. Sage.

Burke, W.W. and Litwin, G. (1989). A causal model of organizational performance. In: J.W. Pfeiffer (ed.), *The 1989 Annual: Developing Human Resources*. University Associates.

Burke, W.W. and Litwin, G. (1992). A causal model of organisational performance and change. *Journal of Management*, 18(3), 523–545.

Burns, J.M. (1978). *Leadership*. Harper and Row.

Butcher, D. and Atkinson, S. (2000). The bottom-up principle. *Management Review*, January, 89(1), 48–53.

Butcher, D. and Clarke, M. (1999). Organisational politics: the missing discipline of management? *Industrial and Commercial Training*, 31(1), 9–12.

Butcher, D. and Clarke, M. (2002). Smart management: how to be a good corporate politician. *Training Magazine*.

Butler, A.S. (2000). Developing your company's e-business. *Journal of Business Strategy*, pp. 38–44.

Butts, D. (1999). Spirituality at work: an overview. *Journal of Organisational Change Management*, 12(4), 328–331.

Calori, R., Baden-Fuller, C. and Hunt, B. (2001). Managing change at Novotel. *Long Range Planning*, 33, 779–805.

Cameron, K.S. and Quinn, R.E. (1998). *Diagnosing and Changing Organizational Culture, Based on the Competing Values Framework*. Addison-Wesley.

Cannon, D. (1997). *Generation X*. Demos.

Cannon, F. (2003). Organisational climate: a proven tool for improving business performance. *Human Resources and Employment Review*, Croner.

Carrington, L. (2002). Goodson's Global Challenge. *Training Magazine,* November.

Carroll, G., Delacroix, J. and Goodstein, J. (1990). The political environment of organizations: an ecological view. In: B.M. Staw and L.L. Cummings (eds), *The Evolution and Adaptation of Organizations*. JAI Press Inc., pp.67–100.

Caulkin, S. (1995). Take your partners. *Management Today*, February.

Cavanagh, G.F. (1999). Spirituality for managers; context and critique. *Journal of Organisational Change Management*, 12(3), 186–199.

CBI/TUC Submission to the Productivity Initiative (2001). *The UK Productivity Challenge*. CBI/TUC.

Chandler, A.D. (1962). DuPont – creating the autonomous divisions. In: *Strategy and Structure*. MIT Press, Chapter 2 (available at http://tigger.uic.edu/~jwalsh/ORG447.html).

Chan Kim, W. and Mauborgne, R. (2003). Tipping point leadership. *Harvard Business Review*, March/April. 60–69.

Chappell, T. (1993). *The Soul of a Business: Managing for Profit and the Common Good*. Bantam Books.

Cheung-Judge, M-Y. (2001). The self as instrument: a cornerstone for the future of OD. *OD Practitioner, Journal of the Organization Development Network*, 33(3), 2001.

Chorn, N. and Nurick, I. (1997). *Strategic Alignment*. Psychometrics Canada Ltd.

Church, A.H., Hurley, R.F. and Warner Burke, W. (1992). Evolution or revolution in the values of organizational development. *Journal of Organizational Change Management*, 5(4).

CIPD (2001). *Raising Productivity: Why People Management Matters*. CIPD.

CIPD (2002). *Recruitment and Retention: Survey Report, May 2002*. CIPD.

CIPD (2003). *Recruitment and Retention: Survey Report, June 2003*. CIPD.

CMI (2003). *CMI Workplace Survey (2003)*. Chartered Management Institute.

CMI Survey (2003). *Business Continuity and Supply Chain Management*. Chartered Management Institute.

Colenso, M. (1998). *Strategic Skills for Line Managers*. Butterworth-Heinemann.

Collins, J.C. (2001). *Good to Great: why some companies make the leap and others don't*. Random House Books.

Collins, J.C. and Porras, J. (1994). *Built to Last: successful habits of visionary companies*. Harper Business Books.

Conger, J. (1989). *The Charismatic Leader: behind the mystique of exceptional leadership*. Jossey-Bass.

Conger, J. (1990). The dark side of leadership. *Organizational Dynamics*, Autumn, 44–55.

Conner, D.R. (1988). The myth of bottom-up change. *Personnel*, 65(10), 50–52.

Conner, D.R. (1998). *Leading at the Edge of Chaos: How to Create the Nimble Organization*. John Wiley & Sons.

Connolly, S. (2003). Spare the axe. *People Management*, 23 October.

Connor, D. (1988). *The Art of Winning*. Thorsons.

Cook, R.A. and Lafferty, J.C. (1987). *Organizational Culture Inventory*. OCI, USA; Plymouth MI, Human Synergistics.

Cooper, R. (1997). Executive EQ: Emotional intelligence in the workplace, Orion Publishing Co.

Covey, S.R. (1997). Sense of stewardship. *Executive Excellence*, 14.

Crenshaw, A.B. (1994). The myth of the mobile worker. *Washington Post*, 28 December.

Crouch, N. (2003). Actions speak louder than words. *People and Performance*. Fit for the Future.

Csikszentmihalyi, M. (1992). *Flow: the Psychology of Optimal Experience*. Harper and Row.

Cully, M., Woodland, S., O'Reilly, A. and Dix, C. (1999). *Britain at Work, The 1998 Workplace Employee Relations Survey*. (WERS), London, Routledge.

Cunninghan, S., Ryan, Y., Shedman, L., Tapsell, S., Bagdon, K., Flew, T. and Coldrake, P. (2000). *The Business of Borderless Education*, DETYA, Canberra.

Damon, N. (2002). Fresh bait. *Personnel Today*, 19 February.

Davenport, T.H. and Prusak, L. (2003). *What's the Big Idea? Creating and Capitalizing on the Best Management Thinking*, Harvard Business Press.

Davis, S. and Botkin, J. (1994). A monstrous opportunity, *Training and Development*, May.

Deal, T.E. and Kennedy, A.A. (1982). *Corporate Cultures*, Addison-Wesley.

Deal, T.E. and Kennedy, A.A. (2000). *The New Corporate Cultures*. Texere.

Dean, B.V. and Cassidy, J.C. (1990). *Strategic Management: Methods and Studies*. Elsevier Science and Technology Books.

Dearlove, D. and Coomber, S. (1999). *Heart and Soul and Millenial Values*. Blessing/White.

Dearlove, D. and Coomber, S. (2000). *Architects of the Business Revolution: The Ultimate E-Business Book*. Capstone.

De Bono, E. (1992). *Serious Creativity*. Harper Collins.

Deering, A. and Murphy, A. (1998). *The Difference Engine: achieving powerful and sustainable partnering*. Gower Publishing.

De Geus, A.P. (1988). Planning as learning. *Harvard Business Review*, 66(2), 70–74.

De Geus, A.P. (1997). *The Living Company*. Nicholas Brealey Publishing.

Dehler, G.E. and Welsh, M.A. (1994). Spirituality and organizational transformation. *Journal of Managerial Psychology*, 9(6), 17–26.

Delbecq, A.L. (1999). Christian spirituality and contemporary business leadership, *Journal of Organisational Change Management*, 12(4), 345–349.

Devine, M. (2000). *A Guide to Effective People Management during a Merger or Acquisition*. Roffey Park Institute.

Devine, M., Garrow, V., Hirsh, W. and Holbeche, L. (1999). *Mergers and Acquisitions: Getting the People Bit Right*. Roffey Park Institute.

DfEE (1997–8). *Workplace Trends*. DfEE.

DfES (2003). http://skillsbase.dfes.gov.uk/ (accessed June).

Doke, D. (2003). Pulling power – people management is the key, *Personnel Today Magazine*, 25 February.

Douglas, C. (1999). Organization redesign: the current state and trends. *Management Decision*, 37/8, 621–627.

Drory, A. and Romm, C. (1990). The definition of organisational politics. *Human Relations*, 43(11), 1133–1154.

DTI (2002). *High Performance Workplaces – a discussion paper*. DTI.

Dunbar, E. and Katcher, A. (1990). Preparing managers for foreign assignments. *Training and Development Journal*, September, 45–47.

Dunphy, D., Griffiths, A. and Benn, S. (2003). *Organizational Change for Corporate Sustainability*. Routledge.

Eastman, L.J. (1995). *Succession Planning*. Center for Creative Leadership, Greensboro, NC.

Eggebrecht, P. (2003). Striking a balance between head, heart and soul. *Personal Learning Journal*.

Eglin, R. (2000). Training flaw that costs firms billions. *Sunday Times*, 14 July.

Eisenberger, R. (1989). *Blue Monday: The Loss of the Work Ethic in America*. Paragon House.

Ellsworth, R.E. (2002). *Leading with Purpose*. Stanford Business Books.

Emmott, M. (2003). Five models for staff representation. Personneltoday.com, 22 July.

Ettore, B. (1993). A Brave New World – managing international careers. *Management Review*, April.

Evans, C. (2003). *Managing for Knowledge: HR's Strategic Role*. Butterworth-Heinemann.

Evans, M. and Gilbert, E. (1984). Plateaued managers: their need gratifications and their effort–performance expectations. *Journal of Management Studies*, 21(1).

Faulkner, D. and Johnson, G. (1992). *The Challenge of Strategic Management*. Kogan Page.

Finn, R. (2004). Five steps to effective human capital measurement, *Strategic HR Review*, January/February.

Fisher, R. and Ury, W. (1991). *Getting to Yes: Negotiating an Agreement Without Giving In*. Business Books.

Fox, M. (2000). *The Reinvention of Work*. Harper Collins.

Freeman, R.E. and Gilbert, D.R. (1988). *Corporate Strategy and the Search for Ethics*. Prentice-Hall.

French, J.R.P. and Raven, B. (1959). Bases of social power. In: D. Cartwright (ed.), *Studies in Social Power*. University of Michigan Press.

Funes, M. and Johnson, N. (1998). *Honing Your Knowledge Skills*. Butterworth-Heinemann.

Furnham, A. (2003). The role of communication in motivation. Presented at the *Motivating in Tough Times* conference, Roffey Park.

Gabel, S. (2002). Leading from the middle. *Leadership and Organizational Development Journal*, 23/7.

Gallup International and Environics International: Global Voice of the People Survey on Trust (2002), update 2004 (available at http://www.weforum.org/site/homepublic.nsf/Content/Survey+on+Trust+2004).

Gardner, H., Csikszentmihalyi, M. and Damon, W. (2001). *Good Work*. Basic Books.

Garrow, V., Devine, M., Hirsh, W. and Holbeche, L. (2000). *Strategic Alliances – Getting the People Bit Right*. Roffey Park Institute.

Germain, R. and Spears, N. (1999). Quality management and its relationship with organisational context and design. *International Journal of Quality and Reliability Management*, 16(4), 371–391.

Gersick, C.J.G. (1991). Revolutionary change theories: a multi level exploration of the punctuated equilibrium paradigm. *Academy of Management Review*, 16(1), 10–36.

Glynn, C. and Holbeche, L. (2000). *The Management Agenda*. Roffey Park Institute.

Glynn, C. and Holbeche, L. (2001). *The Management Agenda*. Roffey Park Institute.

Glynn, C., McCartney, C. and Steinberg, I. (2002). *Work–Life Balance*. Roffey Park Institute.

Glynn, C., McCartney, C. and Steinberg, I. (2002). *Managing Work–Life Balance*. Roffey Park Institute.

Ghoshal, S. and Bartlett, C. (1989). *Managing Across Borders*. Harvard Business School Press.

Ghoshal, S. and Bartlett, C. (1998). *The Individualised Corporation*. William Heinemann.

Goldstein, J. (1994). *The Unshackled Organization*. Productivity Press.

Goleman, D. (1995). *Emotional Intelligence – Why it can matter more than IQ*. Bantam Books.

Goleman, D. (1998). *Working with Emotional Intelligence*. Bantam.

Goleman, D. (2000). Leadership that gets results. *Harvard Business Review*, March–April, 78–90.

Gratton, L. (1999). *People Management*, October.

Gratton, L. (2000). *Living Strategy, Putting People at the Heart of Corporate Purpose*. Prentice Hall.

Greenleaf, R.K. (1998). *The Power of Servant Leadership*. Berrett-Koehler.

Grove, C.L. and Torbiorn, I. (1985). A new conceptualization of intercultural adjustment and the goals of training. *International Journal of Intercultural Relations*, 9(2), 205–233.

Guest, D. (1989). Personnel and Human Resource Management: Can you tell the difference? *Personnel Management*, January, 21(1), 48–51.

Guest, D and Conway, N. (1997). Employee motivation and the psychological contract. *Issues in People Management*, 21, Institute of Personnel and Development, London.

Guest, D and Conway, N. (1999). *Organisational Change and the Psychological Contract*. CIPD.

Guest, D., Michie, J., Sheehan, M. and Conway, N. (2000). *Employment Relations, HRM and Business Performance: An Analysis of the 1998 Workplace Employment Relations Survey*. CIPD.

Gunz, H.P., Jalland, R.M. and Evans, M.G. (1998). New strategy, wrong managers? *Academy of Management Executive*, 12(2), 21–37.

Guzzo, R. and Klein, K. (1991). HR communication in times of change. In: R.S. Schuler and J. Walker (eds), *Managing HR in the Information Age*. BNA Books.

Hackman, J. and Oldman, G.R. (1980). *Work Redesign*. Addison-Wesley.

Hall, D.T. and Mirvis, P.H. (1994). Psychological success and the boundaryless career. *Journal of Organizational Behaviour*, 15, 365–380.

Hall, D.T. and Moss, J.E. (1998). The new protean career contract: helping organizations and employees adapt. *Organizational Dynamics*, Winter, 26(3), 22–37.

Hall, T.B. and Forbes, G.H. (2003). *Modern Christian Spiritualism*, Kessinger Publishing.

Hamel, G. and Prahalad, C. (1990a). *Corporate Imagination and Expeditionary Marketing*, 37(3), 177–184.

Hamel, G. and Prahalad, C.K. (1990b). The core competence of the corporation. *Harvard Business Review*, May–June, 79–91.

Hamel, G. and Prahalad, C.K. (1994). *Competing for the Future*. Harvard Business School Press.

Hammer, M. (2001). *The Agenda: What every business must do to dominate the decade*. Random House.

Hammer, M. and Champy, J. (1993). *Reengineering the Corporation*. HarperCollins.

Hammond, S. (1998). *The Thin Book of Appreciative Inquiry* (2nd edn). The Thin Book Publishing Company.

Hampden-Turner, C. (1994). *Corporate Culture*. Piatkus.

Hampden-Turner, C. and Trompenaars, F. (1993). *The Seven Cultures of Capitalism*. Piatkus.

Handy, C. (1976). *Understanding Organizations*. Penguin Books.

Handy, C. (1984). *The Future of Work*. Basil Blackwell.

Handy, C. (1992). The language of leadership. In: M. Syrett and C. Hogg (eds), *Frontiers of Leadership*. Blackwell.

Handy, C. (1995a). *Beyond Certainty: The changing worlds of organization*. Hutchinson.

Handy, C. (1995b). *The Gods of Management*. Arrow.

Hardy, C. (1996). Understanding power: bringing about strategic change. *British Journal of Management*, 7, S3–S16.

Harung, H.S. and Dahl, T. (1995). Increased productivity and quality through management by values: a case study of Manpower Scandinavia. *The TQM Magazine*, 7(2), 13–22.

Hawk, E.J. (1995). Culture and rewards: a balancing act. *Personnel Journal*, 74(4), 30–37.

Hawkins, P. (1991). The Spiritual dimension of the learning organisation. *Management Education and Development*, 22(3), 172–187.

Hayday, S. (2003). Staff commitment is the key to an improved performance. *Personnel Today*, 10 June.

Heckscher, C. and Donnellon, A. (eds) (1994). *The Post-bureaucratic Organization: New perspectives on organizational change*. Basic Books.

Herriot, P. (1998). The role of the HRM function in building a new proposition for staff. In: P. Sparrow and M. Marchington (eds), *Human Resource Management: The New Agenda*. Financial Times and Pitman.

Herriot, P. and Pemberton, C. (1995). *New Deals: the revolution in managerial careers*. Wiley.

Hewitt Associates (2000). People issues; a top challenge for companies trying to compete in today's e-world. Press release, June 1.

Hiltrop, J.M. (2002). Mapping HRM: an international perspective. *Strategic Change*, 11(6).

Hipp, K.A. and Huffman, J.B. (2000). How leadership is shared and visions emerge in the creation of learning communities. *Annual Meeting of the American Educational Research Association, New Orleans*, April, 24–28.

HM Treasury (2000). Productivity Report. HM Treasury (available at http://www.archive.official-documents.co.uk/document/hmt/pbr2000/chap03.htm).

Hofstede, G. (1991). *Cultures and Organizations: Software of the Mind*. McGraw-Hill.

Holbeche, L. (1994). *Career Development in Flatter Structures*. Roffey Park Institute.

Holbeche, L. (1997a). *Career Development: The Impact of Flatter Structures on Careers*. Butterworth-Heinemann.

Holbeche, L. (1997b). *Motivating People in Lean Organizations*. Butterworth-Heinemann.

Holbeche, L. (1998). *High Flyers and Succession Planning*. Roffey Park Institute.

Holbeche, L. (1999). *Aligning HR and Business Strategy*. Butterworth-Heinemann.

Holbeche, L. (2003a). *Politics in Organizations*. Roffey Park Institute.

Holbeche, L. (2003b): *The High Performance Organization Checklist*, Roffey Park Institute.

Holbeche, L. (2004). *Politics for the Greater Good*, Roffey Park Institute.

Holbeche, L. and Springett, N. (2004). *In Search of Meaning in the Workplace*. Roffey Park Institute.

Holbeche, L. (2005). *Understanding change: theory, implementation and success*, Elsevier Butterworth-Heinemann.

Holbeche, L. and Glynn, C. (1998, 1999). *The Management Agenda*. Roffey Park Management Institute.

Holbeche, L. and McCartney, C. (2002–4). *The Management Agenda*. Roffey Park Institute.

Holman, T. and Devane, P. (1999). *The Change Handbook*. Berrett-Koehler.

Holt, G. (2000). Best practice. *Personnel Today*, 31 October.

Horn, C. (2002). Assessing true potential. *Personnel Today*, 12 November.

Hoyle, E. (1982). Micropolitics of educational organisations. *Educational Management and Administration*, 10(2), 87–98.

Huber, G.P. and Glick, W.H. (1993a). A theory of the effects of advanced information technologies on organizational design. *Academy of Management Review*, 15, 47–71.

Huber, G.P. and Glick, W.H. (1993b). Sources and forms of organizational change. In: G.P. Huber and W.H. Glick, *Organization Change and Redesign*. Oxford University Press.

Hudson, M. (2004). Unpublished Doctoral Thesis.

Hunt, J.G., Buglia, J.R., Dachler, H.P. and Schriasheim, Ch. A. (Eds). (1988). *Emerging Leadership Vistas*. Lexington.

Hunter, J.E., Schmidt, F.L. and Judiesch, M.K. (1995). Individual differences in output variability as a function of job complexity. *Journal of Applied Psychology*, 75, 28–42.

Hurley, A.E., Fagenson-Eland, E.A. and Sonnenfeld, J.A. (1997). An investigation of career attainment determinants. *Field Report*, Autumn.

Huselid, M. (1995). The impact of Human Resource Management practices on turnover, productivity, and corporate financial performance. *Academy of Management Journal*, 38, 972–991.

Iles, P.A. (1997). Sustainable career development: a resource based view. *Career Development International*, 2(7), 347–353.

Ingham, J. (2003). How to implement a diversity policy. *People Management*, 24 July.

Institute of Management (2002). *Leadership: The Challenge for All*. Institute of Management.

IPA Study (2001). Sharing the challenge ahead. *Consultation – the IPA Statement and Report on Best Practice*. IPA (available at http://www.partnership-at-work.com/cgi-bin/webdata_ipapaw.pl?Subject=Consultation+-+the+IPA+statement+and+report+on+best+practice+%282001%29&cgifunction=Search).

IRS (2002). Facing the retention challenge. *IRS Employment Review*, 750, 29 April.

IRS (2003). Public sector boosts job scene. *IRS Employment Review*, 767, 10 January.

Itoi, N.G. (2001). E-Business: Hail to the e-chief. IT executives are versatile innovators, managers, and counselors. If they do their jobs well, 'e-business' becomes just 'business'. *Industry Week*, 250(12), 27–30.

Jacobs, R.W. (1994). *Real Time Strategic Change: How to involve an entire organisation in fast and far-reaching change*. Berrett-Koehler.

Javenpaa, S.L, Knoll, K. and Leidner, D.E. (1998). Is anybody out there? Antecedents of trust in global virtual teams. *Journal of Management Information Systems*, 14(4).

Javidan, M. (2001). Organizational dimensions of global change: no limits to cooperation (Review). *Administrative Science Quarterly*, June.

Jennings, P.L. (2004). Strategic adaptation: a uni or multi-dimensional concept? *Strategic Change*, 13(1), 1–10.

Johns, G. (1983). *Organizational Behaviour: Understanding Life at Work*. Scott, Foresman and Company.

Johnson, D. (2003). The war for talent. *People and Performance*, Fit for the Future.

Johnson, G. (1987). *The Process of Strategic Change: A management perspective*. Basil Blackwell.

Johnson, G. (1990). Managing strategic change: the role of symbolic action. *British Journal of Management*, 1(1), 183–200.

Johnson, G. (1992). Managing strategic change: strategy, culture and action. *Long Range Planning*, 25(1).

Johnson, G. and Scholes, K. (2002). *Exploring Corporate Strategy* (6th edn). Prentice Hall.

Johnson, R. (2001). On message. *People Management*, 30 August.

Jones, J.E. (1981). The organisational universe. In: *The 1981 Handbook for Group Facilitators*. University Associates.

Kanter, R.M. (1979). Power failure in management circuits. *Harvard Business Review*, Article, July–August.

Kanter, R.M. (1983). *The Change Masters: Innovation for productivity in the American corporation*. Simon and Schuster.

Kanter, R.M. (1989). *When Giants Learn to Dance*. Simon and Schuster.

Kanter, R.M., Stein, B.A. and Jick, T.D. (1992). *The Challenge of Organizational Change*. Free Press.

Kaplan, R.S. and Norton, D.P. (1996). *The Balanced Scorecard: Translating strategy into action*. Harvard Business School Press.

Kenton, B. and Moody, D. (2002). *Coaching*. Roffey Park Institute.

Kenton, B. and Moody, D. (2003). *The Internal Consultant*. Roffey Park Institute.

Kets de Vries, M.F.R. and Mead, C. (1993). *The Development of the Global Leader Within the Multinational Corporation*, cited in Pucik, V. (1992). *Globalising Management – Creating and Leading in the Competitive Organization*. John Wiley & Sons, 187–205.

Kiechel, W. (1990). The organization that learns. *Fortune*, 6, 75–77.

Kiechel, W. (1993). How will we work in the year 2000? *Fortune*, 127, 38–52.

Kiechel, W. III (1994). A manager's career in the new economy. *Fortune*, 4 April, 68–72.

Kiedel, R.W. (1995). *Seeing Organizational Patterns: A new theory and language of organizational design*. Berrett-Koehler.

Kilmann, R.H. and Associates (eds) (1985). *Gaining Control of the Corporate Culture*. Jossey-Bass.

Kilmann, T., in Kindler, H.S. (1996). Managing conflict constructively. *Training and Development*, 50.

Kingsmill, D. (2003). *Accounting for People*, UK, DTI.

Klein, J.I. (2000). *Corporate Failure by Design: Why Organisations are Built to Fail*, Quorum Books.

Knell, J. and Harding, R. (2000). *New Jerusalem: Productivity, wealth and the UK economy*. The Industrial Society.

Kohn, A. (1993a). Rethinking rewards. *Harvard Business Review*, November–December, 71(6), 37.

Kohn, A. (1993b). Why incentive plans cannot work. *Harvard Business Review*, September–October, 71(5), 54–63.

Konz, G.N.P. and Ryan, F.X. (1999). Maintaining an organizational spirituality: no easy task. *Organizational Change Management*, 12(3), 200–210.

Kotter, J.P. (1985). *Power and Influence*. Free Press.

Kotter, J.P. (1988). The leadership factor. *McKinsey Quarterly*, Spring.

Kotter, J.P. (1990). *A Force for Change: How leadership differs from management*. Free Press.

Kotter, J.P. (1995a). *The New Rules. How to succeed in today's post-corporate world*. Free Press.

Kotter, J.P. (1995b). Leading change: why transformation efforts fail. *Harvard Business Review*, March–April, 59–67.

Kotter, J.P. and Heskett, J.L. (1992). *Corporate Culture and Performance*. Free Press.

Kouzes, J.M. and Posner, B.Z. (1988). *The Leadership Challenge*. Jossey-Bass.

Kouzes, J.M. and Posner, B.Z. (1990, 1995). The credibility factor: what followers expect from their leaders. *Management Review*, January.

Kouzes, J.M. and Posner, B.Z. (1997). *Leadership Practices Inventory* (2nd edn). Jossey-Bass.

Kozmetsky, G. (1985). *Transformational Management*. Harper and Row.

Kransdorff, A. (1995). Succession planning in a fast changing world. *Training officer*, 31(2), 52–53.

Kubicek, M. (2003). Distance no object. *Training Magazine*, February.

Laabs, J. (1995). Balancing spirituality and work. *Personnel Journal*. September, 60–76.

Lawler, E.E., Nadler, D.A. and Cammann, C. (eds) (1980). *Organizational Assessment: Perspectives on the measurement of organizational behavior and the quality of work life*. John Wiley & Sons.

Lawrence, P.R. and Lorsch, J.W. (1969). *Developing Organizations*. Addison-Wesley.

Lawrie, J. (1990). The ABCs of change management. *Training and Development Journal*, March.

Lewin, K. (1952). *Field Theory in Social Science*. Tavistock.

Lewis, D. (1994). Organizational change: relationship between reactions, behaviour and organizational performance. *Journal of Organizational Change Management*, Vol. 7(5), 41–55.

Lillrank, P. (1995). The transfer of management innovations from Japan. *Organization Studies*, 16(6), 971–989.

Lillrank, P., Shani, A.B. and Lindberg, P. (2001). Continuous improvement: exploring alternative organizational designs. *Total Quality Management*; 12(1), 41.

Littlefield, D. (2001). No need to shout about it. *People Management*, 5 April.

Litwin, G.H. and Stringer, R.A. (1984). *Motivation and Organisational Climate*, Harvard Business School Press.

Louis, M.R. (1983). Organizations as culture-bearing milieux. In: L.R. Pondy, R.J. Frost, G. Morgan and T.C. Dandridge (eds), *Organizational Symbolism*. JAI Press.

Lundberg, C.C. (1994). Toward managerial artistry: appreciating and designing organisations for the future. *International Journal of Public Administration*, 17(3/4).

MacLachlan, R. (1998). HR with attitude. *People Management*, August 13.

Maclagen, P. (1998). *Management and Morality*. Sage.

Mahoney, C. (2000). Ward winners. *People Management*, 28 September.

Maitland, R. (2002). Due consideration. *People Management*, 24 January.

Marks, M. and Mirvis, P. (1997). Revisiting the merger syndrome: dealing with stress, *Mergers and Acquisitions*, 31(6), 1–10.

Marshall, J. and McLean, A. (1988). Reflection in action: exploring organizational culture. In P. Reason (ed). *Human Inquiry in Action*. Sage.

Maslow, A. (1968). *Towards a Psychology of Being*, 2nd edn. Van Nostrand Reinhold.

McBain, R. (2000). Managing emotions and moods. *Manager Update*, 12(2).

McCalman, J. and Paton, R. (2000). *Change Management: A Guide to Effective Implement Action*. Sage.

McCartney, C. (2002). *E-Business: What are the human implications of transformation?* Roffey Park Institute.

McCartney, C. and Holbeche, L. (2003). *The Management Agenda*. Roffey Park Institute.

McEnrue, M.P. (1989). The perceived fairness of managerial promotion practice. *Human Relations*, 42(9), 815–827.

McGovern, P. (1995). Learning from the gurus: managers' responses to The Unwritten Rules of the Game. *Business Strategy Review*, Autumn, 6(3), 13–25.

McKeown, M. (2000). *E-customer*. Financial Times, 1st edn. Prentice Hall.

McLagan, P.A. (2003). The change-capable organization. *Training and Development*, January.

McLuhan, R. (1999). The homecoming. *Personnel Today*, 4 March.

McLuhan, R. (2000). Smooth handover. *Personnel Today*, 3 October.

McNulty, T., Roberts, J. and Stiles, P. (2003). *Creating Accountability Within the Board: The Work of the Effective Non-executive Director*. DTI.

Means, G.E. and Faulkner, M. (2000). Strategic innovation in the new economy. *Journal of Business Strategy*, 21(3), 25–29.

Mercer, W.M. and Friedman, D. (2000). William M. Mercer survey. *Survey of Work/Life Initiatives 2000*.

Mercer's *International Assignments Survey* (2003).

Meyer, A.D. (1982). Adapting to environmental jolts. *Administrative Science Quarterly*, 27.

Meyerson, D.E. (2001). Radical change, the quiet way. *Harvard Business Review*, 92–100.

Miles, R. (1997). *Corporate Comeback*. Jossey-Bass.

Miles, R.E. and Snow, C.C. (1986). Organizations: new concepts for new forms. *California Management Review*, 28, 62–73.

Miller, E.J. (1993). *From Dependency to Autonomy Studies in Organization and change*. Free Association.

Millman, J. and Ferguson, J. (1999). Spirit and community at Southwest Airlines. *Journal of Organisational Change Management*, 12(3), 221–233.

Mindell, A. (1992). *The Leader as Martial Artist: An Introduction to Deep Democracy*. Harper SF.

Mintzberg, H. (1979). *The Structure of Organisations*. Prentice-Hall.

Mintzberg, H., Quinn, J.B. and Ghoshal, S. (1995). *The Strategy Process*, European edn. Prentice Hall.

Mirvis, P. (1997). 'Soul work' in organizations. *Organization Science*, 8, 193–206.

Mitroff, I.I. and Denton, E.A. (1999). A study of spirituality in the workplace. *Sloan Management Review*, 40(4), 83–92.

Moran, J.W. and Brightman, B.K. (2001). Leading organizational change. *Career Development International*, 6(2), 12–27.

Morgan, G. (1986). *Images of Organization*. Sage.

Morgan, G. (1993). *Imaginization: The Art of Creative Management*. Sage Publications.

Morrison, E.W. (1994). Role definitions and organizational citizenship behaviour. *Academy of Management Journal*, 37(6), 1543.

Morrison, M. and Mezentseff, L. (1997). Learning alliances – a new dimension of strategic alliances. *Management Decision*, 35/5, 351–357.

Morrison, I. and Schmid, G. (1994). *Future Tense-Preparing for the Business Realities of the Next Ten Years*. Morrow.

Morton, C. (1998). *Beyond World Class*. Macmillan.

Moynagh, M. and Worsley, R. (2001). *Tomorrow's Workplace: Fulfilment or Stress?* CIPD.

Nadler, D.A. and Tushman, M.L. (1989). Organizational frame bending: principles for managing re-orientation. *Academy of Management Executive*, 3, 194–204.

Nadler, D.A., Hackman, R. and Lawler, E.E. (1979). *Managing Organizational Behavior*. Little Brown.

Neck, C.P. and Milliman, J.F. (1994). Thought self-leadership: finding spiritual fulfilment in organizational life. *Journal of Managerial Psychology*, 9(6), 9–16.

Nel, J., cited in Doke, D. (2003). Pulling power – people management is the key. *Personnel Today*, 25 February.

Oberg, K. (1960). Cultural shock: adjustments to new cultural paradigms. *Practical Anthropology*, 7, 177–182.

O'Reilly, N. (2001). UK firms get top marks for consultation. *Personnel Today*, 17 July.

Owen, H. (1997). *Open Space Technology: A User's Guide*. Berrett-Koehler.

Owen, T. (2000). Not flowing around. *Manufacturing Systems*, April (available at http://www.manufacturing.net/articles/msys/2000/0401/article1.html).

Panter, S. (1995). *Summary Report of a Qualitative International Research Survey*. Ashridge Management College.

Parker, M.M. (1995). *Strategic Transformation and Information Technology*. Prentice-Hall.

Parker, P. and Inkson, K. (1999). New forms of career: the challenge to Human Resource Management. *Asia Pacific Journal of Human Resources*, 37(1), 69–78.

Parry, I.J., Tranfield, D., Smith, S. *et al.* (1998). Reconfiguring your organisation: a teamwork approach. *Team Performance Management*, 4(4), 166–176.

Pate, J., Martin, G. and Staines, H. (2000). Exploring the relationship between psychological contracts and organizational change. *Strategic Change*, 9(8), 481–493.

Peters, T.J. (1987). *Thriving on Chaos*. Knopf.

Peters, T. and Waterman, R. (1982). *In Search of Excellence*. Harper Row.

Pettigrew, A. (1985). *The Awakening Giant*. Blackwell.

Pettigrew, A.M. (1990). Is corporate culture manageable? In: D.C. Wilson and J. Rosenfeld Pfeffer (1981). *Power in Organizations*. Pitman.

Pettigrew, A.M. and Whipp, R. (1991). *Managing Change for Competitive Success*. Blackwell.

Pfeffer, J. (1981). Management as symbolic action. In: L.L. Cummings and B.M. Straw (eds), *Research in Organizational Behaviour*, Vol. 3. JAI Press.

Pfeffer, J. (1992). In Bolman, L. and Deal, T.E. (1997). *Reframing Organizations*, 2nd edn. Jossey-Bass.

Pfeffer, J. (1996). When it comes to 'Best Practices' why do smart organizations occasionally do dumb things? *Organizational Dynamics*, Summer.

Pfeffer, J. (1998a). Six myths about pay. *Harvard Business Review*, June.

Pfeffer, J. (1998b). *The Human Equation*. HBS Press.

Philipson, I. (2002). *Married to the Job: Why We Live to Work and What We Can Do About It*. Free Press.

Philpott, J. (2002). *Perspectives: Productivity and People Management*. CIPD.

Pichault, F. (1993), cited in Bolman, L. and Deal T.E. (1997). *Reframing Organizations*, 2nd edn. Jossey-Bass.

Pickard, J. (1996). A fertile grounding. *People Management*, 24 October.

Pickard, J. (2001). Prophet sharing. *People Management*, 27 December.

Pickard, J. (2003). Cadbury defends apartheid business. *People Management*, 24 October.

Pondy, L.R., Frost, R.J., Morgan, G. and Dandridge, T.C. (eds) (1983). *Organizational Symbolism*. JAI Press.

Porter, M. (2003). *UK Competitiveness: Moving on to the Next Stage*. DTI.

Purcell, J., Marginson, P., Edwards, P. and Sissons, K. (1987). The industrial relations practices of multi-plant foreign owned firms. *Industrial Relations Journal*, 18(2), Summer.

Quinn, J.B. (1978). Strategic change: Logical incrementalism. In *Sloan Management Review*, Fall, 7–21.

Rana, E. (2002). Flying information. *People Management*, 7 November.

Reichers, A.E. and Wanous, J.P. (1997). Understanding and managing *cynicism* about organizational change. *Academy of Management Executive*, 11(1), 48.

Revens, R.W. (1983). Action learning: kindling the touch paper. *Management Development*, 21(6).

Rhinesmith, S.H. *et al.* (1989). Developing leaders for the global enterprise. *Training and Development Journal*, April.

Rice, V. (2001). The Cost of Customer Support. *eWEEK* (available at http://www.zdnet.com/ecommerce/stories/main/0,10475,2706274-6,00.html).

Richer, J. (1995). *The Richer Way*. Emap Business Publications.

Roddick, A. (2000). *Business as Unusual: The Triumph of Anita Roddick*. Thorsens Publishers.

Rodgers, K. (2003). Delivering training on a shoestring. *Personnel Today*, 8 April.

Rosener, J.B. (1990). Ways women lead. *Harvard Business Review*, November–December, 119–125.

Rosener, J.B. (1996). *America's Competitive Secret: Utilizing Women as a Management Strategy*. Oxford University Press.

Rothwell, S. (1992). The development of the international manager. *Personnel Management*, 24, 33–35.

Rousseau, D.M. (1995). *Psychological Contracts in Organizations*. Sage.

Rousseau, D.M. (1996). *The Boundaryless Career*. Oxford University Press.

Rowden, R. (2001). The learning organization and strategic change. *Society for the Advancement of Management Journal*, 66(3), 11–16.

Rucci, A.J., Kim, S.P. and Quinn, R.T. (1998). The employee–customer–profit chain at Sears. *Harvard Business Review*, 76(1), 83–97.

Sadler, P. (2003). The company with a shining soul. *Human Resources and Employment Review*, Croner, Vol 1(1).

Sandelands, L.E. (1998). *Feeling and Form in Social Life*.

Sanders, P. (2000). How to get the best from an EAP. *People Management*, 12 October.

Scarborough, H. (2003). Why your employees don't share what they know. *Knowledge Management Review*, 16(2).

Schein, E. (1993). *Organizational Culture and Leadership*, 2nd edn. Jossey-Bass.

Schneider, B. (1994). HRM – a service perspective: towards a customer focused HRM. *International Journal of Service Industry Management*, 5(1), 64–76.

Seel, R. (2000). Culture and complexity: new insights into organizational change *Organizations and People*, 7(2), 2–9.

Selmer, J., Torbiorn, I. and de Leon, C. (1998). Sequential cross-cultural training for expatriate business managers: pre-departure and post-arrival. *Human Resources Management*, 9(5), 832–840.

Semler, R. (1993). *Maverick*. Arrow.

Senge, P.M. (1990). *The Fifth Discipline: The art and practice of the learning organization*. Doubleday.

Sergiovanni, T. (1984). Leadership and excellence in schooling. *Educational Leadership*, February, 4–13.

Shafritz, J. and Ott, S. (eds.) (2000). *Classics of Organization Theory*, 5th edn. Harcourt College Publishers.

Shaw, M. (2001). *Ten Secrets to Living a Successful and Fulfilling Life*. Trafford Publishing.

Shaw, P. and Phillips, K. (1998). *A Consultancy Approach for Trainers*. Gower.

Simon, H.A. (1960). The New Science of Management Decisions. Harper and Row.

Simpson, P. (2002). Victory disease. *Personnel Today*, 5 November.

Sinclair, A. (2003). Re-winning the war for talent. *Human Resources and Employment Review*, July.

Smith, A. and Sinclair, A. (2003). *What Makes an Excellent Virtual Manager?* Roffey Park Institute.

Sparrow, S. (2001). Power surge. *Training Magazine*, June.

Spekeman, R., Isabella, L., MacAvoy, T. and Forbes, T. (1996). Creating strategic alliances which endure. *Long Range Planning*, 29(3), 346–357.

Spilsbury, D. (2001). *Learning and Training at Work (2000)*. IFF Report for the Department for Education and Employment (DFEE Research Report 269).

Springett, N. (2004). Corporate purpose as the basis of moral leadership of the firm. *Human Resources and Employment Review*, 2(3).

Stacey, R. (1999). *Strategic Management and Organisational Dynamics*, 3rd edn. Pitman.

Stanford, N. (2004). *Organization Design*. Butterworth-Heinemann.

Stevens, R. (2003). Guidance and training underpin good practice (available at http://www.partnership-at-work.com/ezine_plus/pawpub/story237.shtml).

Stewart, R. (1991). *Managing Today and Tomorrow*. Macmillan.

Stewart, R. (1995). *Leading in the NHS*. Palgrave Macmillan.

Stewart, V. (1990). *The David Solution – How to liberate your organization*. Gower.

Stokes, H. and Harrison, R. (1992). *Diagnosing Organizational Culture*. Pfeiffer & Co.

Strange, T. (1993). The human organisation. *Management*, November.

Stuart, R. (1995). Experiencing organizational change. *Personnel Review*, 24(2), 3–88.

Suff, P. (2000). *Knowledge Management*. Industrial Relations Services London, Eclipse.

Sull, D., cited in Arkin (2000). Motional intelligence (Profile: Donald Sull). *People Management*, 6(21), 56–58.

Tate, W. (1997). *The Business of Innovation*. Prometheus Consulting.

Thomas, J. (1985). Force field analysis: a new way to evaluate your strategy. *Long Range Planning*, 18(6), 54–59.

Thompson, P. and McHugh, D. (2002). *Work Organizations: A Critical Introduction*. Macmillan.

Thorne, K. (2003). *Blended Learning*. Kogan Page.

Tichy, N.M. and Devanna, M.A. (1986, 1990). *The Transformational Leader*. John Wiley & Sons.

Tischler, L. (1999). The growing interest in spirituality. *Journal of Organizational Change Management*, 12(4), 272–279.

Toffler, A. (1991). *The Third Wave*. Pan.

Tourish, D. and Pinnington, A. (2002). Transformational leadership, corporate cultism and the spirituality paradigm: an unholy trinity in the workplace? *Human Relations*, 55, 147–172.

Trahant, W. and Burke, W. (1996). Creating a change reaction: how understanding organizational dynamics can ease re-engineering. *National Productivity Review*, 15(4), 37–46.

Trice, H.M. and Beyer, J.M. (1984). Studying organizational cultures through rites and ceremonials. *Academy of Management Review*, 9(4), 653–669.

Trompenaars, F. (1993). *Riding the Waves of Culture*. Brealey.

Trompenaars, F. (1998). The making of the international manager. *Human Resource Management International Digest*, September–October.

Trompenaars, F. and Hampden-Turner, C. (1993). *The Seven Cultures of Capitalism*. Doubleday.

Tulgan, B. (1998, 2000). *Recruiting the Workforce of the Future*, 2nd edn. \\HRD Press.

Tyson, S. (1995). *Human Resource Strategy*. Pitman.

Uddin, K. (1998). Inter-organisational relationships: growth and management. *Topics ER Consultants*, 75(2).

Ulrich, D. (1997). *Human Resource Champions: The Next Agenda for Adding Value and Delivering Results*. Harvard Business Press.

Ulrich, D., interviewed by MacLachlan, R. (1998). HR with attitude. *People Management*, 13 August.

Ulrich, D. and Lake, D. (1990). *Organizational Capability: Competing from the inside/out*. John Wiley & Sons.

Ulrich, D, Smallwood, N. and Zenger, J. (2000). Building your leadership brand. *Leader to Leader*, 15, 40–46.

Upton, R. (2003). Star gazers. *People Management*, 24 July.

Van de Vliet, A. (1994). Order from chaos. *Management Today*, 62. November.

Van Maurik, J. (1996). *Discovering the Leader in You*. McGraw-Hill.

Van Oech, R. (2001). *Creative Whack Pack*. United Games Systems.

Vecchio, R.P. and Appelbaum, S.H. (1995). *Managing Organizational Behaviour*. Dryden.

Volberda, H.W. (1992). *Organizational Flexibility, Change and Preservation: A flexibility audit and redesign model*. Wolters-Noordhoff.

Volberda, H.W. (1998). *Building the Flexible Firm*. Oxford University Press.

Vroom, V. (1994). *Work and Motivation*. Jossey-Bass.

Waddock, S.A. (1999). Linking community and spirit: a commentary and some propositions. *Organisational Change Management*, 12(4), 332–344.

Walton, E. and Nadler, D.A. (1994). Diagnosis for organization design. In: D.W. Bray (ed.), *Diagnosis for Organizational Change. Methods and Models*. The Guilford Press, S. 85–112.

Waterman, R.H. Jr. (1993). *Adhocracy: The Power to Change*, W.W. Norton.

Waterman, R.H. Jr. (1994). *The Renewal Factor*. Bantam.

Waterman, R.H. Jr. *et al.* (1995) *Harvard Business Review*. Toward a Career Resistant Force.

Waters, C. (2003). Input at Roffey Park Seminar on Work–Life Balance.

Watkin, C. (2001). How to improve organizational climate. *People Management*, 28 June.

Watson, G. and Crossley, M. (2001). Beyond the rational. In *Educational Management and Administration*. Sage.

Weber, M. (1922). Legitimate power and bureaucracy. In: L.E. Boone and D.D. Bowen (eds) (1987). *The Great Writings in Management and Organizational Behaviour*. Irwin.

Webster, A. (2002). *Wellbeing*. SCM Press.

Weick, K.E. (1977). Enactment processes in organisations. In: B. Staw and G. Salancik (eds), *New Directions in Organizational Behavior*. St Clair Press.

Weick, K.E. (1993). Organizational redesign as improvisation. In: G.P. Huber and W.H. Glick (eds), *Organization Change and Redesign*. Oxford University Press.

Weidman, D. (2002). Redefining leadership for the 21st century. *Journal of Business Strategy*, 23, 16–18.

Weisbord, M. (1987). *Productive Workplaces: Organizing and Managing for Dignity, Meaning and Community*. Jossey-Bass.

Weisbord, M. and Janoff, S. (2000). *Future Search: An action guide to finding common ground in organizations and communities*. Berrett-Koehler.

Welch, J. (2001). *Jack – What I've learned leading a great company and great people*. Warner Books.

Wenger, E.C. and Snyder, W. (2000). Communities of practice: the organisational frontier. *Harvard Business Review*, January–February, 139–145.

West, M., Nicholson, N. and Fees, A. (1990). The outcomes of downward managerial mobility. *Journal of Organizational Behaviour*, 11, 117–134.

Whatmore, J. (1993). *Managing Creative Groups*. Roffey Park Institute.

Whipp, R., Rosenfeld, R. and Pettigrew, A. (1989). Managing strategic change in a mature business. *Long Range Planning*, 22(6), 92–99.

Whiteley, P. (1999). Staff loyalty plummets in developed nations. *Personnel Today*, 22 October.

Wilber, K. (2001). *A Theory of Everything: An integral vision for business, politics, science and spirituality*. Gateway.

Wilkins, A. (1989). *Developing Corporate Character: How to Successfully Change an Organisation Without Destroying It*. Jossey-Bass.

Williams, K. and Hart, J. (1999). Getting Oracle back to basics. *Management Accounting*, 80(10), 36.

Williamson, C.L. *et al.* (2002). Policy capturing as a tool to enhance recruiting. *Career Development International*, 7(3), 159–166.

Wilson, N. (2004). Rewarding values at Loop Customer Management. *Strategic HR Review*, January–February.

Womack, J.P., Jones, D.T. and Roos, D. (1991). *The Machine that Changed the World*. Harper Business.

Woodruffe, C. (1999). *Winning the Talent War: A strategic approach to attracting, developing and retaining the best people*. John Wiley & Sons.

Woodruffe, C. (2000). Employability: a strategic role for training. *Training Journal*, February.

Zohar, D. (1997). *Rewiring the Corporate Brain*. Berrett-Koehler.

Zohar, D. and Marshall, I. (2000). *Spiritual Intelligence – The Ultimate Intelligence*. Bloomsbury Publishing.

Zuboff, S. (1988). *In the Age of the Smart Machine: The Future of Work and Power*. Oxford University Press.

Index